THE MERTON ANNUAL

1

THE MERTON ANNUAL

Studies in Thomas Merton, Religion, Culture, Literature & Social Concerns

THE MERTON ANNUAL will publish articles about Thomas Merton and about matters of major concern in his life and work. Its purpose is to enhance Merton's reputation as a writer and monk, to continue to develop his message for our times, and to provide a regular outlet for substantial Merton-related scholarship. *THE MERTON ANNUAL* will also include as regular features reviews, review-essays, a bibliographic survey, interviews, and first appearances of unpublished, or obscurely published, Merton materials, photographs, and art. Essays about related literary connections or events which Merton has influenced will also be considered. Manuscripts and books for review may be sent to any of the editors.

THE MERTON ANNUAL

Studies in Thomas Merton,
Religion, Culture, Literature & Social Concerns

Volume 1   **1988**

Edited by

Robert E. Daggy

Patrick Hart, O.C.S.O.

Dewey Weiss Kramer

Victor A. Kramer

AMS Press, Inc.
New York

THE MERTON ANNUAL

LC 87-47815   ISBN-0-404-63800-7 (set)

ISSN 0894-4857   ISBN-0-404-63801-5 (v. 1)

THE MERTON ANNUAL, 1
was set in Chelmsford *type
and camera-ready copy prepared
at the Thomas Merton Studies Center
Bellarmine College, Louisville, Kentucky.*

Manufactured in the United States of America

THE MERTON ANNUAL

Volume 1   1988

O

○

○

○

○

○

o

REVIEWS

Introduction

This volume of articles and reviews about Thomas Merton and his writings appears two decades after his untimely death. It is a reflection of Merton's prodigious energy which has generated a large body of writing about him, his life and work, and relationships to wider issues. The diversity of Merton's interests is demonstrated in the subtitle for this new scholarly publication, "Studies in Thomas Merton, Religion, Culture, Literature, & Social Concerns." As a contemplative and a writer, he was interested in all these subjects. Our intent as editors of this publication is that *The Merton Annual* represent the best in contemporary scholarship about Merton's wide-ranging interests.

The need for such a scholarly avenue for Merton related scholarship has been recognized for a long time. We believe that substantial materials will be produced in years to come for inclusion in *The Merton Annual* as still more Merton manuscripts, letters, and journals are studied and published. As editors we hope to accomplish several things with *The Merton Annual*. Primarily, this annual volume will provide an outlet for scholarly investigations which are of a length sometimes difficult to place in journals, which are limited by space considerations. We hope to publish lengthy studies of Merton, but length is not our main concern. This annual's most important function will be to provide a carefully edited and refereed organ for scholarship related to Thomas Merton's accomplishments as monk and artist.

As is reflected in this first gathering, we will seek to use items in the annual which include art and photography by Merton and also unpublished, or obscurely published, writings by him which will help to further his reputation. We hope to include lectures and papers from Merton symposiums, conferences and commemorations which occur with ever-increasing frequency. We also plan to include interviews of persons who knew him, as well as articles which may be speculative in the sense of relating to Merton's work in a concrete, but sometimes, indirect fashion. Therefore essays on subjects as diverse as the peace movement, or race relations, or Christian art, which are in the spirit that Merton cultivated will always be welcome. Another regular feature of this publication will be its inclusion of a bibliographic essay which provides commentary about all the significant (and perhaps the insignificant) Merton scholarship which appears during the preceding year. The editors will also solicit reviews and review-essays on the most important books by, and about, Merton.

This annual is edited in a spirit which the editors hope Merton would acknowledge as valuable. We want to provide an organ which will encourage scholars to examine all aspects of his life and work. Everything which a scholar can bring to bear on Merton's writing and life -- from biography to textual bibliography, from theology to sociology, from close readings to studies of culture -- will be welcome. Merton's energy, insight, love, and compassion are more and more appreciated as additional readers and scholars come to appreciate his life's work. We want *The Merton Annual* to reflect Merton's own best characteristics.

The Editors

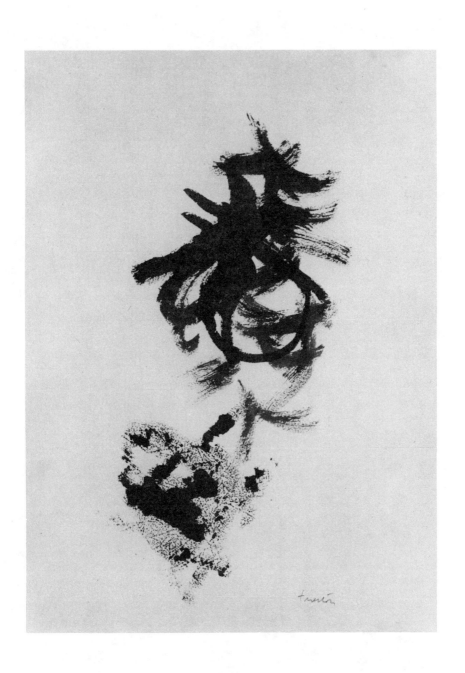

THE ZEN INSIGHT OF SHEN HUI

By **Thomas Merton**

Edited by **Patrick Hart**, O.C.S.O.

EDITOR'S NOTE

When preparing the first volume of The Merton Annual, this unpublished manuscript by Thomas Merton was unearthed at the Merton Studies Center of Bellarmine College. It was suggested that a brief explanation be given to fill in the historical context of the introduction so that it could appear in the first number of the annual. The letters of Thomas Merton to Richard S. Y. Chi have been included in the first volume of Merton letters, which mentions the project of an introduction to the translations of Shen Hui which Dr. Chi was planning (see The Hidden Ground of Love: The Letters of Thomas Merton on Religious Experience and Social Concerns, selected and edited by William H. Shannon, New York: Farrar, Straus & Giroux, 1985, pp. 121-125).

In the opening letter of the correspondence, dated December 26, 1967, Merton wrote: "As you know, Lunsford Yandell has forwarded to me the excellent ms. on Shen Hui, and I am reading it with real pleasure." He continued by saying that he had some ideas about its publication in case the Indiana University Press did not bring it out. After inviting Dr. Chi to visit Gethsemani, he suggested publishing selections from Shen Hui in Monks Pond, a literary journal Merton edited in 1968. There were only four issues, and as it turned out, selections of Shen Hui in English were included in the first and fourth numbers. Incidentally, as this first volume goes to press, plans are in the offing for a facsimile reprint edition of the four numbers of Monks Pond, edited by Robert E. Daggy and published by the University Press of Kentucky.

For those unfamiliar with Shen Hui, suffice it here to say that he was the successor to the Sixth Zen Patriarch Hui Neng as the leader of the Southern (Sudden

Enlightenment) School of Ch'an (Zen) Buddhism, and was a figure of decisive importance in the development of Chinese Ch'an Buddhism. After several exchanges of letters between Merton and Chi, as well as a visit by Dr. Chi to Gethsemani, Merton wrote in appreciation of an article by Hu Shih, which Chi had forwarded to him: "It was just what I needed to make everything fall into place. The draft of the introduction is finished and it is now being typed. A very enjoyable and interesting task. . ." (April 3, 1968).

After receiving the introduction, Dr. Chi replied to Merton on April 23: "Your introduction is really a masterpiece. This is the first time I have seen anything written by a non-Chinese with such a deep understanding of Ch'an. It will be immortal, and the work of Shen Hui will also be immortalized by your introduction." But such was not to be the case. Now after nearly twenty years, the volume of Shen Hui in English has still not appeared.

The last letter of the exchange was written by Thomas Merton on December 21, 1968, from Darjeeling, India, less than three weeks before his death: "I have been having a very fruitful trip in Asia. I have been in India over a month, mostly in the Himalayas, and have had good conversations with the Dalai Lama and with many others high in Tibetan Buddhism -- including some extraordinary mystics. . . ." He continues his letter by giving Dr. Chi his address in Indonesia, where he was going from Bangkok following the monastic conference, to direct a retreat for the Cistercian Community at Rawa Seneng. He again mentions the Shen Hui book, and wonders if it has been published, as he wanted a copy sent to the Dalai Lama and others whom he met. He concluded his letter by telling Dr. Chi that he was adding to his knowledge of Madhyamika (the School of Mahayana Buddhism developed by Nagarjuna in the second century A.D., which stressed the notion of emptiness): "I am eager to reread Shen Hui in the light of this study and look forward very much to seeing your book -- or any other studies you may be doing on Buddhist topics. In any case, I would be glad of suggestions, some people to see, especially in Taiwan. . . ."

Thomas Merton ends his introduction by making it clear that when he writes about the religious genius of the Far East as having achieved a resolution of the age-old conflict between action and contemplation, he is not criticizing Christian spirituality as such, although the following lines may sound like a prophetic warning: "In the West we are still hung up in an inexorable division between activists who run around in circles claiming that their hectic and ulcer-forming busyness is 'prayer' and contemplatives (so-called) who are completely immersed in liturgical projects, or devout pieties which are justified as supremely efficacious activities." In truth, Merton saw "a fatal division in Western thinking which makes this kind of split almost inevitable. The ground of the division is the Western obsession with will, achievement, production, self-affirmation and power." He concludes by reminding us that Shen Hui is actually talking about the ground of existence and not about a religious system, which should be obvious. Let us hope that this introduction to the Zen insight of Shen Hui will help us all understand it better whether we be activists, contemplatives or a mixture of both.

With a minimum of editing, we are happy to present Merton's introduction to Shen Hui, with the hope that it will open up a new world to many Western readers who have not as yet made their acquaintance with this great spiritual master of the East. It may even act as a catalyst for some enterprising publisher to bring out a volume of Shen Hui in English. What a signal event that would be in the advancement of the East/West dialogue and in Asian studies.

THE ZEN INSIGHT OF SHEN HUI

by **Thomas Merton**

The discovery of ancient Buddhist manuscripts in the Tunhwang Caves is comparable to the more recent finds made at Qumran in Palestine. The Qumran manuscripts have made a decisive contribution to the study of Judaism and early Christianity. The Tunhwang texts have opened up to the modern scholar a revolutionary period in Chinese culture and religion. More than that, however, they have put into our hands documents which are absolutely necessary for the understanding of Ch'an Buddhism (more familiar by the Japanese name Zen). If Ch'an, which is characteristically "anti-scriptural" and "anti-authoritarian," can be said to have "authoritative documents" in China, the highest importance is to be attributed to those of the eighth century Master, the so-called "Seventh Patriarch," Shen Hui.

The teachings of Shen Hui are not only scholarly but alive with Zen insight. Many scholars think that works attributed to the Sixth Patriarch, Hui Neng, are actually the work of Shen Hui and his disciples. Whether or not this is true, the whole corpus of documents which represent the teaching of the Southern School of Ch'an in the seventh and eighth centuries -- the teachings of Hui Neng, Shen Hui and their followers -- are completely decisive in the development of Chinese Buddhism. It is with these Masters that Ch'an attained its purest and most authentic expression as a perfectly Chinese creation. Later growth brought further refinements and perhaps more paradoxical methods of teaching, but the central insights of Ch'an, and its fantastic wedding of simplicity and depth, sophistication and directness, paradox and clarity, was achieved in the Southern School. It can be said without serious fear of contradiction that Shen Hui possessed all these qualities in a most unusual degree. It was he who gave Ch'an its final and mature shape.

But there is more to Shen Hui than this. Unlike the simple, unlettered peasant, Hui Neng, and unlike so many other Ch'an masters who lived silent and remote in mountain hermitages, Shen Hui was an active and in some ways revolutionary figure in the intellectual and religious world of his time -- which was one of the most civilized and creative in the entire history of humanity. It is enough to say that he was in close contact with poets like Wang Wei as well as with the religious and political figures who appear dimly to tease him with their enigmatic questions. More than that -- and here we run into a paradox that is not the least of those we find in Ch'an -- he was able to propose an essentially revolutionary teaching within the framework of a religious and political establishment which sought to use him for what one might call counter-revolutionary ends. At first, because his teaching attracted large crowds, Shen Hui was exiled to a distant place -- lest he be tempted to overthrow the imperial government. A revolution did indeed occur, but he was not implicated in it. After its overthrow, in 757, Shen Hui was called back to preach a monastic renewal which was to have interesting consequences for the government: the tax on profession-licenses of monks and nuns was intended to meet the defense budget.

Shen Hui's teaching, on highly official occasions, operates on two levels: that of a popular Buddhism for the masses, and that of Ch'an insight for the advanced. Nor was this a matter of clever policy. Shen Hui maintained that it was an expression of Ch'an itself. His *dhyana* (meditation) and *prajna* (contemplative insight, wisdom) were not only confined to moments of "quiet sitting" in the forest or meditation hall: his preaching itself was both *dhyana* and *prajna* in one. Those who understood would intuitively realize this. Those who did not understand would still be, without realizing it, in contact with the immediate manifestation of what they were obscurely seeking, and might awaken to it in their own way. Evidently the crowds who listened to Shen Hui *believed* this.

The temptation to compare Shen Hui with the Western Gnostics must be avoided here. Buddhism has no room in it for Gnosticism, though the *chio* ("knowledge"), which is identical with the union of *dhyana* and *prajna*, might conceivably be translated "gnosis" (taken in a non-"gnostic" sense). Gnosticism is profoundly dualistic, and there is no dualism in Ch'an. Shen Hui would never have claimed that there was one level of Ch'an for an elite and another for *hoi polloi*. There was one insight for everyone, but not everyone *saw* it. Perhaps the extraordinary impact upon large crowds of his teaching may have been due to the fact that those who did not *experience* what he said nevertheless believed it.

I am no student of Chinese history, and what I have said so far about Shen Hui as a "revolutionary" I have taken on trust from a modern Chinese scholar, Hu Shih, who also happens to have been one of the leaders in the Chinese literary revolution after World War I. In the famous debate between Hu Shih and the Japanese Zen scholar, Daisetz Suzuki (which centers on the Ch'an of Shen Hui) one may be inclined to side with Suzuki who has recaptured the authentic spirit of Ch'an insight. Suzuki was speaking from his own experience and not only from his research. But at the same time Hu Shih's essay is full of important information. The reader is charmed and absorbed by the way Hu Shih intuitively identifies himself with the eighth century master and projects his own ideals into the revolutionary situation of a former time.

It might be useful to quote a few lines from him here. They will bring to life if not Shen Hui himself, at least the Shen Hui that Dr. Hu Shih imaged and venerated.

> His lifelong popular preaching of a new and simple form of Buddhism based on the idea of sudden enlightenment, his four time banishment, and his final victory in the official recognition of his school as the True School -- was historically not an isolated event but only part of a larger movement which may be correctly characterized as an internal reformation of revolution in Buddhism, a movement that had been fermenting and spreading throughout the eighth century in many parts of China. . . Shen Hui himself was a product of a revolutionary age in which the great minds in the Buddhist and Ch'an schools were, in one way or another, thinking dangerous thoughts and preaching dangerous doctrines. . . Shen Hui was a political genius who understood the signs of the times and knew what to attack and how to do it. So he became the warrior and statesman of the new movement and fired the first shot of the revolution. His long life, his great eloquence and, above all, his courage and shrewdness saved the day and a powerful orthodoxy was crushed. What appeared to be an easy and quick victory was probably due to the fact that his striking tactics of bold and persistent offensive attacks and his simple and popular preaching. . . had won for himself and his cause a tremendous following among the people.

Dr. Hu Shih concludes this somewhat exuberant description by showing how the poets, intellectuals, and all the radical and liberal elements gathered together with the Ch'an iconoclasts to win a sweeping revolutionary victory (in the cultural rather than in the military sense). And he concludes: "To them the victory must have meant a great liberation of thought and belief from the old shackles of tradition and authority."[1]

It is possible to stand back from these statements of Hu Shih and view them a little critically. They do reflect the conceptions and even cliches of a mind trained in American universities such as Columbia and Cornell, impregnated with pragmatism and with the influence of Dewey, as well as with the standard notions of a democracy shaped by European and American history, the enlightenment, and so on. There is nothing exactly wrong

---

1. Hu Shih, "Ch'an (Zen) Buddhism in China: Its History and Method," in *Philosophy East and West*, Vol. III, No. 1, April 1953, University of Hawaii Press, Honolulu, p. 13.

with this, but it does give a slightly distorted perspective, as if Shen Hui were at the same time a kind of Luther and also something of a Voltaire, or indeed a Lenin. He comes out looking very much like a revolutionary activist of the European type. But if we get this impression, we fail entirely to see the uniqueness of a purely Asian approach, founded not in the dynamics of reasoned strategy and well-planned attack, but in the totally different insights that emanate from the void and from *wu-wei* (non-action). What is remarkable in Shen Hui is not just strength of character and tactical genius -- though we need not deny him these qualities. But what really marks him out as extraordinary is that his action was at the same time his Ch'an, his "contemplation" (though the word simply does not apply here). The impact of his action, preaching and teaching derived not from strength and application of will-power (still less of will-*to*-power) but from a will-less-ness endowed with lucid and total efficacy and a mind-less-ness that was free from pedestrian political figuring. But Shen Hui was not an irrational, pseudo-mystical demagogue on the Fascist pattern. Far from it. How then are we to comprehend a life of contemplative action grounded in non-action and no-mind?

It must be made clear that on this point there is a radical difference between East and West, and if this difference is overlooked one will fall into the sin of finding "Zen" here, there and everywhere in Western literature when it is in fact seldom found there at all. Take for example the literature of "the absurd" in the West: Kafka, Camus and so on. The mere fact that this literature represents a reaction against the heritage of bourgeois rationalism and liberal enlightenment does not make it in any sense "Zen." Western literature, philosophy and religion are underlain by a tendency to regard the universe either as mystery or as antagonist: a mystery to be entered by some awesome mystic initiation or an antagonist to be opposed with stoic courage. Greek tragedy and philosophy set the tone for this; modern science and technology have amplified it a hundredfold. Western man is essentially Promethean, and therein lies both his greatness and his absurdity. He does possess ways of escape from the dilemmas into which he is thrown by his endemic willfulness. The kenotic theology of Christian self-emptying is the most radical of them all -- but it seldom really appeals to him. Another is his sense of humor. The great comic writers of the West, from Cervantes and Rabelais to Joyce (and in a much lesser way Brecht, Kafka and Camus) have tried to help with their potent exorcisms. But still they show the comic epic hero in his pitiable humanity and isolation opposing the antagonistic world with all that he has. And (says a critic) "it is not much -- merely free will and a capacity for love."[2]

The East on the other hand does not try to beat or cajole the universe or the gods. It tries to join them. So of course does the Western stoic. But the Western stoic regards this problem as one of antagonistic *wills*, to be reconciled by obedience or overcome by dogged refusal -- "Better to reign in hell than serve in heaven!" The East regards it more as a matter of ignorance and enlightenment. Ch'an, and especially Shen Hui, further simplifies the question: to fight nature and the world is sheer illusion, for this assumes that we are somehow outside the world and not really part of it. Furthermore, the world itself is not an objective whole of which we are a part -- nor is it one great pantheistic substance -- but is itself void. There is then nothing to oppose and nothing to join. There is nothing to be reconciled. The opposition itself is the radical illusion. What is to be done then is to stop thinking in terms of this illusion. But all "thought" is affected by the illusion. Should one then stop thinking altogether? No. For that would perpetuate the same illusion (the illusion that one could effectively will to stop thinking).

This question of no-mind and non-action, which is absolutely central to the Ch'an of Shen Hui, is not accounted for by the historical analysis of Hu Shih, brilliant though it may be. Daisetz Suzuki grasped this, and demolished Hu Shih's argument that the insight of Shen Hui was rational and intellectual -- a kind of enlightened debunking of religious superstition --when it was in fact much more. The *chih* (knowledge, insight, gnosis-in-act) of Shen Hui is much more like what Kitaro Nishida called "pure experience" which is not "experience of" any special object or objects, but the very awakening of the ground of all existence. Thus the action of Shen Hui was in no sense a planned operation in which an objective was envisioned, willed and then attained. Shen Hui, of course, saw that the Northern School of Ch'an was somehow a stuffy and narrow conservatism allied with a backward political establishment. This does not mean that he conceived and cleverly executed a revolutionary plan to discredit this outdated doctrine. His attack on the Northern School was in some sense an attack on *will*, on the volitive execution of reasoned plans, the carrying out of system in Ch'an. But he did not overcome volition with volition. He did it with insight.

Nothing could be more misleading than to say, as someone has said, that Shen Hui (and Hui Neng) represented a "quietist trend" in Ch'an

---

2. Anthony Burgess, *Re Joyce*, Norton & Co., New York, 1968, p. 22.

because they preached a "sudden enlightenment" which was not the result of systematic discipline and effort. On the contrary, it was the Northern School that was profoundly quietistic, even though it was at the same time profoundly voluntaristic. The Northern way of gradual enlightenment -- preached by another Master whose name is so like Shen Hui that it must be read carefully to avoid disastrous confusions (Shen Hsiu) -- advocated the practice of enforced, studied, systematic tranquillity. One *willed* to withdraw, one *willed* to meditate, concentrate, to "wipe the mirror" of the mind clear of all "dust" -- or all taint of conceptual thought. One *willed* to empty the mind in order to converge in purity and emptiness. This was all planned and directed to a *willed* consummation: the "realization" or "illumination" of a perfectly pure emptiness as the ground of all. Shen Hui's reply to all this was:

> To converge one's mind with volition, to adhere to the concepts of voidness and purity, to seek to realize enlightenment and nirvana, all these are illusory. Only by avoiding volition will the mind be rid of objects. A mind unconscious of any object is void and tranquil by nature.[3]

This is of course a quotation that cannot be understood outside the context of Shen Hui's whole teaching. If we read it superficially we will inevitably tend to fall back into the same error Shen Hui is refuting: the error of concluding "if the mind that is unconscious of an object is tranquil, then I must empty my mind of all objects." This is the teaching of the Northern School. Shen Hui's teaching is not that the mind *must be* emptied, but that it is empty in the first place, and what "fills" it is the ground of volition or craving that Buddhism calls *avidya*, the ignorance that wills itself as a willing self. To will the mind to be empty is to fill it with a ground of willed content and therefore to will it to be not-empty. What then? Should we will to destroy will? Should we will to be will-less? This too is absurd.

> Destruction of affectivity should not be called *nirvana*; realization of the fact that affectivity has never come into being at all can be called *nirvana*.[4]

In the debate between Hu Shih and Daisetz Suzuki, one of the main issues was whether or not Shen Hui can be called "logical." If we consider carefully the statements above in the light of the controversy between the two schools, it must be admitted that the most rigorous and sophisticated logic is on the side of Shen Hui. The Northern School suffers, like so many artificial systems, from a basic illogicality. It is built on self-contradiction. But Suzuki (who always emphasized the apparent irrationality of Ch'an) is

---

3. Kitaro Nishida, "Comments on Zen," *Psychologia*, Kyoto, 1960, III, pp. 80-82.
4. *Ibid.*

also right when he insists that the validity of the Ch'an "argument" rests not so much on a correct sequence of propositions but on an original intuition which gives an internal consistency to all that follows.

The apparent irrationality of Ch'an is in fact what Nishida called the "rationality of anti-rationality."[5] If our existence, as Nishida says, [is] fundamentally self-contradictory (since for him we are the "self-negation of the absolute"), we affirm ourselves only by denying ourselves. And this, by the way, is close to the existential logic of the Gospels and the New Testament. The real affirmation is beyond affirmation and negation (is in fact no-affirmation). It is the *kensho* or insight into the ground-nature attained by penetrating to the very root of our "contradictory self-identity." Anti-rational rationality is not, Nishida says, irrational. It is the result of thinking-through that entirely exhausts the thinking self and empties it at once of self, of logic and of thought. It is the final stripping away not only of all opinions and all dogmas but of the self that affirms and contradicts itself in the same breath every time it says "I think therefore I am." (For the Buddhist this *also* means "I think therefore I am not.")

Though Daisetz Suzuki was perhaps going too far in giving the impression that Zen *defied* logic at every turn, his views were right insofar as he was protesting against Hu Shih's short-sighted implication that Shen Hui was a sort of rationalist a la enlightenment. Nothing could be further from the truth.

It now becomes important to clarify one main point. What precisely was the essence of Shen Hui's Ch'an teaching? It is extremely important to know this; otherwise we will tend to view the struggle of the Northern and Southern Schools in terms of the doctrinal battles with which we are so familiar in the West. The term "orthodoxy" is very unfortunate in this connection. It should never be used of someone like Shen Hui. True, the historical struggle did take on the character of a struggle for official recognition. True, the revolutionary "victory" of Shen Hui which made the heart of Hu Shih beat faster was canonized by the declaration that Hui Neng was the Sixth Patriarch and Shen Hui was the Seventh. This was the same as saying they had transmitted the pure *dharma*. But the public and official declaration must be weighed against the statement of Shen Hui, that there is no *dharma*, and there is nothing in Buddhism that can be the object of a meaningful official approval; to canonize the pure is at the same time to canonize the impure along with it.

---

5. *Ibid.*

Curious that Shen Hui could at the same time "defeat" the Northern School and assert that the doctrine of gradual enlightenment was all wrong. Strange that he should want people to know this, and to embrace the way of sudden enlightenment: yet at the same time he should say that there "is no way." Logical? Contradictory? Here we must admit that from the viewpoint of a short-sighted and merely empirical logic, Shen Hui is being absurd. But yet from a higher and more sophisticated viewpoint he is being utterly logical.

A concrete example of Shen Hui's logic is this: the *kasaya* or *dharma* mantle of succession assumed tremendous official importance in the struggle between the Northern and Southern schools. The disciple who received the *kasaya* from his dying Master was approved as his true successor: he was entitled to speak with authority in the name of *dharma*. A certain kind of "logic" assumed that if one stole the *kasaya* one had the authority along with it. We are even told that things reached the point where monks were ready to kill each other for the *kasaya*. What about Shen Hui?

When Hui Neng died, Shen Hui came down the mountain with the *kasaya*. Naturally everyone wanted to know if he were the official successor. They asked:

> Has it been transmitted to you?
>
> It is not with me.
>
> Who has received it?
>
> If anyone has received it, he must know that himself. And if such a one preaches, the true law is spread everywhere and thereby vanishes of its own accord.

That gives a good insight into the mind of Shen Hui. Obviously what matters is not a "sign" of authenticity but authenticity itself. And true authenticity is not authentic doctrine, but, one might say, the absence of an "authentic doctrine" and the presence of an authentic mind. The task of the preacher — which Shen Hui accepted without qualms — was not correct exposition of orthodox theology, but a manifestation of the Buddha mind. This manifestation was not just a matter of revealing the Buddha as "another" mysteriously present behind or "in" the preacher himself, mystically shining through to the hearer. To impose this expectation upon the hearer was to make it impossible for him to grasp the true teaching. If the Master were to communicate to others that there is a direct knowledge without medium between the knower and the known, then he must not place any medium between them. He must not put his teaching in the way, or himself in the way. He must teach them in the simplest language that there *is no teaching*.

Yet this must be set in a framework of language. Shen Hui took as his framework the familiar Buddhist teaching about *sila* (morality), *dhyana* (meditation) and *prajna* (wisdom, insight, contemplation) and presented them in a revolutionary form.

Instead of starting out to be virtuous and to practice good works, especially the work of meditation; instead of willing to attain to contemplative wisdom; instead of starting out to "follow a way" -- one "leaves the way" (my expression is borrowed from St. John of the Cross). Instead of finding the "right road" one recognizes that there is no road. And there is no road because there is nowhere to go. Thinking that there is somewhere to go, that there is something that must be attained, is the basic illusion. *Sila*, then, *is not to let this illusion arise* in us. *Dhyana* is freedom from this illusion by non-volition -- including not wanting to attain anything. *Prajna* is awareness that there is no illusion anyway. And these three, Shen Hui adds, are all the same. They are the recognition that no-seeing is the true-seeing.

This may sound a little obscure, but it has momentous consequences in concrete life. It is by no means esoteric. It shows that the Northern School has got the whole of Buddhism turned upside down and standing on its head because of the ingrained defect of voluntaristic quietism. But at the same time, this static, inert, dead, self-defeating routine of concentration lends itself very well to the purposes of a conservative and authoritarian social establishment. The imperial government was well aware of the fact that a flourishing monastic order, with thousands of monks engaged in concentration, provided a stabilizing religious base for society. Somehow it seems that the government did not fully realize to what extent Shen Hui was denouncing all this as mystification and fakery.

On the other hand it would be absolutely wrong to suppose that the Ch'an of Shen Hui dispensed entirely with all "practice." If Shen Hui asserted that the Northern School was wrong in trying to attain illumination by practice and systematic effort, it was because he saw that such effort was meaningless and wasted if they were based on an illusory objective: and that unless there was some experience to begin with, practice would remain an obstacle and an illusion. This is the real meaning of the doctrine of sudden enlightenment. In the Ch'an of Shen Hui, one does not gradually build up to an experience but one *begins with an experience*. This experience is not the fruition and confirmation of a doctrine, but is an explosive realization that doctrines and systems are built on illusion. Once this realization is present, then one can and must develop it in meditation and action. But the meditation and action are only further expressions of the experience itself. In simple words, the Ch'an of Shen Hui is based on the radical assertion that unless one has some enlightenment one cannot even begin to meditate for he does not know what he is doing. Until one has oneself awakened, the thing to do is to live with an awakened Master -- who fully knows what he is doing -- and hope to be awakened by him. The Master however will take great care to avoid giving any impression that the awakening is something systematic or the result of a magically efficacious technique.

Thus Shen Hui made it perfectly clear that this obsession with *nirvana* as an end to be attained through will and effort was completely self-defeating. What is self-defeating is deadly. It eventually fills the whole atmosphere of society with the odor of corruption. As Shen Hui put it, concentration in inertia will lead only to the complete failure of meditation.

> When a hovering bird stays motionless at a point in the sky it will inevitably fall to the ground. Similarly when one practices the "non abiding mind" and yet still abides in something, he will not be emancipated.

This brings us to the real point. If *dhyana, prajna, sila* are all one, and if they are nothing but life itself, then the thing to do is not to stop life, like the bird stopping itself in mid-flight, but to *go on living* even though life may be a contradiction. Instead of being like a bird with an absurd project to stop dead in mid-air and thus attain *prajna*, one should go on flying with the awareness that *prajna, dhyana* and *sila* are *not something other than the flight itself.* Life itself is all of these. Therefore, Ch'an does not consist in stopping life in mid-flight, but in flying and living as spontaneously as a bird. Is there nothing more? There is much more: there is the sudden enlightenment in which life is *fully experienced* as at once illusionless and mindless: as *prajna. At this point meditation and morality can really begin.* Once one "sees" life as it is, illusionlessly, mindlessly, unfettered by compulsion and artificiality and formalism, once one sees that there is nothing else to it: that meditation is not *more than* living, or anti-living, but living without explanation and without attachment to the self-contradiction which is life. Life lived without attachment is itself meditation and enlightenment. One does not meditate in order to live, or live in order to meditate, one lives meditating and meditates living, and the two are not separate. They are a living-dying life in which one is not aware of meditating on death or on life.

It was here of course that Ch'an became supremely dangerous. Conservatives attacked it furiously as total lawlessness, as "godlessness" (if a somewhat inexact word may be used), as utter impiety and revolution. And it was. For evidently, though the masses did not all at once become "enlightened" in the Buddhist sense, they seem to have grasped some of the implications of this radical kenoticism. In any event, it is clear that Shen Hui's Ch'an is anything but unworldly, inert, or static. It is anything but an evasion of ordinary life, though the reader who is mystified by the verbal fencing in his dialogues and the formal Buddhism of his discourses may be disturbed by something so remote and unfamiliar.

A modern Chinese scholar, Liang Chi Ch'ao, saw how much this Ch'an had in common with the vitalism of a Bergson and regretted that it was not better known in the West. Since then, writers like Suzuki have made it well known, and the effect upon thinkers like Heidegger, Tillich, Fromm and others has not been negligible. But still, the dialogue with Ch'an has yet really to begin. Too many Westerners are still obsessed with the idea of a Ch'an or Zen that is purely a matter of introversion, concentration, and head-splitting ventures in attaining *satori*. The Ch'an of Shen Hui is the exact opposite of any such thing. In Liang Chi Ch'ao's words, it "can truly be considered as practical Buddhism and worldly Buddhism . . . . It enables the way of renouncing the world and the way of remaining in the world to go hand in hand without conflict."

The religious genius of the Far East, China and Japan is the *only one* that has so far achieved this perfect resolution of any possible conflict between "action and contemplation." In the West we are still hung up in an inexorable division between activists who run around in circles claiming that their hectic and ulcer-forming busyness is "prayer" and contemplatives (so-called) who are completely immersed in liturgical projects, or devout pieties which are justified as supremely efficacious activities. This is not to criticize Christian spirituality as such: but there is a fatal division in Western thinking which makes this kind of split almost inevitable. The ground of the division is the Western obsession with will, achievement, production, self-affirmation and power . . . . Perhaps this reminder that Shen Hui is talking about the ground of existence and not about a religious system may help you to understand him better.

ZEN INFLUENCE
ON THOMAS MERTON'S
VIEW OF THE SELF

by **Bonnie Bowman Thurston**

"If you want the kernel you must break the shell."
Meister Eckhart[1]

"Descartes made a fetish out of the mirror in which the self finds itself.
Zen shatters it."[2]

Thomas Merton realized that "you can hardly set Christianity and Zen side by side and compare them. That would almost be like trying to compare mathematics and tennis."[3] Problems like those of emptiness vs. God, nirvana vs. salvation, and wisdom vs. faith loomed large in his mind. And yet he did, in fact, set the two side by side and, without unduly distorting either, gleaned from them a remarkable approach to human identity. He understood so well because he understood from both positions.

---

1. R. B. Blankney, *Meister Eckhart: A Modern Translation* (New York: Harper and Bros., 1941), p. 148.

2. Thomas Merton, *Conjectures of a Guilty Bystander* (New York: Image Books, 1968), p. 285. Hereafter appears in text as CGB.

3. Thomas Merton, *Zen and the Birds of Appetite* (New York: New Directions, 1968), p. 33. Hereafter appears in text as ZBA. In so far as possible, I have kept to primary material in the text of this essay and put references to secondary material in the notes.

Editors' Note: This essay appeared originally in *Japanese Religions* Vol. 14, No. 3, December 1986, and is reprinted here by permission of The Center for the Study of Japanese Religions, Kyoto, Japan.

This question of identity, or of the self, was for Merton the key issue in a Zen-Christian dialogue.[4] From Murti, Merton understood that the "Buddha neither said 'there is a self' or 'there is not a self' . . . among many Buddhists there appears to be a kind of dogmatism that says 'there is not a self' instead of taking the true middle . . . Buddha replied [to Vacchagotta] by silence because he considered the *condition of the questioner*. . . Buddha did not say 'there is no self'. . . ."[5] So for Merton, if not for us, the question of whether or not there was a self to ponder was not the issue. For Christians (and I believe he thought for Buddhists) human persons are "selves" involved in a crisis of identity.

In some of the last materials Merton put together before his death, he defined identity.[6]

> . . . For practical purposes here we are talking about one's own authentic and personal beliefs and convictions, based on experience of oneself as a person, experience of one's ability to choose and reject even good things which are not relevant to one's own life.
>
> One does not receive "identity" in this sense along with life and vegetative existence. To have identity is not merely to have a face and a name, a recognizable physical presence. Identity in this deep sense is something that one must create for himself by choices that are significant and that require a courageous commitment in the face of anguish and risk. . . . In this sense, identity is one's witness to truth in one's life. (CWA, p. 78)

Merton understood the truth in our lives to be forged by a process of consciously made decisions to act and to believe. In Christian terms, we are partners with God in creating the truth of our selves. In Zen terms, we can discipline our selves into their "native nakedness."[7] In each case the process has an element, call it gift or grace or mystery, which is not rationally comprehensible or controlled.

It is the process of creating identity in this sense, coming to a ridding of self, that most fascinated Merton and that will be explored as a point of dialogue here.[8]

---

4. Indeed, Raymond Bailey (*Thomas Merton on Mysticism*, Garden City, New York: Doubleday Image Books, 1974) believed it was the key to all Merton's work. "In every period of his life and in every major title published over his name, he attacked the problem of the real and illusory selves" (p. 205).

5. Naomi Burton, Patrick Hart, James Laughlin (eds.), *The Asian Journal of Thomas Merton* (New York: New Directions, 1973), p. 104. Hereafter referred to in the text as AJ.

6. Thomas Merton, *Contemplation in a World of Action* (New York: Image Books, 1973), p. 19. Hereafter referred to in the text as CWA.

7. Suzuki Teitaro Daisetz, "Self the Unattainable" in *The Buddha Eye*, Frederick Franck (ed.), (New York: Crossroad Publishers, 1982), p. 15. Hereafter referred to in the text as BE.

8. Readers unfamiliar with Merton on the subject are referred to "Nirvana" (ZBA, pp. 79-88) and to "Mystics and Zen Masters" in the volume by that title (New York: Delta Books, 1969), pp. 3-44. (Hereafter referred to in the text as MZM). See also Raymond Bailey (note 4 above), "East meets West," pp. 189-210.

I. The Christian Self

> . . . there was this shadow, this double, this writer who had followed me into the cloister.
>
> He is supposed to be dead.
>
> But he stands and meets me in the doorway of all my prayers, and follows me into church. He kneels with me behind the pillar, the Judas, and talks to me all the time in my ear.
>
> And the worst of it is, he has my superiors on his side. They won't kick him out. I can't get rid of him.
>
> Nobody seems to understand that one of us has got to die.[9]

This passage from *The Seven Storey Mountain*, the autobiography written in Merton's early monastic life, articulates the psychology which undergirds his later writing on self. Its clearest expression is in chapters 5-9 of *New Seeds of Contemplation*. Here Merton states that we are all "shadowed by an illusory person: a false self." The false self "wants to exist outside the reach of God's will and God's love -- outside of reality and outside of life."[10] This false self harbors illusions, desires which confuse ego gratification with the inner needs of the soul, and is, therefore, the root of sin.

> All sin starts from the assumption that my false self, the self that exists only in my egocentric desires, is the fundamental reality of life to which everything else in the universe is ordered. Thus I use up my life in the desire for pleasures and the thirst for experiences, for power, honor, knowledge and love, to clothe this false self. . . and I wind experiences around myself. . . like bandages in order to make myself perceptible to myself and to the world . . . .
>
> But there is no substance under the things with which I am clothed. I am hollow, and my structure of pleasures and ambitions has no foundation.
>
> (NSC, pp. 34-35)

The false self is mirrored in its own activities rather than in an identity begun in relationship to Jesus Christ at baptism. Merton explains in *No Man is an Island*, chapter 9, that, because of Christ's sacrifice, we do not have "to do" but "to be."[11] When we are unable simply to be, we fill our lives with

---

9. Thomas Merton, *The Seven Storey Mountain* (New York: Doubleday Image Books, 1974), pp. 496-497. Hereafter referred to in the text as SSM. Much of this discussion on the Christian self appears in an article I wrote for *Cistercian Studies*, "Self and the World: Two Directions of the Spiritual Life," Vol. XVIII, 1983:2, pp. 149-155. I thank them for permission to use it here.

10. Thomas Merton, *New Seeds of Contemplation* (New York: New Directions, 1972), p. 34. Hereafter referred to in the text as NSC.

11. Thomas Merton, *No Man is an Island* (New York: Image Books, 1967). Hereafter referred to in the text as NMI.

doing and become, to use Merton's image, like a madman who sleeps on the street rather than in the safety and comfort of his house.

The result of "doing" to fill our false selves, of laboring for the "food which perishes" (St. John 6:27), is that we become enamoured by our labels or roles. We are not "teachers," "secretaries," "priests," "monks," "wives," or "fathers" and, if we think these labels contain our identities, we are on very thin spiritual ice. The point is exemplified in St. Paul's letter to the Galatians. He writes, "Am I now seeking the favor of men or of God? Or am I trying to please men? If I were still pleasing men, I would not be a servant of Christ" (Galatians 1:10). In Merton's terms, all activities, regardless of their "goodness," if done to curry the favor of other persons, are motivated by the false self. On the other hand, actions done in response to God's love, and for His sake alone, are from the true self.

Merton used the example of the desert monastics to show how some have realized society gives us false images of the self and have rejected those images. The desert monk chooses

> . . .to lose himself in the inner, hidden reality of a self that was transcendent, mysterious, half-known, and lost in Christ. He had to die to the values of transient existence as Christ had died to them on the cross, and rise from the dead with Him in the light of an entirely new wisdom.[12]

St. Paul serves to move us to an understanding of the true self: "Put off your old nature . . . and be renewed in the spirit of your minds, and put on the new nature created after the likeness of God. . ." (Ephesians 4:22-24). This new nature made after the likeness of God is found by looking within. St. John records, "You know him, for he dwells with you, and will be in you" (St. John 14:17). After St. John, in *New Seeds of Contemplation* Merton relates his belief that human personality is created by the Word (the speaking of God) exactly as everything else is created.

> God utters me like a word containing a partial thought of Himself.

> But if I am true to the concept that God utters in me, if I am true to the thought of Him I was meant to embody, I shall be full of His actuality and find Him everywhere in myself, and find myself nowhere. I shall be lost in Him: that is, I shall find myself. I shall be "saved." (NSC, p. 37)

In Merton's terms, to be "born again" is to rediscover within ourselves the God Who uttered our lives. Again, as Jesus says in St. John, "You are already made clean by the word which I have spoken to you. Abide in me, and I in you" (St. John 15:3).

---

12. Thomas Merton, *The Wisdom of the Desert* (New York: New Directions, 1960), p. 7. Hereafter referred to in the text as WD.

True identity, the *insitum verbum*, is spoken in the inner silence of
an individual life, and this speaking takes place within historical time and
place.

> His presence is present in *my own presence*. If I am, then He is. And
> knowing that I am, if I penetrate to the depths of my own existence and *my*
> *own present reality*, the indefinable "am" that is myself in its deepest
> roots, then through this deep center I pass into the infinite "I am" which is
> the very Name of the Almighty.
>
> My knowledge of myself in silence . . . opens out into the silence and the
> "subjectivity" of God's own self.[13]

Merton believes that, in fact, we do not "know" ourselves so much
as we "are known" by God. We are not so much speakers as we are spoken.
This mystery leads us to submit to the truth of our own experience. We are
(as so many of Merton's poems demonstrate) part of the world around us.
As he explains:

> The world as pure object is something that is not there. It is not a reality
> outside us for which we exist. . . . It is a living and self-creating mystery of
> which I am myself a part, to which I am myself, my own unique door.
> When I find the world in my own ground, it is impossible for me to be
> alienated by it.[14]

The secret of identity, of the True Self, "is hidden in the love and
mercy of God. . . in Whom is hidden the reason and fulfillment of my
existence" (NSC, pp. 35-36). We discover the true self by discovering God
Who utters Himself in us. By becoming one with the God within, we "share
with God the work of *creating* the truth of our identity" (NSC, p. 32).
Because God speaks Himself in each person, the discovery of the True Self is
the discovery of all persons, the apex of community and of mystical union.[15]

II. The Point of Dialogue

For Merton, true identity speaks of a unity of individual, God, and
other. This unity is the True Self. It shatters the falseness of what, in many
places, Merton calls the Cartesian consciousness.[16] In writing of Kitaro

13. Thomas Merton, *Thoughts in Solitude* (New York: Farrar, Straus & Giroux, 1977), p. 70. Hereafter
referred to in the text as TS. See also ZBA, p. 75ff on the person as "actualized" in union with Christ.

14. Thomas Merton, "Is the World a Problem?" in *Commonweal*, 3 June 1966, p. 308.

15. See also William H. Shannon, "Thomas Merton and the Discovery of the Real Self," *Cistercian
Studies*, Vol. 13, 1978:4, pp. 298-308.

16. See, for example, ZBA p. 22 and p. 67 or MZM p. 26 and p. 241. Also William H. Shannon, *Thomas
Merton's Dark Path* (New York: Penguin Books, 1981), pp. 206-212.

Nishida (1870-1945), Merton begins his remarks with a discussion of "the *unifying* intuition of the *basic unity of subject and object in being* or a 'deep grasp of life' in its essential concreteness 'at the base of consciousness.' " This basic unity is being itself "prior to all differentiations and contradictions" (ZBA, p. 68). True Self, then, is participation in Being.[17] Merton's discussion expands on this point.

> Buddha taught us that all evil is rooted in the "ignorance" which makes us take our individual ego as our true self. But Nishida is not confusing the "person" with the external and individual self. Nor is the "person" for him simply the "subject" related to various objects, or even to God in an I-Thou relationship. The root of personality is to be sought in the "true Self" which is manifested in the basic unification of consciousness in which subject and object are one. Hence the highest good is "the self's fusion with the highest reality." Human personality is regarded as the force which effects this fusion. The hopes and desires of the external, individual self are all, in fact, opposed to this higher unity. They are centered on the affirmation of the individual. It is only at the point where the hopes and fears of the individual self are done away with and forgotten "that true human personality appears." (ZBA, p. 69)

There are clear parallels here between the Christian coming to True Self and the Zen Buddhist coming to *sunyata* (emptiness or "enlightenment of the nature of essencelessness").[18] Merton suggests that

> Buddhism and Biblical Christianity agree in their view of man's present condition. Both are aware that man is somehow not in his right relation to the world and to things in it, . . . they see that man bears in himself a mysterious tendency to *falsify* that relation, and to spend a great deal of energy in justifying the false view he takes of his world and of his place in it. (ZBA, p. 82)

In both traditions, the fundamental impediment to True Self is the concept of an individual ego, "a subject for whom his own self-awareness...is absolutely primary." Such an attitude creates a "solipsistic bubble of awareness -- an ego self -- imprisoned in its own consciousness, isolated, and out of touch" (ZBA, p. 22). "For this very reason it is basic to Zen . . . and to Christian mysticism . . . to *radically and unconditionally question the ego*" (ZBA, p. 73). In both Christianity and Zen this impediment is, unfortunately, strengthened by striving for externally defined identity and by focusing on the imperfectly understood self.[19]

In *Conjectures of a Guilty Bystander*, Merton remarks that the

---

17. "Enlightenment is an experience of absolute unity; it is beyond subject and object; the empirical ego is so submerged that there is no longer "I" and "it" but pure existence or 'is-ness'." William Johnston, *The Still Point: Reflections on Zen and Christian Mysticism* (New York: Fordham University Press, 1970), pp. 20.

18. S. B. Dasgupta quoted in AJ, p. 405.

19. For a parallel discussion see Donald K. Swearer, *Dialogue: The Key to Understanding Other Religions* (Philadelphia: Westminster Press, Chapt. 3, "It is No Longer I Who Live," especially pp. 78-83).

enlightened Zen man is not one who seeks Buddha, but an ordinary man with nothing left to do. "The man who is ripe discovers that there was never anything to be done" (CGB, p. 282). In the same book Merton asserts that one does not gain possession of wisdom; wisdom seizes one.

> To be wise is, in a sense, to abandon every attempt at gaining wisdom, and to enter into a whole new dimension of existence, where the division of subject and object, ends and means, time and eternity, body and soul either appears in a totally new perspective or vanished altogether. (CGB, p. 291)

Similarly, D. T. Suzuki (with whom Merton corresponded) wrote that *ani-kalpajnana* ("the sense of nondiscrimination") is not acquired by means of learning or experience. "It has nothing to do with accumulated knowledge. It comes out of one's innermost being all at once, when the zero-self becomes identified with the totality of infinity" (BE, p. 21).[20]

Striving, externally or intellectually, tightens one in the vice grip of the false self with its round of activity and labelling and social compulsion. Nor does focusing on the "self which strives" provide an escape. Merton asserts that it worsens the situation, that a great need of modern man is precisely "liberation from his inordinate self-consciousness, his monumental self-awareness, his obsession with self-affirmation" (ZBA, p. 31). "What is important is not liberation from the body but liberation from the mind. We are not entangled in our own body but entangled in our own mind" (AJ, p. 90).

Merton understands that in both Christianity and Zen (with some qualifications), liberation from false self is a process of self-emptying which leads from isolation to unity. The Preface to the Japanese Edition of *Thoughts in Solitude* describes the process as follows: "As Christ said, the seed in the ground must die. To be as a seed in the ground of one's life is to dissolve in that ground in order to become fruitful. One disappears into Love, in order to 'be Love.' "[21] In order for the seed to dissolve, we must doubt all we have seen in ourselves.

> The "doubt" dissolves our ego-identity. Faith gives us life in Christ, according to St. Paul's word: "I live, now not I, but Christ lives in me" (Galatians 2:20). To accept this is impossible unless one has profound hope in the incomprehensible fruitfulness that emerges from the dissolution of our ego in the ground of being and Love . . . . To accept our own dissolution would be inhuman if we did not at the same time accept the wholeness and completeness of everything in God's Love. We accept our emptying

---

20. Note that both Zen and Christian descriptions of coming to True Self stress unity and universality.

21. Robert E. Daggy (ed.), *Introductions East and West: The Foreign Prefaces of Thomas Merton* (Greensboro, North Carolina: Unicorn Press, 1981), p. 96. Hereafter referred to in the text as *IEW*.

> because we realize that our very emptiness is fulfillment and plentitude. In
> our emptiness the One Word is clearly spoken. (*IEW*, pp. 96-97)

In a discussion of D. T. Suzuki, Merton points to Eckhart's belief that
"it is precisely in this pure poverty when one is no longer a 'self' that one
recovers one's true identity in God: This true identity is the 'birth of Christ
in us'" (*ZBA*, p. 12). The relationship Merton points to between the Christian and the Zen True Self centers around what Christians would call
kenosis and what Zen might call self-emptying.[22]

> The "mind of Christ" as described by St. Paul in Philippians 2 may be
> theologically worlds apart from the "mind of Buddha" -- this I am not
> prepared to discuss. But the utter "self-emptying" of Christ -- and the
> self-emptying which makes the disciple one with Christ in *His* kenosis --
> can be understood and has been understood in a very Zen-like sense as far
> as psychology and experience are concerned. (*ZBA*, p. 8)

Let us address the question Merton skirts. To what extent may Christian *kenosis* and Zen self-emptying be similarly understood?

III. The "Problem" of *Kenosis*

Most who have read Merton on Zen agree that he has effected a
remarkable synthesis with Christianity "as far as psychology and experience
are concerned." His work on identity, however, raises a question. Are
Buddhist self-emptying and Christian *kenosis* for the same end? Can we
with truthfulness to both traditions equate unity with God (and thus Other)
and Emptiness?

John Cobb, Jr. suggests in *Beyond Dialogue* that both being and
nirvana are names for ultimate reality. "Emptiness," he says, "for much of
Mahayana becomes the preferred way of naming ultimate reality."[23]

> To be empty is to lack any boundaries, any determining content of one's
> own, and filter through which the world is experienced. To be empty is to
> be perfectly open to what is there, whatever that may be. It is to be
> completely defenseless and with nothing to defend. (*BD*, p.. 90)

---

22.   The noun form, *kenos*, occurs in the papyri in the literal sense of "empty" (see St. Luke 1:53; 20: 20-11
or Ephesians 5:6), though it is used metaphorically in the New Testament to mean "vain" (especially in I Corinthians 15) and also "hollow" or pretentious (Acts 4:25 or James 2:20). The verb form means "to deprive of
power" or "to make of no meaning." When it occurs with the reflexive pronoun (my self, my own), it is
usually translated "to give up or lay aside what one possesses" or "to divest one's self of one's prerogatives."
It is so used in the Philippian passage that most concerns us here, 2:5-8, especially verse 7. (It may be straining
grammatical interpretation to point to the use of the aorist as past time which may either be momentary or
prolonged.)

23.   John B. Cobb, Jr., *Beyond Dialogue: Toward a Mutual Transformation of Christianity and Buddhism*
(Philadelphia: Fortress Press, 1982): pp. 88-90. Hereafter referred to in the text as *BD*.

Ultimate reality is empty; so the "True Self" of Zen equals emptiness. As Masao Abe suggests "what is beyond all affirmation and all negation --that is, Ultimate Reality -- should not be 'Him' or 'Thou'...."[24] But Merton has said the Christian True Self is "Christ within" (Galatians 2:20) or God Who utters Himself in us (NSC, p. 37).[25] On the surface it seems that self-emptying and *kenosis* lead to two different and incomparable ends: Emptiness and God (or Christ). But suppose God (or Jesus Christ) is understood by the Christian to be empty in terms that a Buddhist could accept?

In *Beyond Dialogue* Cobb discusses "God and Emptiness." He argues that asserting ultimate reality is Emptiness does not necessarily sever the connection the Christian makes between God and ultimate reality. In fact, it clarifies the conceptual confusion between God and being, by helping us to see the difference between ultimate reality and its divine manifestations and by helping us to recognize "that the God of the Bible... is a manifestation of ultimate reality, not the name of that reality" (BD, p. 111). Further, "manifest" is a misleading term for the relationship between God and ultimate reality, because "God also actualizes and embodies that reality" (BD, p. 112). "Acceptance of the view that ultimate reality is Emptiness rather than being can free us from a tendency to place it at the top of a hierarchy in which its actualizations are located in ontologically subordinate roles" (BD, p. 112).[26]

While Cobb conceeds that "to date, no formulation of the Christian understanding of God is compatible with the Buddhist vision," he believes a key requirement in rethinking God in Buddhist terms is that "God be understood to be wholly, unqualifiedly empty" (BD, p. 113). Though perhaps not in an unqualified state, I maintain that this formulation has always existed.

In the early sagas of the Old Testament, God remains unknowable or "empty" by refusing to give a name (Genesis 32:29), and thus, in Cobb's terms, remains without boundaries or determining content. When a name is given (Exodus 3:14), it is so opaque that scholars still argue about what it means. What of Jesus of Nazareth? The substance of the synoptic gospels is

---

24.   Quoted in Hans Waldenfels, *Absolute Nothingness: Foundations for a Buddhist-Christian Dialogue* (New York: Paulist Press, 1980), (J. W. Heisig, trans.), p. 141. Hereafter referred to in the text as *AN*.

25.   Waldenfels notes that about ten years ago Nishitani placed just this point (from the perspective of Zen) before theologians in Basel and Marburg. "I find a statement in Paul which I, coming out of Zen-Buddhism, believe I understand only too well. He says he has suffered a death: 'I live now not with my own life but with the life of Christ who lives in me.' That makes sense to me immediately. Allow me only to ask you this: Who is speaking here?" (AN, p. 157).

26.   This is an especially appropriate point for Christian theologians who have wrestled with the doctrine of the Trinity and the problem of explaining to non-Christians (especially Muslims) the separate-but-One-and-equal-God.

an attempt to determine for non-believers who He is. One of His own answers appears in St. John when Phillip asks to be shown the Father. "Do you not believe that I am in the Father and the Father in me? . . . . The Father who dwells in me does His works" (St. John 14:10). Jesus is a manifestation of the God Who is unknowable! (I shall return to this presently.)

St. Augustine of Hippo (354-430) at least hints at an empty God along these lines:

> What then, brethren, shall we say of God? For if you have been able to comprehend what you would say, then it is not God . . . . If you have been able to comprehend Him as you think, by so thinking you have deceived yourself. This then is not God, if you have comprehended it. But if it be God, then you have not comprehended it. Therefore how would you speak of that which you cannot comprehend?[27]

That which I cannot comprehend (or am unable to know) is certainly, at least on a conceptual level, an emptiness to me. (Of course that I do not "know" God, or that God is an emptiness to me, does not mean that God does not exist. Emptiness is pure possibility, open to all, denying nothing. See Cobb above.)

A less orthodox source of the formulation God equals emptiness, but one which is still within the Christian tradition is the mystical theologian Dionysius the Areopagite (c. 500).[28] His writings attempt a synthesis between neo-platonism and Christianity and stress the intimate union between God and the soul which is realized by a process of "unknowing" (leaving behind the senses and the intellect). In Chapter 7 of *The Divine Names*, a section is devoted to "how we know God, which is neither intelligible, sensible, nor in general some being among beings. It is never true to say that we know God in terms of its nature . . . . We know God in terms of the order of all beings which are projected out of it and which have some similarity and likeness to its divine paradigms."[29]

We might worry about the problem of "manifestation" which Cobb speaks of were it not for the following remarkable statement:

> God is
>   all in all,
>   nothing in none,
>   known to all in reference to all,
>   known to no one in reference to nothing.[30]

---

27. St. Augustine, Sermons on Selected Lessons of the New Testament 52:16 (quoted in Robley E. Whitson, *Mysticism and Ecumenism* (New York: Sheed & Ward, 1966), pp. 23-24.

28. *The Ascent to Truth* makes it clear that Merton knew this work. Elena Malits in her study of Merton (*The Solitary Explorer*, New York: Harper & Row, 1980) notes Merton's knowledge of Pseudo-Dionysius in the context of a discussion of Zen (see p. 102).

29. John D. Jones (trans.), Pseudo-Dionysius Areopagite, *The Divine Names and Mystical Theology* (Milwaukee: Marquette University Press, 1980), p. 178.

30. *Op. cit.*, p. 179.

God is nothing in none, Absolute Nothingness! The editor of the work, John D. Jones, has given this expression in response to Dionysius the Areopagite.

> The divinity of all that is,
> Apart from all that is: nothing.
> Divinity: nothing.[31]

We could continue to quote Christian sources which intimate an equation of God and emptiness,[32] but certainly Dionysius the Areopagite has established the connection.[33] What of the equation of Jesus Christ and emptiness?

A simple (and flip!) answer can be offered by engaging in a bit of grammar school logic. If God is Empty and God is Jesus, then Jesus is Empty. Hans Waldenfels makes the connection more satisfactorily in the section of his book *Absolute Nothingness* entitled "Jesus Christ: The Figure of the 'Empty' God." He begins by warning that we are dealing here not with an "'emptiness' without content. . . but with an emptiness of comprehension" (AN, p. 155).[34] Jesus Christ is the "emptiness" of God taken form. As St. Paul wrote in the letter to the Philippians:

> Have this in mind among yourselves, which you have in Christ Jesus, who, though he was in the form of God, did not count equality with God a thing to be grasped, but emptied himself, taking the form of a servant, being born in the likeness of men. And being found in human form he humbled himself and became obedient unto death, even death on a cross. (Philippians 2:5-8).

Waldenfels quotes Rahner to describe the nature of Jesus' self-emptying; in it "the one who loves makes a total surrender of everything pertaining to the movement of his own personal history toward fulfillment." "The fundamental attribute of the figure of Jesus," Waldenfels notes, "is that . . . it continually and radically points away from itself" (AN, p. 160). Jesus Christ constantly turns us to God; He understands Himself as belonging to God in obedience (St. John 10:30). There is nothing in Him which He holds fast for Himself.[35] This, for Paul Tillich, is the central event of Christianity.

It is a personal life, the image of which, as it impressed itself on his

---

31. *Op. cit.*, p. 103.

32. For example, in the *Summa Theologica*, St Thomas Aquinas says we have no means for considering how God is. Another obvious source would be St. John of the Cross whom Merton knew thoroughly (See *The Ascent to Truth*).

33. There is a great deal to be done in comparing the work of Pseudo-Dionysius with Zen statements, perhaps after the manner of *Mysticism East and West*.

34. This bears out my point above.

35. Again, see Merton, ZBA, pp. 75ff.

followers, shows no break in his relation to God and no claim for himself in his particularity. What is particular in him is that he crucified the particular in himself for the sake of the universal.[36]

And what is "the universal" toward which Jesus points if it is not the self-emptying God? God empties Himself to be born of a virgin, to become human. Rahner thus defines man as the "self-emptying" of God: "If God wills to become non-God, man comes to be." Waldenfels continues:

The high point of the kenosis of God, is realized in two steps, with the radical and total correspondence of the self-emptying of God and the self-emptying of man. That is precisely what Christian belief confesses in the figure of Jesus Christ and in no other. The self-surrender of God to the world in his Logos corresponds to the radical obedience of Jesus of Nazareth in his total self-surrender to his "other" which he calls "God" and whom he addresses as "Father." In Jesus of Nazareth the self-emptying of God and the self-emptying of man coincide. (AN, p. 158)

The God Who is empty (in the sense of unknowable or without content) empties Himself to become a man. Jesus Christ desires or grasps at nothing for Himself and empties Himself to become nothing in the world. Jesus Christ thus "embodies" the emptiness of God. The Christian, like Jesus, must strive to be an "embodiment" of emptiness. By "putting on" Christ, as St. Paul says, are we not "putting on" emptiness?

If there is any accuracy in this way of viewing God, Jesus Christ, and Emptiness, then we can rightly speak of a connection between Zen self-emptying and Christian *kenosis* in the process of realizing identity, True Self. The question is, "Does Thomas Merton explicitly make the connection?"

IV. The Conclusions

The answer to the question of whether or not Merton explicitly connects Emptiness with God or Christ in Christian *kenosis* must, at best, be but a qualified "yes." The imagery he uses to describe the Christian True Self hints at emptiness when, for example, he discusses "hollowness" (NSC, p. 35) and being "lost in Christ" (NSC, p. 37). In writing about Zen he joins "nothingness" and the figurative terms Christian mystics use to speak of God.[37] Merton goes so far as to say that "the quiet meditation of Dogen

---

36. Paul Tillich, *Christianity and the Encounter with World Religions* (New York: Columbia University Press, 1965), p. 81.

37. See MZM, p. 20 and p. 30.

could in fact turn into supernatural contemplation." Faith effects this transition

> because it would provide not merely a psychological assurance that one had gained possession of his object, but, as St. John of the Cross teaches, since "faith is the proximate means of union with God" as He is in Himself, in His invisibility and seeming "emptiness" (as regards our intellect, to which He is "pure darkness" and "night"), if one's meditation is a resting in faith, then it does in fact attain to the infinite source of all supernatural light. (MZM, p. 37)

Admittedly these connections are casual. But it seems to me valid to read them in light of a statement Merton made to Brother David Steindl-Rast. Merton made the point that when one belongs to Christ, there is no self to justify. Brother David asked if "he could have come to these insights if he had never come across Zen. 'I'm not sure,' he answered pensively, 'but I don't think so. I see no contradiction between Buddhism and Christianity.' "[38] Certainly it is true that in his later writings on human identity, Zen and Christian insights on the nature of God and of Emptiness occur side by side.

For example, writing of *kenosis* in the Preface to the Japanese Edition of *The Seven Storey Mountain*, Merton speaks both of the Emptiness of Christ and of the emptiness required of Christians.

> But if the Truth is to make me free, I must let go my hold upon myself, and not retain the semblance of a self which is an object or a "thing." I too must be no-thing. And when I am no-thing, I am in the All, and Christ lives in me. But He who lives in me is in all those around me. He who lives in the chaotic world of men is hidden in the midst of them, unknowable and unrecognizable because he is no-thing. (*IEW*, pp. 44-45)

Does Merton intend "no-thing" to mean "without corporeal existence" or to suggest a more Zen-like notion? I opt in favor of the latter on the basis of another statement he makes on the same subject but in another essay (in August, 1963 and March, 1965 respectively). "The Cross of Christ means more than the juridical redemption of man from the guilt of evil-doing. It means the passage from death to life and from nothingness to fullness, or to fullness in nothingness" (*IEW*, p. 71). And note here the similarity to Merton's description of *sunyata* "which is described as emptiness only because, being completely without any limit of particularity it is also perfect fullness . . . Buddhism prefers to speak of 'emptiness' not because it conceives the ultimate as mere nothingness and void, but because it is aware of the nonlimitation and non-definition of the infinite" (ZBA, p. 85).

---

38. Brother David Steindl-Rast, "Man of Prayer," in *Thomas Merton/ Monk: A Monastic Tribute*, Brother Patrick Hart (ed.), (New York: Sheed & Ward, 1974), p. 88.

In the same essay, "Nirvana," Merton recognizes the need for "a serious discussion, with Buddhists, of the idea of God" (*ZBA*, p. 85). In a sense, he initiates it in the Preface to the Japanese Edition of *Seeds of Contemplation* (1965). Writing of the goal of the contemplative, he says:

> It is the transcendent ground and source of being, the not-being and the emptiness that is so called because it is absolutely beyond all definitions and limitation. This ground and source is not simply an inert and passive emptiness, but for the Christian it is pure act, pure freedom, pure light. The emptiness which is "pure being" is the light of God which, as St. John's Gospel says, "gives light to every man who comes into the world."
>
> (*IEW*, p. 69)

Here is the notion suggested earlier that God is empty by virtue of being unknowable, "beyond all definitions and limitations."

Did Zen bring Merton to the intuition that the metaphysical ground of being and knowledge is void? Note the similarity of the previous passage to one on Hui Neng.

> The infinite emptiness is then infinite totality and fullness. The ground of the void is *sunyata*, but the pure void is also pure light, because it is void of all (limited) mind: and the light of the pure void manifests itself in act. But since this can be translated into positive terms, pure void is pure Being. And pure Being is by that very fact pure illumination. And the illumination springs from pure Being in perfect Actuality. (*MZM*, p. 39)

In spite of his attraction to apophatic theologians like St. John of the Cross (mentioned in connection with Hui Neng), when Merton speaks of ultimate reality which is the end of Christian contemplation, he reaches out, like the opening chapters of St. John's Gospel, for words which express light.[39]

And, thanks to Hui Neng, Merton interprets *prajna* in terms of light, being, and void.

> The ground of all Being is pure Void (*sunyata*-emptiness) which is *prajna*, light illuminating everything in a pure Act of being-void without any limitation. The ground-Being is not distinct from itself as Light and as Act . . . . And to this basic constitution of being there corresponds . . . the act of realization, or *prajna*, in which the void and light are so to speak let loose in pure freedom and power to give and spend in action this self which is no-self, this void which is the inexhaustible source of all light and act, and which has broken through into our own life, bursting its limitations and uniting us to itself so that we are lost in the boundless freedom and energy of *prajna*-wisdom. (*MZM*, p. 40)

The context here is "an *experience* of the ground of being as pure void

---

39.   In this context, see also the fascinating passage in the *Asian Journal* on the "three doors which are one door" (*AJ*, pp. 153-155). It brings together both the major themes in the issue of identity and the recurring metaphors which occur in that context.

which is light and act because it is fullness and totality" (*MZM*, p. 40). It is not a mystique of passivity and withdrawal "resting in one's own interiority but a complete release from bondage to the limited and subjective self" (*MZM*, p. 41). In the Rinzai tradition, which is broadly Merton's subject, this means fulfillment in love.[40] And in the Christian tradition, it is certainly orthodox to say "God is Love."

It would be satisfying if we could conclude here and say that Merton understands Zen self-emptying and Christian *kenosis* to converge in love. If *dharmakaya* can be equated with love ("all matter, all life, is charged with dharmakaya... [sic] everything is emptiness and everything is compassion" (*AJ*, p. 235), and if *nirvana* is, indeed, "the void which is Absolute Reality and Absolute Love" (*ZBA*, p. 86), Merton does suggest this. But it would be dishonest to omit Merton's closing remarks on Hui Neng: "We must also look to the transcendent and personal center upon which this love, liberated by illumination and freedom, can converge. That Center is the Risen and Deathless Christ in Whom all are fulfilled in One" (*MZM*, p. 42).

Perhaps we are left with Merton's own statement that the chief difference between the self emptying and enlightenment of the Buddhist and the self-emptying and enlightenment of the Christian is that "the former is existential and ontological, the latter is theological and personal" (*ZBA*, p. 76). However, as I hope these remarks and quotations indicate, Merton has raised the possibility of a more profound engagement between Zen and Christianity in precisely the place where each manifests itself --individual lives and their witness to truth.

> "Myself." No-self. The self is merely a locus in which the dance of the universe is aware of itself as complete from beginning to end -- and returning to the void. Gladly. Praising, giving thanks, with all beings. Christ light -- spirit -- grace -- gift. (Bodhicitta) (*AJ*, p. 68).

The Christian monk raises many questions and gives few answers. In this, he is our good Zen Master.

---

40. ". . . for Daisetz Suzuki, who is certainly the most authoritative . . . interpreter of Rinzai, the 'most important thing of all is love.' " Merton, in *MZM*, p. 41.

HARPO'S PROGRESS

Notes Toward an Understanding
Of Merton's Ways

by **Robert Lax**

There was a hermit who lived in the woods. He spent his days and nights in prayer, and in peaceful works that gave praise to the Lord. Though his spirit rested always in the heart of his Creator, his hands and feet were seldom idle, and neither was his mind. It might be said that the things he made were useless (he didn't weave baskets, he didn't make shoes), or if useful, only to the spirit: only to the soul in its journey toward God.

What were his works? Tracts, translations, poems, fables, drawings, photographs, dancing and drumming. So many works and all of the spirit? So many works, and all from a single source, toward a single end.

His tracts were concerned with mystical theology, both the problems and the glories of the contemplative life: but the language in them was always as simple as possible, and his examples and illustrations clear. No problem ever seemed too complex for him to tackle, and he never dropped one until he had found a solution: an insight, at least, that he was capable of explaining.

---

*   **HARPO** is a pseudonym which Merton used in writing his "anti-letters" to Robert Lax.

Editors' Note: This paper was written originally for "The Maritain/ Merton Symposium" held in Louisville, Kentucky, 25-26 September 1980. It was not presented at the symposium and is published here for the first time.

His translations: some were from Latin, from the writings and sermons of the early Church fathers; but just as many were from French, Spanish and even Chinese: poems and fables he'd found and admired and wanted to put into English so others could read them.

His own poems and fables, dramas and songs were works of the spirit, praise of the Lord, particularly of His mercy: sometimes directly, sometimes by inference; sometimes simply by the fact of their being. Ever creative, seldom didactic, they were always superabundantly alive.

The drawings, the photos? Filled with that same joy (the joy of David dancing before the Ark of the Covenant): a cause for rejoicing.

The dancing, the drumming? New dancing, new drumming: new song for the Lord. And (once when he travelled) the hermit and his friends, all dancing, all drumming, all rejoicing in His love.

Did he write letters, too? He wrote them and wrote them. Some light, some heavy. Some addressed to problems in the world, others purely to matters of the spirit: some only to include a song, some only for laughter. Yet all from a single impulse of the heart.

Where find the time for so much writing? He rose early and had no other work but to praise the Lord.

A new kind of life, and a classic one, too. In all the ages of Christianity there have been at least a few joyous hermits who have filled the world about them with divinely inspired joy. And this hermit, without at all forcing his way, is of their number. A dolphin-like personality with a lively approach to all matters divine is not new in the Christian tradition, yet each time one appears it's as though a new star were in the sky.

How did his work relate to his prayer? The work took its rise from prayer and returned to prayer. The work itself was prayer and was informed by prayer. There was no conflict between work and prayer: if conflict arose it was resolved by prayer. It was resolved (turned from conflict to creation) in the poet's -- the hermit's -- full dedication to contemplative prayer: to union with God.

Drumming: surely it's possible to pray without drumming; but not (for this hermit) to drum without praying.

Dancing, the same.

Singing, the same.

Preaching, photographing, drawing: the same.

And so with the employment of all his gifts and talents. He might, and often did, pray without visible movement. But none of his outward actions were ever unaccompanied by prayer. Nor was the final purpose of any one of them less than the ultimate goal of his whole life of prayer.

It was the force, the strength, the weakness, too, of this whole life of prayer that gave life to the works, and gives life still, even though the hermit appears, at least for the moment, to have left the woods.

---

being given over entirely to the love of the Lord
he did what he did with joy and energy
he did not doubt, since there was only one goal in
mind: to serve the Lord

and who is the Lord and how should he serve Him?
he learned more and more each day

he learned to express himself more and more clearly
on the nature of this love, on the meaning of the life
he had entered upon, as a river runs into the sea

(when a river runs into the sea it stops being a
river: its molecules are invaded by the molecules of
the sea, and while it loses nothing, it gains new
being in the sea)

the closer he came to knowing God, the closer he
came
to knowing himself, his true self

the closer he came to knowing God and himself, the
more clearly he saw how they were related: how like
they were, and how unlike

his work was work
his play was play

his play was work
his work was play

his work and play
were prayer

his prayer was
work and play

did he play
lightly?

he played
lightly

did he play
seriously?

he played
seriously

lightly and
seriously
at once?

lightly
and seriously
at once

HARPO
FINDS
THE LORD

he looked for him
and found him

found him
living
within his
own heart

he hadn't gone
to see him
to steal
fire

he had gone
to see him
because he
knew he
should

if he is the
ruler

it is the
ruler
i must
find

all the skeins
that had been
twisted

now came straight
for him

all the knots
that had been tied
now came
undone

he knew he had
found

the one he
sought

and now
could speak
quite
freely

could point out
a path

that others
might take

to find
the one

he had
found

the road moved
in only
one direction

(once one
had found it)

the paths
through the
woods

which led
to the road

were
wandering

one needed
a guide

for every
step
of the
way

whom would he have gotten along with
in history?

with rabelais?
surely

with donne?
yes

with blake?
yes, yes

with augustine?
surely

chaucer, shakespeare?
yes

louis armstrong?
yes

how would he have felt
about the abbey of
theleme?

he might not at all
have disliked it

not by wanting
but by doing

not by doing
but by being

not by being
but by growing

he grew to be
the person

he knew
he was

he chose
& kept
choosing

chose &
stood firm
by his
choices

took on
the jobs
he was meant
to do

took on,
and carried
them through

sees
&   can say
what he
sees

the closer
he comes

to the
center
of the
circle

the better
he sees
the whole

with speed &
direction

certainty
& joy

he bowls
down the
hall

like a
ball
of light

or, sitting
at ease

his back
erect

he plays
the bongos
between his
knees

hands hover,
fall & fly

his fingers
fly   on the
                        white
                        paper

his thumbs
beat out
the rhythm

what do his
drawing brushes
do?

fly, too

flight &
control

they leave
a character

that of the
moment

What of his dancing?   His dancing
was a dance of grace and wit: a ritual that
consumed itself in performance. Not just
anyone's dancing, but his own: own limbs and
sinews responding to the music of his spirit:
a celebration and a cause for joy.

And so, in all he did, he praised the
Lord; in all he did, rejoiced in the gift of
living.

A four-year-old child is seated at a desk, his
feet planted squarely before him. He is writing
or drawing; absorbed in his work. His sitting
posture is erect; his expression serious. He is
engaged in a work he enjoys. Events will interrupt this moment, but it will be resumed years
later, when seeds of this early planting flower.

he rejoices
in the Lord

rejoices in
the liberty
of the children
of light

rejoices in
it and turns
it to song

rejoices,
and turns it
to light

he draws
his song

from the
wells
of contemplation

and the song
leads back
to the
source

his world

is just like
the one
we know

but it has
more dimensions

his world
contains
discoveries
and wonders

news, good
news, that
rings
with joy

a child
of light
rejoicing
in light

he lives,
not he,
but Christ
lives in him;

in praising
him,

we praise
the Lord

LOOKING BACK TO MERTON:

Memories and Impressions /

An Interview

by **Matthew Kelty,** O.C.S.O.

Edited by Dewey Weiss Kramer

This interview has been edited from a tape made for the "Thomas Merton Oral History." It was conducted by Victor A. Kramer on 26 October 1982 at the Abbey of Gethsemani.

Matthew (Charles) Kelty, born in South Boston in 1915, has been a monk of Gethsemani since 1960. He joined the Cistercians at forty-five after having been a member of the Society of the Divine Word for over fifteen years, serving as priest in the S.V.D. mission in New Guinea (1948-1951), then as editor of the S.V.D. magazine. He was novice under Merton for two and a half years. After his solemn profession in 1969, Kelty became Superior of a small experimental foundation at Oxford, North Carolina, then spent nine years as a hermit (still a member of Gethsemani) in Papua New Guinea, the same mission where he had served twenty-five years earlier. He returned to the Abbey of Gethsemani in 1982 where he continues to live the monastic life. A gifted homilist, in demand as a spiritual director and retreat master, Kelty has published several books, among them the autobiographical meditation on his New Guinea hermitage, *Flute Solo,* and *Sermons in a Monastery.*

> "His last appearance among us was in that monstrous casket in
> our sanctuary while we did our last service to him. He was Jonah
> in the belly of the whale. He was the man totally committed
> to the mercy of God, about to be cast on the eternal shores.
> Mercy was his other name."

Kramer: We are talking about biographical problems and the recent Furlong biography.[1]

Kelty: Now, just what were you saying -- about Monica Furlong? I read rapidly a copy that was here -- the manuscript. It was being printed when I was home the last time, home from New Guinea where I lived the solitary life from 1973 to 1982 and had come home for six months during that period. There were several things I would have questioned. But I knew nothing of it while it was being written. But in reference to what you were just saying, there was a point where Furlong referred to the monastery as being very bright and light. (**Kramer**: Yes, yes.) And it wasn't. It was very dark and gloomy, the old monastery. (**Kramer**: Yes, I've seen photographs of it.) That shows you how tricky it is because she placed Merton in terms of the present. It was nothing like this. (**Kramer**: Very good point.) The church was dark and gloomy, not depressing, but dark, the whole house was dark, being even dirty compared to now. The church wasn't painted. It hadn't seen paint for God knows how long. That was deliberate because the monks knew someday they were going to redo it anyhow, and it would have wasted money to make an effort in that direction. Anyway, I came in 1960, it was November, dark and gloomy, and I saw Fr. Andrew who was the Guestmaster and I was there three or four days and then I wanted to enter. The first one to receive me was Fr. John Eudes Bamberger who was the psychiatrist. And he didn't give you much attention. He just asked a few, almost blase, questions, nothing very striking. I didn't think they were very telling. He just said they get a lot of priests coming here who were just coming to get away from their orders or societies. . . . And then Merton came along and just asked a few simple questions. It was not very astonishing.

Kramer: And in 1960 Merton would have been the Novice Master?

Kelty: Yes. And that's all. And both of them were about as indifferent as if they couldn't care less. That was deliberate; I realized that after a while. They probably, even today, do that. They don't entice you, and beg you, or cajole you or make any effort at all to coax you to enter or something like that.

---

1. Monica Furlong, *Merton: A Biography* (San Francisco: Harper & Row, 1980).

Kramer: So you wondered, do I really want to do this?

Kelty: Yes, it's up to you. They just, both of them, sat. Actually, it's up to you. If you want to try it . . . that's about as much interest as they showed. The Abbot, Dom James Fox, was a little more positive. And that was the first meeting. And then when I came, I came in January or February 1960, then Merton was Novice Master.

Kramer: So at that point you would have had some contact with him?

Kelty: From then on you were under him because we lived separately then, and we had a conference from him everyday, and he ran our little community. (**Kramer**: Of about how many novices?) About a dozen or sixteen, twelve to sixteen . . . very mixed, young high school kids, graduates, and some from college, couple of businessmen, couple of priests, It was a very wide variety. Paul Quenon was one the novices; Timothy Kelly [now Abbot of Gethsemani] was one of the novices then. How would I describe Merton in those days? I always thought he was very British. I don't know if people would agree with that. I grew up in the Boston area, and there was a strong British influence in Boston. I went to public schools and the teachers were all maiden ladies, "secular nuns," "protestant nuns." He had a lot of that. At least I thought he did. His humor, I thought, was British. He could be very cutting . . . maybe even sarcastic. I don't want to put this out as being critical, but the British (Anglo-Saxons) are pretty good at the "put-down," but with "class." He could seem very British. His humor was on the dry side.

Kramer: At that point, were the novices much more separated from the rest of the monks, more than today?

Kelty: Yes. We lived in the rear. . . it's gone now. But there was a back wing, and we had our own bootroom where we would change our clothes. And we had our own study hall, and our own conference room. And the dormitory. . . we had a separate chapel. We were more segregated in those days. (**Kramer**: So your actual contact with the professed monks?) Was little. We worked with them and we went to choir, of course. We blended with them, but we were more separated than they are today. There was a certain point in it. And so it did tend to make a group, a community, out of the Novitiate. Now there aren't as many and it would be more difiicult. Beside the Abbot, Merton would be the one we had most contact with, like assigning your work, for example in the morning after Prime. And he was very shrewd at that. (**Kramer**: And this was done everyday? So you never knew what you would be doing?) After Prime. Never knew. And he could be really demanding. Many in the community thought he was kind of a pushover as Novice Master, but he wasn't. He didn't mind imposing discipline. (**Kramer**: And what kind of work did you do? Outdoor work?) Indoor, outdoor. You know you'd get a beautiful day like this, say in February, and Kentucky in February can be kind of grim, but you get occasionally a beautiful sunshiny, lovely day, and you'd just love to go outside and do something. He'd assign me to type stencils for him. That was his work style. He used to write out, type out his articles, and then revise them, I think in red, and then revise them again in black, and then we would type it out on a stencil and mimeograph it, and then he would send it out to a lot of his friends. He would get their reactions, and then he would go into the feedback. Having some kind of assessment of the article, he would do it again and then maybe send it out to a magazine. It would appear in a journal and there would be more feedback and ultimately [it would] find its way into a book. I'm not a typist. There were only one or two typists in the group. It was tedious work. And then you'd find things you couldn't read, where he'd make these corrections in his cramped hand, and I simply couldn't read it, and he would get very annoyed. You weren't supposed to bother him. He was very strict on this. Once the man was at his work, you left him alone. This was a lesson to us. (**Kramer**: So, he'd put everybody to work, and he'd go off and do his thing?) Yes, we were supposed to respect people when they were working. Don't bother people; imposing on others, you know, taking advantage of them on the point of their work. You were expected to be charitable. You'd have to go to his door. He would be annoyed.

Kramer: Were the other novices aware of the fact that he was a writer, that he wrote a lot of things?

Kelty: Oh, yes. But we knew very little. The Abbot never talked about it, and he never talked about it. He was seeing people all the time, but we knew very little. No, it was very low key. They made nothing of him in the Abbey.

Kramer: So, in terms of the attitudes of some of the other monks toward Merton, you didn't get any feeling that here was a man who had written a lot of books?

Kelty: Oh, no! Famous man, or something? Oh, Lord, no. And I thought a lot of the reason was he didn't think of himself that way. He didn't think of himself as famous, or interesting, or a character, or a well-known writer. He simply didn't take himself that seriously; and when you don't, nobody else will. They will react to you the way you react to yourself. And they took him very casually. They treated him just like any other monk. And we would hear very little about his impact on the literary world in any case. The books, when they did appear, were up in the library on the table and nothing specially would be made of them. I don't remember any of his books being read in refectory but they did read one or two, I think, before my time. There was no big announcement made. We had no idea, in fact, that he was well-known. (**Kramer**: More than, say, Fr. Raymond?) Fr. Raymond was a little different because he started as different. He was perhaps more a "writer" than Merton; you know, this is not said critically. It's just that their styles were quite different. But we had no idea that Merton's impact was as great as it was. It was a bombshell to most of us to find out how great a man he was.

Kramer: In some ways, it's been only in the years since his death that he's really become so well known. So, in a sense, in 1960 he would have been recognized and his books would have been distributed over the country, but he wouldn't have been known that well among Cistercians.

Kelty: Occasionally he would share guests with us; you know, get them to talk to the Novices. The Abbot would let him... (**Kramer**: For instance?) The Berrigans did, once or twice. But he did that with the community, too. Then we had Evans. He was a Dominican. (**Kramer**: What was his first name?) Illtud. I think it's a British name. He was editor of "Blackfriars." He talked to us one day. I remember him particularly. He's very British. He's learned...a Dominican, you know, a very learned man, the kind of man that Merton loved, and he had toured the States and he came especially to see some of the abbeys. He visited Collegeville and then there was a friary in St. Louis, built in very modern style; then there was another one out in Rhode Island some place. These were a little bit advanced in their style. He was praising them and I could remember, we novices didn't go along with him. We told him we didn't like these new monasteries, these great German masses of concrete. We thought it was hideous. And we said we thought that the

National Shrine of the Immaculate Conception, which was just being finished in Washington, was much more typical of the United States. (**Kramer**:
What did he say about the remodeling of this monastery, though?) I don't
think it was along yet. I don't think we had started it. I don't remember. We
hadn't finished the church yet. He didn't comment on Gethsemani, but he
was proud of the fact the monastic orders had the most advanced architecture. We said we didn't agree with that. I mean we weren't saying the Shrine
of the Immaculate Conception was all that great, but it was typical of the
American Catholic viewpoint, and the American Bishops, that it would be
much more representative of the Catholic Church than St. John's in Collegeville would be. St. John's would be for an elite, a very small group. But
this is what I was getting to, that Merton would take it very much amiss if
you criticized his guests or disagreed with them or spoke out, didn't treat
them with great civility. We weren't uncivil to Evans. But I didn't realize that
Merton would get very annoyed. Finally Dom James told me, "Don't do
that, don't pick on his guests." Well, we had a very quiet life. We saw
nobody, and we were restricted here in this confine, then much more than
now, and we were all new at it, we had just come. You move into an
environment where all outside stimulus is cut off, there's no input. It's to
awaken the inner life. So there's nothing coming in from outside. But all of
his friends were intellectually stimulating, original thinkers, and many of
them were professional. They were speakers, lecturers, and they deliberately set out to antagonize you, to stimulate you by making extraordinary
statements. These people would come in to us novices and in no more than
ten minutes, we'd be jumping out of the chairs. He'd get very annoyed.

Kramer: Do you remember other persons who came as guests?

Kelty: Oh, it would take a while. It was twenty years ago. If I talked, I could
get it.

Kramer: We can pursue that another time. Let's change the subject and
ask you to say something about Merton's physical appearance, as you recall
it. I read the essay you wrote which was in Br. Patrick Hart's book, and you
did a beautiful job there of saying something about Merton's manner.[2] But I
just wondered what comes to mind?

---

2. "The Man" in *Thomas Merton/ Monk: A Monastic Tribute*, Kalamazoo: Cistercian Publications, 1983,
pp. 19-35.

Kelty: Yes. . . not big and heavy. . . with the Charlie Chaplin feet?. . . how his feet were spread? And he thought of himself, I'm sure he did, as physically capable, but I thought he was dangerous with an axe. He thought of himself as not exactly athletic, for he talked about his failure as a rower with the boats. (**Kramer**: I know, oarsman) That was mentioned, but he wasn't all that coordinated. He wasn't handy. Let's put it that way. He wasn't handy with stuff, tools and things.

Kramer: But he must have realized that and also have had a sense of humor.

Kelty: Well, I think he did. I remember one day we were all coming in from work or something. It was the afternoon, around three or something, and there was an enormous black cloud of smoke up there on the hill. It would have been right in the dry time, in the fall sometime. Fires can be very dangerous here. And so he rounded us all up and we all went just as we were, robes and all, we went galavanting up the hill, and he took charge. And he wouldn't let us run; he made us walk fast. And we all had brooms; there was a fire broom each of us took along. And the whole woods was a roaring fire because one of the neighbors was burning something in the back of his yard, and it had gotten out of hand. And of course his hermitage was right in the middle of all that. But I never forgot it because he was showing more than just ordinary concern, telling us: "All right, men, now, go here, now we'll do this," shouting orders. We got it out, though. It was so unlike him. It was so out of context, as the military leader leading this expedition to put out this fire.

Kramer: Do you think he was conscious of how he appeared?

Kelty: Not impressive, a poor dresser. Didn't know how to wear clothes. Even in the habit, he didn't look very good. He was just not gifted that way. It was the same in New Guinea. The people on the coast are aware of clothes and what you can do with them. People in the highlands are not. You know, you either have this gift or you haven't. Even people who don't have much in terms of a body, if they have a feeling for clothes they can always look good, you know, with a little bit of class. But he had nothing of that. Funny. Of course, he was indifferent to it, too. That didn't help it any. No. . . a very modest, humble person, unassuming, unpushy, the kind people, I'm sure, could talk to easily. They wouldn't be afraid of him.

Kramer: You mentioned some of the duties you had when you were a novice. Later, did you have other duties which brought you into contact with Merton?

Kelty: Yes, because of what they call vocations. I would interview the men who were interested. (**Kramer**: So you were the Vocation Director?) Well, you call it that. What it meant was that you got the mail that came in, and you sorted out the absolutely hopeless and didn't encourage them to waste their money. We would engage in a little preliminary correspondence and send them some stuff, some pamphlet or booklets and then eventually they'd come for a weekend retreat when they could. And then I would talk, just see what they sounded like and then Fr. Eudes would see them, the psychiatrist. If they were interested in entering Merton would be the third one, and then it wasn't a final judgment. It was just kind of an assessment whether there was any hope in pursuing this any further. It used to be quite awkward at times because they would get here Friday night, and wouldn't know whether they were going to have these interviews or not; and then sometime Saturday morning or Saturday afternoon, Merton would have to see them in order to get it done in time for the Abbot to see them on Sunday morning. So, if Fr. Louis was busy or had company or was working on something, it would be a little awkward at times to squeeze that in.

Kramer: During that period when he was writing and distributing a lot of material in mimeograph form to get reactions, do you think he sometimes felt frustrated because he often couldn't get things published quickly or because he wasn't sure he could get permission from the censors?

Kelty: Well, I never got the impression that he felt crushed. He would talk about it occasionally, but I never thought of it as anything more than anyone else in the church would be subject to. That was the feeling I had.

Kramer: So you'd say his attitudes toward his life at Gethsemani during that whole period were clearly very, very positive?

Kelty: Oh, yes, yes.

Kramer: See, that's the thing. If you read Monica Furlong's book, she stresses this poor Fr. Louis who felt frustrated. (**Kelty**: It was overdone.) I think so too. (**Kelty**: It may be all correct.) But I think it's out of context. My feeling is that she was looking for a problem chapter by chapter, and so she would find a problem upon which to build the chapter. But she's ignoring the larger rhythm.

Kelty: I really wouldn't say that what she said was not true, but it's not the whole truth. And I'm not saying either that this is an easy thing to do, to assess a character like Merton, a person like that. No, no. He would frequently bitch about the Abbot and we always understood this to mean that, you know, he criticized the Abbot. He'd find fault with him, the Abbot did this or that. (**Kramer:** You're talking about the Abbot at that time?) Dom James, yes. And we novices, we understood this perfectly. The idea was that the Abbot is a human being. He is the head of this monastery. You take vows to God Almighty through the hands of this Abbot. If you cannot live with his imperfections and human frailty, well, don't get involved then. If your faith isn't deep enough to go beyond this, you're simply out of your element. In other words, he wasn't out to put the Abbot up as some glorified figure, the Christ figure, whom you would find it easy to obey. You took your vows to God through this man, and this man was a human being, and he wouldn't pull any punches. He would tell us what this old man's job was, what this man was up to. So it was done frankly but without this sneering backbiting sort of thing. Very objective.

Kramer: There has been some writing about Merton's wanting to change Orders, to become a hermit and so on, and you get a kind of one-sided view of that sometimes, too.

Kelty: He told me himself that he was an artist, a poet, he was a romantic, he was a dreamer, he had a new idea every week, and he would get all worked up over these ideas, and then he would go running off to the Abbot with them, and the Abbot would sit and listen to him patiently and, of course, eventually tell him the whole thing was just a dream. Then he'd bitch a bit and then go back where he was and start over again. And he told me himself that Dom James was the kind of Abbot that he needed. If he had had a soft-hearted, easy, benevolent Abbot, he would have ended up a disaster. His gifts were so strong and so wild that he needed this control if they were going to amount to anything. And he told me that himself.

Kramer: So you might say that, although it was difficult for a monk to be a monk and a writer, it wasn't any more difficult for him to be a writer here than it would have been somewhere else.

Kelty: It's him. It was the gift that made it difficult for him. Any artist has this problem.

Kramer: And would you say Merton would think, "O.K. I'm an artist, but first I'm a monk?"

Kelty: He had it straight. The monks used to think he was kind of a wild one, you know, that he got away with a great deal. And he would give you this impression, you know, because he was not out to create a following. He hated that. He did not want a cult; he was vehement on this. He'd get wild if he thought people were cultivating him, you know, or were making a fetish out of him. But Dom James himself told me that he had no more obedient monk than Merton. He would bitch and make a lot of noise about something, but when it came to a showdown, he'd obey. And the Abbot knew this. This is why the Abbot could give him a great deal of rope, because he could trust him. But in the end, if he said "No" it was finished. He'd give him a real good talking to and the matter was settled. And those were the principles Fr. Louis taught us. Being a good, obedient monk didn't mean that you lived forever in a kind of equanimity with your Abbot on every single issue. There were many areas where you could be in disagreement, and even in contention if you thought it was serious enough; but in the end the decision was the Abbot's, and that's the way the life is set up. And he lived up to it.

Kramer: Do you remember if he ever indicated any special concerns about the monastery? What kinds of things would he get worked up over?

Kelty: Before I forget, he did feel very badly about the Peace book. . . that he wrote. . . it was something about peace, and the Abbot General turned it down.[3] The Abbot General was a patriot and De Gaulle had decorated him. He was a super French patriot, you know, and I know that hurt Merton but then it was not so long after that Pope John came out with his *Pacem in Terris* and he was delighted. Merton said, "He said everything I wanted to say and said it better." But, the biggest thing. . . (**Kramer**: I was inquiring about the kinds of things he would be concerned about at Gethsemani.) Earlier in his life, that would have been the *environment*. I think in the

---

3. Probably *Peace in the Post-Christian Era* (1962), never published as a book, but various articles appeared separately. See listings in Marquita E. Breit / Robert E. Daggy, *Thomas Merton: A Comprehensive Bibliography* (New York: Garland, 1986).

Abbey that was probably the thing that he made the biggest stink about, and with certain departments, you know, that would be the Cellarer, Brother Clement, who was in charge of the farm and who was a modern farmer, and who did everything just like right out of a book. I never saw a farm like the one we had. I came from a different order and at our seminary we had a farm. We were in some ways more of a monastery than this place was. We grew our wheat and made our own flour and baked our own bread. The equipment was old hand-me-downs and poor stuff and you had to fix it up, you know. I mean it was antiquated. And this place was modern, up-to-date, and that meant going along with all that involved; pesticides, for instance, to make the crops grow because our land is not that good. And then they watered all these fields with these irrigation pipes, you know, and lakes they made. (**Kramer**: They needed the ponds so they could irrigate?) Sure, because it gets dry here. It doesn't rain maybe for a month or so. And then it all had to be sprayed with pesticides. And Merton would go wild over this, because it would kill everything, bugs and birds, bees and butterflies, in order to make this alfalfa. You know our alfalfa would be up to your waist and the neighbors' would be like clover around your ankles. (**Kramer**: They didn't stop using the pesticides, I don't suppose.) No! No! Then they . . . down in the bottoms . . . you don't know it, but out back there, there's the so-called "bottoms" . . . there was a creek that wandered through the fields. (**Kramer**: Behind the buildings?) Yes, along in there, and it was more fertile ground because it's lowland, and there was a creek wandering through it but the creek wandering through it made it very difficult to cultivate it, and so they moved the creek, put it over on the further side. Well that went on, I think, for months, day and night, or at least they worked in the moonlight, you know. They moved that creek over to the one side so that they could, you know, do the corn or whatever it was in one clean sweep. He bitched about that without end, because he couldn't sleep at night. He'd write nasty notes. (**Kramer**: So he wasn't concerned about the environment; he was concerned about how he couldn't sleep!) Well, he didn't like the idea of tearing up this creek anyhow. Later on the water returned. I don't know how it is today. I think the water . . . (**Kramer**: Went back?) Yes! . . . but bulldozers, pawing through, tearing up woods and spreading chemicals. This sort of thing annoyed him no end.

Kramer: How about the environment within the monastery?

Kelty: Noise, excitement . . . big to-do over anything. Life used to be much more exciting than it is now. There was much more pandemonium. The Office was longer and complicated, feast days were apt to be very elaborate with very long Offices. Whenever they would do anything, they'd tend to make it big. (**Kramer**: He didn't like that?) Down on it. He was very low key. I remember the class a year ahead of me, before I came. They took one little room off of the office in the Novitiate, before Christmas, and tore everything out and then built a crib, a big Christmas scene inside. He was very annoyed. Because they wasted valuable time. Just because of Christmas, because the room was for Christmas, you don't have to make work out of it. Oh, he'd get very, very nasty. (**Kramer**: Who would the crib have been for?) For the novices. Oh, he didn't mind a little decoration, but all that running out to the woods and bringing in all kinds of green, spending all day working on it. And then they used to have a Corpus Christi procession in the cloister. You've seen pictures of it in Europe? This got more and more elaborate every year that I was here because you'd have to go out and gather all these flowers, and because there weren't enough flowers, they'd go out and gather greens, and grind them up in one of the farm machines, so you could handle them. You'd get different colored kinds of grass and gravel. (**Kramer**: And where was all this done?) The whole cloister floor was covered with this carpet of flowers and greens in designs.

Kramer: Do you think that Merton's years as a hermit were satisfactory?

Kelty: Yes. But after he was living up there a while, it got to be known where he was, and priests from the area used to come. They knew that you could park on the highway up there and cut across the fields, and then climb over the fence to the woods. And it got to be so bad that, in the end, in the afternoons, you'd find him out in the woods because people would come to him. But he told me, too, that priests, like in Louisville, which is what we were talking about, "If they need me, I would gladly spend myself for them. I would give up my solitude." What he resented was people coming to him just like they were tourists or something. If people had problems and worries or wanted somebody to talk to, he would be very glad to see them. He never would turn them away.

Kramer: Now, you said he told you this. Did you have much personal association with him, after you ceased to be a Novice?

Kelty: Well, I'd see him every time there would be somebody entering or who wanted an interview. (**Kramer**: So you would see him on a more or less regular basis?) Often. And as you know, there would always be small talk, something in the air at the moment. It wouldn't be just business.

Kramer: Would you say that your own personal association with him was valuable?

Kelty: Oh, yes. He was an interesting person. He was difficult, not the easiest person to work with, but I enjoyed working with him. I never thought of it in terms of whether it was valuable or not. He was an interesting man. (**Kramer**: Very well disciplined in some ways?) Oh, yes, extremely. But he didn't give you this impression. Hard work was his basic discipline and he was more mortified than many thought. For instance, I can remember problems sometimes with the food he was given. I won't criticize certain people. The cooks sometimes get, you know, kind of tired. You know Merton didn't pay attention to his health. He was supposed to get certain foods and was not to get others.

Kramer: Sometimes it has been said that his health deteriorated because the food wasn't good, but I think part of it was that he just didn't think. He didn't think, am I eating a balanced diet?

Kelty: The cooks' attitudes, too. . . they just didn't like fussing over it with the people. He didn't like fussing over it either. I know he told me this several times, that he just went down to dinner and he couldn't eat anything because what they gave him he wasn't supposed to get, and he knew if he did eat it, he would get sick. And he would never complain. I know this, because the monk he complained to me about for doing such a shitty job was the monk who told me that Merton never complained. So I got it from both sides. And it doesn't mean this particular man was evil! Well, you just get tired of cooking for a lot of different people.

Kramer: Would you say today that if a monk needed some special attention, right now, in this monastery, he'd probably stand a better chance?

Kelty: Yes. Today we don't have the cult of severity, or the rigor. See, the cult of the day was, if it's tough, it's good. If it's hard, it's better. You know, this was in the air. It was dying in Merton's time, but it was still very strong, and this was the environment in which he was living. So in that context, it is very difficult to develop a certain kind of tenderness toward people who needed a little bit of special consideration, especially if the person doesn't demand it, or insist on it. Do you follow me?

Kramer: Yes, yes, I do. Do you think persons were attracted to the religious life because of Merton? I mean because of his writings?

Kelty: I would think so. (**Kramer**: When the men came here and spoke with you, did they mention that?) Sometimes, yes. They knew his books often. Dom James used to say he sure brings them, but that doesn't keep them. (**Kramer**: Would you agree with that?) Yes. 'Cause they get like anybody else, a romanticized version of the life. He didn't romanticize it, but they did.

Kramer: I have a monk friend at the Monastery of the Holy Spirit near Conyers. He says, you know, one out of twenty-five will stay a while.

Kelty: Yes, it looks different from the gallery, you know. It doesn't mean they're supermen, but it does take a peculiar combination of gifts to be able to make a life of frugal experience.

Kramer: Some people have said that Thomas Merton would write about one thing and then he would change his mind and he would take another opinion, or that he was easily swayed in his opinions. You mentioned that he would have a new idea every week and so on.

Kelty: Not so much the way he did it. I think he was seeing it from so many aspects, from so many sides. I don't know much about intellectuals. I sometimes get the impression that intellectuals love stimulating dialogue, and he could do this. He could be very exciting in his talks, lectures and so on, and say really outrageous things and then come back tomorrow and, without batting an eye, contradict everything he said yesterday. (**Kramer**: And enjoy it!) Without, you know, thinking that there's any reason to apologize, because he's seeing it today from this side, and yesterday he was seeing it from that side. And it was up to you to figure it out.

Kramer: Did you go to any of these Sunday afternoon conferences?

Kelty: Very few, because I just had enough of him. In this context, in this life too much excitement is not good for you, too much emotion, too much, you know. And he used to get me excited, even annoyed, get me all worked up. Reading him is different, but hearing him. . . I should have gone. It was sinful not to, but they'll all appear in print eventually, his literary criticism. (**Kramer**: Yes, he spoke on several poets and Faulkner.) Faulkner. I've read a comment by people, I think John Eudes said it, that this was where he was superb, as a literary critic, apart from his spiritual area, which was probably the best. But as a literary critic, he was very gifted, and that's what he was doing on Sunday afternoons. When I think of it. . . I didn't even bother going.

Kramer: You know there were tapes made.

Kelty: Yes, they're all down. You heard the story of how that started? (**Kramer**: I've heard someone explain a little bit of it.) 'Cause that was an accident. The brothers used to go down and cut up the vegetables for dinner, early in the morning, four o'clock or something. . . and they resented it as time went on, and when the new look began to come into the life, they wanted more time for reading. A lot of this was make-do work, wasn't really necessary. . . sometimes it was, but sometimes it wasn't. And so they began to fall off; they figured let the cooks do it themselves. And then we had an eager beaver, a young father, appointed to be Master of the Brothers, and he was wanting to get all the Brothers down there in the morning, because those who went resented the fact that others didn't come, you know, the usual community thing. And in order to entice the Brothers to come to work, he would tape Merton's conferences to the Novices today at eleven o'clock and would play it the next day at four o'clock in the morning, because in those days, there was no contact between the different departments. Merton might just as well have been anywhere as far as they were concerned, because they never heard him talk. At most maybe once a year, in a Chapter talk, and you couldn't go to confession to him. You weren't allowed to speak to him, seeing him occasionally, that's all. And they had no awareness of his spiritual teaching because it wasn't yet available. And so one day we went to a conference at 11:15, I think it was, and there was a microphone hanging in front of him. He said, "Today we're on the air." And I said, "Who's listening to you?" "Well," he said, "the Brothers will." I said, "How are the Brothers listening to you, because there's nobody in the house." He said, "The Brothers down in the workroom." I said, "They're not down in the workroom now." He said, "It's on tape. It's going to be put on tape." Tape was fairly new then; tape recorders weren't everywhere. Well, I thought, for Heaven's sake! And we were surprised that he went along with it, because he didn't have much sympathy for electronic business. So then they started and all the Brothers flocked to the workroom. They went, because it was the first time they had heard him. Well, that started them to work. It was a trick to get them there. And then from then on, they recorded all of his conferences, and then they were better in the original because... well the originals were better than the printed form, because his talks were always preceded by his little... you know, small talk around the Abbey, little jokes, and then questions from the audience and that sort of thing. And then they went on further, and began to record any address that he made, and by the time he died, they had a whole cabinet full. (**Kramer**: Yes, they do have a lot of them. You're right. They will eventually be made available.) It was Gerard Majella, that's the Father's name, Bryan. He's gone now. He left. He was the Father Master for the Brothers. It was his idea.

Kramer: I wanted to ask you a question since you lived in Asia and because you may have thought about some of the Eastern connections. (**Kelty**: South Pacific. I lived in New Guinea.) You'd have a better feel for Eastern views than most Americans. Have you read Merton's writings about the East? (**Kelty**: Not many.) I just wondered if you had some sympathetic feelings about them, the way he became so interested in Eastern philosophy and religion and so on toward the end of his life, then the trip, of course.

Kelty: Yes, the last card he wrote me. He sent a card from Singapore when he was on his way to Bangkok, because I had been in Singapore and he knew that. And I had talked to him about the Cargo Cults in the Pacific. And that would be typical of the way he did things. We would be in what he called a rap session, direction, you know, every two weeks or so, you had a half an hour. (**Kramer**: But he asked you specifically about the Cargo Cults?) It must have come up in conversation, and I talked about it to him, and he was interested, and then what would he do... (**Kramer**: He hadn't been reading about them?) No. He knew a little bit about it, and what he would do, he would write for books, I mean to the University Library, and they would send them back. He would just ask for books on the Cargo Cults, and they would send them back. You know, boxes of books, and then he would read that all through. Then he would do several papers on it. That's the way he worked; he would delve deep into a subject. (**Kramer**: But what do you remember? What did you tell him about Cargo Cults?) Well, it was simply talking about it in reference to the fact that it was the reaction of a primitive people to maintain the role of the world of spirit in society. Western man thinks the Pacific people are barren of religion and they cannot understand this. We do not integrate faith or beliefs and action in the secular world and the spiritual world. We don't integrate this, and they do. (**Kramer**: So they figure it has to be integrated?) Has to be. When we deny it, they say we're either lying, or we're deceiving them, or hiding it from them. And so actually the cult is not a thing to get money, which is the way most Europeans think of the Cargo Cults. They think it's rubbing your hand in spiritual techniques in order to get wealth. That's a very crude interpretation. Merton denies this too. What they're trying to say is that there is a spiritual world, a dominion, a dimension to every secular action, and it's not evident in the Westerner. (**Kramer**: That's a very good way to explain it.) Why is it? And when you ask about it, we deny there is any and then they say, you're hiding it. And this then is where crooked characters are out there, too. Because we're "hiding it," they think we have special techniques for producing things, and this is how it can get perverted, and then it becomes a cult for money.

Kramer: That's very interesting, though, that you knew about the Cargo Cults. (**Kelty**: It's still there.) And you talked with Merton, and then he started reading and making notes, and then he ended up writing a whole section in the book *The Geography of Lograire*, which is really very much about Cargo cults, and about the fact that Western ideas have had a bad influence upon these native cults.

Kelty: Indeed! You see, this would be the point, I think, of his contact with the East, because the East would be traditional and has a much better integrated spiritual world along with their material world. Their material world may not be, or at least traditionally hasn't been, as advanced as ours has been, but they have had this spiritual dominion, you know, the Contemplative East, and we lack this dreadfully; and it's very difficult to have anything like a contemplative life or live in a monastery, when the people who are in it come from this kind of a background. And this Western mentality continues to be the problem in New Guinea. They would make elegant monks, contemplative monks. In fact, they're contemplative already, in terms of their ability to reflect and to ponder, even though it's low level, not sophisticated. . . (**Kramer**: But they're ready for it, they're ready for it, just as the people in Africa are ready for it.) They have the gift. They're normal. They're healthy human beings, that's what it amounts to. But all Western materialism is gross in its secularity, and even the spiritual people who become priests, the brothers and sisters and so on, are tainted with it, and it's very hard to see very much spirituality even in them; in other words, it's not integrated. You follow me? (**Kramer**: Right, right.) The difference between the plantation manager, the government men, and the priest, they see this. They're quite aware there's a real difference, but it's as much their insight as their gift. Because they look the same, dress the same, they all have Hondas or they have Toyotas, they eat the same; there was precious little difference. The Father may be a bit more moral, and he's a celibate and they appreciated this; but then they do know he prays and they do know he has his sacraments and so on, and so, even though on the evidence there isn't a great deal to distinguish them, the local is very much aware of the fact that this man's a priest, but it's sharp insight on their part.

Kramer: How many Christians are there in the area of New Guinea where you lived?

Kelty: They'd be predominantly Christian, predominantly Catholic in that area. Most of New Guinea has been colored with Christianity, and they take it seriously. They consider themselves a Christian country. Areas would be Lutheran and other areas would be so-called United Church, that would be the British Baptists or whatever they were, and then other whole areas would be Catholic. But no religion they would see is as important in the elemental aspect of life as they would have it. Even if they are not individually pious, and they might not go to Mass or something, neglect many things, religion is important to them.

Kramer: So this word "integration" is the key and this would be what Merton would be interested in, the fact that something is wrong, fundamentally wrong, with Western society.

Kelty: This is *the* problem there now because they're headed toward a secular society. The new University has nothing to identify it as Christian. It's government sponsored. They're building a big government center near Port Moresby. There's no cross there, there's no Madonna, there's no

Christ, there's nothing, no chapel, nothing to indicate a spiritual orientation. This is not in conformity with primitive thinking, and they will move into a secular society because they want it to be Western. They want to have our ways. They do! They wear the kind of clothes we do. They like Americans, they love jeans and boots, the whole show. But if they do, they will blow it in one generation, because they came yesterday from a rich, integrated culture, and they're going to be moving into a barren desert with a lot of toys. I mean they'll have clothes if the economy holds up. They'll have a lot of material things and they will discover too late that these things do not provide what they're looking for. I told this to a young Father, an Irish priest in the Cathedral in Madang. I said, "You know, Father, it ain't going to be very long, a generation maybe, and you're going to have young men and women who are successful. They've got a nice education, they've got nice government jobs, they have a cute little house, they've got one or two kids, they've got a motorcycle or a car, they eat better than the typical locals. In terms of the average New Guinean, they're sophisticates." But I said, "They're going to come to you and tell you that inside they're empty. 'Empty drums' is their expression. 'Life has no meaning.'" And he told me, he said, "Father, that ain't coming. It has come. I have young people coming to me telling me, 'I got everything and my life is empty, and it leads to drink and worse.'" Because, you see, they come from just yesterday. We are schooled, we have a tradition of Christianity going back a thousand years, and we're living on the remnants of it, and furthermore, we've been schooled in will power and ego expression and aggression and Western modes of thinking over a long, long period. We have been doing this for a couple of hundred years; this secular society has been a slow process, and we're tough, and even we, as Jung said, we're sick people, and the sickness is no faith now.

Kramer: I wanted to ask just a couple of other questions which lead back to Merton and monasticism. You know he had a lot of ideas, expressed mostly in essays written toward the end of his life, about monastic renewal and renewal in the Church. Do you think he was instrumental in bringing about some change within the monasteries, or would you think that most of the changes within monasteries which have taken place would have been effected if Thomas Merton had stayed in New York City and had never come to Kentucky?

Kelty: I think he had a really powerful role within the Order. (**Kramer:**

Within the Cistercian Order?) Yes. I think that would be admitted, because of his research and his studies.

Kramer: And so the things that he published would have been read carefully and would have had an effect?

Kelty: Oh, they did! They had an impact, yes. As a spiritual writer in the monastic area, he was widely accepted in the Order, even universally. And his strictly spiritual writing, there was no question that they loved him and followed him. There was no doubt that he was a real leader and a real influence within the Order. If he hadn't been there, the impact would probably have come from others, but it would have been a great loss, a great loss.

Kramer: Do particular writings come to mind?

Kelty: Well, all of his so-called monastic writings. I'd have to get a list.

Kramer: His books about monasticism and books having to do with matters of spirituality, and so on?

Kelty: And history, monastic history. The kind of stuff he was giving the Novices. He'd get into the social areas, war and peace, and the monks were a little bit skittish there. Today they're not. He was never a popular figure when it came to war and nonviolence, this kind of thing. There his influence was not what it could have been. Today, perhaps, it comes into its own, because now we're faced with things which are not better. (**Kramer**: They're worse.) Much worse, much worse. But this particular house was superbly blessed by God. Because we had Dom James who was a superb Abbot. He was an authoritarian character, an old-fashioned kind of an Abbot, but a holy man, and a shrewd operator. He knew men when he had them. And he was blessed with good men. He had this brother, Clement Dorsey, who completely revitalized the whole economics of the place. Then he had John Eudes who was a doctor, and he sent him off to study psychiatry and he did much to improve the psychiatric tone of this place, because there were a lot of nutty things going on here. Even in terms of things like diet. Also the "climate" was really quite weird. Then we had Chrysogonus Waddell, a musician, superb. And then we had Merton for the spirituality. And that combination, I mean, if you couldn't build a good monastery with them!

Kramer: Dom James Fox knew this. He knew what he was doing, right?

Kelty: And he was completely different from many in these modern Orders who are stingy with dealing out power.

Kramer: Someone should have told, probably someone did tell, Monica Furlong about this and she missed it when she wrote her book about Merton since you just get the one thing about Dom James.

Kelty: It's a pity, because he wasn't that kind. It's not fair. He *was* authoritarian, there's no question of it, that's the way he did things, but so was the whole monastic set-up run that way. But when he found a good man, he would give power and that meant the money, too. I mean I'd come from an active Order. The active Orders are not nearly as democratic as the old ones, and you didn't get nearly the power, and power means also the money, because these people, these brothers, they built this farm, and they didn't have to run to him every few minutes to get permission to spend ten dollars. They were given authority and it was sink or swim. If you failed, it's your neck, you know. If you succeed, it's to your credit. And they would die for him. (**Kramer**: That makes them feel like they're doing it, you know, and they're doing it as a community, and that's the beauty of it.) And that builds a really strong community.

Kramer: I've got one last question, and that is, if you were to put in a few words what you think the most important thing to be remembered about Thomas Merton is, what would you say?

Kelty: The most important thing about him? I would always think of him not as being brilliant and an intellectual and all that, I think of him as being poor, and simple, and little, and fragile and dearly loved. Do you follow me? (**Kramer**: Yes.) I'm not an intellectual, so I don't understand all that. People think of him as brilliant and all this, but he thought of himself as a poor sinner whom God infinitely loved. He reflected this in his whole manner and that's the way he affected people. He did not impress you. He was not an impressive person. He was not an impressive figure, even his face was plain. This isn't to criticize other people, some people exhibit power and strength, but he didn't. And his lesson was how good God is, how sweet

God is and how loving God is, even for the littlest and poorest and the most fragile of us. Do you follow me?

Kramer: Right, I do, and that's very important because, see, if we can provide this information for people some twenty, thirty years from now, then it would be a matter of fitting it back into the context of how he lived day by day in the atmosphere of this monastery. It wasn't a matter of somebody who produced a bibliography which was so long, or somebody who corresponded with 1700 people.

Kelty: Some of his earlier poetry reflects these things, especially the one on the death of his brother, and some of them are very touching in their simplicity. . . in their utter modesty.

Kramer: That's very good. Thank you. Now would you want to give a final reflection on Fr. Louis?

Kelty: His last appearance among us was in that monstrous casket in our sanctuary while we did our last service to him. He was Jonah in the belly of the whale. He was the man totally committed to the mercy of God, about to be cast on the eternal shores. Mercy was his other name.

THOMAS MERTON

AND THE LIVING TRADITION

OF FAITH

by **William H. Shannon**

To talk about a "living tradition of faith" is to talk about a particular way of the old meeting the new and the present confronting the past in the faith-experience of a community of believers. There are at least three ways of dealing with this conjunction of the old and the new, the past and the present. The first is to give one's total loyalty to the past and ignore the demands of the present, with the hope that somehow they will go away. When a faith-tradition becomes a desperate clinging to the past at all costs, it comes dangerously close to an antiquarianism that makes faith a museum piece. A faith that will not let itself be challenged by the needs and questions of the present is in process of becoming a dead tradition, with little relationship to the lives people are actually living.

A second way of dealing with the coincidence of the past and the present is to become so completely absorbed in the needs and questions posed by the present situation that one closes the book on the past and refuses to allow that the accumulated wisdom of the past has anything to say to the problems of the present. This approach becomes the process of inventing the wheel all over again. It is to lock oneself in the present with no way out. For it is one thing to say that the past cannot answer all our questions, quite another thing to believe that it has nothing to say to us.

The difficulty with these two approaches to the meeting of the past and the present is that they tend to absolutize the one or the other. Yet neither the past nor the present can make absolute claim to our allegiance. To absolutize the past is to have answers, but answers that often do not fit the actual questions we may have in the present. On the other hand, to absolutize the present is to have the right questions perhaps, but with little hint of the direction in which we need to move to locate viable answers that will enable us to adapt to the new without losing our identity.

There is, however, a third way of handling the conflux of the past and the present; and that is to let them meet in creative tension. In such creative tension the old meets the new in a decisive encounter so that what is dead in the old and simply ephemeral in the new are both put aside. In such a process the truth in the old meets the truth in the new: they strengthen one another and the total truth shines the more brightly.

This, of course, is to express an ideal. Seldom do past and present meet in such congenial fashion. Oftentimes the new questions which the present generates, especially in cataclysmic times like our own, admit of no easy or readily discoverable answers, either from the past experience of the faith-community or from what it is experiencing in the present. Such times call for a ruthless honesty and an adamant refusal to be content with inadequate answers, whether inherited from the past or generated in the present. We may have to live a long time with certain questions before we come up with answers that are truly adequate and meet the honest demands of those questions. But it is surely possible to live as authentic persons without having all the answers to the questions that trouble us. Such authenticity is not possible, however, if -- for the sake of security -- we are willing to settle for answers that are less than adequate.

There are, then, I suggest, three possible ways of dealing with the meeting of the past with the present: the first lets the past suffocate the present; the second drowns the past in the present. The third lets the two meet in a tension that ultimately is creative: for allowing the present freely to challenge the past and the past to scrutinize the present, with equal freedom, makes possible the emergence of truth that is at once vibrant and alive, in living continuity with our past and at the same time reflecting the productive initiatives and the hitherto unseen visions of our own times. This last is what I mean by a "living tradition of faith." It means connecting past and present, new and old, in what Thomas Merton -- writing in 1967 -- calls a "current of uninterrupted vitality." "Tradition," he writes, "is not passive submission to the obsessions of former generations."

> It is a living spirit marked by freedom and by a certain *originality*. Fidelity to tradition does not mean the renunciation of all initiative, but a new initiative that is faithful to a certain spirit of freedom and of vision which demands to be incarnated in a new and unique situation.[1]

It took Merton a good while to arrive at this understanding of tradition. It is the intent of this essay to show that Thomas Merton experienced, at different times in his life, all three of these approaches to the meeting of the old and the new (and, indeed, in his later years went beyond all of them). In his younger years (at least into his early twenties) he drifted on a sea of aimlessness, a-morality and lack of faith. There were no moorings to tie his ship to and no rudder to direct it on the open sea. He was locked into a present that offered him little light and a lot of uncertainties.

In 1938 he entered the Catholic Church and found the certainties he had unwittingly been searching for. Indeed, he found them with a vengeance! The Church he was initiated into in 1938 was a Church that clung to its past with great tenacity. It was a Church of *imposition* which showed little inclination to *accommodate* itself to the questions and needs of the times. It had something of the character of a medieval walled city, with moats around it to protect it from whatever was outside. It was a self-contained structure with a rigid discipline, especially in matters of faith and morals, that brooked no opposition. Orthodoxy was clearly defined. Plurality of theological expression was not just frowned upon; it was simply not allowed. The only thinking allowed in the Roman Catholic Church of the first half of the twentieth century was "thinking with the Church" (*sentire cum ecclesia*). Thinking with the Church meant accepting what Rome taught. "Faith" was like a blank check which believers signed, leaving Rome -- or rather Roman theologians --to fill in the correct sum. Roman Catholic Theology had become, at least since the 17th century, increasingly a prepackaged retailing of answers to any and all questions. It was theology become ideology: more a propaganda machine than a creative effort to express the faith experience that was going on in the Christian community. It was a theology that had been trivialized by reducing it to a question of authority and obedience. Its aim was unbendingly apologetic and polemical: it needed to prove that Catholics were right and all others were wrong.

---

1. Thomas Merton, *Contemplation in a World of Action* (Garden City: Doubleday, 1971), pp. 41-42.

There is a Brendan Behan story that aptly captures the mentality of this pre-Vatican II theology. The story is about the Catholic bishop of Cork in Ireland. One morning as he was having his breakfast, his secretary entered the episcopal dining room and said: "Your Lordship, I have unexpected news for you. Last night the Church of England bishop of Cork died in his sleep." The Catholic bishop of Cork took a sip of his Irish breakfast tea and then said, rather matter-of-factly, to his secretary: "Now he knows who is the real bishop of Cork." His lordship was at once a product and a bearer of that early 20th century Roman Catholic theology. It was a theology that forgot nothing old and learned nothing new. It brought the past into the present; and it was the past that dictated Catholic reaction to and understanding of the present. There was little inclination to allow the present to react to or to interact with the past. Oblivious of history, living in fact in a world of absolutes that transcended history, the Church enjoyed the security of an impregnable fortress, with nothing inside or outside allowed to challenge that security.

Thomas Merton, like many converts who found their way into the Church after years of aimless drifting, initially welcomed that security as an attractive alternative to the undisciplined life he had lived prior to his conversion. The unquestioned and unquestioning certitude that went along with being a Roman Catholic in the 1940s replaced the doubts and uncertainties of his former way of life. Basking in the sunlight of ecclesial certainty, he worked hard -- after he had entered the monastery -- to master the official theology of the day, studying the appropriate theological manuals (Tanqueray, Noldin and the rest), which were standard fare for those preparing for the priesthood. By the time he came to write *The Seven Storey Mountain* (probably begun in 1944, though there is some question as to when he actually did begin it), his theological outlook had all the narrowness and rigidity that defined the thinking of the vast majority of his fellow Catholics.

Reading *Seven Storey Mountain* in the late 1980s is like taking a trip back to the Roman Catholic Church of four decades ago: a Church that today exists only in the nostalgic intransigence of a relatively small number of Catholics who remain convinced that nothing of significance has happened in the Church since the Council of Trent. If *Seven Storey Mountain* continues to appeal to readers (as it surely does), this is not because of its theology but in spite of it. The magnanimity of the writer somehow transcends the narrowness of his theology. The narrowness of Merton's early Catholicism is all there. There is the smugness of belonging to the "right" church, the frequent "put-downs" of other Christian churches, the brushing aside of Eastern religions as worthless. Catholics were a breed apart from other Christians. They went to church on Sunday to praise God; most Protestants went to show off their new clothes. *Seven Storey Mountain* draws a sharp cleavage between the supernatural and the natural. Sermons and feverinos, not unlike those Catholics were hearing from the pulpit, are scattered through the text: like the one scolding Catholic parents who were derelict in their responsibility of sending their children to Catholic schools. Protestants who read the book (and many did) experienced its power, but were somewhat bewildered by its obvious bias. Naomi Burton Stone's step-child summed up their feeling as well as anyone when she wrote: "I wish he wasn't so vituperous about Protestants. Are they *that* misled?"

Seven Storey Mountain, which marked the beginning of Merton's career as a famous author, also marked the beginning of the end of his literary flirtation with 20th century scholastic theology. He did have one more affair with it, however. This was the book which he first called *The Cloud and the Fire*, then *The School of the Spirit*, and finally published as *The Ascent to Truth*. It was a book he agonized over and found difficult to complete.

In *Seven Storey Mountain* the scholastic theology is there, but it is subordinated to the odyssey of the author. In *The Ascent to Truth*, the methodology of scholastic theology, as it had become since the 17th century, is all too evident. It was a deductive approach to theological reasoning that began with a thesis. The thesis itself is accepted as true and not open to questioning. The task of the theologian is simply to defend the thesis with proofs from the Scriptures, the Fathers of the Church and reason, while at the same time refuting the "errors of adversaries." *The Ascent to Truth* is not so baldly scholastic in its methodology as were the manuals; but the "thesis-mentality" is very much apparent throughout the book.

Merton considered *The Ascent to Truth* his "worst book, except for two early ones."[2] There are a number of reasons for Merton's dissatisfaction with this book and specifically with the methodology of the thesis. One of these reasons is that he had discovered, within the Roman Catholic tradition, another way of doing theology that was more congenial to his temperament. This was monastic theology and, closely akin to it, the theology of the mystics. The Fathers and the mystics were not abstract thinkers who speculated about God and things divine. They were more inductive in their

---

2. Letter to Etta Gullick, 5 March 1961 (*The Hidden Ground of Love* (New York: Farrar, Straus & Giroux, 1985), p. 341). The two early ones were *Exile Ends in Glory* and *What Are These Wounds?*.

methodology. They wrote about their experience in reading the scriptures and, even more importantly, their experience of encountering God.

The Sign of Jonas:
Initial Signs of a Shift in Methodology

The shift in Merton's methodology, from speculation to experience, is well articulated in the important Prologue to *The Sign of Jonas*, published in 1953.

> I have attempted to convey something of a monk's spiritual life and of his thoughts, not in the language of speculation but in terms of personal experience. This is always a little hazardous, because it means leaving the sure plain path of an accepted terminology and traveling in byways of poetry and intuition. I found in writing *The Ascent to Truth* that technical language, though it is universal and certain and accepted by theologians, does not reach the average man and does not convey what is most personal and most vital in religious experience. Since my focus is not upon dogmas as such, but only on their repercussions in the life of a soul in which they begin to find a concrete realization, I may be pardoned for using my own words to talk about my own soul.[3]

These clear choices (though not without a sense that they were "hazardous!" [Or was this remark inserted for the sake of the censors?]) of "experience" over "speculation," of "poetry and intuition" over "accepted terminology" are a forecast of what we are to expect increasingly in the writings of Thomas Merton.

The Sign of Jonas was indeed for Merton a courageous step in a new direction. It was a step prepared for, though somewhat timidly, by an earlier work *Seeds of Contemplation* (published in 1949 -- four years earlier than *Jonas*) and definitively established as his approach in a book published two years after *Jonas*, namely, *No Man is an Island* (1955). *Seeds* and *No Man* are similar in format to one another: both are cast in the literary genre, made popular by Pascal, of *pensees*.

---

3. *The Sign of Jonas* (New York: Harcourt Brace, 1953), pp. 8-9. Hereafter referred to in the text as *SJ*.

Seeds of Contemplation:
Timid Steps toward a New Methodology

Seeds, which Merton describes as a "collection of notes and personal reflections" about the interior life, is a kind of "half-way house," in which Merton shows himself cautiously poised on the brink of moving from a strict adherence to dogmatic formulas handed down from the past toward a kind of writing that will give greater play to experience. I say "cautiously" because he feels constrained in the introduction to the book to say: "We sincerely hope it does not contain a line that is new to Catholic tradition or a single word that would perplex an orthodox theologian."[4]

Yet popular though this book was (and it became a kind of latter day *Imitation of Christ* for many sincerely seeking a deeper spirituality), there is evidence that Merton was not satisfied with it. On July 9, 1949, he confided to Jacques Maritain: "I am revising the *Seeds of Contemplation*, in which many statements are hasty and do not express my true meaning."[5] A couple of weeks later (on July 15) he wrote, in the same vein, to Sr. Therese Lentfoehr: "I am preparing a second edition of *Seeds* with a few emendations, hoping to tie up the loose ends and make things less likely to lead people astray."[6]

The edition with these "emendations" was published in December of 1949. It is not to be confused with the large-scale rewriting of *Seeds* that appeared in 1962 under the title of *New Seeds of Contemplation*. The December 1949 edition of *Seeds* does not eliminate or modify any of the contents of the earlier printings of the book. What makes it a "revised edition" is the addition at the beginning of four important pages which are entitled, "Preface to the Revised Edition." In this new preface the author, after warning his readers not to look for a systematic study of the spiritual life, goes on to say: "The author is talking about spiritual things from the point of view of experience rather than in the concise terms of dogmatic theology or metaphysics."[7]

This statement of December 1949 represents a hesitant crossing of the theological Rubicon. Though firm as ever in his desire to be faithful to the faith-formulations of the past, Merton is inching his way toward an

---

4. *Seeds of Contemplation* (New York: New Directions, 1949), p. 14.
5. Thomas Merton Studies Center, Bellarmine College, Louisville, Kentucky.
6. Merton Center, Columbia University, New York.
7. *Seeds of Contemplation* (revised ed.), p. xii.

understanding of Catholic tradition that will more and more submit that tradition to the test of actual experience. Another way of putting this is to say that Merton is beginning more and more to trust his own experience and leaning in a direction in which he will gradually become more comfortable using, what (as we have already seen) he will later call (in *Jonas*), "the byways of poetry and intuition" to articulate that experience. His understanding of the tradition of faith will more and more begin to take on a dynamic and dialogic character in which age-old formulas must be tested in the crucible of experience.

No Man is an Island:
Definitive Move to a New Methodology

No Man is an Island, published in 1955, represents a clear breakthrough to a definitive position in understanding tradition from which there will be no departure or turning back. This work, which Merton saw as a sequel to *Seeds* is, he says, a sharing with his readers of his own reflections on the spiritual life. It is intended, he tells us, "to be simpler, more fundamental and more detailed than *Seeds*."[8]

The phrase "more detailed" is worth noting. Several years later in 1959 (January 13) he wrote to Sr. Therese Lentfoehr and suggested that "long-winded" might be a more appropriate description of *No Man is an Island*. At the time he was sending her the typescript of an unpublished work called *Sentences*. Telling her that it is the rudiments of what eventually became *No Man is an Island*, he remarks: "I think these short phrases [in *Sentences*] are better than the long-winded finished book."[9] He mused that he might some day publish the *Sentences*.

Sentences, which is dated on the concluding page of the typescript: "Feast of the Sacred Heart, 1952," does not speak of tradition as such. It does have a number of references to "experience." In Sentence # 79, Merton speaks of the capacity we have for "vision and for disinterested love." This capacity, which Merton calls "the summit of the spirit" in us, is

---

8. *No Man is an Island* (New York: Harcourt Brace, 1955), p. x. Hereafter referred to as *No Man*.
9. Merton Center, Columbia University, New York.

brought to perfection in us only through experience. It is impossible to reach this summit by "retiring from experience." In Sentence # 80 he identifies that "summit" with the image of God. To become conscious of that summit is to experience myself as the "image of God." To quote Merton directly: "When the summit of my being lies open to consciousness, I *know by experience* that I am the image of God." I quote this passage from *Sentences* to show how in 1952 Merton was remaining true to the commitment of December 1949 to talk "about spiritual things from the point of view of experience."

No Man is an Island, published three years after the completion of this earlier and much shorter draft, speaks explicitly about "tradition." In Section # 8, which deals with the general topic of "Vocation," Merton speaks of "the transforming and life-giving effect" of tradition. His remarks are about the "monastic tradition," which he says "is rooted in the wisdom of the distant past, and yet is living and young, with something peculiarly new and original to say to [people] of our own time." But what he says about monastic tradition can easily be applied to the notion of tradition in general and to the tradition of Christian faith. He writes:

> Tradition is living and active. . . . [It] does not form us automatically: we have to work to understand it . . . . [It] teaches us how to live and shows us how to take full responsibility for our own lives. *Tradition, which is always old, is at the same time ever new because it is always reviving -- born again in each generation, to be lived and applied in a new and particular way* . . . . Tradition is creative. Always original, it always opens out new horizons for an old journey . . . . Tradition teaches us how to live, because it develops and expands our powers, and shows us how to give ourselves to the world in which we live . . . (Italics added) (*No Man*, pp. 150-151).

This passage shows dramatically how far Merton has moved from the rigidity of *Seven Storey Mountain* to an understanding of tradition that involves a vital and creative meeting of the old and the new. And the meeting place is experience.

Yet, as I have pointed out earlier, this meeting of the old and the new in the reality of concrete experience is not always a congenial meeting. Quite the contrary, it may be jarring at times: questions, hitherto unasked, may come to the fore and, more often than not perhaps, admit of no immediately evident answers. That is why Merton's growing affinity for a methodology of experience (one that is more inductive than deductive) inevitably moved him toward a kindred methodology: the methodology of the question. It would be going too far afield in this article to discuss how his acceptance of the methodology of the question was actually a revisit to the tradition of the golden age of scholasticism, when it was the *quaestio* rather than the *thesis* that was at the center of theological reflection. After all, St. Thomas Aquinas begins his reflections on God, not with the *thesis*: "God exists," but with the *quaestio*: "Does God exist?"[10] It was not really till the later part of the 17th century that the *thesis* replaced the *quaestio* in theological discourse.

Bernard Lonergan, the brilliant Canadian theologian, who spent a lifetime studying methodology has helped us to see the crucial importance of the question in theological enterprise. In clarifying the function of the question, Lonergan has made it clear that it is not just the answer to our question that enlightens us: the steps we take to get to the answer may be as enlightening as the answer itself.

As far as I know, Merton was not well acquainted with the writings of Lonergan; but in his own way and in the more unsystematic kind of theology he wrote, he did discover, as Lonergan had, the critical importance and the vital function of the question. This discovery is clearly set forth in the Prologue to the book we have been talking about (*No Man is an Island*), where he writes about "spiritual insecurity," which, he says, is "the fruit of unanswered questions." He continues:

> But questions cannot go unanswered unless they first be asked. And there is a far worse anxiety, a far worse insecurity, which comes from being afraid to ask the right questions -- because they might turn out to have no answer. One of the moral diseases we communicate to one another in society [and also in the Church?] comes from huddling together in the pale light of an insufficient answer to a question we are afraid to ask.
>
> (*No Man*, p. xiii).

No Man stands, then, as a kind of centerpiece in the Merton corpus: a key that opens the door to his more mature appreciation of the meaning of "the living tradition of faith." The writings which precede this book ready the way for this definitive commitment to "experience" and "the question" as his chosen methodology. The writings that follow emerge from the context of this commitment.

---

10. In *Conjectures of a Guilty Bystander*, Merton remarks about the structure of the articles of St. Thomas's *Summa Theologica*: "In the usual structure of his articles, St. Thomas first lines up the arguments he finds not fully satisfactory, then gives his own view, and finally discusses the arguments he first set forth. Note the way I have expressed this -- one is usually inclined (by the bad habit acquired in seminaries) to say that 'he first lines up the *wrong opinions*, then gives the *right answer*, then *demolishes the wrong answers*.' Very often St. Thomas has better insight into . . . the opinion which he does not fully accept than the ones who themselves hold it. Very often, too, his answer, is not a refutation but a placing in perspective, or a qualified acceptance, fitting the seemingly adverse opinion into the broader context of his own view."

The Case of *The Inner Experience*

One of his books which lavishly displays the use of this methodology is *Conjectures of a Guilty Bystander*. Before discussing *Conjectures*, however, I want to digress for a moment to discuss a book that Merton worked on four years after the publication of *No Man is an Island*. During the summer of 1959 he did an extensive reworking of some earlier materials. The very title he gave to the book that emerged from this rewriting seems to highlight the growing experiential thrust of his writings: he called it *The Inner Experience*. Yet it is a puzzling book. In a letter of September 22, 1959, to Sr. Therese Lentfoehr, he makes reference to this new book: "I *finished* a book this summer called 'The Inner Experience' which started out to be a simple revision of *What is Contemplation* but turned into something new, and just about full length. It *has to be revised* and has been sitting here on the desk waiting for revision for some time. . ." (Italics added).[11]

This enigma of a book which is "finished" and yet still "has to be revised" is a problem that continues to vex Merton scholars. Equally puzzling is the question: why did Merton say in his Trust Agreement that *The Inner Experience* was not to be published "as a book?" Was it because he wanted to do the revision that was needed? Yet one cannot help but ask: if the book was in need of revision, why did he refer to it as a book that he had "finished?" Further, it must be said that a large portion of this work has closer affinities with *The Ascent to Truth* and *Seeds of Contemplation* than with *No Man is an Island*. Much of it, in its approach and basic content, antedates the spirit of *No Man is an Island*, even though it was put together four years later. I do not wish to delay on something that is outside the main thrust of this article. Yet I think that, in the context of that thrust, it is worth pointing out two possible ways of understanding the problem that *The Inner Experience* poses. First, it may well be said that what we have here is an indication that Merton was not always consistent in his thought: it was quite possible for him at times (as I presume it is for any writer) to retreat, perhaps without even realizing he was doing so, from the advances he had made in his thinking. A second possibility is that, as a writer, he was reluctant to put aside some of the materials he had given so much time and energy to in the past, even though he realized that, in terms of where his thought had progressed since he had first dealt with those materials, much of what was there was in fact "old hat." Surely such nostalgia is quite understandable. Many people like to cling to old hats!

---

11. Merton Center, Columbia University, New York.

Conjectures of a Guilty Bystander:
The "Triumph" of a Methodology

Whatever we say about this work -- that it represents inconsistency or "over-attachment" -- it is clear that one must look beyond it to see the growth of Merton's thought.[12] And *Conjectures of a Guilty Bystander* is a good place to look. This work might well be described as the "triumph" of the methodology of the question in Merton's writing. *Conjectures* is a difficult work to identify in terms of literary genre. Published in 1966, it represents Merton's thought over a fairly long and especially productive period. It is not a journal, though it is made up of materials taken from journals which Merton kept from 1956 on (unfortunately, the items are undated; hence without the journals, whose use is still restricted, it is not usually possible to know exactly when Merton wrote a particular item). The items are generally too long to be classified, like *Seeds*, as *pensees*, yet too short and unfinished to be designated as essays. One might say that these reflections, which grew out of his reading, his correspondence and his prayer, resemble somewhat the parables of the Gospels: not in the form they take (they are not stories like the parables), but in their invitation to involvement in the question. Like the parables of Jesus, they are a challenge to dialogue: what do you think or how do you feel about this issue?

"Conjectures" in the title is intended, it seems clear, to mean more than guesses, but much less than definitive stands. "Bystander" suggests that Merton sees himself as one who, for all too long a time, has stood aloof from the demands of the times. Further, he wants to say that this aloofness begets a kind of existential guilt. Since this book is surely an entrance into the human fray (if only a literary entrance), it may perhaps be said that "guilty bystander" is less a designation of where Merton is than it is of where he has come from.

Whatever one might be inclined to say about the genre or the title, the book's methodology and general contents are quite clear. In his *Preface* the author tells us that these pages are not "pure soliloquy." This is an important and significant methodological statement. Not a few of Merton's earlier works could be described as "soliloquy"; in them he speaks with a certitude that neither asks for a reply nor expects one. *Conjectures* clearly adopts a different approach: it is billed as "an implicit dialogue with other

---

12. This is not in any way to deny that there is valuable material in *The Inner Experience*. See my book *Thomas Merton's Dark Path* and also the serialization of *The Inner Experience* in recent issues of *Cistercian Studies*.

minds." More than that: it is a dialogue "in which questions are raised." Merton hastens to add, however, that his intent is not to give the readers "his answers." For, he says, "I do not have clear answers to current questions." At the same time he is committed to the methodology of the question. "I do have questions," he states, "and, as a matter of fact, I think a person is known better by his/her questions than by his/her answers."[13] Nor is he willing to be satisfied with glib answers that fail to come to grips with real questions.

In a later passage in Conjectures, he expresses his distress that some people, who ask him for articles on all sorts of different topics, seem to take it for granted that he can simply reach into the back of his mind "for a dish of ready-to-serve Catholic answers about everything under the sun" (CGB, p. 49). While willing to accept his share of blame for anything he has done that might seem to have encouraged such an attitude, he suggests that people who make these kinds of requests have not really read his works. If they had, they would realize that he never intended to pose as one who had "all the answers."

> It seems to me that one of the reasons why my writing appeals to many people is precisely that I am not so sure of myself and do not claim to have all the answers . . . . In fact, I often wonder quite openly about these "answers," and about the habit of always having them ready. The best I can do is to look for some of the questions. (CGB, p. 49)

It should be obvious that when Merton talks about questions, his reference is not to queries that admit rather readily of a "yes" or "no" answer. He is referring -- and this constitutes the general content of his book -- to issues, problems, attitudes that concern the way we live and order our lives in terms of faith-commitment. He is talking about life-and-death matters that impinge on our understanding of human dignity, equality and freedom as well as the meaning we give to Christian faith and the demands that that faith makes upon us in the context of contemporary life. Describing his theological position in what are perhaps overworked political terms, he writes:

> For my part I consider myself neither conservative nor an extreme progressive. I would like to think that I am what Pope John was -- a progressive with a deep respect and love for tradition -- in other words a progressive who wants to preserve a very clear continuity with the past and not make silly and idealistic compromises with the present -- yet to be completely open to the modern world while retaining the clearly defined, traditionally Catholic position. (CGB, p. 312)

---

13. Conjectures of a Guilty Bystander (Garden City: Doubleday Image, 1968), p. 5. Hereafter referred to in the text as CGB.

"*Continuity* with the past" yet *completely open* to the modern world" seems to say well what Merton means by "a living tradition of faith." Yet one has to deal with what I can only call the perplexing conclusion of that statement. What does he mean by "retaining the clearly defined, traditionally Catholic position"? Does not this phrase say the same thing as "continuity with the past"? If it does, then why is it repeated? If it does not, then it seems to cancel out "completely open to the modern world." The least that can be said about this phrase is that it is either tautological or ambiguous. Yet perhaps we should not be too demanding of Merton in expecting him to express his position clearly and unambiguously. If he is over-cautious, as he certainly appears to be here, it is perhaps helpful in understanding him to note the time at which he was writing. And this happens to be one of the texts from *Conjectures* for which we can suggest a likely date. Clearly the text was written after Pope John XXIII's death --which would place its writing in 1963 or later. Now, as everyone knows, these were unsettling times in the Roman Catholic Church: times when "openness to the world" meant for some people accommodation to what-ever happened to be the whim, opinion or idiosyncrasy of the current moment. A lot of absurd and stupid things were done in the name of "contemporaneity."

Perhaps in fairness to Merton, it would be correct to say that he was trying to strike a balance. In seeking to reach such a position, one does perhaps have to take note of whatever extreme attitude or mood may be seeking at the moment to tip the scales in its favor. That Merton did feel, rightly or not, the need to defend the authentic heritage of the past against what he saw as obviously aberrant accommodations to modernity must not in any way move us to question Merton's genuine belief in a living tradition that embodied continuity and openness. This understanding of tradition is evidenced in countless examples that are easily discoverable in the pages of *Conjectures*.

Merton's conscious effort to achieve a proper balance of the claims of the past and the present is well expressed in a statement that comes fairly late in the book: "What is new in modern theology is not the essential message, but our rethinking of it, our rediscovery in it of insights we had lost" (*CGB*, p. 322). In this statement, Merton is saying three things, I believe, about theology and the tradition which theology attempts to embody: (1) the essential message is not new; (2) what is new is our rediscovery in that message of insights we had lost; and (3) what is also new is our discovery of insights we had never had before. It is fair, I think, to say that this third point is implicit in Merton's careful wording: "our rethinking of [the essential message]." Rethinking is a step beyond "rediscovery."

There is not the time nor is there the need to discuss in detail the many questions dealt with in this book (such matters as technology, racism, nuclear war, non-violence, the role of the church in the modern world, the place of monastic life in contemporary society, attitudes toward death, the abuse of language, solitude, prayer, Zen and a host of other issues). A look at the brief index of the book will give ample indication of the kinds of issues about which the author wishes to dialogue with his readers.

Thus far I have discussed how tradition is shaped by past and present meeting in creative tension in a faith-community of believers. What we have been discussing is what happens to form tradition in a particular household of faith. But tradition can be shaped not only from within the community of faith but also from without. By this I mean that a tradition may be shaped by a community of faith entering into dialogue with other communities of faith as well as with other purveyors of religious experience that are outside one's own faith-tradition. Thus there can be *inter-faith* dialogue of Christians, institutionally separated, but professing faith in one Lord, one Spirit, one Baptism. There can also be *inter-religious* dialogue.

Enriching Tradition by Going Beyond It

In the beginning of this article I spoke of three ways in which tradition can be shaped in the life of a faith community. Each had to do with a particular way in which the old and the new, the past and the present, were brought into configuration with one another. I suggested that at different stages of his life Merton experienced all three. I suggested, further, that in his later years he went beyond all three. What I mean is that in the 1960s (and to some degree even earlier) Merton had reached a point of personal growth when he could no longer limit the shaping of his understanding of tradition to what was happening within the Roman Catholic Church. He was, in other words, no longer content to explore his faith-tradition simply *from within*; he needed to enrich that tradition by contact with *outside* traditions; not only those outside the Roman Catholic tradition (but still within the context of Christian Faith) but even those that were outside the pale of Christian Faith. His own growth coincided with, and in a sense received a mandate from, what was happening in his own Church. Thus he writes in *Conjectures*:

> If the Catholic Church is turning to the modern world and to the other Christian Churches, and if she is perhaps for the first time seriously taking note of the non-Christian religions in their own terms, then it becomes necessary for at least a few contemplative and monastic theologians to contribute something of their own to the discussion. (*CGB*, p. 7)

Openness to the World and to Other Christian Churches

These three movements (opening to the world, opening to other Christian Churches and opening to non-Christian religions *in their own terms*), which Merton sees as important agenda for the Roman Catholic Church, also help to define his life and activities in the 1960s. He was open to the world: "the world of the bomb, the world of race hatred, the world of technology, the world of mass media, big business, revolution and all the rest" (*CGB*, p. 157).

He was also in much closer contact with other Christian communities. He met regularly with groups of Protestants from Vanderbilt University, Lexington Theological Seminary (then the College of the Bible), and Southern Baptist Theological Seminary in Louisville. He corresponded extensively with Anglicans. Thus, he wrote to Canon A. M. Allchin of his admiration for Anglicanism (what a change from the attitude expressed in *Seven Storey Mountain*!) and his feeling that Roman Catholics, in their transition to the vernacular, had much to learn from Anglicanism.

> It seems to me that the best of Anglicanism is unexcelled . . . . For my part I will try to cling to the best and be as English a Catholic as one in my position can be. I think it is terribly important for Roman Catholics now plunging into the vernacular to have some sense of the Anglican tradition.[14]

In response to another Anglican friend, the late Etta Gullick, who asked him whether his faith commitment obligated him to consider her a heretic, he replied:

---

14. *The Hidden Ground of Love: The Letters of Thomas Merton on Religious Experience and Social Concerns*; ed. William H. Shannon (New York: Farrar, Straus & Giroux, 1985), p. 26. Hereafter referred to in the text as *HGL*.

> I suppose in some theoretical sense you may be so to one on my side of the
> fence, but personally I have long since given up attaching importance to
> that sort of thing, because I have no idea what you may be in the eyes of
> God, and that is what counts.... I do think, though, that you and I are one
> in Christ, and hence the presence of some material heresy (according to
> my side of the fence) does not make that much difference. (*HGL*, p. 358)

And when Etta wrote of her anguish over the fact that there was dim
hope, in the foreseeable future, of any kind of union between Anglicanism
and Roman Catholicism that would allow for inter-communion and recognition of one another's institutional structure, Merton said:

> I can understand your being a bit anguished about the obvious fact that
> there can be little hope of institutional or sacramental union between
> Anglicans and Romans. Perhaps on the other hand I am too stoical about it
> all, but I frankly am not terribly anguished. I am not able to get too
> involved in the institutional side of any of the efforts now being made....
> This kind of thing is for others who know more about it. To me it is enough
> to be united with people in love and in the Holy Spirit, as I am sure I am
> and they are, in spite of the sometimes momentous institutional and
> doctrinal differences. (*HGL*, pp. 377-378)

This is an important statement for understanding Merton's "ecumenical" stance. He makes clear in *Conjectures* that he is not writing
"professional ecumenism." What he intends to do in his book is to share
what he has learned from his readings and from other contacts he had with
people who, while they may have differed from him in the religious traditions which they embraced, were nonetheless not far from him in the
religious experiences going on in their lives. Merton was convinced that
doctrinal differences did not necessarily mean differences in religious
experience. And his concern was much more with the latter than the
former. It is this approach that enables him to read with profit and to
identify in many ways with people whose doctrinal positions differed from
his own. *Conjectures*, as Merton himself put it, is simply about one Catholic
"sharing the Protestant experience -- and other religious experiences as
well." This sharing of religious experience was something Merton felt was
very important, not just for the good of religion, but for the peace of the
world. To Ananda Coomaraswamy's widow, Dona Luisa, he wrote (January
13, 1961) of his admiration for Ananda as a man who was able to unite in
himself the spiritual traditions of East and West. One of the needs in
preparing the way for peace, he told her, was the formation of people who
would be able "to unite in themselves and experience in their own lives all
that is best and most true in the various great spiritual traditions" (*HGL*,
p. 126). Such people would be "sacraments of peace" in a so often alienated
world. This was not a new idea to him. There is the oft quoted passage from

Conjectures (which in its original form comes quite early, April 28, 1957) in which he says much the same thing:[15] "If I can unite *in myself* the thought and the devotion of Eastern and Western Christendom, the Greek and the Latin Fathers, the Russians with the Spanish mystics, I can prepare in myself the reunion of divided Christians" (*CGB*, p. 21).

Wherever he looked in the fields of religious thought and experience, he sought areas of common affirmation rather than points of disagreement. He would be a better Catholic, he thought, not if he was able to refute Protestant positions, but rather if he affirmed the truth of Protestantism wherever he could. This he felt not only about other Christian faiths, but also about other religions such as Islam, Hinduism, Buddhism and all the rest. This does not mean that Merton favored a kind of vapid indifferentism or a syncretism that somehow made everything one. No, he realized well the rules of dialogue. One must be faithful to one's own tradition. This fidelity will mean that there will be things in other religious traditions which as a Catholic he could not affirm and accept. But, first, he says, one needs to say "yes" to all the things that he/she can.

> If I affirm myself as a Catholic merely by denying all that is Muslim, Jewish, Protestant, Hindu, Buddhist, etc., in the end I will find that there is not much left for me to affirm as a Catholic: and certainly no breath of the Spirit with which to affirm it. (*CGB*, p. 144)

Openness to Non-Christian Religions on Their Terms

If Merton's "ecumenical" concerns in the 1960s meant openness to the world, to other Christian Churches and to non-Christian religions listened to "on their own terms," it may perhaps be said that the last of these became for him a special preoccupation. Thus, Merton felt a special kinship with that religious tradition out of which Christianity first emerged: Judaism. It was with genuine joy that he read Abraham Joshua Heschel's books and welcomed him on his visit to Gethsemani on July 13, 1964. One of the subjects they discussed was the Vatican Declaration on Jewish-Christian Relations. Merton anguished with Heschel over a Declaration that, in its second draft, had been notably weakened, apparently for political reasons.

---

15. Michael Mott, *The Seven Mountains of Thomas Merton* (Boston: Houghton Mifflin, 1984), p. 306.

This turn of events prompted a long letter from Merton to Cardinal Augustine Bea of the Secretariat for Christian Unity. Merton wrote with strong feeling:

> I am personally convinced that the grace to truly see the Church as she is in her humility and in her splendor may perhaps not be granted to the Council Fathers, if they fail to take account of her relation to the anguished synagogue . . . . The deepest truths are in question. The very words themselves should suggest that the *ekklesia* is not altogether alien from the *synagogue* and that she should be able to see herself to some extent, though darkly, in this antitypal mirror. (*HGL*, p. 433)

Even stronger (possibly because less official) are his words in a letter of February 15, 1962, to Rabbi Zalman Schachter, who was at the time teaching at the University of Manitoba in Winnipeg, Canada:

> The Jews have been the greatest eschatological sign of the twentieth century . . . a sign from God. Telling us what? Among other things, telling Christians that if they don't look out, they are going to miss the boat or fall out if it, because the antinomy they have unconsciously and complacently supposed between the Jews and Christ is not even a very good figment of the imagination. The Suffering Servant is one: Christ, Israel. There is one wedding and one wedding feast . . . . There is one bride. There is one mystery, and the mystery of Israel and of the Church is ultimately to be revealed as One. (*HGL*, p. 535)

Merton's interest in other religions extended, with a growing enthusiasm, to religious traditions far removed geographically and doctrinally from Christian Faith. His interest in Sufism, the mystical strain in Islam, came rather late in his life. Though in somewhat superficial contact with Islam for some years through Louis Massignon, it was in 1967 and 1968 that he began reading steadily in Islamic literature and giving lectures to the monks at Gethsemani on Sufism.

His interest in Zen was long standing and deeply earnest. In 1961, New Directions published a dialogue between him and D. T. Suzuki, which was later to appear in a 1968 New Directions Merton publication, *Zen and the Birds of Appetite*. Merton and Suzuki were in agreement that meaningful parallels could be found between some of the Christian mystics, like Eckhart for instance, and the Zen Masters. On June 20, 1964, Merton received permission to fly to New York City, where he had two treasured visits with the 94-year old Suzuki. In Suzuki Merton felt that he had met "the true man of no title," of which the Zen Masters speak. It was an important experience for him: the discovery of so deep an understanding between himself and this extraordinary and simple man whose books he had been reading for many years.

Merton was taken, too, with Chinese religious thought: he wrote about it and, with the help of Dr. John C. H. Wu, managed to make his own "translation" of the Taoist philosopher, Chuang Tzu, in what turned out to be without doubt one of his most delightful books, *The Way of Chuang Tzu.* Dr. Wu, to whom the book was dedicated, was ecstatic in his praise: "This is exactly what Chuang Tzu would have written had he known English. You have made Chuang Tzu relive in these beautiful poems."[16] Merton was especially happy with *The Way of Chuang Tzu.* He wrote to Sister Emmanuel de Souza e Silva in Brazil: "The Chuang Tzu book is one of my favorites" (*HGL*, p. 195).

In May of 1964 he welcomed at Gethsemani a group of Hibakusha people (those who had survived the bombing of Hiroshima) and he continued to correspond with their leader, Hiromu Morishita. In June of 1966 the Vietnamese monk-poet, Thich Nhat Hanh, in company with John Heidbrink, paid a brief visit to Gethsemani. In an article that appeared in the August issue of *Jubilee*, Merton spoke of the close ties he felt with this monk from the East. In this brief tribute, called "Nhat Hanh is My Brother," he wrote:

> We are both monks and we have lived the monastic life about the same number of years. We are both poets, both existentialists. I have far more in common with Nhat Hanh than I have with many Americans and I do not hesitate to say it. It is vitally important that such bonds be admitted. They are the bonds of a new solidarity and a new brotherhood which is beginning to be evident on all the five continents and which cut across all political, religious and cultural lines to unite young men and women in every country in something that is more concrete than an ideal and more alive than a program.[17]

And finally, of course, there was the great adventure: the face to face meeting with the Asia he had visited so many times in word, thought and imagination: the journey that began so ecstatically in San Francisco and ended so tragically in Bangkok. As his plane left San Francisco on October 15, 1968, Merton wrote: "I am going home to the home where I have never been in this body."[18] The story of this direct meeting with Asia, after so many meetings mediated through books or personalities, is told in *The Asian Journal*: a book at once fascinating and disconcerting -- fascinating, because one is swept up into his enthusiasms for the places he visited and

---

16. Merton Center, Bellarmine College, Louisville, Kentucky.

17. Thomas Merton, *The Nonviolent Alternative*; ed. Gordon C. Zahn (New York: Farrar, Straus & Giroux, 1981), p. 264.

18. *The Asian Journal of Thomas Merton*; ed. Naomi Burton Stone, Patrick Hart, James Laughlin (New York: New Directions, 1973), p. 5. Hereafter referred to in the text as *AJ*.

the Hindu and Buddhist scholars he met; disconcerting, because one looks almost in vain for some prophetic judgment on the grim poverty, the over-population, the starvation, the disease that are so strikingly evident in modern-day India. Yet the Thomas Merton who was so sharply critical of social injustices at home seems curiously detached when he sees the same things -- and perhaps worse -- in India. It seems almost as if Merton is determined to project on Asia the image of it he had brought with him. There is something defensive in his statement of November 18: "Now suppose some loon comes up to me and says: Have you found the *real* Asia? I am at a loss to know what one means by the 'real Asia'. It is *all* real, as far as I can see. Though certainly a lot of it has been corrupted by the West" (*AJ*, pp. 149-150). As one puts down *The Asian Journal*, it is with the strong feeling that sooner or later "some loon" does have to put that question.

Still, in all fairness to Merton, it must be remembered that he, of course, never got to edit *The Asian Journal*. It was put together by Naomi Burton Stone, Brother Patrick Hart and James Laughlin from the notebook jottings that Merton kept so meticulously. The journal evidences the care and skill with which these editors managed to decipher what were often-times little more than scribblings and put the contents of two different notebooks into a comprehensible whole. Yet grateful though we may be to them, it does not detract from their good work to say that the journal would have been a better book had Merton edited it himself -- after he had put time and distance between himself and his Asian experience. One suspects that from such a perspective, he might himself have been the "loon" who would have asked: "Did I find the *real* Asia?" Indeed, his intent to revise these hastily written notes is implicit in a notation recorded, curiously, on November 18 (the same day he made the "loon statement" quoted above) in which he reflects that there must be "a reassessment of this whole Indian experience *in more critical terms*" (italics added) (*AJ*, p. 148). But such was not to be: on December 10, 1968, the designs of an inscrutable Providence called him to a reassessment, not of his Asian journey, but of his whole life, as a mysterious and fatal accident joined him to the company of the "burnt men."

What happened at that Grand Assize is hidden from us so long as we remain on this side of the Great Divide. Yet there is nothing to prevent us from being a bit "loon-like," projecting our fancies beyond the eschatological curtain, and imagining what Thomas Merton, who wrote so well from the base of that seven storey mountain, might say to us from above its summit. Our fancy would expect to see it in writing. After all, he had said:

"Perhaps I shall continue writing on my death bed and even take some asbestos paper with me in order to go on writing in purgatory" (*SJ*, p. 233). No need to consign him to purgatory, surely; but the writing: that is a different matter. We would expect to be able to peer at the heavenly scroll:

"My sisters and brothers, I have struck too many typewriter keys, writing about God and what it means to be aware of His Presence. I would have been better occupied, had I been content simply with the experience without feeling the need to verbalize it. But, as you well know, writing was the "sting of the flesh" which I asked God to deliver from me, only to be told -- as Paul was -- 'my grace is sufficient for you.'

"And I have known that grace: Mercy within Mercy within Mercy. The Mercy that created me and brought me on the outward journey 'from Prades to Bermuda to St. Antonin to Oakham to New York to Cambridge to Rome to New York to Columbia to Corpus Christi to St. Bonaventure to the Cistercian Abbey of the poor men who labor in Gethsemani.'[19] That Mercy has also led me on the inner journey, which is 'a matter of growth, deepening, and an ever greater surrender to the creative action of love and grace in our hearts' (*AJ*, p. 296). In that interior journey I have moved from the aimlessness of youth to the security of the monastery and finally to the wide-open plains of religious experience that Mercy has spread out for me to see. As time passed, I became more and more convinced, as I said in *Conjectures*, that my task was 'to clarify something of the tradition that lives in me and in which I live: the tradition of wisdom and spirit. . .' (*CGB*, p. 194). And I have been able, much more precisely as time went on, to locate the various places where that tradition is to be located. It 'is found not only in Western Christendom but in Orthodoxy, and also, at least analogously, in Asia and in Islam' (*CGB*, p. 194).

"All this is to say that, as my inner journey continued, the Divine Mercy, which in 1938 brought me to a Roman Catholicism that I embraced irrevocably, led me, besides,

---

19. Thomas Merton, *The Seven Storey Mountain* (New York: Harcourt Brace, 1948), pp. 422-423.

into a World Catholicism. I discovered I was more, not less, a Catholic, when I was willing to recognize all the things that God was doing outside the parameters of the institutional structure of which I was a part. I could not be Catholic by holding God captive in a single religious tradition, but only by realizing that He was above all religious traditions as Saviour and Judge of all. What I know now that I only obscurely understood before, is that our God is not a Christian God, in the sense of belonging only to Christian people; He is a Catholic God, that is, a God of all peoples and places, who lives in all and acts in all and leaves traces of His Presence in everything that is authentic and genuine in religious rituals, stories and symbols in whatever part of the world they may be found.

"My sisters and brothers, dialogue with other religions will not (or at least need not) obscure or compromise your own faith-commitment; on the contrary, it can increase that commitment. I once wrote to James Baldwin: 'I am . . . not completely human until I have found myself in my African and Asian and Indonesian brother [and sister], because he [/she] has the part of humanity that I lack.'[20]

"Now I would want to add: I am not completely Catholic until I have found myself in my Protestant, Jewish, Muslim, Hindu, Buddhist brother and sister; for they have a part of the totality that being Catholic means -- which I lack without them. This insight may not be a grace that comes to all; but those who receive it, receive a great grace indeed.

"You are a community of believers. If your faith is to be alive, it must bring together the past and the present, the new and the old, in a creative tension that is a fruitful meeting. But that meeting will achieve its full potential and be truly Catholic, only if it pushes the frontiers of that creative tension to the very ends of the earth and is willing to listen to the voice of our God speaking -- sometimes in different, or even muted tones, but still speaking -- in the religious experiences of a total humanity."

---

20. Thomas Merton, *Seeds of Destruction* (New York: Farrar, Straus & Giroux), 1964, p. 305.

THE EXPERIENCE OF GOD
AND THE EXPERIENCE OF NOTHINGNESS
IN THOMAS MERTON

by **James Conner,** O.C.S.O.

"Leave nothingness as it is. In it, He is present."[1]

In these words, Thomas Merton expresses what may be the central message of all his writings. However this expression took gradual shape over the course of the years. He himself acknowledged the fact that his earlier writings contained a certain element of naivete which colored his approach to the life of contemplation. One of his earliest books was entitled *Exile Ends in Glory*, the life of a Cistercian nun; and the original title of the work which will be studied here was *The Dark Path*. This change of imagery, from glory to darkness, expresses the progression of his writings and of his life. This also expresses the extent to which Merton's writings moved from a theory about contemplation to the fruit of his own experience of the contemplative life. As his experience matured, it took on more of the flavor of that dark night through which one passes on the way to oneness with God.

---

1.   Thomas Merton, *The Inner Experience*, Edited by Brother Patrick Hart and published in *Cistercian Studies* in eight installments during 1983 and 1984; see Section VI, page 150. Hereafter referred to in the text as *IE*.

Editors' Note: This essay is based on a talk given at "The Third-God Conference," sponsored by the New Ecumenical Research Association in San Juan, Puerto Rico, 28 December - 4 January 1984.

John F. Teahan has pointed out that most studies of Merton have strangely ignored one of the major aspects of his work: his appropriation of the apophatic tradition in Christian mysticism.[2] Merton himself wrote:

> Now while the Christian contemplative must certainly develop by study the theological understanding of the concepts about God, he is mainly called to penetrate the wordless darkness and apophatic light of an experience beyond concepts, and here he gradually becomes familiar with a God Who is "absent" and as it were "non-existent" to all human experience.[3]

Many studies have been done on the apophatic aspect of Christian mysticism.[4] In contemplation God is known in darkness, by not knowing Him. God is sought and is found through not finding Him. In a taped lecture given to the monks of Gethsemani, Merton quotes Meister Eckhart: "Seek God so as never to find Him."[5] The point Eckhart is making is that, once you seem to have found God, it is not He Whom you have found. Once you seem to grasp God, He eludes you. For God is not an object or a thing alongside other objects and things. He is not even a person alongside other persons. God is the All Whom we can discover only in the experience of not discovering Him.

In developing such a point, Merton was totally faithful to the whole of Christian tradition. God Himself had said: "No one can see Me and live" (Exodus 33:20). God refused to give a Name to Moses other than simply "I AM." Any other name or expression runs the risk of becoming an idol. St. Thomas Aquinas, the great teacher of Western Scholasticism, says that anything that can be affirmed about God must also be denied of Him, for our concepts are all limited and can be applied to God only in an analogical manner.[6]

However it is not principally reason that taught Merton this, but more particularly experience itself. Life is being constantly affected by our experiences. Edward Schillebeeckx says that experience means learning through "direct" contact with people and things.[7] New experience is

---

2. Cited in William H. Shannon's *Thomas Merton's Dark Path*; rev. ed. (New York: Farrar, Straus & Giroux, 1987), p. 11.

3. Thomas Merton, *Contemplation in a World of Action* (Garden City: Doubleday, 1971), p. 7.

4. See William Johnston, S.J., "The Experience of God in Christian Apophatic Mysticism" in *God: The Contemporary Discussion*; ed. by Frederick Sontag and M. Darrol Bryant (New York: Rose of Sharon Press, 1982), pp. 363-375.

5. Thomas Merton, *The Merton Tapes/* Series III, Chappaqua: Electronic Paperbacks, 1983, tape 4 ("The Ways of God"), side 1.

6. Thomas Aquinas, *Summa Theologica* I, Q. 13, art. 10.

7. Edward Schillebeeckx, *Christ: The Experience of Jesus as Lord* (New York: Seabury Press, 1980), p. 31. Hereafter referred to as *Schillebeeckx*.

always related to the knowledge that we have already gained. Consequently there is a reciprocal relationship between knowledge and experience, states Schillebeeckx:

> The connection between experience and thought is that the constantly unforeseen content of new experiences keeps forcing us to think again. On the one hand, thought makes experience possible, while on the other it is experience that makes new thinking necessary. (*Schillebeeckx*, p. 31)

Though we are constructive, rational beings, reality remains the final criterion. Reality confronts the human tendency to build idols and keeps us from erecting a theoretical system which would only serve as a bulwark against the incursion of the living God. It shows us the total inadequacy of our concepts and attempts to express the ineffable Mystery in words or even in dogmas.

Schillebeeckx speaks of that "permanent resistance of reality to our rational inventions" which forces us to "constantly new and untried models of thought." This is the desert which the Israelites of old had to experience in order to purify their understanding of the "I AM" who was leading them. This is the same desert which every person must encounter in his / her openness to the living God. By coming up against resistance, our planned search is continually forced to follow a new direction. In this way, "truth" directs our ever wider searching.

> In view of the negativity or the "refractoriness" in all this, one might say that the intensity but also the authority of the experience of life culminates in "suffering", in the suffering of disaster and failure, in the suffering of grief, in the suffering of evil, in the suffering of love. Here are the great elements of the revelation of reality in and through men's *finite experience*. (*Schillebeeckx*, p. 36)

It was precisely such elements in Merton's own life which led him, as it has led every person open to reality, to formulate his experience of God more in a negative fashion. And yet for him this very negativity was not separate from its basis in the reality of faith. The human is simply a creature of God. Job said: "Were He to recall his breath, to draw His breathing back into Himself, things of flesh would perish altogether and man would return to dust" (Job 34:14-15). Because of this we are totally dependent upon God and are but nothing of ourselves. However as a result of the Fall, we have forgotten that we are nothing. We have the "illusion" that we are something of ourselves, and a great part of our lives is spent in striving to maintain this illusion for ourselves and for one another.

The struggle between this illusion, or what Merton calls the "false self," and the attempts of Reality to break through to the "true self" forms the basis for his study on *The Inner Experience*. This struggle can be seen particularly in a section which is entitled "Sacred and Secular." This division is not the same as that made by many theologians in past years, separating all reality into that which is *objectively* "sacred" or pertaining to God and the realm of the holy, and "secular" or pertaining to the worldly or mundane. Since Merton is speaking of an inner reality, his distinction pertains more to the *attitude we have in dealing with all* reality.

> Secular life is a life of vain hopes, imprisoned in the illusion of newness and change, an illusion which brings us constantly back to the same old point, the contemplation of our own nothingness. In the words of Pascal: "Nothing is so unbearable to a man as to be completely at rest, without passions, without busyness, without diversion, without study. He then feels his nothingness, his forlornness, his insufficiency, his dependence, his weakness, his emptiness . . ." (Pensees, 131). (*IE*, III, 10)

Merton says that "secular society" is by its nature committed to what Pascal calls "diversion," that is, to the frantic effort at quieting our "anguish." This anguish arises whenever reality threatens to break through the illusion that we have so carefully erected. Such an anguish forces us to a fork in the road of life. The sacred and the secular reflect two kinds of dependence. The secular depends on things it needs for diversion and for escape from its own nothingness. The world makes use of this spirit to create artificial needs which it then pretends to "satisfy." In actual fact, it is simply a complicity on both sides to maintain this illusion of our own false strength and greatness, of our "false self."

> In the sacred society, on the other hand, man admits no dependence on anything lower than himself, or even "outside" himself in a spatial sense. His only Master is God. He rules us by liberating us and raising us to union with Himself *from within*. And in so doing He liberates us from our dependence on created things outside us. We use them and dominate them, so that they exist for our sakes, and not we for theirs. (*IE*, III, 213-214)

In an article on "Buddhism and the Modern World," Merton treats this same point. He quotes Shin'ichi Hisamatsu, a Zen scholar, as saying:

> In Zen, true authority is that Self which is itself authority and does not rely on anything . . . . True authority is where there is no distinction between that which relies and that which is relied upon.[8]

This Self is the "True Self" which is the Self the Father created and loved from all eternity. It is the Self in Christ. It is the Self God looked upon when He said: "Let us make man in our own image and likeness" (Genesis 1:26).

---

8. Thomas Merton, *Mystics and Zen Masters* (New York: Dell Publishing Company, 1969), p. 283. Hereafter referred to in the text as *MZM*.

This Self is one with God and finds its meaning and true reality only in Him. St. Paul reminded the men of Athens that "in Him we live and move and have our being" (Acts 17:28). This is the true authority which does not rely on anything and has no need of anything outside itself. "I can do all things in Him who strengthens me" (Philippians 4:13). Our strength comes from this God Who has given Himself to be our own deepest Self, and consequently there remains no distinction between "that which relies and that which is relied on."

Professor Hisamatsu speaks of the root problem of social and psychological alienation. Merton calls this a "modern and western term for a condition that Zen has been at grips with since it began: the condition of servile dependence on something which is really one's own but which is experienced as outside, above, more perfect than one's self" (*MZM*, p. 283). Because we despair of this inner authority and strength, because we forget that all that we are is a sheer gift from God, we succumb to the "secular" mentality and desperately try to avoid the awareness of that nothingness which is all that we are of ourselves. Merton reminds us that, if we have true faith and trust in the God Who is our All, then we can begin to take on that "sacred" mentality.

> The truly sacred attitude toward life is in no sense an escape from the sense of nothingness that assails us when we are left alone with ourselves. On the contrary, it penetrates into that darkness and that nothingness, realizing that the mercy of God has transformed our nothingness into His temple and believing that in our darkness His light has hidden itself. Hence the sacred attitude is one that does not recoil from our own inner emptiness, but rather penetrates into it with awe and reverence, and with the awareness of Mystery. (*IE*, pp. 213-214)

The sacred attitude enables us to be open to that truth "which comes to us by the alienation and disorientation of what we have already achieved and planned" (*Schillebeeckx*, 35). Reality of life situations shows that the self we have imagined ourselves to be is false. But it also shows that the God Whom we have imagined to be separate from us is also false, for He is nearer to us than we are to ourselves. Consequently we do not have to try to build a false self, even a virtuous one, to confront this "God."

> It is therefore a matter of great courage and spiritual energy to turn away from diversion and prepare to meet, face to face, that *immediate* experience of life which is intolerable to the exterior man. This is possible only when, by a gift of God (St. Thomas would say it was the Gift of Fear or sacred awe) we are able to see our inner selves not as a vacuum but as an *infinite depth*, not as emptiness but as fullness. This change of perspective is impossible as long as we are afraid of our own nothingness, as long as we are afraid of fear, afraid of poverty, afraid of boredom -- as long as we run away from ourselves. (*IE*, p. 214)

And yet this emptiness and nothingness which we discover in ourselves need not be feared. It is not a negative quality which would make us
distant from God. On the contrary, it is the very title that we have to lay
claim that God be "my God." As Merton says elsewhere:

> The man who has truly found his spiritual nakedness, who has realized he
> is empty, is not just a self that has *acquired* emptiness or *become* empty.
> He just "is empty from the beginning," as Dr. Suzuki has observed. That is
> to say he loves with a purity and freedom that spring spontaneously and
> directly from the fact that he has fully recovered the divine likeness, and is
> now fully his true self because he is lost in God. He is one with God and
> identified with God and hence knows nothing of any ego in himself. All he
> knows is love.[9]

In Merton's dialogue with Dr. Suzuki on the question of Emptiness,
reference was made to the Commentary of Meister Eckhart on the beati-
tude "Blessed are the poor in spirit." The Zen Master stated:

> As Buddhists would say, the realization of Emptiness is no more, no less
> than seeing into the nonexistence of a thingish ego-substance. This is the
> greatest stumbling block in our spiritual discipline, which in actuality
> consists not in getting rid of the self but in realizing the fact that there is no
> such existence from the first. "Being poor" does not mean "becoming
> poor;" "being poor" means to be from the beginning not in possession of
> anything and not giving away what one has. Nothing to gain, nothing to
> lose; nothing to give, nothing to take; to be just so, and yet to be rich in
> inexhaustible possibilities -- this is to be "poor" in its most proper and
> characteristic sense of the word. This is what all religious experience tells
> us. To be absolutely nothing is to be everything. When one is in possession
> of something, that something will keep all other somethings from coming
> in. (*ZBA*, p. 109)

Suzuki says that this can be so because Buddhism sees the equation
as being "zero equals infinity and infinity equals zero." The "zero" is not a
mathematical symbol. It is the infinite -- "a storehouse or womb of all
possible good or values." This is what Paul means when he speaks of
"having nothing, yet possessing all things" (2 Corinthians 6:10). It is precisely the experience of nothingness within ourselves which opens the way
to possess the fullness of God. This is also an expression of that "true
wisdom" in contrast to the "foolishness of human wisdom" which Paul
speaks of in I Corinthians Ch. 1 and 2. "As Scripture says: 'If anyone wants to
boast, let him boast in the Lord'" (1 Corinthians 1:31). One who has the
"sacred" attitude can "glory in our infirmity in order that the power of
Christ may abide in us" (2 Corinthians 12:9). Merton developed this even
further in a later article:

---

9.   Thomas Merton, *Zen and the Birds of Appetite* (New York: New Directions, 1968), p. 129. Hereafter
referred to in the text as *ZBA*.

> The utter "self-emptying" of Christ -- and the self-emptying which makes the disciple one with Christ in *His* kenosis -- can be understood and has been understood in a very Zen-like sense as far as psychology and experience are concerned. (*ZBA*, p. 21)

Like Suzuki, Merton makes use of Meister Eckhart to express this experience. Eckhart says:

> A man should be so poor that he is not and has not a place for God to act in. To reserve a place would be to maintain distinctions . . . . For if God wants to act in the soul, He Himself must be the place in which He acts -- and that is what He would like to do . . . . It is here, in this poverty, that man regains the eternal being that once he was, now is, and evermore shall be.
>
> (*ZBA*, p. 23)

Since it is only the "poor in spirit" who can experience this, it means that one must be willing to face this poverty in daily experience of life. Paul refers to those "unutterable groanings" with which the Spirit of God Himself intercedes on our behalf since we do not know even how to pray. James Dunn comments on this passage from Galatians as follows:

> What Paul seems to have in mind is the only form of prayer left to the Christian believer when he comes to the end of himself, frustrated by his own weakness and baffled by his own ignorance of God and God's Will. Here we see the two sides of charismatic consciousness -- the consciousness of human impotence and the consciousness of divine power in and through that weakness. It is this consciousness that the Spirit is acting in and through his complete impotence at the most fundamental level of his relationship with the Father which gives him confidence that the Spirit is at work in all his other relationships and circumstances: "in everything He (the Spirit) cooperates for good with those who love God."
>
> (Romans 8:26-28)[10]

In contrast to all of this is the person whose view of life is purely "secular." Unless one can accept this inner poverty and seeming emptiness with humility and trust in God, one will react against it and ultimately come to hate oneself. Merton says:

> He hates himself in the sense that he cannot stand to be "with" or "by" himself. And because he hates himself, he also tends to hate God, because he cannot abide the inner loneliness which must be suffered and accepted before God can be found. His rebellion against his own inner loneliness and poverty turns into pride. Pride is the fixation of the exterior self upon itself, and the rejection of all other elements in the self for which it is incapable of assuming responsibility . . . . The basic and most fundamental problem of the spiritual life is this acceptance of our hidden and dark self, with which we tend to identify all the evil that is in us. (*IE*, p. 214)

When one comes face to face with the inner poverty which opens us to the presence of the Divine, the reaction is normally a profound sense of

---

10.   James D. G. Dunn, *Jesus and the Spirit* (Philadelphia: Westminster Press, 1975), p. 241.

our own sinfulness. Such was the experience of Isaiah when he found himself before the throne of God (Isaiah Ch. 6). Such was also the experience of Peter when confronted by that miraculous catch of fish which could have been effected only by the divine power: "Depart from me, Lord, for I am a sinful man" (Luke 5:8). Merton says that there is a subtle but inescapable connection between the "sacred" attitude and the acceptance of one's inmost self. As we recognize this emptiness of the true Self, we become aware of the extent to which we are a potentiality not only for the luminous presence of the divine, but also a potentiality for darkness and sin. He says:

> This implies humility, or full acceptance of all that we tend to reject and ignore in ourselves. The inner self is "purified" by the acknowledgment of sin, not precisely because the inner self is a sea of sin, but because both our sinfulness and our interiority tend to be rejected in one and the same movement by the exterior self, and relegated to the same darkness, so that when the inner self is brought back to light, sin emerges and is liquidated by the assuming of responsibility and sorrow. (*IE*, p. 214)

It is once again the mysterious paradox that we find God in not finding Him, that we arrive in seeming to be further away, that it is only when we despair of our own power that the power of God can reveal itself in us. "For power is made perfect in infirmity" (2 Corinthians 12:9). Merton says:

> Thus the man with the "sacred" view is one who does not need to hate himself, and is never afraid or ashamed to remain with his own loneliness, for in it he is at peace, and through it he comes to the presence of God.
> (*IE*, p. 215)

Moreover as a result of such an experience he can see others as they also truly are and has no need either to identify them with their sin. This engenders a spirit of true compassion and love for the other.

> He is able, in them also, to see below the surface and to guess at the presence of the inner and innocent self that is also the image of God. Such a one is able to help others to find God in themselves, educating them in confidence by the respect he is able to feel for them. Thus he is capable of allaying some of their fears and helping them to put up with themselves, until they become interiorly quiet and learn to see God in the depths of their own poverty. (*IE*, p. 215)

Thus the acceptance of our own inner poverty brings us to a true compassion for others, a true love of them as God loves them with that creative love which enables them to become what they are. This opens the way to the further mission of the person of faith. Since we are one with God in our deepest self, we are also one with all mankind, and the path we walk and the search we pursue is done not only for ourselves but for all.

The contemplative is one who is, like the Servant of Yahweh, "acquainted with infirmity," not only with his own sin but with the sin of the whole world, which he takes upon himself because he is a man among men, and cannot dissociate himself from the works of other men. The contemplative life in our time is therefore necessarily modified by the sins of our age. They bring down upon us a cloud of darkness far more terrible than the innocent night of unknowing. Contemplation in the age of Auschwitz, Solovky and Karaganda is something darker and more fearsome than contemplation in the age of the Church Fathers. For that very reason, the urge to seek a path of spiritual light can be a subtle temptation to sin. It certainly is sin if it means the frank rejection of the burden of our age, an escape into unreality and spiritual illusion, so as not to share the misery of other men. (*IE*, IV, p. 149)

This oneness with humanity brings us to the even deeper level of the way in which we experience God in nothingness. For we not only experience God in our own nothingness, but we enter into an experience of the very Nothingness of God. It would be relatively easy to accept our own nothingness if that were accompanied with a profound sense of the power of God within us. But we find that in this attempt to come before the Lord with open hands and heart, we are left only with that even greater sense of nothingness. And yet that in itself is the surest indication of the fact that we have come into the presence of the living God, the great and tremendous Mystery of God, rather than some fabrication of our own making.

Nietzsche, speaking for our world, proclaimed that God was dead. And that is why, in our contemplation, God must often seem to be absent, as though dead. But the truth of our contemplation is in this: that never more than today has He made His presence felt by "being absent." In this, then, we are most faithful: that we prefer the darkness, and in the very depths of our being value this emptiness and apparent absence. We need not struggle vainly to make Him present, if such struggles are a mockery. Leave nothingness as it is. In it, He is present. (*IE*, p. 150)

This brings us to the very heart of the matter. Since God is God, that is, since the only way of adequately describing Him is as the Ultimate Mystery, this Mystery most surely reveals Himself to us in this very experience of emptiness and nothingness. Anything else that we might experience would not truly be that Mystery, but rather something of our own making or simply an experience of our own self.

Another way of expressing this can be seen in the oneness that exists between God and ourselves as a result of the outpouring of His Love, which is what our True Self really is. Another Japanese Zen Master, Keiji Nishitani, has developed possible connections between Christianity and Zen Buddhism. He admits that our encounter with God's transcendence and omnipresence in an existential way can be termed a personal relationship between God and man; yet it must be so in a very different sense from what is usually meant by "personal," that is, a relationship of the "I-Thou" type. Seen from this perspective, it should rather be called "impersonal." Yet this "impersonal" is not seen as being the opposite of the personal. It is not impersonal in the usual sense of the word. To avoid this problem, he suggests that such a relationship be called "impersonally personal" or "personally impersonal." Such seemingly contradictory terms are not meant simply to confuse the issue, but rather to impress on us that the relationship we have with God is like nothing else in our human experience. Rather it parallels that relationship within the life of the Trinity Itself.

> In Christianity, what is called the Holy Spirit possesses such characteristics. At the same time that It is thought of as one persona in the Trinity of "personal" God, it is not other than God's Love Itself, the breath of God: a sort of impersonal person or personal imperson, as it were.[11]

He is suggesting that just as Christianity can recognize the Holy Spirit as One Person within the Trinity, though still not having Three Gods because of that complete Oneness that exists within the Trinity, so we could recognize that what seems to be the absence of God is simply an experience of that profound oneness between God and ourselves. That oneness has been given to us in Jesus Christ, giving us His own Spirit to be our very own Spirit. Merton speaks of this:

> It is evident that the Holy Spirit has been given to us as a true and literal gift of God! *Donum Dei Altissimi*. He is truly our possession, which means to say that He becomes as it were our own spirit, speaking within our own being. It is He that becomes our spiritual and divine self. . . . The life of contemplation is then not simply a life of human technique and discipline; it is the life of the Holy Spirit in our inmost souls. (*IE*, p. 209)

It is striking that a Zen Buddhist should understand this reality more profoundly than we Western Christians do. The extent to which this is connected with the Mystery of God the Trinity and the Mystery of True Self is perhaps closer to what is experienced in that mysterious process of piercing through the meaning of a koan. Nishitani says:

> Despite the great similarity between Zen and Christian mysticism, we should not overlook an essential difference between them. Pseudo-Dionysius calls that which is beyond all affirmation and negation by the term "Him." Many Christian mystics call God "Thou." In Zen, however, what is beyond all affirmation and all negation -- that is, Ultimate Reality --should not be "Him" or "Thou" but "Self" or one's "True Self." I am not concerned here with verbal expressions, but the reality behind the words.
> (*AN*, p. 141)

---

11.   Quoted by Hans Waldenfels in *Absolute Nothingess*, Foundations for a Buddhist-Christian Dialogue (New York: Paulist Press, 1980), p. 142. Hereafter referred to in the text as *AN*.

Perhaps the answer to this can be found in the Pauline "koan" used by Nishitani when talking with the theologians of Basel:

> I find a statement in Paul which I, coming out of Zen Buddhism, believe I understand only too well. He says he has suffered a death. "I live now, not I, but Christ lives in me." That makes sense to me immediately. Allow me only to ask you this: Who is speaking here? (*AN*, p. 157)

Nishitani's European colleagues made no reply to his question. And yet contained in that "koan" is the whole mystery of this absence and presence, of this emptiness and fullness, of this sacred and secular.

Merton realized that the life of contemplation cannot be relegated merely to the realm of the objectively sacred. He saw that it must become an all-pervasive attitude which touches and affects every aspect of our life. If it does not, then the "secular" attitude will vitiate even those areas which are seen as more "holy."

> The visible and symbolic expressions of the divine tend to become opaque in their constant use by men, so that we stop at them and no longer go through them to God. Hence Holy Communion, for instance, tends to become a routine and "secularized" activity when it is sought not so much as a mystical contact with the Incarnate Word of God and with all the members of His Mystical Body, but rather as a way of gaining social approval and allaying feelings of anxiety. In this way even the most sacred realities can be debased and, without totally losing their sacred character, enter into the round of secular "diversion." (*IE*, p. 213)

Even those sacred realities or times can be used as a way of evading that sense of emptiness in which we encounter that God Who is the very "ground" of our being. At that level of our being, which is to be activated in every part of our life, we develop that sacred attitude which is "one of reverence, awe and silence before the mystery that begins to take place within us when we become aware of our inmost self" (*IE*, p. 215).

> The sacred attitude is then one of deep and fundamental respect for the real in whatever form it may present itself. The secular attitude is one of gross disrespect for reality, upon which the worldly mind seeks only to force its own crude patterns. (*IE*, p. 215)

Such a fundamental attitude is what Merton is trying to inculcate in his writing. It expresses itself in that openness to all things and all people as a revelation of the divine. Merton says that "it is this delicate instinct to yield to the slightest movement of God's love that makes the true contemplative."

This same phenomenon can be found in Christian tradition in the figure of Christ hanging on the Cross. The emptiness of God is manifested in the pouring out of His Love in Jesus Christ and the emptiness of man is seen in the radical obedience of Jesus, in His total surrender to this "other" whom He calls "God" and Whom He addresses as "Father." In Jesus of Nazareth the self-emptying of God and the self-emptying of man coincide. Only in death are things shown to be what they really are. For only in the radical letting go of life is it revealed

> whether the fullness reached in death is the previously only disguised emptiness and nothingess of man, or vice versa, whether the emptiness that shows itself in death is only the appearance (deceiving to us who have not yet died) of a true fullness. (*AN*, p. 159)

The fullness of life is revealed only in death, just as the complete presence of God and all creation is revealed only in that moment of absolute solitariness when one confronts that mystery of death. It is only this final experience which can ultimately break through the illusions and refuges that we cling to, even in the most remote parts of our heart. It is then that we will finally yield ourselves into the hands of the One Whom Jesus Christ revealed to us as being "at one with us as He is at one with the Father; that they may be perfectly One" (John 17).

By looking at these passages in Merton we see that his awareness of darkness and nothingess evolved so that traditional Christianity and the insights which he had learned from Buddhism were not contradictory, but rather complementary. It is especially useful to realize that Merton was totally faithful to Christian tradition while he also was able in writings, such as in *The Inner Experience*, to reach out to other world traditions.

Paradise.

THE PEACEMAKER:

Merton's Critique and Model

by David Steindl-Rast, O.S.B.

Honored friends of Thomas Merton, brothers and sisters. It is a great honor and joy to be with you this evening.* And it is very festive. I sometimes wonder how Thomas Merton would feel in this situation, sitting between Terence Cardinal Cooke and the President of Columbia [William J. McGill]. I think he would think it's a big joke.

I am afraid if we take it all too seriously, the joke will be on us, but if we take it very lightly, we will find that this is, after all, a very serious moment. It is very serious because one can hardly fail to hear somewhere the echoes of Jesus' own words in the Gospels, "You hypocrites. You are building sepulchers for prophets and adorning the tombs of the just. And so you become guilty with your fathers who killed the prophets."

Thomas Merton stands before us as a prophet. Another prophet of our time, Father Daniel Berrigan, very rightly said about Thomas Merton, "Enticed as he was, enticed as we all are by a corrupt culture that asks us to become celebrities at the expense of life and death issues, he never yielded. And it is in this way that he became truly a prophet."

*   This address, delivered in Low Memorial Library Rotunda on 1 December 1978, was the *Inaugural Thomas Merton Lecture* of the Merton Center at Columbia University and the initial event of the 1978 "Merton Commemoration." © 1978 by Hallel Communications.

There are two ways of becoming celebrities. One is to stay within the environment, to stay within one's community, and to conform, and not to speak out. The other one is to get out and to criticize from the outside. But the prophet lives with this terrible tension of remaining within and yet speaking out. It is precisely that tension which characterizes Thomas Merton's life as it characterizes Daniel Berrigan's life. The question before us is, then, how should we honor a prophet without making a celebrity of him? How should we celebrate the memory of Thomas Merton? Certainly not by building sepulchers. What is to be celebrated here cannot be buried. It is alive.

Not by adorning monuments, as people do who have Merton's works in beautiful editions and never read them. But by understanding the message. That means by standing under the judgment that this message implies. By living out the consequences each in our own way. You might say, using the terminology of the title of this lecture, by applying Merton's model to our lives, Merton's model of peacemaker to our peacemaking. But here we come across a serious problem. We cannot really apply Merton's model because if we submit to Merton's critique of the peacemaker, it shatters all models. Because Merton's critique is not a critique of a peacemaker who criticizes warmakers but it is a radical critique of "would-be" peacemakers in the light of the one and only peacemaker and that is the spirit and the power of God. On this insight that God is the only peacemaker -- that *God* is the *only* peacemaker -- on this insight hinges everything that Thomas Merton ever thought, taught, and suffered in the cause of peacemaking. So we could ask ourselves in celebrating Thomas Merton's memory: what were for him the consequences of this model-shattering insight that God is the one and only peacemaker?

The first consequence was, if you want to express it somewhat paradoxically, that Merton no longer sought peace, no longer, at any rate, the illusory peace of our willful manipulations but he sought to know God whose will is our true peace. Or you may put it this way: he no longer attempted to rush into doctoring up the world, but he, rather, tried to hold still long enough to allow the Great Peacemaker to heal his heart. That is more difficult. This meant for him entering a monastery. Now, this fact raises some very difficult questions. The first question might be: Well, is then the monastic life, for Thomas Merton, the model of peacemaking?

The answer is a clear "No." It is one form among many forms of channelling God's peacemaking into our world. We might ask: Well, why was it Merton's form of peacemaking? And the answer, in Merton's words, would simply be:

"It is God's will. And God's will is our peace."

God's will was not revealed to him through some voice that whispered into his ear and said that he should become a monk, but in a very confused and everyday way, feeling a certain attraction and circumstances conspiring to allow it. That's all! Very much in the way anyone's vocation comes about. Then he found himself a monk and then he tried to channel peace through this medium into his world because it simply was his calling.

But then you might ask: if Merton lived as a monk a life so foreign to most people, of what help can he be to them? The answer is that the forms are many, but the authentic inner gesture is one for all of us. The only difference may be that the monk has no alibi, no excuse, for making that inner gesture while most of us in other walks of life have all sorts of other things with which we can busy ourselves and which we could put in the foreground instead of making that one identical gesture, the gesture that is identical for all of us, the gesture of finding God and God's will because his will is our peace.

There is no model and monasticism itself is no model and for those who are not so well acquainted with monasticism, it might seem like a nice and well-defined model but when you come to look more closely at monasticism itself, it is a model-shattering model in itself. You have within one and the same monastic world stability, as one form of living out monastic commitment, and *peregrinatio*, never resting anywhere, from one place to another. Both for the same reason.

You have, on a much more superficial level, those monks that never let their hair be touched by scissors. There is no model even in haircuts in monastic life. You have the poverty of security. Benedictine poverty is a poverty of security. If you get into that monastery, you've made it. And you have the poverty of absolute insecurity. One is not more monastic than the other. You have, within one and the same monastic community, obedience of following orders and obedience of giving orders. The monk who followed orders yesterday may be the Abbot tomorrow and may be giving the orders. There is no model of obedience that says that you follow anybody else's orders because no one is quite as autonomous in the Church as a Benedictine Abbot. Almost. Well, of course, all of us want models for the sake of security and monks also are no exception to that. Merton had to take a very strong prophetic stance not to follow anybody's model. He kept repeating: "Don't call me a hermit. I'm not going to live up to anybody's standards of what a hermit should be like." And when he referred to himself, he would say: "A hermit of sorts." Or something like that -- very qualified.

In many other ways, faithful to the monastic tradition, that model-shattering monastic tradition, he became rather disturbing to monastic convention. But because he doesn't fit any preconceived model of monk, that makes him a monk in truth. So what is emphasized, when the particular form of life loses its ultimate importance, is life itself. Aliveness. When the focus shifts away from the form of life, the source of life comes into focus. God. The Great Peacemaker. In the Rule of St. Benedict, the rule, as you probably all know, that Thomas Merton followed as a Trappist, there is one decisive criterium for the acceptance or rejection of a candidate. "Si vero Deum vult." One criterium --"If he truly seeks God, nothing else matters." But, obviously, this is a life and death criterion, not only for monks, but for all of us. Do we truly seek God? Do we ultimately seek God and so find ourselves for, "God is more intimate for each one of us than we are to ourselves." Or as Merton used to say, paraphrasing St. Augustine: "God isn't somebody else."

Do we seek ourselves and so lose ourselves in the very seeking? Of course we can never be sure of the answer. We can never be safe from self-deception either inside the monastery or outside the monastery. Yet the human heart cannot find peace unless we continue to let that question spur us on. It is precisely this question which unites Merton with all monks and with all human beings. It was a great discovery for him when he met Thich Nhat Hanh, the Vietnamese Buddhist monk, to discover how deeply they shared. When he met Tibetan monks later towards the end of his life, he experienced their deep union in the monastic quest. Not only with monks is he united but with all of us because that question, "Do we truly seek God?", is the life and death issue for all of us. We all long for that healing that comes from encounter with God --that healing which Christian tradition calls salvation or peace. Peace and salvation in Jewish-Christian Biblical tradition are practically interchangeable.

There are four great terms for the reality of salvation in our Biblical tradition and they are "salvation," "blessing," "righteousness" and "peace." Another consequence of Merton's insight that God is the only peacemaker was that he was thrown directly into the hard reality of that Biblical paradox of peace, not by speculating about it as a theologian but by living it out, by suffering it out, in his life. Salvation in Biblical terms means the saving encounter with God, an encounter that takes place in history and in community. The response is joy. Blessing -- very similar, with only a slight change of accentuation -- means the communication of life from God in history, in community, and the response is thanksgiving. Righteousness is the term which is most misunderstood in popular theology today. Righteousness is very close in its meaning to salvation and blessing. It is not rooted in a legal notion nor is it exhausted in a legal notion. It is not socio-ethical but religious. Justice is not a virtue we possess, not primarily, but rather a realm we enter -- the realm of God's justicing. God makes whole and thus, entering that realm of wholeness, we can respond in holiness. All these -- salvation, blessing, righteousness -- are summed up in the notion of peace in the Bible because peace stands for that fullness of communion with God -- in history and beyond history. Here the response is universal love, the fullness of communion with God and God's will, all of which St. Augustine calls *"tranquillitas ordinis,"* the dynamic "stillness of order," order as the form in which love celebrates its creative freedom. Merton entered into this reality by seeking God alone.

It was perfectly clear to him that the initiative comes from God, and that is the characteristic of the Biblical notion of salvation, blessing, righteousness, and peace. The initiative comes from God. A key quotation in this context is the one that Cardinal Cooke used in his introductory remarks this evening: "Nonviolence is not primarily the language of efficacy, but the language of *kairos*, of God's own good time." God chooses when it is time. Nonviolence does not say "we shall overcome" so much as it says "this is the way of the Lord and whatever happens to us, He shall overcome." I think that Merton might have said today: "She shall overcome."

Let us not forget that this saving event takes place in concrete historical circumstances. That is the second important aspect of the Biblical notion of salvation, blessing, righteousness, and peace. It takes place in history, in concrete history. Therefore, Merton could say:

> In practice, the way to contemplation is an obscurity so obscure that it is no longer even dramatic. There is nothing left in it that can be grasped and cherished as heroic or even unusual. And so for a contemplative, there is a supreme value in the ordinary routine of work and poverty and hardship and monotony that characterizes the lives of all the poor and uninteresting and forgotten people in the world.

That again is a bond of communion. The response to God's initiative in history, the response of joy, of thanks, of love, of wholeness and holiness is the response that comes from the heart and that is where we are most truly ourselves and most intimately united with all others and with God -- the place where we are really together -- a togetherness that is the very opposite of alienation, violence, and war. So, the realization that God is the

only peacemaker makes us aware that all other "would-be" peacemaking
that does not flow from God as its source either comes from alienation or
leads to alienation -- or both. Therefore, Merton had to confront within
himself and around him (and that was another consequence of his realization that God is the only peacemaker) the brokenness of the Western
tradition of peacemaking which is cut off from its Biblical roots. He had
bitter things to say about it at the end of his life. In one of the last things he
wrote, he said:

> The decline of the classic Graeco-Roman civilization that first flowered in
> Homer, the nobility, the idealism, the chivalry, the humanity that we
> encounter in our cultural tradition have become a pile of non-descript
> linguistic rubbish -- sentimental jargon without any real force, based on
> no deep experience of life but rather devised to justify alienation and
> evasion.

We encounter clearly that linguistic rubbish and alienation from the
true tradition that Merton suffered when we find, for instance, law and
order opposed to justice and peace, when justice should be the root and
fruit of law and order, should be the root and fruit of peace. An image that
comes to mind when I think of the brokenness of the Western tradition of
peacemaking that Merton suffered is an image that many of you may have
seen and so I would like to call it to mind. A film was made about Father
Daniel Berrigan when he was in hiding from the FBI. The one part of the film
which most impressed me was a long scene in which Berrigan's mother was
interviewed. You only heard the voice of the interviewer and saw the face
of this old farmer woman. It was a moment in which the brokenness of our
peacemaking tradition was brought home to her and to all those who
watched her. The interviewer first asked her whether she agreed with what
her son was doing and she said, "Yes." Then he said, "But it's against the
law." There was this long silence in which you simply saw the woman's face
trying to make sense of these words -- a woman who had lived all her life in
a simple, rural community -- trying to make sense of what law meant for
her. Then she said, "But it isn't God's law." That was the only answer and
that brings home to us that brokenness, that brings home to us the Bible's
words: "My thoughts, says the Lord, are not your thoughts. Neither are
your ways my ways. For as the heavens are higher than the earth, so are my
ways higher than your ways, and my thoughts than your thoughts."
Merton, almost paraphrasing this if we listen carefully, said:

> The chief difference between violence and nonviolence is that violence
> depends entirely on its own calculation. Nonviolence depends entirely on
> God and God's word.

God's word. Not some Bible reading that we occasionally listen to, but God's creative word that makes everything what it is, that makes us what we are, that makes peace of all. As the wonderful Psalm verse says: "I am listening. What is God saying?" What God is saying means peace, a peace that may be a very disturbing peace. Since the creative word of God which means peace makes each thing what it is and makes each one of us what we are, it will mean for us peace in that full sense that it has in Hebrew and in the Bible. That is a good time. It will be a good time even when it is a hard time.

That brings me to another consequence that directly flows from Merton's insight that God is the only peacemaker, and that was his choice, the crucial choice, of opting for a good time in the sense of genuine self-fulfillment in the freedom of obedience rather than becoming a "do-gooder." There is a wonderful passage in the prologue to the Rule of St. Benedict and it runs something like this: "The Lord, looking for His workmen in the crowd, cries out and says 'Where is the man who wants life? Where is the man who wants to see a good time?' And if you hear that and say 'That's me,' then the Lord says: 'If you really want to have true and eternal life then seek peace and chase after it.'" St. Benedict comments on this and says: "Oh, my brothers, what can be sweeter to us than that voice of the Lord inviting us. Oh look, in His Fatherly Love He shows us the way to life." To seek peace, that is to listen to that word of God which each one of us is and so to become truly ourselves. That option includes the option against the "do-gooder."

Merton saw that, and when he talked to his novices, he said:

> If we make the monastic life a constant project of seeing ourselves doing good, we are in trouble. Wanting to see ourselves doing good is a real source of trouble around here.

And he prayed:

> If You send me work I shall embrace it with joy and it will be rest to me, because it is Your Will. And if You send me rest, I will rest in You. Only save me from myself. Save me from my own, private, poisonous urge to change everything . . . . Let me rest in Your Will and be silent . . . . This is what I live for. Amen, amen.

He kept emphasizing that the good of this world, including the monastic world, vastly outweighs all evil. He certainly had a good time. If there is anything that is characteristic about Merton, it is that he had a good time. I am delighted to see Brother Patrick [Hart] nod because he knew him a lot better than I did.

Particularly in solitude he found this good time, because that was the word that God spoke in his heart. He had great compassion for people who would not be able to spend any time in solitude. He said so. For him that was the word. He said:

> So much do I love this solitude that when I walk out among the roads to the old barns that stand alone, far from the new buildings, delight begins to overpower me from head to foot and peace smiles even in the marrow of my bones.

We may say that that is very romantic but what is the purpose of all of that? If we ask that question, we stand already under the judgment of Merton's message. We need more than purpose to survive. If it helps you to think of a little bit of purpose, think of the solitude of the monk as an antenna but an antenna for meaning, relatively free from the static of purpose. After all that, not everything has to be useful. In fact, the most meaningful realities in our lives, when we look closely, turn out to be largely useless. Merton said that beautifully in one passage where he writes:

> The rain has stopped. The afternoon sun slants through the pine trees and how those useless needles smell in the clear air. A dandelion, long out of season has pushed itself into bloom between the smashed leaves of last season's day lilies. The valley sounds with the totally uninformative talk of creeks and wild water. And the quails begin their sweet whistling in the wet bushes. Their noise is absolutely useless and so is the delight I take in it.

It isn't that "do-gooders" were not well-intentioned in their purposefulness. Yet you start doing good to others and the next thing is that you know best what is good for others and then you find that they just don't know what is good for them, and then you might end up killing them in their own best interest. We have all seen it happen. Merton writes: "The greatest inhumanities have been perpetrated in the name of 'humanity,' 'civilization,' 'progress,' 'freedom,' 'my country,' and of course, 'God.'" If I had the courage to admit to myself that I seek a good time, then I soon realize that the good time one has is not really fully a good time until all have a good time. That is a different approach to peacemaking, or as Merton says: "Life should be joyful and easy in our uselessness. Then I don't have to sell myself to the world, but I am happy to be what I am."

That should be the happiness of the peacemaker or, rather, of that channel for God's peacemaking. To be happy as who I am. To be happy with what I am. I think that was, in a sense, the core and the most easily accessible expression of Merton's peacemaking. It clearly shows that there is no model to it, because there is no model to what each one of us can be if we are truly ourselves and become truly ourselves. As I was preparing thoughts to share with you -- these thoughts -- it seemed to me several times that I almost heard Merton speak. I had this beautiful picture of a friend and brother of mine, a portrait made of him, kind of looking over my shoulder and I kept hearing him say: "Don't give them too much abstract thought. Why don't you read a poem to them? And be sure it's not one of my own." So I would like to read a poem to you in celebration. It is a poem that is quite central to his thought and quite central to the notion of peacemaking about becoming who you can be, about being happy with what you are, and about having a good time. It is a poem of which Merton himself was very fond. You might remember that, at one time, he wanted to write his thesis here at Columbia on Hopkins and then ended up writing it on Blake, but Hopkins was very close to his heart all his life. I will read this poem hoping that it is familiar to many of you because it doesn't come across all that easily. Then I would like to illustrate it with a few parallels from Merton's own writings. It's the sonnet "As Kingfishers Catch Fire."

> As kingfishers catch fire, dragonflies draw flame;
>   As tumbled over rim in roundy wells
>   Stones ring: like each tucked string tells, each hung bell's
> Bow swung finds tongue to fling out broad its name;
> Each mortal thing does one thing and the same;
>   Deals out that being indoors each one swells;
>   Selves -- goes itself; *myself* it speaks and spells,
> Crying *What I Do Is Me: For That I Came.*
> I say more: the just man justices;
>   Keeps grace: that keeps all his goings graces;
> Acts in God's eye what in God's eye he is -- Christ.
>   For Christ plays in ten thousand places,
> Lovely in limbs, and lovely in eyes not his
>   To the Father through the features of men's faces.

It almost sounds like a paraphrase on this when Merton writes: "The forms and individual characters of living and growing things, of inanimate beings, of animals and flowers and all nature, constitute their holiness in the sight of God. Their inscape." That word obviously gives away Hopkins, "Their inscape is their sanctity. It is the imprint of His wisdom and His reality in them." That holds not only for things, that holds for everyone of us if we have what Merton calls "the humility to be myself." He writes: "If I find him, I will find myself, and if I find my true self, I will find Him. . . The only One Who can teach me to find God is God Himself, Alone."

There is a beautiful passage which I recommend to you to read. It's in *The Sign of Jonas*, on page 275, somewhere around there, and I can only read you the last passage but again it has to do with this "selving," with this being yourself. After describing how a hawk came down and swooped up a starling in a field with many, many starlings, Merton writes:

> I tried to pray afterwards. But the hawk was eating the bird. And I thought
> of that flight coming down like a bullet from the sky behind me and over
> my roof, the sure aim with which he hit this one bird, as though he had
> picked it out a mile away. For a moment . . . I understood the terrible fact
> that some men love war. But in the end, I think that hawk is to be studied
> by saints and contemplatives; because he knows his business. I wish I
> knew my business as well as he does his.

He describes again and again in his work, you will remember, all
these wonderful things in which God dwells, and who live out of God, and
who glorify God. He says:

> And in the midst of them all, I know you. And I know your presence and
> you love me. And my love is precious because it is yours rather than my
> own. Precious to you because it comes to you from your own son but
> precious even more because it makes me your son.

Through being himself, from living out of that word -- that creative word
that makes each thing what it is and makes each one of us what we are
--through living it out, Merton's recognition that God is the only peacemaker drew him deeper and deeper into the mystery of the heart as the
source of nonviolent power. He wrote: "To be here with the silence of
sonship in my heart is to be a center in which all things converge upon you
God and this is surely enough for the time being."

In this center of his own heart where he listened to the word of God,
he felt deeply at one, deeply united with all. He also tapped that source of
power for nonviolence. He wrote:

> The basic problem is not political, it is apolitical and human. One of the
> most important things to do is to keep cutting deliberately through
> political lines and barriers and emphasize the fact that these are largely
> fabrications, and that there is another dimension, a genuine reality, totally
> opposed to the fictions of politics. The human dimension which politics
> pretends to arrogate entirely to themselves. This is the necessary first step
> along the long way toward the perhaps impossible task of purifying,
> humanizing and somehow illuminating politics themselves.

From that heart he also saw clearly because there is no eye with
which we can truly, clearly, see except the eye of the heart. He saw the task.
This is why, if we really want to be channels of God's peace, we have to go to
the heart and open the eyes of our heart to see the task. The task, as Merton
saw it, is to work for the total abolition of war. There can be no question
that, unless war is abolished, the world will remain constantly in a state of
madness and desperation in which, because of the immense destructive
power of modern weapons, the danger of catastrophe will be imminent
and probable at every moment and everywhere. The task of abolishing war
totally he saw as the great Christian task of our time. Everything else is

secondary. For the survival of the human race itself depends upon it. We must at least face the responsibility and do something about it. Now, the crucial moment came when Merton, because of the choice he made in light of the fact that God is the only peacemaker, because of the choice to become a monk, was silenced about peace. He was not allowed to write about peace. That was the crucial point of his peacemaking. He faced, as squarely as anyone else would have faced, the situation, and wrote:

> Now you will ask me: How do I reconcile obedience, true obedience, which is synonomous with love, with a situation like this? Should I just blast the whole thing wide open, or walk out, or tell them just to jump in the lake?

And his answer was:

> I am who I am. I have freely chosen this state and have freely chosen to stay in it when the question of a possible change arose. I am a disturbing element. All right. I am not making a point of being that but simply of saying what my conscience dictates and doing so without seeking my own interests. This means accepting such limitations as may be placed on me by authority , and not because I may or may not agree with the ostensible reasons why the limitations are imposed, but out of love for God who is using these things to attain ends which I myself cannot at the moment see or comprehend.

In hindsight, we can clearly see that God had reasons which were greater than anything that one could have comprehended at that time. But that also meant that by recognizing that God is the only peacemaker, Merton had to pay the price for what Eliot calls "a condition of complete simplicity, costing not less but everything." He wrote:

> He who is called to be a monk is precisely the one who when he finally realizes that he is engaged in the pure folly of making an impossible demand, instead of renouncing the whole thing, proceeds to devote himself even more completely to the task. Aware that precisely because he cannot meet it, it will be met for him.

Here we have reached the final point:

> Here where love burns with an innocent flame. The clean desire for death. Death without sweetness, without sickness, without commentary, without reference and without change. Clean death by the sword of the spirit in which is intelligence and everything in order purges and delivers us.
>
> For my part my name is that sky, those fence-posts, and those cedar trees. I shall not even reflect on who I am and I shall not say my identity is nobody's business because that implies a truculence I do not intend. It has no meaning.
>
> Now my whole life is this -- to keep unencumbered. The wind owns the fields where I walk and I own nothing and am owned by nothing and I shall never even be forgotten because no one will ever discover me. This is to me a source of immense confidence.

Only when we have somehow reached a point where we realize that beyond this point is the Merton whom we will never discover, have we gone to where we should be when we commemorate the prophet. We can ask ourselves: Do we seek peace or do we seek the source of peace -- God? Can we live with the Biblical paradox of Christ who is our peace and yet says: "I have not come to bring peace but a sword"? Can we face the brokenness of our Western tradition of peacemaking? Can we make the crucial choice of opting for a good time? Do we dare to stand at the place of the heart? Are we willing to pay the price for a condition of complete simplicity costing not less but everything? This is how Merton prayed. This is how he might pray at this point:

ALMIGHTY AND MERCIFUL GOD, in your will is our peace.

Help us to be masters of the weapons that threaten to master us.

Help us to use our science for peace and plenty, not for war and destruction.

Save us from the compulsion to follow our adversaries in all that we most hate, confirming them in their hatred and suspicion of us.

Resolve our inner contradictions which now grow beyond belief and beyond bearing.

Teach us to be long-suffering in anguish and insecurity.

Teach us to wait and trust.

Grant light.

Grant strength and patience to all who work for peace.

Grant us prudence in proportion to our power;
wisdom in proportion to our science;
humanness in proportion to our wealth and might.

But grant us, above all, to see that our ways are not necessarily your ways.

That we cannot fully penetrate the mystery of your design.

And that the very storm of power now raging on this earth reveals your hidden will and your inscrutable decision.

Grant us to see your face in the lightning of this cosmic storm, oh God of holiness, merciful to all.

Grant us to seek peace where it is truly found.

In your will, oh God, is our peace. Amen.

MERTON,

NONVIOLENCE

AND THE BISHOPS' PASTORAL

by **Paul E. Dinter**

---

1. Merton's Contemporary Witness to Sanity

Although writing between fifteen and twenty years ago, Thomas Merton's understanding of the moral and political crisis of those years is startlingly contemporary, if not prophetic. His keen insight into the workings as well as the charades practiced by the society from which he "withdrew" in 1941 has been noted long before now, so it remains for us to do more than lionize him for his insight and prophetic charism.

I wish, then, in this essay to turn to Merton's writings to shed some light on the contemporary crisis of our culture, that is, whether we can long endure the threat to our lives, institutions and everything else that the nuclear arms race poses. What is more, I wish to examine these writings as a basis for understanding how the two foundational documents which underlie the recent pastoral letter *The Challenge of Peace* still have something to say to us today. Without these earlier works, *Pacem in Terris* of Pope John XXIII and the Second Vatican Council's Pastoral Constitution *Gaudium et Spes*, the bishops' pastoral would have been unthinkable.

Editors' Note: This essay is based on a talk given at St. Mary's College, Notre Dame, Indiana, on 10 December 1983, the fifteenth anniversary of Merton's death.

But my purpose here is as much critical as it is historical, for I wish to use Merton's writings and their critique of our culture as a background against which to judge the adequacy of the pastoral letter twenty years after Merton's incisive wisdom was lost to us. At this early stage of the pastoral's reception, certainly any of my critical judgments are necessarily provisional and are undertaken in a spirit of gratitude for the effort of the Catholic bishops of this country. At the same time, the nature of the challenge of peace requires every effort we can muster to refine our response to God's promise.[1]

Let me begin, then, by stating that Merton's comments on the arms race and our attendant nuclear idolatry were so pellucid back in the 1960s that they could easily be describing our political and moral predicament today. I would like to take a look at some of them to establish anew, as it were, his credentials as a critic of contemporary culture.

Commenting on the need for alternatives to the arms race, Merton anticipated the notion, if not the language, of the Freeze by calling for a remedy that would "slow down our activity, especially all activity concerned with the production and testing of weapons of destruction."[2] He wanted this to be immediately followed by the reduction and elimination of nuclear weapons stockpiles; yet he was no "pollyanna" about this expectation. In another article he counsels:

> Realize what we are up against. The military-industrial-political-academic complex, with the mass media at its disposal, is sold on military defense and the arms race and is obviously interested in ridiculing or discrediting all nonmilitary forms of defense -- in fact all alternatives to the arms race. (*NVA*, p. 93)

Merton knew that this resistance to alternatives grew not merely from political and ideological reasons but from economic ones as well. But he was strong in his affirmation that "it is not morally licit for us as a nation to refuse the risk because our whole economy now depends on this war effort" (*NVA*, p. 16). In other words, he would have us understand that there is a moral imperative to work for the conversion of our economy from a military to a civilian-based economy, a step the bishops in their pastoral were not so forthright about (cf. *CP* # 271).

Again, anticipating the strategic options examined in the pastoral letter, Merton characterized the admixture of deterrence and

---

    1. For a later critique of *The Challenge of Peace*, cf. M. Gallagher, "Sidestepping the Challenge of Peace?", *Commonweal*, 16 January 1987, pp. 9-13 and E. Doherty, "A Classic Case of Consequentialism," p. 11.

    2. Thomas Merton, *The Nonviolent Alternative* (New York: Farrar, Straus & Giroux, 1980), p. 16. Hereafter referred to in the text as *NVA*.

counterforce along with the arms race they fuel as a policy of total war and then added a trenchant comment about the way total war is packaged and sold.

> What is essentially a power struggle is presented as an ideological and spiritual struggle, as a battle between light and darkness, and it is presented in a way that *Christians are convinced that there is no other way of defense than military defense.* (NVA, p. 92)

Even more strongly, Merton described an important element of the problem in his portrayal of various kinds of citizens that still accurately describes a frightening proportion of Americans. On the one hand, there are those who were cheered by the invasion of Grenada and our superpower meddling in Lebanon. Merton terms them "fanatics" who "yield to the pressures of inner resentment and frustration, and seek a show-down because they cannot bear the intolerable burden of waiting and uncertainty." On the other hand, there is the significant sector of the population whom he terms "the passive and despairing" who "accept the absurdity of life with a shrug and seek forgetfulness in an automatic drugged existence" (NVA, p. 78).

These latter are not isolated individuals in Merton's understanding but are products of what he calls "the mass mind" both in the Church and beyond who are affected by the "poisonous effect of the mass media that keeps violence, cruelty and sadism constantly present to the minds of unformed and irresponsible people" (NVA, pp. 19, 130). Merton's words regarding the "crude assumptions" which a majority of Americans held and the "state of mind" that accepted the inevitability of nuclear war which he found promoted through a form of thought control by the "American mass media" are strong (NVA, pp. 81, 114). So strong that they almost remind us of the chilling picture in George Orwell's *1984* of the way reality was controlled in fictitious Oceania. At the same time, Merton's opinions of the popular state of understanding and the role of the mass media in sustaining myths are echoed convincingly by a non-fiction writer, former Ambassador, now Professor, George Kennan. In his collection of essays *The Nuclear Delusion* Kennan excoriates the "journalistic establishment" for its role in the uncritical promotion of a "fantastic view of the monstrosity of our Soviet adversaries" that allows our government to pursue no alternatives to confrontation.[3] Kennan lays a good bit of blame at the door of the "commercial media of information" that are dedicated "to the over-

---

3.   George Frost Kennan, *The Nuclear Delusion: Soviet-American Relations in the Atomic Age* (New York: Pantheon, 1983), pp. 186, 196. Hereafter referred to in the text as *Nuclear Delusion*.

simplification and dramatization of reality rather than the education of the public" in much the same way that Merton deplores the "pseudo-news" and "manufactured event" of the print media.[4]

Yet the currency of Fr. Louis' observations goes beyond the stuff of our media-ized culture and its nuclear idolatry. In an essay published in 1961, "Peace: A Religious Responsibility," he takes Christians to task for their passivity with the following (strongly current) indictment: "An American President can speak of warfare in outer space and nobody bursts out laughing -- he is perfectly serious. Science fiction and the comic strip have all suddenly come true" (*NVA*, p. 114). Writing five years later in "Faith and Violence" against the background of ghetto riots, but in a way that is virtually prescient of our relationship to the violence daily committed in Latin America, Merton reveals to his largely white, middle-class readership:

> Modern technological mass murder is not directly visible, like individual murder. It is abstract, corporate, businesslike, cool, free of guilty feelings and therefore a thousand times more deadly and effective than the eruption of violence out of individual hate. It is this polite, massively organized white-collar murder machine that threatens the world with destruction, not the violence of a few desperate teen-agers in a slum. But our antiquated theology, myopically focused on *individual* violence alone, fails to see this. It shudders at the fantasm of muggings and killings where a mess is made on our doorstep, but blesses and canonizes the antiseptic violence of corporately organized murder because it is respectable, clean and above all profitable. (*NVA*, p. 188)

Just before his death, in an essay entitled "War and the Crisis of Language," Merton again pinpointed two grave problems that continue to fog our perception of the depth of the crisis we face. Exposing to view the technological jargon of our political and military planners, he first denounced the discourse of the White House and the Pentagon in starkly contemporary terms as "the language of escalation," which he calls

> the language of power, a language that is all the more persuasive because it is proud of being ethically literate and because it accepts, as realistic, the basic irrationality of its own tactics. The language of escalation, in its superb mixture of banality and apocalypse, science and unreason, is the expression of a massive death wish. We can only hope that this death wish is only that of a decaying Western civilization, and that it is not common to the entire race. (*NVA*, p. 186)

Permit me a second reference from this same powerful essay which will, I trust, further illustrate the kind of prophetic clarity which Thomas Merton can be said to have suffered from.

---

4. Thomas Merton, "Events and Pseudo-Events: Letter to a Southern Churchman," *Katallagete*, Summer 1966, p. 12. Also published in *Faith and Violence* (Notre Dame: University of Notre Dame Press, 1968), pp. 145-164. Hereafter referred to in the text as "ESE".

Looking at the use of language and its corruption regarding arms negotiations, our hermit describes the recent futile Geneva talks as if he were a political commentator present at them. He writes:

> Of course, verbal formulas have to be resorted to, in order to define what force is all about, to set conditions, etc. But the verbal formulas must be kept deliberately ambiguous, unclear. The clear and unmistakable message is not that of the *terms offered* but of escalation itself. In other words there is an *appearance* of dialogue on the verbal and political level. But the real dialogue is with weapons and may be a complete contradiction of what appears to be said in the prose of politics.
>
> The effect of this, of course, is a vicious circle: it begins with a tacit admission that negotiation is meaningless, and it does in fact render the language of negotiation meaningless. (*NVA*, pp. 243-244)

Thus, the scenario that Merton painted, which is even more apt than when he typed the words twenty years ago, brings us in truth close to elements of the society which Orwell himself painted. In Erich Fromm's words, that is a society in which "the military will become dominant (in fact, if not in law)" with the result "that fright and hatred of a possible aggressor will destroy the basic attitudes of a democratic, humanistic society".[5] We can say, then, that Merton's critique of our society and our economy's militarization is at least as pertinent today as it was when shaped by the events of the 1960s.

But to say that everything today is the same as when Merton wrote would be an oversimplification. Beginning in 1963, with the publication of *Pacem in Terris* by Pope John XXIII, a profound change began to overtake the Catholic Church of which Merton was such a critical yet convinced member. Before returning to a more specific look at the crisis we face, I would like to examine Merton's understanding of the emerging Catholic tradition on peacemaking as prelude to presenting a critique of some elements in the bishops' pastoral letter from Merton's perspective on the nature of the challenge of peace.

2. *From* Pacem in Terris *to* The Challenge of Peace

Commenting on John XXIII's final encyclical, Merton wrote that at least part of the significance of *Pacem in Terris* was its recognition that "Catholics themselves were to a great extent out of contact with the rest of the world, enclosed within their own spiritual and religious ghetto"

---

5.   Erich Fromm, "Afterword" in George Orwell, *1984* (New York: Signet/ New American Library, 1961), p. 262.

(*NVA*, p. 30). The publication of the pastoral letter *The Challenge of Peace: God's Promise and Our Response* represents the closing of an initial twenty year cycle that Pope John opened in 1963 with his audacious letter on peace. Though alive for only five of these years, Merton, through his writings, has remained one of the major influences on both theologians and peace-oriented communities in the church and, therefore, can help us understand how it is that *Pacem in Terris* and the Pastoral Constitution *Gaudium et Spes* led Catholics out of their political ghetto and paved the way for the bishops' pastoral in this country. At the same time, an examination of a number of Merton's writings can reveal elements of the tradition which the 1983 letter of the American bishops, for all its strengths, has seriously neglected.

Thus, in a short while, I wish to take up an examination of whether *The Challenge of Peace* measures up to Merton's critique of our culture and, hence, whether it goes far enough in clarifying the real challenge with which "peace on earth" presents us. But, first, I wish to look at Merton's commentary on the papal encyclical and pastoral constitution of Vatican II.

Merton's regard for John XXIII and his profoundly human papacy needs little emphasis.[6] Seeing in the encyclical *Pacem in Terris* a mixture of the "sanity of Aquinas" and the "radiant hopefulness" of Francis, Merton understood it as an important step in the work of moral renewal so long overdue in the West (*NVA*, p. 61). By itself, the letter challenged a host of convenient dualisms by which Catholics, in general, and particularly those in this country were wont to store up treasures in heaven while at the same time engaging in capitalist conquest here below. What appealed to Merton was the Pope's essential fairmindedness -- something he felt was essential if a climate of relative sanity could be restored to the international scene. He defined such a climate in terms of people understanding their plight "without hatred, without fury, without desperation, and with a minimum of good will" (*NVA*, p. 23).

If this was to be accomplished it would be the result of an acceptance of the basic principles of the encyclical: "The dignity of the human person and the primacy of the universal common good over the particular good of the political unit" (*NVA*, p. 23). The essential condition of this acceptance was human freedom which is understood neither in classically "liberal" or "libertarian" terms but as an orientation to truth by which we can "transcend even the most tragic injustices" and be more truly human because of

---

6. See, for example, Thomas Merton, *Conjectures of a Guilty Bystander* (Garden City: Doubleday and Company, 1968), p. 302.

them (*NVA*, 23). In other words, the more freedom of choice available in the capitalist West (but nearly absent in the collectivist East) is *not* enough to ensure the moral freedom necessary for us to make the choice to survive.

Blocking the moral freedom to which Pope John summoned us are the essentially self-righteous attitudes we cultivate towards our political and ideological opponents. The kinds of double standards that are used by both the Pentagon and Kremlin led Merton to observe that

> the extremists on both sides are mirror images of each other . . . . The leaders help to make a myth by their own pronouncements and slogans and because the myth is so willingly believed by the common man they themselves assume that this is a kind of divine ratification. Vox populi vox Dei. (*NVA*, pp. 25-26)

A restoration of human freedom rests upon the rediscovery of how the truly human and personal is discovered and developed not through competition or in dialectic but in the communality by which we contribute to the upbuilding of a society of nations mutually seeking peace and security. *Pacem in Terris* makes the step forthrightly from condemning philosophical individualism to exposing the inadequacy of nationalist individualism and engages in a critique of governmental authority which makes the claim that no form of government or public authority adequately promotes the "universal common good" at this time in history (PT # 135).

Taking his cue from the Pope's teaching, Merton analyzes the concept of authority outlined there and finds both the Marxist and the positivist (or "value-free") solutions to political authority equally dependent on a pessimistic view of human nature. Both social systems that have emerged from them rely on their power to compel obedience by external force rather than on the establishment of an order of justice whose agency is freedom.

Pope John, by contrast, building upon the Christian concept of the human person, expressed confidence that the need for truth was "congenital" with human nature. As a result, granting the certain action of God on the "interior being," believers are exhorted to have the confidence to dialogue with non-believers because they both share "the light of reason" and an attraction to truth. This understanding of human nature redeemed in Christ is not only, from a theological point of view, what makes all people *capax Dei* but is also, from a political point of view, what makes us, in Merton's words, "capable of desiring peace with justice" (*NVA*, p. 60).

Merton developed this Christian and humanist anthropology both as a commentator on *Pacem in Terris* and the Pastoral Constitution and in his own writings. So impressed was he with the centrality of personalism in these documents that he commented that the Constitution could have been entitled "The Human Person in the Modern World."[7] For, it is precisely our personhood and the transcendent human freedom that we are capable of that enables us to overcome what Merton terms "natural necessity" and act in a way that brings a "fully human solution" to the age-old problem of conflict and violence. It is our freedom, activated mainly through nonviolence, that tells us that although "conflict will never be abolished . . . a new way of solving it can become habitual" (*NVA*, p. 217).

Freedom, then, results not merely from a natural state of the human person but from the grace we experience in Christ and in the resulting transcendent character of our human dignity. In the Pastoral Constitution, Merton writes, "The person is defined in terms of freedom, hence in terms of responsibility also: responsibility *to* other persons and *for* other persons." No longer is the Christian "confined merely to a realm of inwardness and of pure intentions. It is not just a matter of interior charity and good will." Rather the context of Christian responsibility requires that we find our true maturity and fulfillment in a relationship of love, in reconciling activity that encompasses "social action, political life, work, and all other practical choices that affect our relations with others in the family, the city, the nation, and the world." Freedom, in brief, is not freedom *from* constraint as much as it is freedom *for* human development (*NVA*, p. 217).

The Council's humanist vision opened up doors to what could be termed a new moral epistemology as well as a new sense of how we fulfill our moral character through global responsibility. From this renewed Christian understanding of humanism (GS # 55) flow the Constitution's conclusions that call for the proper use of science in human development, the extension of education and making available the sources of culture to all people, reforms in the unhappy state of the world's economy that so discriminates against developing peoples and, lastly, a new attitude towards the nation state whose dedication to certain notions of its independence and security have provoked what the Council called the "melancholy state of humanity" as this is evidenced in the arms race. Without rehearsing here the Constitution's stance on the arms race and the nuclear crisis, as well as its explicit commendation of nonviolence, I would just note how positive was Merton's own estimation of the "deeply traditional Christian humanism" of the Pastoral Constitution and its sense of urgency, some-

---

7. Thomas Merton, "Christian Humanism in the Nuclear Age," in *Love and Living*, edited by Naomi Burton Stone and Brother Patrick Hart (New York: Farrar, Straus & Giroux, 1979), pp. 151-170.

thing that his own writings in the last three years of his life increasingly emphasized.

To say that Merton was quicker than most Catholics to understand the import of the documents under discussion would be no exaggeration. The global perspective, not to mention the affirmative anthropology that was expressed in both were foreign elements in a young and proudly chauvinistic American church. But learn we have -- slowly, moved by two opposite pressures: one "from above" as Pope Paul VI continued spelling out the implications in social, political and economic life of the church's mission to be a sign of the joy and hope of humanity and especially of the poor (GS # 1); and by a second pressure "from below" as Catholics in Latin America and activist groups in the United States began incarnating the gospel message more radically. Both these pressures on the Church in general and the United States bishops in particular were to come to fruition during the otherwise somnolent '70s, budding forth at the November 1980 annual meeting of the National Conference of Catholic Bishops. By the time the process begun at that meeting was completed, the fruits of *Pacem in Terris* and *Gaudium et Spes* were more bountiful than ever before. The process of de-ghetto-izing which Pope John began had come very far.

Thus it was that the letter *The Challenge of Peace* took its very starting point from the Pastoral Constitution's treatment of the "supreme crisis" that the human race today faces "in its advance toward maturity" (GS # 77; CP # 1). Similarly, the letter attempts to teach in continuity with the central affirmation of Vatican II which it characterizes as "the transcendence of God and the dignity of the human person" and seeks, in the same ways as the Pastoral Constitution, to address not merely the community of the faithful but the civil community as well (CP # 17-19). The letter describes the Church's role as servant of peace in a new situation by noting that the history of Catholic teaching on war and peace had focused on limiting the resort to violence in human affairs, yet it admits that this task "is not a sufficient response" to Vatican II's challenge to "undertake a completely fresh reappraisal of war" (GS # 80; CP # 23).

Here, however, we must pause to comment that, although the bishops' pastoral letter was developed in clear continuity with its papal and conciliar antecedents, it adopted a humbler tone in its refusal to offer a "final synthesis" of the "new appraisal" of war and peace and in substituting "an invitation to continue" such an appraisal as well as in allowing that "those who assess the factual data of situations differently" could disagree with the letter's moral judgments. These features of the letter

were, no doubt, appropriate and even necessary given the lack of agreement on many issues with the episcopal conferences of some European
countries and with many influential Catholics high in the government
establishment of the United States.

Even here, it can be argued that the bishops had opted to leave their
own episcopal ghetto and risk getting dirty in the political highways and
byways. I cannot help but think that Merton, who himself addressed a letter
to the bishops of the world before the final session of Vatican II in 1965,
would heartily approve.

Beyond these general points of agreement the question can be
raised whether *The Challenge of Peace* is as faithful to the personalist and
humanist perspectives of John XXIII and the Vatican Council as it could be
and whether it might not have profited more from Merton's critique of our
political culture than it did. Hence, I wish to look at some of the premises
adopted in *The Challenge of Peace* and compare them with Merton's
understanding of Christian humanism as a way of determining how far we
in the United States have to go in confronting the real challenge of peace
on earth.

3. The Challenge of Peace and
Merton's Critique of Our Culture

For all its explicit citation of *Pacem in Terris* and the Pastoral Constitution *Gaudium et Spes*, I wish to inquire whether *The Challenge of Peace*
draws out their implications or "incarnates" the elements of the Catholic
tradition to which I alluded above as clearly as it could have. There are two
sticking points for me which only my reading of Merton has helped to
clarify. They deal with the concept of human freedom and with the latter's
emphasis on "defending peace." Examining these issues against the background of Merton's understanding of freedom in the earlier documents
will, I think, be instructive.

As part of its attempt to evaluate war with a new attitude and pay
sufficient respect to human rights and human dignity, *The Challenge of
Peace* calls for a sensitivity both "to the dangers of war and the conditions of

true freedom within which moral choices can be made. Peace, it affirms, "is the setting in which moral choices can most effectively be exercised" (CP 67). While paragraph 17 of the Pastoral Constitution is footnoted here in the bishops' letter, there is to my mind serious question whether the import of the Council's text is the same as that in the letter. For, as was noted in Merton's commentary above, the Constitution's notion of freedom is not something consequent upon the establishment of a peaceful societal arrangement, but part of the transcendent nature of human dignity that empowers us, even in adversity and persecution, to choose the good. Freedom is first of all our orientation to the truth, something that must be elicited, not forced or compelled. But, as the Council text notes, since our "natural" freedom has been damaged by sin, freedom can only come to "full flower" through the action of grace wherein we both discover and act upon the dignity of our restored human nature. Yet we accomplish this, not as one individual over against another, but as persons whose identity "in the image and likeness of God" defines us more deeply than any of the forces that divide us or put us at enmity. According to Merton, it is precisely this freedom that enables us "to transcend even the most tragic injustices" and be more truly human because of them (*NVA*, p. 13).

Somewhat diversely, the bishops' pastoral defines human freedom differently when it equates it with the notion of "human rights" which need to be protected as part of preserving peace in a society. Drawing upon statements of Pope John Paul II warning against "the false peace of totalitarian regimes" and ideologies that hold up the prospect of peace as easily attainable (CP # 78), the letter concludes that there are times when the presumption against war may be overridden "in the name of preserving the kind of peace which protects human dignity and human rights" (CP # 70).

Now there is no doubt that societies differ in their understanding of the exigencies of human dignity and the way human rights are best preserved for their members. Nor is there any doubt that some societal arrangements do a better job at translating basic human freedom into various political liberties. But when the pastoral letter reduces the notion of transcendent freedom to consequent free activity, it ends up adopting an understanding of "peace" that is somewhat self-serving.

What I am saying, if I may be blunt, is that the letter argues from a bourgeois American position that our society fulfills the conditions for peace and freedom and that "theirs" (read: "the Soviet Union") does not. It is because this is an underlying perspective, I believe, that we find in the pastoral letter so many references to "preserving the peace," "defending and protecting peace," "defending society," etc. I am not objecting to the awareness that certain human rights are not enjoyed by most of the world's peoples, but rather that there is a tacit assumption throughout the letter (which is also expressed more openly, cf. 250-254) that we in the United States are in possession of the kind of freedom that ensures human dignity and, hence, of the gift of peace, but others, less fortunate than we, are not.

Frankly, I shudder at the task of questioning both this tacit assumption and explicit expression and, in the confines of this paper, I doubt I could do so sufficiently. I would dare to do so only because I can look to Thomas Merton for a franker appraisal of the political culture in which we live. His critique of the underlying "basically materialistic view of life," which anticipated Pope John Paul II's analysis in *Laborem Exercens* of the similarity between dialectical materialism and pragmatic materialism, would have benefited the bishops greatly in their analysis of how we are to "live the tension" between the kingdom and history (*NVA*, p. 117). But such a critique is sadly lacking, at least in this pastoral.

I have already stated more fully how Merton's understanding of Christian freedom is not so reductionist as that of the pastoral letter. His insistence that we need to be freed from some of our own operative mythologies is not easily heard, but attention to his religious and political writings will stand us in better stead to measure our religious and political crisis more accurately.

A first element we might note strikes at the heart of some popular American and Christian presuppositions. Merton writes:

> It is a serious error to imagine that because the West was once largely Christian, the cause of Western nations is now identified, without further qualifications, with the cause of God. The incentive to do this, and to proceed on this assumption to a nuclear crusade to wipe out Bolshevism, may well be one of the apocalyptic temptations of twentieth century Christendom. (*NVA*, p. 14)

Even more pointedly, he stated:

> The interests of the West, the NATO, and the Church are all confused with one another, and the possibility of defending the West with a nuclear first strike on Russia is accepted without too much hesitation as "necessary" and a "lesser evil." (*NVA*, p. 83)

I am *not* saying that these remarks by Merton are directly critical of the bishops and their pastoral. What I *am* saying is that the bishops underestimate the extent to which our society's attachment to nuclear weapons and our acceptance of their possession, if not their use, results from more than a practical or strategic consideration, but is woven into the warp and woof of our national self-identity. Again, it is Professor George Kennan who writes so perceptively of the moral implications of our willingness to use these weapons when he claims that in 1945 and thereafter

> we embraced nuclear weapons with enthusiasm, used them against the Japanese, took them to our hearts, and unwisely based our military posture very extensively upon their cultivation. And having done this, we proceeded to destroy not only our moral position but our possibilities of effective leadership in efforts for nuclear arms control by declining to renounce the principle of "first-use" -- by insistently reserving to ourselves, that is, the option of using these weapons in any serious military encounter, regardless of whether they were or were not used against us. (*Nuclear Delusion*, p. 184)

By contrast, the bishops' pastoral deals with the issue of "first use" (and clearly supports NATO's adopting a "no first use" policy) without any sense of how deeply ingrained in the mythology of "defending peace" such a policy is. Their treatment is an exercise in casuistry and is likely to draw the response of most casuistic moral reasoning: it may support the convinced but it rarely induces the "change of heart" that Merton and Kennan see required on this issue.

In like manner, a deeper look on the part of the pastoral letter at the reality, rather than the theory, of the "just war" might have been helpful. For, the pastoral's presumption that the "rigorous conditions" of the just war teaching regularly guide our military planners or political decision-makers is wholly gratuitous (the footnoted letter of William Clark notwithstanding). Again, Merton is the far greater realist. He writes in an essay entitled "Target Equals City" that

> it took five years for war to turn the Christian ethic of the "just war" inside out . . . . A country begins a defensive "just war." It starts by declaring its firm adherence to the ethical principles held by its Church, and by the majority of its civilian population. The nation accepts unjust suffering heroically. But then the military begins to grow impatient, seeing that its own methods of retaliation are not effective. *It is the military that changes the policy.* The new, more ruthless policy pays off. The civilian protest is silenced before it begins. (*NVA*, p. 97)

This description of the situation in Britain during World War II was repeated, Merton claims, by Americans in the same war and, as we know, in the bloody conflict which we waged in Vietnam.

By failing to locate the "just war teaching" in either a historical or political context that admitted its dismal failures in the past, the bishops' pastoral overlooks an even more serious moral problem that should have been taken into account. And that is the extent to which just war teaching, in Merton's terms, "implicitly favors the claims of the powerful and self-seeking establishment against the common good of mankind or against the rights of the oppressed" (*NVA*, p. 187). This presumption in favor of established and superior power is what we witnessed in Grenada, a crisis in which no one has bothered to examine whether the "rigorous conditions" of just war teaching, especially "just cause" and "last resort" were at all fulfilled. This presumption is even more the case in our country's arming tyrants who regularly violate not only the principle of "just war" but the even more basic principles of human rights and get away with it. In the absence of Merton's living voice we have had few with the penetrating insight to help us see ourselves as others, especially the poor, see us.

It has not been my desire to submit the bishops' pastoral to a thoroughgoing critique from the perspective of Merton's writing, but rather to inquire whether his understanding of elements in the Church's tradition would not have helped the bishops go further in their spelling out the challenge of peace. Much more could be said in this regard, but I wish here to draw out one more illustration of the viewpoint Merton developed over the years and that we today sorely miss. By and large, not many of us have a taste for the self-critical, but in such an important matter as an honest confrontation with the crisis we face Merton would have us confront our national self-idolatry more squarely.

In his 1966 Letter to a Southern Churchman entitled "Events and Pseudo-Events" he writes:

> My thesis is now clear: in my opinion the root of our trouble is that our habits of thought and the drives that proceed from them are basically idolatrous and mythical. We are all the more inclined to idolatry because we imagine that we are of all generations the most enlightened, the most objective, the most scientific, the most progressive and the most humane. This, in fact, is an "image" of ourselves -- an image that is false and is also the object of a cult. We worship ourselves in this image. . . . In other words, instead of taking care to examine the realities of our political or social problems, we simply bring out the idols in solemn procession: "we are the ones who are right, *they* are the ones who are wrong. We are the good guys, *they* are the bad guys. We are honest, *they* are crooks . . . ." If facts seem to conflict with images, then we feel we are being tempted by the devil , and we determine we will be blindly loyal to our images. To debate with the devil would be to yield. Thus in support of realism and objectivity, we simply determine beforehand that we will be swayed by no fact whatever that does not accord perfectly with our preconceived judgment. Objectivity becomes simple dogmatism.
>   As I say, we can see this mechanism at work in the Communists. We cannot see it in ourselves. ("ESE," p. 13)

By not looking deeply enough into our society's self-deceit, by pretending that we always "defend peace," by ignoring our exportation of violence to countries of the third world, by passing over a deeper understanding of human rights than is provided in the recital of the "range of political freedoms" the Church enjoys (viz. the right to food, shelter, medical care and a job that so many in our society do *not* enjoy), the bishops run the risk of having their pastoral message seriously co-opted, domesticated and largely patronized into meaninglessness. The bishops should have read more of Merton than they did. My final remarks will center on one final problem I have with the pastoral letter, taking my cue from some passages in George Orwell's *1984*.

4. *Doublethink and Deterrence: Is There a Way Out?*

Truly the most frightening element of the society portrayed in *1984* is the existence of "reality control" or what in Newspeak is called "double-think." As it is described in the subversive's manual given to Winston Smith as part of the trap into which he falls,

> doublethink means the power of holding two contradictory beliefs in one's mind simultaneously, and accepting both of them . . . . The process has to be conscious, or it would not be carried out with sufficient precision, but it also has to be unconscious, or it would bring with it a feeling of falsity and hence of guilt . . . .

The result for Oceania, the manual goes on to say is that

> In our society those who have the best knowledge of what is happening are also those who are furthest from seeing the world as it is. In general, the greater the understanding, the greater the delusion: the more intelligent, the less sane.[8]

Now, while many might be reluctant to listen to a serious commentary from a work of fiction, there is every reason to agree with Erich Fromm in his "Afterword" to *1984* when he states "'doublethink' is already with us." To me it manifests itself most clearly in the "illogic of deterrence" which is as accurate an example of doublethink as we have produced.

Deterrence requires that we hold two contradictory beliefs simultaneously, i.e., that we produce quantities of offensive weapons and affirm that they are defensive. Deterrence requires both a conscious intention not to fire the weapons along with the unconscious intention to fire them if necessary. Keeping the intention to use these genocidal weapons unconscious is the chief way we avoid facing the falsity and hence guilt involved. This mental game, or what Michael Novak calls "the complex moral intentionality" of deterrence is flawed however, as is demonstrated by the inevitable

---

8. George Orwell, *1984*(New York: New American Library, 1981), pp. 176-177.

attempts to outwit one's opponent in the deterrence game through the development of first-strike weapons. In fact, our military planners today are fulfilling the scenario which Merton foresaw back in the 1960s when he wrote:

> All the advantage goes to the force that strikes first, without warning. Hence, the multiplication of "hard" weapon sites, and "deep shelters" becomes provocative and instead of convincing the enemy of our invulnerability, it only invites a heavier preemptive attack by bigger bombs and more of them. (*NVA*, p. 117)

When the pastoral letter takes up the issue of deterrence, one has to be impressed by its attempt to engage the full range of issues from the factual character of the deterrent, to the historical development of the policy, to its role in the U. S.-Soviet confrontation and, finally, to the moral issues involved. But when all is said and done, the letter comes up with a "strictly conditioned moral acceptance" or, negatively stated, "lack of unequivocal condemnation" of deterrence, i.e., a moral judgment that leaves everyone exactly where they were before the issue was exhaustively examined. The fault is certainly not in the argument or in the intention of the framers but, I would claim along with Merton, in the premises of the argument. The pastoral clearly does not have the wherewithal to dethrone King Deterrence because it has accepted at the beginning an Augustinian model of the world "marked by sin and conflict of various kinds" (CP # 70), not merely as a physical description but as moral premises. Missing from the pastoral letter is the overarching optimism of *Gaudium et Spes* and its declaration:

> Insofar as men are sinful, the threat of war hangs over them, and hang over them it will until the return of Christ. But insofar as men vanquish sin by a union of love, they will vanquish violence as well and make these words come true: *they shall beat their swords into ploughshares,* etc. (GS # 78)

In other words, the bishops' pastoral moves from a notion of the inevitability of evil to the more hardened position which Merton refers to as "the irreversibility of evil." This slippage results in the acceptance of the premises of deterrence and, because the letter casuistically moves about within them, it produces a *temporary* acceptance of deterrence with no end-term, nor are there any criteria articulated for the "strictly conditioned moral acceptance" of deterrence to reach a point where the conditions no longer hold. Thus, what the pastoral produced, and argues for masterfully, is a case for a *hypothetical deterrence*, a "clean" notion of deterrence deserving of extended treatment by political scientists and moralists. It does not consider deterrence in the real world, although it notes that there are "strong voices" who point out that deterrence "has not, in fact, set in motion substantial processes of disarmament" (CP # 197). What the bishops do not deal with is that Deterrence and its fast-growing sibling First-Strike are the prime components of the "utterly treacherous trap for humanity" against which Vatican II called for "new approaches based on new attitudes" (CP # 81) -- a call the bishops only partially heeded.

The warning from George Orwell is this: in a world where social and economic systems are tied to continuous and escalating arms production, freedom and democracy are endangered. Merton, as well, said it clearly:

> Those who think that they can preserve their independence, their civic and religious rights by ultimate recourse to the H-bomb do not seem to recognize that the mere shadow of the bomb may end by reducing their religious and democratic beliefs to the level of mere words without meaning, veiling a state of rigid and totalitarian belligerency that will tolerate no opposition. (*NVA*, p. 111)

Just as the Party in Orwell's *1984* kept the people in a constant state of frenzy and hate through their invocation of the enemy threat, so we are in danger right now of hardening our Christian and human sensitivities to accept a level of governmental control over the fate of the earth that is both unwise and immoral. Yet, the trap has been set and we have been heading towards it. protesting mildly or demurring internally, but towards the trap nonetheless. Is there a way out?

Allow me to share with you some of what I have learned from Merton and what I believe can be applied to the crisis that we face. I wish to sum up some of his observations and draw specific suggestions from them.

The first recognition that is necessary is a renewed affirmation that the evil of the arms race is not irreversible, nor is the current animosity between the United States and the Soviet Union an expression of God's will or some cosmic divine plan. Hence, it too *can* and *must* change. Let us listen to Merton for a bit when he warns us that

> modern tyrannies have all explicitly or implicitly in one way or other emphasized the *irreversibility of evil* in order to build their power upon it . . . . It is no accident that Hitler believed firmly in the unforgivableness of sin.[9]

By contrast, Merton draws on Thomas Aquinas to develop a deeper understanding of the mystery of evil: "Evil is not only reversible but it is the proper motive of that mercy by which it is overcome and changed into good." But this requires that we first disarm our own hearts. Merton says, "Only the admission of defect and fallibility in oneself makes it possible for one to become merciful to others" (*GNV*, pp. 11-12).

---

9. Thomas Merton, *Gandhi on Non-Violence* (New York: New Directions, 1965), pp. 11-12. Hereafter referred to in the text as *GNV*.

The discovery of a deep "sympathy" for others, responsible like ourselves for the tyrannical and oppressive arms race, is the first step to enacting the transcendent freedom that best corresponds to human dignity. This freedom sets us at liberty from the project of establishing our own righteousness over against those who are sinners. This understanding of our predicament and our liberation from it yields some conclusions that we need to spell out. Once again, Merton advises that

> the evils we suffer cannot be eliminated by a violent attack in which one sector of humanity flies at another in destructive fury. Our evils are common and the solution of them can only be common. (GNV, p. 16)

If we can come to a new, common understanding of our predicament, it will help to create the climate of sanity which Pope John XXIII tried to restore in addressing *Pacem in Terris* to all people of good will. The brief flirtation with such a political climate in the '70s proved only to be a public relations ploy in a political power game. It had no roots and so withered in the heat of conflict. How, then can we move from where we are to renewed sanity? Allow me to articulate some suggestions, based on Merton's understanding of nonviolent actions which seeks "to change relationships that are evil into others that are good, or at least less bad" (GNV, p. 13). The "at least less bad" reminds us that Merton is no doctrinaire pacifist, but an extremely creative thinker whose nonviolence is not pragmatic but is always practical and realistic. If these suggestions possess more than an element of truth, they may demonstrate, beyond the pastoral letter, not merely the "value of nonviolence" but the necessity of it both on a personal and societal level.

My first suggestion is that as citizens we need to change the current climate in which our political leaders can crank out so much hate propaganda against the Soviet Union and its leaders. The insults, often delivered in the name of human rights, are patently hypocritical both because our support of human rights in the other parts of the world is clearly ambiguous and because our denigration of the Soviet Union offends against the dignity of another nation and its peoples no matter how deep the differences are between us.

Secondly, if our initial attempt to restore the climate of sanity requires that we no longer cooperate with the purveyance of self-righteous myths, our next step involves a more direct non-cooperation with the evil of the arms race and the politics that supports it. If the first step is to disarm our hearts, our second is democratically to disarm the mechanism of evil itself -- the testing, production and deployment of new tactical and strategic weapons. In the May 1983 meeting of the National Conference of

Catholic Bishops, Archbishop Raymond Hunthausen proposed that the Church make a "preferential option for noncooperation" which, as the crisis caused by the most recent deployments of missiles in Europe and off our shores demonstrates, cannot be considered a luxury, but increasingly a duty. As it becomes obvious that the current administration does not intend to heed *any* of the policy recommendations of the bishops, noncooperation with this evil becomes a necessity. Morally speaking, the burden of proof that more and deadlier weapons are required lies with the government and the moguls of the arms industry, not with those who refuse to pay a portion of their taxes to support the murderous spiral of preparation for cosmocide. Our opposition to this spiral must be visible and demonstrable as well as loving. Prayer vigils, fasts, and witnesses at research and production facilities are essential if the good news of peace is going to have a chance to save us.

Thirdly, we must begin to act even beyond the recognition that "objective mutual interests do exist between the superpowers" (CP # 255). While this coldly rational approach is superior to the current setting of official disdain, it cannot bring about the kind of change necessary for disarming the mutual hostility and suspicion that has been built up on both sides. The prevention of a nuclear conflict is the first step on the way to building a just world order, but such a world order is not going to be built merely upon "what justice can provide." It can only result from what Vatican II called "the fruit of love" (GS # 78).

Gustavo Gutierrez reminds us that, although "justice" and "love . . . do not often come up in the language of political science . . . the use of the terms . . . recalls to our minds that we are speaking of real human persons."[10] Rediscovering our own common humanity with people constantly portrayed as our enemy is not a mental trick or spiritual intention devoid of concrete actions. It requires "new approaches" that will strain our present categories to their limit.

And so, finally, I wish to propose two "new approaches" or initiatives for nonviolent actions that can seek to enact justice and love in the face of conflict today. The first is more "at home" than directed as far as the Soviet Union, and it takes into account another "preferential option" -- this one "for the poor" which the Church in Latin America made at Medellin in 1968 and reaffirmed at Puebla in 1978. We North American Christians have a burden of repentance to enact for the generations of exploitation in which

---

10.   Gustavo Gutierrez, *The Power of the Poor in History: Selected Writings*; translated from the Spanish by Robert R. Barr (Maryknoll: Orbis, 1979), p. 50.

we have cooperated with the peoples of Central and South America. One concrete way that we can engage in a living witness to our solidarity with the struggle of the poor for dignity and a role in their own social, religious and political development is to support or join in the "Witness for Peace," a grassroots, Christian effort to offer nonviolent resistance to both covert and overt U. S. intervention in Nicaragua. Details can be found in the November 1983 issue of the magazine *Sojourners*.

A second initiative I wish to present to make a first step out of the current impasse is that we encourage a whole range of groups, professional and academic, religious and political to follow the example of the International Physicians for the Prevention of Nuclear War and arrange meetings with their counterparts in the Soviet Union. Overcoming our mutual defensiveness seems unlikely on the governmental level, so we must ask the people to act for themselves and the future. In this way, we can begin to demonstrate how anachronistic purely national governmental institutions are in an age of international relationships. Therefore, against the cultural, historical, political and ideological barriers that separate us we must launch an assault of people of good will from both sides. Why cannot the National Conference of Catholic Bishops request a top level meeting with the Russian Orthodox Church akin to Pax Christi International's consultations to air mutual misunderstanding and build a common hope for peace between Christians, at least? A similar meeting with Soviet and Baptist groups would be of great mutual benefit. And what about university presidents? union leaders? feminists? students?

If we Christians believe that "Christ is our peace who has made the two of us one by breaking down the barrier that kept us apart" (Ephesians 2:14), then we must enact our unity lest the hostility to which we are prone have the last and disastrous say.

Finally, nothing in the current crisis of world conflict will change unless we change. We must rediscover our freedom to act in the face of the enormous evil that confronts us. Once we begin to enact that freedom we will no longer merely be defending the "peace of a sort" that is only another form of oppression, but we can take up the ceaseless process of building up peace (GS # 77), knowing in Merton's words that "love triumphs, at least in this life, not by eliminating evil once and for all but by resisting and overcoming it anew every day" (*GNV*, p. 13).

THE GEOGRAPHY OF SOLITUDE:

THOMAS MERTON'S

"ELIAS — VARIATIONS ON A THEME"

by **Patrick F. O'Connell**

In his long poem "Elias — Variations on a Theme,"[1] Thomas Merton selects one of the most perennially fascinating Biblical characters as a paradigm for his reflections on the theme of spiritual identity and vocation. Wonder-worker, fearless denouncer of the mighty, Elias (Elijah) owes his most enduring reputation to his heavenly ascent in the fiery chariot (4 Kings 2:11-13).[2] This freedom from death led to later speculation about his return as a precursor of the Messiah (cf. Malachi 3:23-24),[3] a role which the

---

1. The version of "Elias" to be discussed here is 25% longer than the text first published in *Thought* 21 (1956), pp. 245-250, and collected in *The Strange Islands* (New York: New Directions, 1957), pp. 36-42; reprinted in *The Collected Poems of Thomas Merton* (New York: New Directions, 1977), pp. 239-245. The longer version, sent by Merton to Sr. Therese Lentfoehr on 16 July 1955 (now in the Lentfoehr Collection at the Merton Center, Columbia University), is substantially identical to the published poem except for an additional typed page, the third of five, consisting of 48 lines of verse, coming after line 97. For an argument that this page was inadvertently omitted when the poem was printed, see my article, "Sunken Islands: Two and One-Fifth Unpublished Merton Poems," *Merton Seasonal* 12:2 (Spring 1987), pp. 4-9.

2. The names of the Biblical books, like that of the prophet himself, correspond to the Latin Vulgate, rather than the more familiar Authorized, or King James, Version, which follows the Hebrew (i.e., 4 Kings for 2 Kings; Elias for Elijah). At the time Merton wrote "Elias," only the first eight books of the Old Testament had been translated from the Hebrew in the new "Confraternity" version, which eventually became The New American Bible; the remainder, including the Books of Kings, were available to Catholics in English only in the Douay version, a sixteenth-century translation from the Vulgate. All Biblical passages will be quoted according to the version which would have been available to Merton in 1954.

3. Interest in Elijah as precursor continues throughout post-Biblical Jewish tradition. For a recent interpretation of this tradition, see Elie Wiesel, *Five Biblical Portraits* (Notre Dame: University of Notre Dame Press, 1981), pp. 33-67.

early Christians would see symbolically fulfilled in the figure of John the Baptist (Matthew 17:9-13).[4] While these aspects of the career of Elias play a part in his poem, Merton is principally interested in the portrait of Elias which emerges from a rather different tradition. Since the time of the early Christian ascetics, Elias had been looked upon as a model for the solitary. In St. Athanasius' *Life of Antony*, the most influential work of primitive monastic literature, the saint "used to tell himself that from the career of the great Elijah, as from a mirror, the ascetic must always acquire knowledge of his own life."[5] It is of course not Elias the adversary of King Ahab to whom Antony primarily looks, but Elias who lived alone at the wadi Cherith (3 Kings 17:2-6), who journeyed through the desert fasting for forty days and nights until he reached Mount Horeb (Sinai), where he heard the Lord speaking in the voice of the gentle breeze (3 Kings 19:1-14).

This conception of Elias the solitary was particularly marked in the early Carmelite tradition, which looked to Elias as the order's "founder."[6] In his essay on "The Primitive Carmelite Ideal," Merton takes note of this tradition and its significance:

> The author of that moving ancient text on the spirit of Carmelite prayer and contemplation, the *Institution* of the first Fathers, interprets the retirement of Elias in typical medieval style. To hide in the torrent of Carith is to embrace the ascetical life, which leads to the perfection of charity by one's own efforts, aided by the grace of God. To drink of the torrent is to passively receive the secret light of contemplation from God and to be inwardly transformed by His wisdom . . . . The Carmelite, then, is the successor of the prophets as a witness to the desert vocation of Israel, that is of the Church: a reminder that we do not have on this earth a lasting city, and that we are pilgrims to the city of God.[7]

It is significant in view of this connection that the "Elias" poem was originally written for the nuns of the New York Carmelite Convent.[8]

---

4. In another stratum of early Christian tradition, found particularly in Luke's Gospel, Elias is seen as a type or predecessor of Jesus himself. See Paul Hinnebusch, *Jesus, the New Elijah* (Ann Arbor: Servant Publications, 1979).

5. Athanasius, *The Life of Antony and the Letter to Marcellinus*, trans. Robert C. Gregg, Classics of Western Spirituality (New York: Paulist Press, 1980), p. 37.

6. The motto of the Carmelites, "Zelo zelatus sum pro Domino Deo exercituum," is taken from Elijah's words in 1 Kings (3 Kings) 19:10: see *The Collected Works of St. Teresa of Avila*, vol. 2, trans. Kieran Kavanaugh, O.C.D. and Otilio Rodriguez, O.C.D. (Washington, D.C.: Institute of Carmelite Studies, 1980), p. 499; cf. also in the same volume St. Teresa's references to "our Father Elijah" in *The Interior Castle*, VI: 7 (p. 401) and VII:4 (p. 448).

7. Thomas Merton, *Disputed Questions* (New York: Farrar, Straus & Cudahy), 1960, pp. 225-226. Hereafter referred to in the text as *DQ*.

8. In the Preface to *The Strange Islands*, Merton writes, "Several of these poems were produced in response to a 'billet' from the New York Carmel. Carmelites have to draw by lot a subject for a Christmas song which they compose and sing at the crib on the Feast of Our Lord's Nativity. 'The Annunciation,' 'Stranger' and 'Elias' are such poems, though 'Elias' hardly turned out to be a carol or even a Christmas poem. It simply represents what the author had going through his head in the Christmas season of 1954."

But Elias is, of course, not simply an ascetic but a prophet, who proclaimed the Word of God boldly, a fact witnessed in the early Carmelite tradition itself, which combined the hermit vocation with a preaching apostolate, in conscious imitation of Elias (*DQ*, pp. 220-222, 226-227). This synthesis, in Merton's view, was not restricted to the Carmelites. In *No Man is an Island* (1955), a book of meditations written at approximately the same time as the poem, Merton concludes his chapter on vocation with a consideration of Francis of Assisi, whom he associates with Elias:

> If there was any recognized vocation in his time that Francis might have associated with his own life, it was the vocation of hermit. . . . He frequently went off into the mountains to pray and live alone. But he never thought that he had a "vocation" to do nothing but that. He stayed alone as long as the Spirit held him in solitude, and then let himself be led back into the towns and villages by the same Spirit.
>
> If he had thought about it, he might have recognized that his vocation was essentially "prophetic." He was like another Elias or Eliseus, taught by the Spirit in solitude, but brought back by God to the cities of men with a message to tell them.[9]

In this perception and in its language, we find the germ of Merton's poem. The figure of Elias, prophet and solitary, becomes the embodiment of the tensions and ambiguities, but also the rich possibilities, of the Christian life in general and of Merton's own in particular. As a meditation on the relationship between contemplation and action, which is also a wrestling with his own identity as monk and writer, "Elias" foreshadows Merton's emergence in the 1960s both as an eloquent spokesperson for peace, civil rights, ecumenism and the renewal of monasticism and Catholicism, and as the first Cistercian since the Middle Ages to live the life of a hermit. But it is also a well-crafted work of literature in its own right, one which richly repays a careful reading, and which can serve as a good starting point for an evaluation of Merton's accomplishment as a poet.[10]

---

9. *No Man is an Island* (New York: Harcourt, Brace, 1955), p. 162. Hereafter referred to in the text as *NMI*. The association of Francis with Elijah is traditional in the Franciscan Order from the earliest days, though with more apocalyptic connotations; see, for example, St. Bonaventure's *Major Life* of Francis, Prol. 1; 4:4, in the Bonaventure volume of the Classics of Western Spirituality Series, trans. Ewert Cousins (New York: Paulist Press, 1978), pp. 180-181, 209.

10. "Elias" has not previously received extensive critical attention, but the poem has drawn favorable notice from Ross Labrie in *The Art of Thomas Merton* (Fort Worth: Texas Christian University Press, 1979), pp. 128-130; from George Woodcock in *Thomas Merton, Monk and Poet: A Critical Study* (New York: Farrar, Straus & Giroux, 1978), pp. 75-77; and more briefly, from Victor A. Kramer in *Thomas Merton*, Twayne's U. S. Authors Series (Boston: G. K. Hall, 1985), p. 81. Sr. Therese Lentfoehr provides helpful background information in *Words and Silence: On the Poetry of Thomas Merton* (New York: New Directions, 1979), pp. 29-33, as does Michael Mott in his biography, *The Seven Mountains of Thomas Merton* (Boston: Houghton Mifflin, 1984), p. 303.

I

The first of the poem's six sections begins with what initially appears to be a straightforward description of a rather unremarkable, even uninviting, landscape:

> Under the blunt pine
> In the winter sun
> The pathway dies
> And the wilds begin.
> Here the bird abides
> Where the ground is warm
> And sings alone. (ll. 1-7)

The dramatic import of the opening lines becomes evident only with the recognition that they are a reworking of the scriptural passage in which Elias, fleeing from the wrath of Queen Jezebel, takes refuge under a juniper tree and wishes only to die: "And he went forward one day's journey into the desert. And when he was there, and sat under a juniper tree, he requested for his soul that he might die, and said: It is enough for me, Lord. Take away my soul, for I am no better than my fathers" (3 Kings 19:4). Far from being an objective description, then, the opening sentence of the poem projects the feelings of near-despair and absolute loneliness of the prophet onto the stark landscape into which he has journeyed. The juniper tree of the Vulgate has become a "blunt pine," reflecting the figure's sense of frustration, of dimmed hopes: deprived of all sense of direction, of purpose, he finds himself at the limits of the familiar, the known, the safe. As the pathway comes to an end, his own inevitable death seems to be presaged: he gives himself up for lost.

The one ambiguous detail of the scene is the winter sun: is the emphasis on the adjective, so that the sun, providing light without warmth, is of a piece with the barren landscape, or is the very fact of its shining an image of hope amidst the deadness without and within? The completion of the scene in the lines which follow suggests that the latter interpretation is the correct one, for in fact the ground beneath the pine, contrary to any expectation, is warm, a detail mysteriously associated with the presence of a bird, who "abides" and "sings alone." Mirroring the prophet's solitude but not his despair, the bird breaks through the pattern of projection and so transfigures the entire landscape. Simply by being what it is, the bird
• incarnates an alternative to the isolation and confusion of Elias and invites a consideration of the world around him, and consequently of his own situation within that world, as it really is. Its role is comparable to that of

the bird described in the final chapter of *No Man is an Island*: "The rain ceases, and a bird's clear song suddenly announces the difference between Heaven and hell" (*NMI*, p. 254). This suggestion of an ultimate meaning for even so hopeless a situation is perhaps conveyed as much by the form of the verse as by its content. In striking contrast with the rather baroque diction of much of Merton's early poetry, this verse possesses unadorned simplicity, a certain rhetorical chasteness, conveying a sense of order and clarity, an underlying calm, which first counters and then coincides with the overt verbal meaning. The short lines of two or three stresses, each a complete phrase, are woven together by a complex series of sound patterns which reminds the reader that, like Eliot's *Four Quartets*, Merton's title suggests a musical analogy.

Each of the stressed syllables of the first two lines has the identical pattern of "n" following the vowel, which in three key words ("Under"; "blunt"; "sun") is the short "u," providing a sort of rhyme to link these lines together; all the others feature "in," whether long ("pine") or short ("In"; "winter"). The dominance of short "i" ("begin") and long "i" ("dies"; "wilds") continues through the next two lines to the key phrase of line 5, "bird abides," where the change from short to long vowel is the main distinction between subject and verb linked by consonance. The terminal "n," submerged in the following two lines ("ground"; "sings") emerges again in the concluding "alone." The functional significance of these patterns is made clear by a look at the words given emphatic position. The last word of the first sentence, "begin," is joined by slant rhyme to the first two lines, thus isolating "dies," with which it contrasts in meaning as well as sound. Yet the long "i" of "dies" is picked up by "abides," which suggests a paradoxical relationship between the two. The final "alone" shares both the initial unstressed short "a" with "abides" and the terminal "n" with "pine," "sun" and "begin," but its long "o" is unique. The effect of this orchestration, besides necessitating a slow and deliberate reading, is to reinforce the positive significance of the landscape suggested by the figure of the bird. This counterstatement becomes explicit, "audible," in the lines that follow, which are perhaps best taken as what the prophet hears in the bird's song:

> Listen, Elias,
> To the southern wind
> Where the grass is brown,
> Live beneath this pine
> In wind and rain.
> Listen to the woods,
> Listen to the ground.
>   (ll., 8-14)

The natural world itself, in its stripped-down, basic simplicity, its patient willingness to be what it is, is an antidote to hopelessness: its rhythms speak not of defeat and despair but of restoration and renewal. The summons to "Live beneath this pine/ In wind and rain" appears to be spoken first to the withered grass by the south wind itself, which forecasts the coming of spring, and only overheard by Elias. But the command to listen indicates that this call to life is addressed to him as well. The woods and ground, beneficiaries of wind and rain, convey the same message, which functions as the angel's command to rise and eat did in the scriptural account (3 Kings 19: 5, 7). This implied parallel between natural and heavenly messengers suggests a sacramental vision of creation in which the natural world, without ceasing to be itself, symbolizes a deeper level of reality: the wind's call to life is thus an image of the life-giving power of the divine Pneuma, the gentle breeze in which Elias hears the voice of the Lord.

This transition from natural to supernatural dimensions is confirmed in the verse paragraph which follows, where the scene has shifted to the theophany on Horeb. While continuity with what preceded is maintained by the repetition of the imperative and the extension of the basic sound patterns ("above," "sun," "one," "fern," "word," "bird," "abides," "bends," "blade," etc.), both the sense of stillness and the message itself are transposed into an explicitly spiritual context, yet without intrusion upon or disruption of the natural setting:

> O listen, Elias
> (Where the bird abides
> And sings alone),
> The sun grows pale
> Where passes One
> Who bends no blade, no fern.
> Listen to His word. (ll. 15-21)

The parenthetical inclusion of the bird here is a reminder that it too has a sacramental dimension. Uniting stillness ("abides") with solitude ("alone") and praise ("sings"), the bird is a perfect image of contemplation, that condition of awareness which is able to perceive the divine Presence inaccessible to the outward senses. Like the "One bird" in "Stranger," the final poem of the collection in which "Elias" appears, it "sits still / Watching the work of God."[11] At the same time, as its song flows into "His Word," the bird suggests the Spirit of God itself, hovering over the creation at the beginning of Genesis as here the bird "abides" above the warm ground;

---

11. "Stranger," ll. 12-13; *The Strange Islands*, p. 101; *Collected Poems*, p. 290.

this very action, moreover, recalls Jesus' repeated use of the same term in the Last Supper discourse of John's Gospel to describe the unity between Himself and His disciples which not even death could destroy (John 15: 4-7, 9-10).

It is precisely this message of re-creation and fidelity which is articulated in the divine word spoken to Elias:

> "Where the fields end
> Thou shalt be my friend.
> Where the bird is gone
> Thou shalt be my son."
> (ll. 22-25)

Here the meaning of the prophet's experience is revealed to be that it is precisely when one appears to be most lost, farthest from one's goal, that God's affirming presence is at hand.[12] The dead-end, the loss of direction and meaning, can now be accepted as the occasion for the end of self-will, a necessary surrender of one's own desires and plans, of one's own very self, to follow the direction of Another. It is a dying which leads not to extinction but to life, to a new identity as friend and son of God, the two most intimate titles given the disciple in the New Testament. The first particularly recalls Jesus' words at the Last Supper, which are linked to the final examples of the verb "abide":

> As the Father has loved me, I also have loved you. Abide in my love. If you keep my commandments you will abide in my love, as I also have kept my Father's commandments, and abide in his love. . . . This is my commandment, that you love one another as I have loved you. Greater love than this no one has, that one lay down his life for his friends. You are my friends if you do the things I command you. No longer do I call you servants, because the servant does not know what his master does. But I have called you friends, because all things that I have heard from my Father I have made known to you. You have not chosen me, but I have chosen you, and have appointed you that you should go and bear fruit, and that your fruit should remain [RSV: abide] (John 15: 9-10, 12-16).

The second couplet, joining the image of the bird to the title of son, recalls not only the Synoptic baptismal scene, in which Christ's Sonship is revealed as the dove descends upon him (Mark 1:11), but the corresponding scene in John's Gospel, where the Baptist gives witness to Jesus:

---

12.   For a later expression of this characteristic theme see section 84 of the long poem *Cables to the Ace* (1967): ". . . But for each of us there is a point of nowhereness in the middle of movement, a point of nothingness in the midst of being: the incomparable point, not to be discovered by insight. If you seek it you do not find it. If you stop seeking, it is there. But you must not turn to it. Once you become aware of yourself as seeker, you are lost. But if you are content to be lost you will be found without knowing it, precisely because you are lost, for you are, at last, nowhere" (*Collected Poems*, p. 452).

> I beheld the Spirit descending as a dove from heaven, and it abode upon him. And I did not know him. But he who sent me to baptize with water said to me, "He upon whom thou wilt see the Spirit descending, and abiding upon him, he it is who baptizes with the Holy Spirit." And I have seen and have borne witness that this is the Son of God (John 1:32-34).

Here the divine Sonship is explicitly associated with the dove-Spirit who "abides" with the Son. Thus the divine revelation to Elias summarizes, clarifies and concludes all that has preceded it. The journey into solitude leads not to despair but to a purified awareness of the truth about oneself in relation to created reality and God. He who loses his life finds it.

Yet the simplicity of these words of divine acceptance does not completely exclude a latent tension, signalled perhaps by the imperfect rhyme of "gone" and "son." For in fact the message to Elias in 3 Kings 19 is one of engagement, involvement, prophetic witness, a note also found in the Last Supper discourse, which speaks not only of Christ's impending death but of the disciples' future sufferings, and in the baptism scene, which is of course the beginning of Christ's public ministry. From this perspective, even the message itself is not without ambiguities: it is after all phrased in the future tense; how can the bird who "is gone" also be the bird who "abides"; even the fields could be said to "end" where settled areas begin, as well as at the entrance to the wilderness. The question arises: what is to be done now? How does one respond to the divine call? The value of solitude has been recognized, but the relation of solitude to witness, of contemplation to action, must still be faced.

The second aspect of Elias' vocation now receives explicit consideration, as the term "prophet" appears for the first time:

> How the pine burns
> In the furious sun
> When the prophets come
> To Jerusalem.
> (Listen, Elias,
> For the fiery wing)[13]
> To Jerusalem
> Where the knife is drawn.
> (Do her children run
> To the covering wing?)
> Look, look, My son,
> At the smashed wood
> At the bloody stone. (ll. 26-38)

While these verses stress both the danger and the active engagement of

---

13. In *Collected Poems*, this line is misprinted "To the covering wing?" as, properly, in l. 35.

the prophetic vocation, they do not refer directly to the career of Elias, who worked not in Jerusalem but in the northern kingdom, Israel. They are, rather, based on the gospel passage in which Jesus identifies himself with both the mission and the fate of the prophet, and laments that Jerusalem will not listen to his message:

> I must go my way today and tomorrow and the next day, for it cannot be that a prophet perish outside Jerusalem. Jerusalem, Jerusalem, thou who killest the prophets, and stonest those who are sent to thee! how often would I have gathered thy children together, as a hen gathers her young under her wings, but thou wouldst not! (Luke 13:33-34).

Thus the prophetic role is represented not only by the figure of Elias but by that of Christ himself: to follow in the footsteps of Jesus is to journey back to Jerusalem. Likewise the reference to "the fiery wing" of the Pentecostal Spirit, which empowered the disciples to proclaim the Word boldly, and "the covering wing" of divine protection (cf. Psalms 90:4), suggest that "where the bird is gone" is into the midst of active involvement in the affairs of the world.

Yet it will soon become evident that this route is neither taken nor recommended at this point. Why? Obvious motives for remaining in solitude present themselves: fear -- the desire to save oneself from "the knife," or frustration -- the sense of helplessness to avert impending catastrophe (the children do not, after all, "run / To the covering wing" even at the word of Jesus). Both of these, of course, played a part in the original flight of Elias into the wilderness, but they have already been confronted and there is no indication that they are now in control.

A careful reading of the opening lines of this section indicates, rather, that it is not the motives for withdrawing but for returning which are being called into question. Once more the focus is on the landscape, again envisioned not according to objective description but subjective projection. The burning pine, and particularly the "furious sun," images of apocalyptic wrath and cosmic judgment, suggest a different scenario for the prophets coming to Jerusalem: they recall the incident at the very outset of Jesus' journey to the Holy City, when two of his disciples are rebuked for misconstruing the prophetic role:

> Now it came to pass, when the days had come for him to be taken up, that he steadfastly set his face to go to Jerusalem, and sent messengers before him. And they went and entered a Samaritan town to make ready for him, and they did not receive him, because his face was set for Jerusalem. But when his disciples James and John saw this, they said, "Lord, wilt thou that we bid fire come down from heaven and consume them?" But he turned and rebuked them, saying, "You do not know of what manner of spirit you

are; for the Son of Man did not come to destroy men's lives, but to save them" (Luke 9:51-56).

The disciples' question echoes the passage in which Elias twice called down fire from heaven to consume his opponents, sent out from Samaria (4 Kings 1:9-12); some textual authorities even add "as Elias did" at the conclusion of the disciples' question.[14] Jesus emphatically dissociates himself from such an attitude: his response stresses the need for discernment of spirits, a recognition that "the fiery wing" is also "the covering wing."[15] Thus the final lines of this section, in which Elias is again addressed by God as "My son," are a summons to see the city of men through the eyes of Jesus, the Son, with compassion and a willingness to take upon oneself its suffering. The "smashed wood" and "bloody stone" can refer equally to the destruction of the city ("not . . . one stone upon another," Luke 19:44) or the martyrdom of the prophet (Luke 13:34), and in fact the two are not intended to be distinguished. The ironic lesson of this section is a warning against a pseudo-righteousness by which prophetic engagement would actually create a false dichotomy between the prophet and the world which does not heed his message. In the face of this temptation, the divine counsel is not to reject the prophetic role absolutely, but to wait, and to grow.

Thus the concluding section of this first "variation" again affirms the need for solitude, but does so in a way which leaves open the question of its relation to active involvement:

> Where the fields end
> And the stars begin
> Listen, Elias,
> To the winter rain.
> For the seed sleeps
> By the sleeping stone.
> But the seed has life
> While the stone has none. (ll. 39-46)

Here all is silence, stillness, patience. At the threshold of mystery, on the boundary between settled and wild, daylight and darkness, Elias is again enjoined to listen, to learn. Although the concerns of the previous verse paragraph may seem absent here, they remain no less central for being "beneath the surface" rather than explicit. In the distinction between seed and stone, one apparently inert, totally passive, unresponsive to anything

---

14. See the note on Luke 9:54 in the Jerusalem Bible.

15. This verse, found in the Vulgate and in the translation Merton would have known, is considered of doubtful authenticity in more recent translations.

beyond itself, the other seemingly the same yet responding, imperceptibly yet ineluctably, to the life-bearing force of the winter rain, the dynamism of true solitude is revealed: it is not evasion but engagement, even though hidden from sight. It seeks not to escape from but to experience profoundly the dying which awaits the prophet, for in solitude identity is found in conforming the self to the pattern of Jesus' words and life: "Amen, amen, I say to you, unless the grain of wheat falls into the ground and dies, it remains alone. But if it dies, it brings forth much fruit" (John 12:24-25).

If the relationship of prophecy to solitude has not been definitely settled, it has been clarified. In the sleeping seed, image of transformation, of process, of growth, is hidden the recognition that what one does must spring from one who is, authentic action from authentic identity, which is not a matter of self-definition or self-fulfillment but of divine gift:

> "Where the fields end
> Thou shalt be My friend.
> Where the bird is gone
> Thou shalt be My son." (ll. 47-50)

The image of the seed, like the future tense of the divine call, now repeated to end the first part of the poem, suggests a promise, a sign of hope to be fulfilled, even if the form it will take is not yet clear.

II

The second variation becomes the occasion for the speaker, obviously someone similar to Thomas Merton, to consider some of the implications of this meditation on the Biblical Elias for his own vocation. The setting has shifted to the present, and the initial mood seems to be one of disappointment that the speaker's experience fails to correspond to the scriptural model:

> There were supposed to be
> Not birds but spirits of flame
> Around the old wagon.
> ("Bring me my chariot")
> There were supposed
> To be fiery devices,
> Grand machines, all flame,
> With supernatural wings
> Beyond the full creek.
> ("Bring me my chariot of fire")
> All flame, beyond the rotten tree!
> (ll. 51-61)

Prosaic and commonplace, the wagon and its birds seem to be pathetically inadequate substitutes for the fiery chariot of the Bible. This complex image combines at least three different referents, each of which contributes to the impression of failed expectations. The most immediate is, of course, the chariot in which Elias was swept up into heaven (4 Kings 2:11): a traditional symbol of mystical elevation as well as the culmination of Elias' prophetic career, the image unites the two dimensions of contemplation and action, but without giving the speaker access to either. He resembles neither Elias himself, ascending to the vision of the Most High, nor Eliseus (Elisha), who sees the chariot and so receives a double portion of his master's prophetic spirit (4 Kings 2:9-10). In its attendant imagery, however, the "fiery devices" and "supernatural wings," the chariot resembles that in the inaugural vision of Ezechiel (Ezechiel 1:4-28), which later reappears (Ezechiel 10:4-23) to carry the Divine Presence from the doomed Jerusalem Temple. Again mystical vision is combined with the summons to prophetic witness, here at the beginning rather than at the end of the prophet's career. Thirdly, the parenthetical quotation, which will continue to appear, antiphon-like (though frequently incomplete), throughout this section, is taken from William Blake's famous lyric, often called "Jerusalem," which prefaces his Prophetic Book *Milton*. Blake uses the fiery chariot of Elias to symbolize his conception of the poet as prophet, the harbinger of a new order:

> Bring me my Bow of burning gold:
> Bring me my Arrows of desire:
> Bring me my Spear: O clouds unfold!
> Bring me my Chariot of fire.
>
> I will not cease from Mental Fight,
> Nor shall my Sword sleep in my hand
> Till we have built Jerusalem
> In England's green and pleasant Land.[16]

By integrating the literary allusion into the poem, Merton is implicitly extending his examination of the tension between engagement and withdrawal, between prophetic speech and contemplative silence, to include the act of writing.[17] The image of the chariot thus becomes the locus of

---

16.   William Blake, *Complete Writings*, ed. Geoffrey Keynes (London: Oxford University Press, 1966), p. 181. These are the first two stanzas of the four-stanza poem. Also pertinent is the quotation from the Book of Numbers which follows immediately after the lyric and before the first book of the poem proper: "Would to God that all the Lord's people were Prophets" (Numbers 11:29). Merton's interest in Blake dates back to his 1939 Columbia Master's thesis, "Nature and Art in William Blake," reprinted as Appendix I in *The Literary Essays of Thomas Merton*, ed. Patrick Hart (New York: New Directions, 1981), pp. 387-453.

17.   This connection of poetry with prophecy is made by Merton in his essay, "Poetry and Contemplation: A Reappraisal," first published in *Commonweal*, 24 October 1958, and reprinted in *Literary Essays*: "The Christian poet is therefore the successor to David and the Prophets, he contemplates what was announced by the poets of the Old Testament: he should be, as they were, a mystic, full of divine fire.

Merton's confrontation with his own vocation, or vocations, as monk and author.

These opening lines, however, seem to indicate a failure on all fronts -- a failure to encounter the extraordinary, the overpowering numinous Presence that overwhelms and transforms the initiate, a failure of the present to meet the criteria dictated by past models of mystical, prophetic, even poetic, vision. The sense of disappointment verges on the petulant as the section begins: "supposed to be" ordinarily means "intended to be," but there is no indication on what grounds such a supposition is based. In fact the phrase can also have the more negative sense of "expected on slight or erroneous evidence," which seems closer to the case here: that is, the reader is likely to give the phrase a different interpretation than that intended by the speaker. In fact when the phrase is repeated four lines later, the arrangement is significantly altered: the removal of the infinitive to the following line has the effect of leaving the verb "supposed" to stand alone, where its connotations of unrealistic, illusory expectations are more evident to the reader, if not to the speaker. Actually the rather grandiose elaborations of the supposed vision in this second description, particularly the mechanistic connotations of "devices" and "grand machines," serve to enhance by contrast the attractiveness of the old wagon's simplicity. Likewise the birds surrounding it, which recall the bird of the opening variation, suggest that there is a genuine and profound experience of God to be found here if only the speaker has the vision to see it.

What follows reveals that he does indeed come to recognize the value of the present. The insight comes first in a negative way, with his awareness that the appeal of the chariot image may not be completely disinterested:

> Flame? This old wagon
> With the wet, smashed wheels
> Is better. ("My chariot")
> This derelict is better.
> ("Of fire.") It abides
> (Swifter) in the brown ferns
> And burns nothing. (ll. 62-68)

He should be one who, like the prophet Isaias, has seen the living God and has lamented the fact that he was a man of impure lips, until God Himself sent Seraph, with a live coal from the altar of the heavenly temple, to burn his lips with prophetic inspiration. In the true Christian poet -- in Dante, St. John of the Cross, St. Francis, Jacopone da Todi, Hopkins, Paul Claudel -- we find it hard to distinguish between the inspiration of the prophet and mystic and the purely poetic enthusiasm of great artistic genius" (p. 344). This passage does not appear in the original version of the essay, "Poetry and the Contemplative Life," first published in *Commonweal* (4 July 1947) and reprinted in *Figures for an Apocalypse* (Norfolk, Connecticut: New Directions, 1947).

The speaker picks up the image of fire, used no less than five times in the previous ten lines, the last time juxtaposed with the "rotten tree." Here the seductive temptation of a desire for sudden apocalyptic purification encountered earlier in the images of the burning pine and "furious sun" (ll. 26-27), is associated with the flames. Again the scene of Elias calling down fire to consume his enemies (4 Kings 1:9-14) is suggested. Likewise the chariot itself, improperly understood, can represent a craving for speed, a desire for instantaneous solutions, immediate bliss: it can also connote a sense of separation from earthly realities, of rising above them, whether it be the prophet leaving the earth or Yahweh abandoning the Temple. Thus the speaker's relinquishing of the chariot for the old wagon, which cannot move and "burns nothing," represents a renunciation of any spurious attitude of separation from or superiority toward the world around him.[18]

The reminiscences of the first section are striking here: like the bird, the wagon "abides," and its location in the "brown ferns" recalls the earlier theophany "where the grass is brown" and "Where passes One / Who bends no blade, no fern" (ll. 10, 19-20). At the same time, the "smashed wheels" of the wagon, recalling the "smashed wood" of Jerusalem (l. 37), suggest that true contemplation involves facing the same reality as that found anywhere. The violence, the dying, is to be found close to home, in the ordinary events which paradoxically are also the stuff of contemplative vision: a derelict in the eyes of the world, the wagon represents a true stability ("abides") which is also filled with inner dynamism ("Swifter").

As the first variation ended not with "the furious sun" but with "the winter rain," so here it is not fire but water, not "All flame" but "wet, smashed wheels," not instantaneous transformation but a nearly over-looked rhythm of renewal, which symbolizes the authentic life of the spirit. This contrast becomes more obvious in the lines which follow, as the Blakean imperative, suitably emended, is incorporated into the speaker's own words.

> Bring me ("Of fire")
> Better still the old trailer ("My chariot")
> With the dead stove in it, and the rain
> Comes down the pipe and covers the floor.
> Bring me my chariot of rain. Bring me

---

18. In terms of Merton's own writing, "Elias" seems to represent a rejection, or strong modification, of the attitude toward the world of such earlier poems as the title piece in *Figures for an Apocalypse*, which includes among its eight parts sections entitled "(Advice to my Friends Robert Lax and Edward Rice, to get away while they still can)" (III), and "In the Ruins of New York" (VI). See *Figures for an Apocalypse*, pp. 13-28; *Collected Poems*, pp. 135-148.

> My old chariot of broken-down rain.
> Bring, bring my old fire, my old storm,
> My old trailer; faster and faster it stands still,
> Faster and faster it stays where it has always been,
> Behind the felled oaks, faster, burning nothing.   (ll. 68-77)

These lines find Merton at his most humorous, even playful, parodying the vatic tone of Blake to describe the trailer with the dead stove (no fire here!) whose pipe leaks rainwater all over the floor. It is precisely the uselessness, the purposeless gratuity, the totally functionless quality of the trailer in the rain, unable even to move by its own power, abandoned by some long-forgotten owner, which provides the speaker's almost giddy sense of release here, marked by the ever more subversive changes rung on Blake's sentence.[19] The speaker realizes that like the trailer, he has nothing to do but to be, but that genuinely to be encompasses everything -- fire, storm, trailer. This sense of simply be-ing is expressed in the play on the word "faster," here meaning not "with greater speed," but exactly the opposite, "more firmly emplaced, more steadfast." The trailer stands fast, it "stands still," a still point in a world of motion without direction.

Yet this sacred space is not conceived as being unrelated to the larger world beyond. The trailer is described as

> Broken and perfect, facing south,
> Facing the sound of distant guns,
> Facing the wall of distance where blue hills
> Hide in the fading rain.   (ll. 78-81)

The opening paradox here finds the trailer a sort of paradigm of human life, which also discovers its perfection not in denying its brokenness but in acknowledging it, an image of redemption and perhaps even of the cross itself. As such it is a sign of contradiction to a world in which weakness cannot be revealed, the world of the distant guns, presumably those described at greater length in "The Guns of Fort Knox" earlier in the same collection.[20] Yet the relationship to the larger world, though admitted and in some sense faced, is still, like the distant blue hills, not clearly seen: the agency of the rain is left ambiguous -- is it "fading" itself, gradually disappearing to reveal the wider landscape, or is its activity one of "fading," of veiling that landscape? The relation of the contemplative awareness to active engagement thus remains unsettled, and unsettling.

---

19. This section foreshadows in a number of ways Merton's important later essay, "Rain and the Rhinoceros," in *Raids on the Unspeakable* (New York: New Directions, 1966), pp. 9-23; he describes there a night spent in the cabin which will become his hermitage, during a rainstorm whose "gratuity" and "meaninglessness" (p. 9) nevertheless intimate "a whole world of meaning, of secrecy, of silence, of rumor" (p. 10).

20. *The Strange Islands*, pp. 21-22; *Collected Poems*, pp. 228-229. The final paragraph of "Rain" reads: "Yet even here the earth shakes. Over at Fort Knox the Rhinoceros is having fun" (*Raids*, p. 23).

But what is not in question is what can only be called the incarnational ground of contemplation, that God reveals Himself through and in the least likely things, the derelict, the broken, the abandoned:

> Where the woods are cut down the punished
> Trailer stands alone and becomes
> (Against all the better intentions of the owners)
> The House of God
> The Gate of Heaven.
> ("My chariot of fire") (ll. 82-87)

Fitting representative of the ravaged landscape itself, the trailer is nonetheless given the two titles used by Jacob to describe his place of encounter with the God of his Fathers: "Truly the Lord is in this place and I did not know it. . . . How awesome is this place! This is none other than the house of God; this is the gate of heaven" (Genesis: 28:16-17). Like Jacob at Bethel (lit. "house of God"), the speaker did not at first recognize the presence of the Lord, but now finds in the seemingly insignificant trailer both the House of God, the divine presence immanent in this world, corresponding to the Temple of Ezechiel's vision, and the "Gate of Heaven," the opening to the transcendent realm corresponding to Elias' own ascent to the skies. The final declaration that the trailer is indeed the authentic "chariot of fire" implies as well an acceptance of the prophetic call to communicate the vision, but as in the first variation there is as yet no explicit consideration of how this summons is to be obeyed.

The conclusion of this second variation, then, has been to bring speaker and reader to an existential awareness of the nature of genuine contemplative experience, a divine epiphany which does not distance the mystic from the world but roots him in it more firmly. Such an incarnational or sacramental focus, which discovers in the created world the medium of God's communication, has definite consequences for a proper understanding of prophecy, of sharing that communication with others, but as yet the dynamics of the interaction between vision and proclamation remain to be worked out.

III

Nevertheless, the third variation seems to consist precisely in proclamation. For the first time in the poem, the speaker emerges as subject, as "I," and speaks in a tone which is assured and confident, even assertive:

> The seed, as I have said,
> Hides in the frozen sod.
> Stones, shaped by rivers they will
> Never care about or feel,
> Cover the cultivated soil.
>
> The seed, by nature, waits to grow and bear
> Fruit. Therefore it is not alone
> As stones, or inanimate things are:
> That is to say, alone by nature,
> Or alone forever.   (ll. 88-97)

Here the comparison of seed and stone, previously found toward the end of Part I (ll. 43-46), is sharpened into opposition. The distinction between "the seed" and "stones" (note the particularity of the one and indefiniteness of the other) is that between potential for activity, for growth, for fruitfulness, and pure passivity, which actually impedes cultivation and growth by being in the way.[21]

This contrast continues through the rest of the section:

> The seed is not incapable of society
> But knows solitude has purpose. Stones
> Resist purpose. There they lie
> Waiting for the military hand,
> Wanting the brain that hates growth,
> Wanting the medical eye
> That aims to kill with blade or gun
> Or with the nearest weapon, namely: stone.
>
> The seed, then, contains society
> Within its own loneliness.
> The stone has a sterile power
> To destroy cities, when hurled upon a prophet.   (ll. 98-109)[22]

Here the focus has shifted from the individual to the social dimension. While the seed "contains society" by its openness to life (and will in time produce many more seeds from itself), stones represent a disruptive, destructive element, the "sterile power" of hatred and war. Thus the section as a whole articulates a kind of negative, inverted synthesis of contemplation and action. The stones are taken by the speaker to signify both meaningless, insensate solitude and violent, divisive activity, also ultimately meaningless. Here the connection between contemplative silence and

---

21.   It would be interesting to know if Richard Wilbur had read these lines. His poem "Two Voices in a Meadow," first published in *The New Yorker* of 17 August 1957, shortly after *The Strange Islands*, provides a perfect rejoinder to the speaker's argument here in the complementary qualities of the milkweed seed and the stone, the "two voices" of the poem.

22.   These lines are not included in the published text of the poem.

prophetic involvement seems to be impressively exhibited both by the act and the content of the speaker's proclamation.

However, the neat dichotomy between seed and stone does not quite ring true; as will become clear later in this analysis, the author does not intend that it should, but even on a first reading, certain elements might leave the reader uneasy. To begin with, the diction is unsatisfying. A certain prolixity intrudes itself in remarks ("as I have said," l. 88; "that is to say," l. 96; "namely," l. 105) which refer to the act of speaking itself, as though the speaker needs to draw attention to his activity. Moreover, the descriptions of the seed are generally more prosaic, perfunctory, even awkward than those concerning the stones. Even in the first verse paragraph, where this might not seem to be the case, the pattern of consonance ("seed," "said," "sod," as well as the reversed "hides") seems more a parody than a continuation of the intricate sound structure of the first variation (particularly in its dependence on the superfluous "as I have said"), and suffers by comparison with the patterns in the lines devoted to the stones ("river," "never," "cover," and the slant rhymes "will," "feel," "soil"). The overall impression created rhetorically is not of a voice in control of the material. Rather than a balanced contrast between seed and stone, the negative example makes more of an impression on the reader as it apparently has on the speaker.

Yet this negative synthesis is itself marked by flawed logic. Whereas the stones are initially described as totally inert, "inanimate," incapable of caring or feeling, in the second half of the variation they are invested with volition, desire: they want to be taken up and used by the forces of destruction. The implication is that there is a natural dynamic in the stone which finds its fulfillment in violence and disorder, an inversion of the seed's potency for growth. Not only is this second description incompatible with the first, it comes dangerously close to a kind of manichean dualism in its attitude toward creation, and calls into question the vision of sacramentality reached at the conclusion of the previous variation. What is at work here is an attitude of projection comparable to that found in the descriptions of the "blunt pine" and the "furious sun" of the first variation, though here the speaker is trying to distance himself from, rather than identify with, the object described. It is actually human intention, rather than some intrinsic quality in the stone itself, which makes it into a weapon.

The inadequacy of the argument is in fact suggested in the description itself. The participle "wanting" (ll. 102, 103), taken to mean "desiring" from its parallel to "waiting for" (l. 101), can also mean "lacking" -- in which case the lines would state that the stones do not possess either brains or eyes, do not hate growth or aim to kill. The ambiguity pits the overt meaning attributing purpose to the stone against a submerged meaning denying the possibility of any such intention. This ambiguity is compounded by the strange phrase "the medical eye/ That aims to kill. . ." The obvious association of a "medical eye" is with healing, not with killing, but the phrase, perhaps suggestive of "we murder to dissect," or even of the perversion of medical science in the Nazi death camps, is a reminder that what is morally neutral or even beneficial can be misused, an implication which subtly undermines the case against the stones.

Thus the comparison between seed and stone, while superficially convincing, is actually quite misleading: it reveals less about the realities described than about the confused state of mind of the speaker, who has attempted to teach what he has not sufficiently learned. Beneath the matter-of-fact presentation of the first, or "contemplative," part of the comparison can be discerned a sense of relief that the seed is not like the stones, a not quite expressed terror of being "alone by nature/ Or alone forever." But as the speaker must painfully come to realize, this simple separation of reality into living and dead, active and passive, while useful to a point, becomes if absolutized a profoundly dangerous distortion which drives a wedge between being and doing. Are inanimate things really alone by nature, alone forever, or are they not an integral part of a larger whole in which aloneness and interconnectedness are reconciled? By choosing the first alternative, an analytic, dissecting approach, the speaker opts for a dualistic view of reality rather than the holistic perspective of the second. It is a worldview of distinctions rather than conjunctions, which evaluates a thing not in its own identity and in its interrelations with the rest of reality, but by means of judgmental comparisons. Specifically, the contrast here seems to represent a subtle preference for doing over being, since the seed, though presently waiting, is still oriented toward activity. Underlying this evaluation is a fundamental mistrust of reality, an existential dread that to be still, simply to be, is to risk vanishing into that abyss where being is indistinguishable from nothingness: it is to be "alone by nature/ Or alone forever."[23] Because his trust is not deep enough, his embrace of be-ing not radical enough, the speaker thereby misperceives and misrepresents reality. His contemplative silence is defective, and consequently any

---

23. Merton later expressed this insight in "Rain and the Rhinoceros" thusly: "The contemplative life. . . must not be construed as an escape from time and matter, from social responsibility and from the life of sense, but rather, as an advance into solitude and the desert, a confrontation with poverty and the void, a renunciation of the empirical self, in the presence of death, and nothingness, in order to overcome the ignorance and error that spring from the fear of 'being nothing' " (*Raids on the Unspeakable*, pp. 17-18).

"prophetic" word of his will be distorted as well.

Thus results the flawed argument of the second, "active" half of the variation. Here too the concluding lines are especially problematic: "The stone has a sterile power/ To destroy cities, when hurled upon a prophet." The last phrase seems enigmatic, incongruous: the sentence would make perfect sense without it, a sense compatible with the earlier depiction of the stone as instrument of violence. As it now reads, the fate of the cities and that of the prophet are somehow linked, but how? Is the verse meant to identify the two, to express that solidarity between messenger and audience which was missing in the first treatment of this theme in Part I? Are the two acts simply contemporaneous, or is there a causal connection? If the speaker is alluding to the only explicit Scriptural reference to stoning prophets, the connection is not one of parallelism but of opposition, since it is the city which stones its prophets and so is left without vision, a condition which has its own destruction as the eventual consequence: "Jerusalem, Jerusalem, thou who killest the prophets, and stonest those who are sent to thee!" (Luke 13:34). Thus the apocalyptic mentality which the speaker seemed to have renounced in the second variation has subtly reinsinuated itself here. Implicitly identifying himself with the prophet, the speaker manages to suggest his own righteousness -- as target of the stones, the prophet can have none of the negative qualities associated with them. This seems to be an instance of projection in the clinical sense, a simultaneous denial and expression of the speaker's inner violence. While the equilibrium found at the conclusion of the previous variation seems to continue through the third section, the tensions and lack of coherence beneath the surface of the speaker's balanced but specious arguments portend an explosive disintegration of this tentative effort to assume the mantle of prophet. This is precisely what takes place in the fourth variation.

IV

This section[24] opens with a description of a storm reminiscent in its violence (and perhaps in its element of wish fulfillment as well) of Lear's speech on the heath:[25]

---

24. This section is missing in the published text, though ll. 116-119, 129-132, 135-140 are quoted by Lentfoehr in *Words and Silence* (pp. 31-32) as part of what she misleadingly refers to as a "first draft" of the poem (p. 29).

25. *King Lear*, III, ii, 1-9.

> Last night when the busting winds
> Buffeted the planets and the sun
> The sea came down. The world was bullied and drowned.
> Cities and churches fell. Such force
> The clouds of winter have when they come out and speak.
>   (ll. 110-114)

The cataclysmic scope of the tempest, along with the specification that it took place "last night," suggests the speaker is dealing, literally, with a nightmare. The vision of apocalypse rejected but not totally exorcised by the waking mind now bursts forth with all the fury of the Biblical flood, bringing cosmic upheaval and the world's destruction. This is the voice of the stormclouds, confirming prophecies of doom.

But the dream is far from over. The speaker himself appears, as commentator and participant:

> Well, this is my argument, of evening and of night,
> Of finding myself hurled, here, in the high wood
> Without a stone or a light
> A corner under a cliff, or any cover
> When the whole world is run over.   (ll. 115-119)

Initially "this is my argument" could be taken to mean that he regards these events as supportive evidence, confirmation of his own point of view, but it immediately becomes evident that his position, rhetorically and literally, is blown sky-high. He is not exempted from the storm's fury, but is subjected to the same buffeting as the rest of creation. The irony of the situation is signalled by his choice of vocabulary: it is not now the stone which is hurled upon the prophet, but the would-be prophet himself who is "hurled" by the winds, and who searches in vain for "any cover," even "a stone," the very object he had previously criticized for covering the fields. His "argument" now seems to refer more appropriately to the debate going on within the speaker between a tendency to be self-righteous and judgmental and an attitude of compassion for and identification with the world's ills.

The adequacy of the first stance is called further into question by the results of the storm:

> Dynamite and traffic and huge
> Wars are born in a forest valley
> Ruining the timber and the gorge.   (ll. 120-122)

The wish for a cataclysm to purify the world and enable it to begin afresh proves delusory: the storm does not end the cycle of human iniquity, but seems to spawn it anew, violence begetting violence. The inclusion of the apparently incongruous "traffic" here is particularly instructive: not only does it relate, as microcosm to macrocosm, to the image of the world being "run over" in the previous line, but it suggests, paradoxically (in the logic of dreams), the continuation of business as usual, and even lends the aura of normalcy to the dynamite and huge wars.

The nature and consequence of the storm force the speaker to come to terms with the basic issue underlying this phantasmagoria, the assumptions and expectations he has of God:

> In the strength of these storms
> Was God found? Was his decree
> Heavy in the vast tree without lights?
> Was it not His curse man-handled and rolled
> Black cedars with both fists? O, No
> I think it was not God.   (ll. 123-128)

The speaker's answer to his own questions represents a definite reliquishing of an image of God as cosmic avenger, setting things right by the sheer exercise of power. But the struggle to reach this conclusion is perceptible in the progression of the questions themselves. The first could legitimately be given either a positive or negative response, depending on the mode of presence considered (i.e., a "no" answer should not be construed to mean that there is a natural force independent of God). The second is both more abstract ("His decree") and more abstruse: the "vast tree without lights" might suggest the world-tree of myth, a Christmas tree *manque*, even the pine of Part I (blunted by the heaviness of the divine decree?), but it remains mysterious, and one could be excused for being unsure of the right answer. Only with the highly anthropomorphic imagery of the last question, in which the cedars[26] are "man-handled" (a particularly telling verb) not by "His decree" but by "His curse," is the matter clarified sufficiently to elicit a response, though even here the phrasing ("Was it not. . .") which normally calls for a positive answer, suggests the tenacity of the apocalyptic mentality even as it is rejected.

Of course the speaker's experience here parallels that of Elias on Mt. Horeb, where God was not present in the wind, or the earthquake, or the fire (3 Kings 19:11-12). The conclusion of the dream likewise has affinities with the divine epiphany in the still, small voice, the gentle breeze:

---

26. The suggestion that "Elias" is a sort of palinode in relation to some of Merton's earlier poetry is supported by the mention of "black cedars, bowing in the sleet" (l. 6) in the poem "Winter Afternoon" (from *Figures for an Apocalypse*), which concludes (ll. 18-22; *Figures*, pp. 80-81; *Collected Poems*, pp. 185-186):

> And oh! From some far rock some echo of your iron, December,
> Halts our slow steps, and calls us to the armored parapet
> Searching the flying skyline for some glare of prophecy.

> We thought we heard John-Baptist or Elias, there, on the dark hill
> Or else the angel with the trumpet of the Judgement.

> Only the wind bullied my sore ears
> Only the winter's trumpet boxed my sides and back
> Tumbled me with no bones broken
> Redfaced into the city of the just, half-frozen
> Until I sat, never forgetting
> The small voice, outside, on which the stars stand focused,
> Poised as on a clear center, with no thought of storms,
> Always balanced and never turned over, not upside
> Down but always balanced and still, untoppling on
> The One, Other voice differing from all storms and calms
> The Other, silent Voice,
> The perfectly True. (ll. 129-140)

There seems to be a sense in which the storm does, after all, function as an instrument of the divine will, though not in an apocalyptic fashion, since "Only the winter's trumpet" is heard, not that announcing the final Judgement. For the speaker is now carried from "the high wood" to "the city of the just," an eschatological image but not an apocalyptic one, since it is a final reality which is already present, in mystery, within time.[27] This change of scene signals an ironic reversal of expectations, as he comes to the city not to speak but to listen, not to act but to sit still, not as a righteous man to the unjust and confused but as an unjust and confused man to the righteous -- he is appropriately "redfaced," not only from the cold wind's buffeting but from shame and embarrassment at his pretensions to wisdom and his presumption to disseminate it.

It is into this setting, then, that the Horeb theophany of Elias, the encounter with the "small voice," the "clear center," is transposed. This experience is no less cosmic than the storm -- it is specified that the voice is "outside," not just a private, interior revelation but an awareness of universal order and harmony like Dante's final vision of "the Love that moves the sun and other stars" or the creation hymns of the Psalms, Job, and Second Isaiah.[28] This voice is not the opposite of the storm, but rather is beyond the distinction between storm and calm, act and stillness. It is the "One, Other voice," totally different from any other yet the One without which no other would exist; it is the "silent Voice" which transcends the neat dichotomies

27. The theme of the two cities is central to Merton's verse play, "The Tower of Babel," which immediately follows "Elias" in *The Strange Islands* (pp. 43-78; *Collected Poems*, pp. 247-273). The second epigraph, from Augustine's *City of God*, xiv, 28, contrasts the two kinds of love, *cupiditas* and *caritas*, which have built the two kinds of city, corresponding to the two halves of the play, PART I -- THE LEGEND OF THE TOWER, and PART II --THE CITY OF GOD. It should be noted that the figure of the prophet plays an important role in Part II by encouraging the exiles from Babylon to wait in hope for the City of God, but does not appear at all in the first half of the play, in which the tower rises and falls.

28. Dante, *Paradiso*, XXXIII, 145, and see Psalms 33:6, 147:4; Job 9:9, 38:7, 31-32; Isaiah 40:26. The first scene of Part II of "The Tower of Babel," entitled "Zodiac," uses the pattern of the constellations as a symbol of divine order (*The Strange Islands*, pp. 63-66; *Collected Poems*, pp. 261-263).

of human concepts, the "perfectly True" which both creates and reveals the ultimate meaningfulness of what is, from the stars to the human spirit. The series of participial phrases which make up the last six lines, most immediately taken as parallel with "focused" and therefore as describing the stars,[29] could also be in parallel with "forgetting" and thus refer to "I."[30] This is the goal, to be centered on the "perfectly True," to be "always balanced," in harmony with the Creator and the rest of creation, as the stars are. The process is reflected even in the structure of the verse, one long sentence which reaches its equilibrium, its balance, only in the final three lines, as the enjambments of "upside/ Down" and "untoppling on/ The One. . ." are succeeded by the end-stopped, ever more concise descriptions of the Voice, which are themselves finally absorbed into the silence.

This profound stillness with which the fourth variation concludes suggests the cathartic function of the dream. If the speaker's problems are not resolved, they have at least come to the surface where they can be confronted and dealt with.[31]. The storm, a manifestation not of divine wrath but of the speaker's own unacknowledged inner turmoil, suggests his own complicity in all that he opposed, his restless unwillingness to be still, his desire for sudden, violent, definitive eradication of the world's ills. Shaken by its force, he is freed by the storm's passing to become aware of God's presence in the order and clarity of the night sky, and to recognize that the same call to be what he has been created to be is addressed to him. This is the secret nexus of contemplation and action, the resolution of his dilemma. What now remains is the necessary but painful task of integrating this insight into his waking life.

V

Just how difficult a task this will be becomes evident in the fifth variation, in which the speaker is subjected to devastating criticism, which in turn prompts even more ruthless self-criticism. While the speaker seems aware only of how flawed his perceptions and motivations have been,

---

29. Here there is a direct reversal of the final stanza of "In the Ruins of New York" (Part VI of "Figures for an Apocalypse"), which begins "And we are full of fear, and muter than the upside-down stars/ That limp in the lame waters" (*Figures*, p. 25; *Collected Poems*, p. 146).

30. Lentfoehr (pp. 31-32) states that these lines modify "voice" (l. 133), which seems grammatically impossible, since "voice" (l. 138) is object for the last participle, "untoppling on."

31. The revelatory role of dreams is also central to another poem from the same collection, entitled "Nocturne" (*The Strange Islands*, p. 23; *Collected Poems*, p. 230).

in fact this experience of spiritual destitution represents not a regression but a deeper purification, a more radical death to self, which is the unavoidable prelude to any authentic enlightenment.

The section begins with the unexpected arrival of rain:

> Here where in the summertime no waters
> Covered the shale, and where October
> Filled the creek with leaves and ruins
> Now voluble streams, sent on their perfect
> Mission, announce the fate of December.
> Where do so many waters come from on an empty hill?
> Rain we had despaired of, rain
> Which is sent from somewhere else, descended
> To fix an exhausted mountain.   (ll. 141-149)[32]

This is the counterpart in the waking world of the dream-storm, but with an effect as profoundly different as the Biblical scene it evokes, not the storm on Horeb but the story of Elias on Mt. Carmel in 3 Kings 18, when the long drought is brought to an end after Elias' contest with the prophets of Baal. But unlike Elias, the speaker is not ready for the rain, not waiting with the patient expectation of a person of faith. His limited perspective, which saw only the "empty hill" and did not extend beyond what he could see, to "somewhere else," was inadequate to the situation.

Ironically, it is the waters themselves, "sent on their perfect/ Mission" (transmitting the "perfectly True" voice of the previous variation) which function prophetically here: they "announce the fate of December," which is of course to die and to be reborn as the new year. They also have a word for the speaker:

> Listen to the waters, if possible,
> And discern the words "False prophet"
> False prophet! So much better is the water's message,
> So much more confident than our own. "It is quite sure
> You are a false prophet, so 'Go back'
> (You have not had the patience of a rock or tree)
> Go back into the cities. They want to receive you
> Because you are not sent to them. You are a false prophet."
> (ll. 150-157)[33]

The sound of the waters, channel of affirmation earlier in the poem, becomes the voice of condemnation, as the speaker in his lack of faith and

---

32. Lines 141-145 are the last of those omitted from the printed text of the poem.

33. In both the typescript and the printed text, the quotation marks are placed before "So" (l. 152), which could not have been spoken by the water since it contrasts "the water's message" to "our own." This sentence must be the speaker's own words (cf. "we had despaired," l. 147). I have therefore emended by placing the quotation marks at the beginning of the next sentence, in which the speaker is addressed in the second person.

hope is identified not with Elias but with the false prophets of Baal (note the change to first person plural in ll. 147, 153). As the pagan prophets gashed themselves and called out in ecstatic frenzy in an effort to force their god's hand on Mt. Carmel, the speaker "had despaired" of the rain because it did not arrive according to his timetable -- he lacked "the patience of a rock or tree" (of stone and seed, now united in witness against him). Unlike the rain, which "is sent" and has a "message," the speaker is "not sent" and has, we later learn (l. 177), "no message." His identity as false prophet refers first perhaps to his "oracle" in the third variation (not "thus saith the Lord" but "as I have said"), but more immediately to his unexpressed but obvious desire to speak, to act, to assume a prophetic role, which would be favorably received not because he proclaims the truth but because he articulates his listeners' own attitudes, just as the false prophets of the Lord in 3 Kings 22 tell King Ahab what he wants to hear -- predictions of success, assurances of visible results. Thus the repeated command to "go back," an ironic echo of the words to Elias on Horeb, "Go, and return on thy way" (3 Kings 19:15), is not a summons to prophesy but a caustic directive to rejoin those whose alienation resembles his own.

The speaker would be so acceptable, and so useless, for people in the cities because both his life and theirs are marked by the same divided consciousness, the same effort to affirm that one is alive by compulsive activity rather than a willingness to accept life as gift:[34]

> Go back where everyone, in heavy hours,
> Is of a different mind, and each is his own burden,
> And each mind is its own division
> With sickness for diversion and war for
> Business reasons. Go where the divided
> Cannot stand to be too well. For then they would be held
> Responsible for their own misery.   (ll. 158-164)

This description of fragmentation and depersonalization is both strikingly modern and thoroughly Scriptural: "each is his own burden" suggests the isolation and individualism which refuses Paul's admonition to "bear one another's burdens" (Galatians 6:2); the mind which is "its own division" recalls the Scriptural theme of *dipsychia*, or double-mindedness, as in the description of a"a double-minded man, unstable in all his ways" (James 1:8); the divided who "cannot stand to be too well" recall the words of Jesus that "a house divided against itself cannot stand" (Matthew 12:25),

---

34.   This same point is made in "The Tower of Babel," when Raphael says of the tower-builders, "Activity is their substitute for faith. Instead of believing in themselves, they seek to convince themselves, by their activity, that they exist" (*The Strange Islands*, p. 50; *Collected Poems*, p. 251).

with perhaps a play on their own mistrust of be-ing ("well" can be read both adjectivally, referring back to "sickness" two lines earlier, and adverbially, with "to be" taken in an absolute sense).[35] It is a world of inert passivity masked by frenetic and purposeless motion, a world where doing has no relation to being because the demands of freedom, the need to take responsibility for one's actions, have been avoided and renounced.[36] The interior division and alienation give rise to the macrocosmic counterpart of war, the rationale for which is busyness as well as business. Recognition of the dignity of the person, which depends not on what one does but on who one is, has disappeared with the loss of contemplative awareness, and requires the restoration of that awareness for its own return. This is the world to which the speaker is encouraged to "go back."

Despite his physical separation, the speaker acknowledges his own complicity in the world just described. His confession exemplifies a change from condemnation of others to self-condemnation, a surrender of all claims to self-righteousness:

> And I have been a man without silence,
> A man without patience, with too many
> Questions. I have blamed God
> Thinking to blame only men
> And defend Him Who does not need to be defended.
> I have blamed ("defended") Him for Whom the wise stones
> (Stones I lately condemned)
> Waited in the patient
> Creek that is now wet and clean of all ruins.   (ll. 165-173)

Here the failure of prophecy is clearly a consequence of a failure of contemplation. His lack of silence means that words become not vehicles of God's Word, but a means of avoiding solitude; they function as a substitute for silence, rather than an epiphany of silence.[37] This lack of interior stillness is mirrored by outward impatience, dissatisfaction with the way the world is going, which leads in time to questioning and to more words, attempts to answer the questions in one's own way. The word "blame" here is the key to distinguishing the speaker's words from authentic prophecy.

---

35. This theme is, of course, central to "The Tower of Babel," in which the appearance of unified effort masks the divisiveness which will cause the tower to fall. See especially *The Strange Islands*, pp. 50-51; *Collected Poems*, pp. 251-252.

36. Again, "The Tower of Babel" provides an appropriate gloss: Raphael says, "Their ambition is only the occasion for a failure they certainly seek. But they require that this failure come upon them, as it were, out of the stars. They want to blame their ruin on fate, and still have the secret satisfaction of ruining themselves" (*The Strange Islands*, p. 50; *Collected Poems*, p. 251).

37. The second scene of Part I of "The Tower of Babel," entitled "The Trial," focuses on the use and misuse of language. The captain accuses words of being "in league with sense,/ Order and even silence" (*The Strange Islands*, p. 56; *Collected Poems*, p. 255), and as the scene ends, silence is crucified as Falsehood is acclaimed as Lord of Babylon (*The Strange Islands*, p. 62; *Collected Poems*, p. 260).

· The prophet is called to strip away illusions and show a situation as it actually is -- to speak the truth -- so as to make conversion possible. To assign blame for a situation is a defensive reaction, an attempt to satisfy one's own desire for a psychologically acceptable explanation of what is wrong, usually in such a way as to protect oneself from any culpability. It is more interested in analyzing a set of circumstances than in changing them: in fact it indicates a fundamental doubt in the possibility of change. It is the refuge of a static, deterministic perspective which divides people into "seeds" and "stones," the quick and the dead. It is the voice of hopelessness, and so finally, as the speaker now realizes, a denial of the power of God Himself, who becomes the ultimate object of blame. Like the people themselves, the speaker has refused to consider them truly "responsible," capable of responding to their situation. However similar to the prophetic stance it may superficially appear, his attitude is directly counter to it: it is the voice of despair.

To this attitude the "wise stones" become the countersign, the emblem of absolute availability,[38] being so grounded in God, in reality, that they are continually open to *kairos*, to the right time of redemption and transformation: they were waiting not for "the military hand" (l. 101) but for the divine act of cleansing and restoration. They suggest in particular the desecrated altar rebuilt by Elias on Carmel at the proper time:

> Elias said to all the people: Come ye unto me. And the people coming near unto him, he repaired the altar of the Lord, that was broken down. And he took twelve stones according to the number of the tribes of the sons of Jacob, to whom the word of the Lord came, saying: Israel shall be thy name. And he built with the stones an altar to the name of the Lord.
> (3 Kings 18:30-32)

Here the repair of the altar, whose stones correspond to the tribes of Israel, clearly represents the possibility of the restoration of Israel's identity as the People of God, who are invited by Elias to "come unto me." But in the speaker's message of blame there is no "come unto me," as there was no rebuilt altar in his condemnation of the stones. But with the rain, sign of renewed life, comes the recognition of his self-righteousness and the confession of his sin. As always in the Biblical view, this admission of failure, the willingness to be "held/ Responsible," is the indispensible prerequisite

---

38. The symbolism of stones as building blocks recurs throughout *The Strange Islands*: see the words of the Prophet on the City of God in "The Tower of Babel: "But you, my brothers, and I are stones in the wall of this city"; also "Early Mass," l. 20: "These mended stones shall build Jerusalem"; and the entire poem "In Silence," which begins, "Be still/ Listen to the stones of the wall/ Be silent, they try/ To speak your// Name. Listen/ To the living walls" (*The Strange Islands*, pp. 66, 89, 87; *Collected Poems*, pp. 263, 282, 281).

to further spiritual growth.[39]

Nevertheless, this variation ends with what seems to be an admission of defeat and the abandonment of any claims of a prophetic dimension to his vocation:

> So now, if I were to return
> To my own city (yes my own city), I would be
> Neither accepted nor rejected.
> For I have no message,
> I would be lost together with the others.   (ll. 174-178)

Recognizing his spiritual kinship with those he had desired to preach to (in "my own city"), the speaker seems to renounce all activity: he has no message, nothing to bring to "the others," because he suffers from the same spiritual sickness as they. So the choice seems to be simply to abandon them to their own lostness so as to save himself from the same fate. But it must be stressed once again that this is not a choice of contemplation over action, but a renunciation of action due to a failure of contemplation; he is not choosing one or the other but confessing his lack of both. The connection between action and contemplation is actually being affirmed here: genuine prophecy is seen to be impossible unless rooted in contemplative union with God.

It may appear that this variation, together with the last, represents a regression, a failure to retain and deepen the sense of the divine presence experienced earlier. But the journey within the self represented by the dream, and the self-condemnation which follows, do not invalidate or cancel out the revelatory moment: rather, they plant it deeper in the soul. The process of letting-go which has occurred on the more superficial levels of the personality has to penetrate to the very core of a person's being. This process is painful precisely because it reveals how deeply the roots of pride, fear and self-love extend, and what a death is required to extirpate them. They have become so much "me" that to destroy them seems to mean being destroyed oneself. It is this more radical surrender which the speaker is now driven to make; yet by the paradoxical logic of spiritual growth, the renunciation of his own projects, his own will, his own image of himself, will prove to be the crucial step in discovering the authentic and lasting fulfillment of an identity at once contemplative and prophetic.

---

39. In *Thoughts in Solitude* (New York: Farrar, Straus & Cudahy, 1958), "written in 1953 and 1954" (p. 11) though not published for four years, Merton discusses this topic: "A false conscience is a false god, a god which says nothing because it is dumb and which does nothing because it has no power. It is a mask through which we utter oracles to ourselves, telling ourselves false prophecies, giving ourselves whatever answer we want to hear. . . . Hence the beginning of wisdom is the confession of sin. This confession gains for us the mercy of God. It makes the light of His truth shine in our conscience, without which we cannot avoid sin" (pp. 77-78).

VI

It is precisely the frustration of efforts to reach the city at the conclusion of the fifth variation which serves to realign the speaker with Elias, who likewise sought after his victory on Carmel to return to the city only to find himself forced by Jezebel's threats to flee into the wilderness, where "he requested for his soul that he might die, and said: It is enough for me, Lord. Take away my soul, for I am no better than my fathers. And he cast himself down, and slept in the shadow of the juniper tree" (3 Kings 19:4-5). This is, of course, the situation in which we find Elias at the beginning of the poem, compelled to renounce his own plans, his own itinerary, in order to become available to the divine presence and will. Thus it is only at this point that the speaker is truly ready to make the experience of Elias his own. It is quite appropriate, then, that the final section quite literally begins as a variation of the first:

> Under the blunt pine
> I who am not sent
> Remain. The pathway dies,
> The journey has begun.
> Here the bird abides
> And sings on top of the forgotten
> Storm. The ground is warm.
> He sings no particular message.
> His hymn has one pattern, no more planned,
> No less perfectly planned
> And no more arbitrary
> Than the pattern in the seed, the salt,
> The snow, the cell, the drop of rain.   (ll. 179-191)

The most obvious change here is that "I," the speaker, is now present beneath the pine; but equally significant is the fact that this will be the last time that a subjective reference occurs in the poem: the speaker appears only to disappear, to "be lost" in a much more profound, and salvific, sense than the rootless alienation which would await him in the city. Remaining in stillness, beneath the pine, he is nevertheless said to begin a journey, one in
• • which further paradoxes are resolved: the loss of self and the discovery of true identity, freedom and the divine plan, silence and speech, contemplation and action.

As in the opening variation, the focus shifts to the mysterious bird, which once again serves as a revelatory sign. The negative connotations of "I who am not sent/ Remain," a carry-over from the previous section, are countered by the parallel with the bird, which still "abides," and is further said to sing "on top of the forgotten/ Storm," a suggestion not only that the upheavals of the past are over, but that the bird, like the stars in the fourth variation, was able to transcend the storm because of its own inner calm. But more crucial is the statement that "he sings no particular message." Here indeed is the beginning of the resolution to the problem with which the speaker has wrestled throughout the poem. For the bird has no "message" in the sense that its song is not something extrinsic, "added on" to its essential nature as bird, not something produced to influence or impress the outside world; it is simply the outward expression of its own deepest identity: there is no division, no distinction, between what it is and what it does. The vision here is comparable to that found in Hopkins' sonnet "As kingfishers catch fire":

> Each mortal thing does one thing and the same:
> Deals out that being indoors each one dwells;
> Selves -- goes itself; *myself* it speaks and spells,
> Crying What I do is me: for that I came.[40]

By being itself, by living out its own freedom, the bird is the incarnation of its hymn of praise, and the hymn the self-expression, in the most profound sense, of the singer. The pattern of its song is not imposed from without but is a manifestation, an epiphany, of the bird's God-given identity, comparable, despite its classification as "activity," with the structure found in "the seed, the salt,/ The snow, the cell, the drop of rain."

Thus the song of the bird not only reveals the bird's own identity, but draws the listener into the mystery of creation as a whole; suddenly the song is part of a chorus of voices, in which spontaneity and order are united, specificity and universality are one:

> (Snow says: I have my own pattern;
> Rain says: no arbitrary plan!

---

40. *The Poems of Gerard Manley Hopkins*, ed. W. H. Gardner and N. H. MacKenzie, 4th ed. (London: Oxford University Press, 1967), p. 90. Hopkins was the catalyst for Merton's conversion and was to be the subject of his doctoral dissertation: see *The Seven Storey Mountain* (New York: Harcourt, Brace, 1948), pp. 215, 255. Echoes of this sonnet can be found in "Canticle for the Blessed Virgin" from *Figures for an Apocalypse*: "Then will obedience bring forth new Incarnations/ Shining to God with the features of His Christ" (ll. 75-76, *Figures*, p. 46; *Collected Poems*, p. 163) reworks Hopkins' "Christ plays in ten thousand places,/ Lovely in limbs, and lovely in eyes not his/ To the Father through the features of men's faces" (ll. 12-14), as does "Hagia Sophia": "He speaks to us gently in ten thousand things, in which His light is one fulness and one Wisdom" (*Collected Poems*, p. 366, noted by Lentfoehr, p. 49); the line "All her goings graces" in "The Ladies of Tlatilco" section of *The Geography of Lograire* (*Collected Poems*, p. 485) is an ironic allusion to Hopkins' "the just man justices;/ Keeps grace: that keeps all his goings graces" (ll. 9-10). The movement from external objects to "the just man" in the sonnet is paralleled in "Elias" by the shift from natural objects to "the free man" (ll. 199 ff.). Both Hopkins and Merton were strongly influenced by the thirteenth-century Franciscan Duns Scotus, especially his ideas on the sacramentality of the natural world and *haecceitas*, individual identity. For the importance of Scotus to Hopkins, see John Pick, *Gerard Manley Hopkins: Priest and Poet* (London: Oxford University Press, 1942), pp. 32-37, 156-159; in *A Reader's Guide to Gerard Manley Hopkins* (Ithaca: Cornell University Press, 1981), Norman H. MacKenzie says of "As kingfishers catch fire": "This sonnet contains the most striking poetic illustrations of Hopkins' Scotist theory of the inscapes to be found among natural and man-made things" (p. 148). Merton studied Scotus at Columbia with Daniel Walsh and St. Bonaventure's with Fr. Philotheus Boehner, and the long sections on Scotus in the original manuscript of *The Seven Storey Mountain* (omitted from the published text) indicated "that Merton was under the spell of Duns Scotus" (Mott, p. 231).

> River says: I go my own way.
> Bird says: I am the same.
> The pine tree says also:
> Not compulsion plants me in my place,
> No, not compulsion!)   (ll. 192-198)

Here each of these natural objects testifies to its own *logos*, that principle of harmony implanted within each as its deepest identity; together they provide a revelation of cosmic freedom, realized by each in its own particular way but pointing to a common ground of absolute Freedom which coincides with absolute Order in the divine Logos, the creative Word which called them into being.

In his ability to "hear" these voices and to resonate with their disclosures, the speaker shows himself to be possessed of a kind of contemplative awareness, what Merton, borrowing from the Greek Fathers, elsewhere calls "*theoria physica*, or 'natural contemplation,' which arrives at God through the inner spiritual reality (the *logos*) of the created thing."[41] Here the theme of the sacramentality of the created world receives its most explicit affirmation.[42] But he recognizes further that these creatures, in which the divine wisdom shines forth, provide a kind of paradigm of integration. Simply by being themselves, truly and completely, they are at once contemplative and prophetic, living hymns of praise to the Creator and witnesses to the divine will for all creation -- including the human, as he has now come to realize:

> The free man is not alone as busy men are
> But as birds are. The free man sings
> Alone as universes do. Built
> Upon his own inscrutable pattern
> Clear, unmistakable, not invented by himself alone
> Or for himself, but for the universe also.   (ll. 199-204)

In these lines the central dilemma of the entire poem, the tension between being and doing, contemplation and prophecy, is not so much solved as it is

---

41. "Poetry and Contemplation: A Reappraisal," *Literary Essays*, p. 347; this passage is not found in the 1947 version of the essay (see above, note 17). Merton discusses this same concept in "The Inner Experience," the radical revision and expansion of his 1948 essay, *What is Contemplation*? Merton left instructions that this work, dating from 1959, was not to be published as a book, evidently because he did not consider it to be in final form, but it appeared, slightly abridged, in *Cistercian Studies*, 18-19 (1983-1984). For his discussion of *theoria physike*, see *Cistercian Studies*, 18:4 (1983): pp. 297-298.

42. In "Poetry and Contemplation" (another passage added to the original), Merton writes: "But the true poet is always akin to the mystic because of the 'prophetic' intuition by which he sees the spiritual reality, the inner meaning of the object he contemplates, which makes that concrete reality not only a thing worthy of admiration in itself, but also and above all makes it a *sign of God*. All good Christian poets are then contemplatives in the sense that they see God everywhere in His creation and in His mysteries, and behold the created world as filled with signs and symbols of God. To the true Christian poet, the whole world and all the incidents of life tend to be sacraments -- signs of God, signs of His love working in the world" (*Literary Essays*, p. 345).

exposed as a pseudo-problem, resulting from a misunderstanding of both the nature of authentic solitude and that of genuine prophetic speech.[43] To be truly alone ("as birds are") has nothing to do with isolation or alienation -- these are traits rather of those whose frantic activity makes community impossible. The real opposition is not between solitude and communion or between contemplation and action, but between "busy men" who strive to invest their lives with meaning through their business, and "the free man" who is free precisely because he is aware that his meaning is already present as gift, one that integrates him into a larger whole. The free man is "alone" because he identifies with all that is, in a solitude which is not exclusive but inclusive, an experience not of separation but of participation; thus he "sings/ Alone as universes do."[44] Here the dualistic perspective which marked the third variation has given way to a holistic one, which suggests a healing of both interior and external divisions.

But the very structure of the lines serves to stress not only that the "free man sings/ *Alone*" but that the "free man *sings.*" Like the bird, the human person has the capacity, in Hopkins' phrase, to "deal out that being indoors each one dwells." Authentic self-expression (which includes, but is not limited to, artistic expression) is a constitutive dimension of human selfhood. The dichotomy between being and doing does not exist for one who is truly free. Thus in the deliberately fragmentary sentence which follows, the participle "Built" modifies equally well the free man and his song, since the second is the outward articulation of the first, the expressed *logos* of true identity.[45] Yet the song, like his very being, is "not invented by himself alone"; it is given in the act of creation by the divine Logos, the Word of God, yet paradoxically this makes it not less but more his own: the task of human freedom is to actualize, to incarnate, the true self eternally

---

43. In "The Inner Experience," Merton writes, "One of the strange laws of the contemplative life is that in it you do not sit down and solve problems: you bear with them until they somehow solve themselves. Or until life itself solves them for you. Usually the solution consists in a discovery that they exist only insofar as they were inseparably connected with your own illusory exterior self." This passage, from the second page of the manuscript, is not included in the version printed in *Cistercian Studies*, but is quoted by William H. Shannon in *Thomas Merton's Dark Path: The Inner Experience of a Contemplative* (New York: Farrar, Straus & Giroux, 1981), p. 114.

44. See the conclusion of "Notes for a Philosophy of Solitude," in *Disputed Questions*, p. 207: "But the deep 'I' of the spirit, of solitude and of love, cannot be 'had,' possessed, developed, perfected. It can only *be*, and *act* according to deep inner laws which are not of man's contriving, but which come from God. They are the Laws of the Spirit, who, like the wind, blows where He wills. This inner 'I,' who is always alone, is always universal: for in this inmost 'I' my own solitude meets the solitude of every other man and the solitude of God. Hence it is beyond division, beyond limitation, beyond selfish affirmation. It is only this inmost and solitary 'I' that truly loves with the love and spirit of Christ. This 'I' is Christ Himself, living in us: and we, in Him, living in the Father." For a discussion of the evolution of this essay, much of which (though not this passage) dates back to 1955, see Richard A. Cashen, *Solitude in the Thought of Thomas Merton* (Kalamazoo: Cistercian Publications, 1981), pp. 29-31.

45. The distinction between immanent and expressed *logos* goes back to the Stoics, and was used by the early Fathers to explain the relation between Father and Son in the Trinity; see J. N. D. Kelly, *Early Christian Doctrines*, 5th ed. (San Francisco: Harper & Row, 1978), pp. 18-19, 95-101.

known and loved by God. In the mystery of divine-human synergy, the song is completely God's and completely his. The more freely one acts, the more one conforms to "his own inscrutable pattern" of identity, and by so doing points toward the Source and Ground of that identity. Merton's essay "In Silentio," written at about the same time as the poem, provides the best commentary on these lines:

> Then, in the deep silence, wisdom begins to sing her unending, sunlit inexpressible song: the private song she sings to the solitary soul. It is his own song and hers -- the unique, irreplaceable song that each soul sings for himself with the unknown Spirit, as he sits on the doorstep of his own being, the place where his existence opens out into the abyss of God. It is the song that each of us must sing, the song God has composed Himself, that He may sing it within us. It is the song which, if we do not listen to it, will never be sung. And if we do not join with God in singing this song, we will never be fully real: for it is the song of our own life welling up like a stream out of the very heart of God.[46]

But the song represents not only the synthesis of being and doing, and of the divine and the human. Because personal identity is grounded in communion with the whole of reality, its outward expression resonates with the needs and hopes of others: the free man lives, and sings, not for himself alone but "for the universe also." Since this concern for the wider world is not something extrinsic, but constitutive of the free man's identity, there is a quality which can be called prophetic built into his song. But it is now clear that the true prophet is not one who is preoccupied with results, who calculates the consequences of his words, but simply one who lives out his pattern, who sings the song given him by God, and leaves the effects in God's hands. He does not depend upon his "message" to affirm, still less to create, his identity; rather the words are the expression of that which is created and affirmed by Another:

> Nor does he make it his business to be recognized
> Or care to have himself found out
> As if some special subterfuge were needed
> To get himself known for who he is.   (ll. 205-208)

Again the essay "In Silentio" provides an apt gloss:

> To understand that one has nothing special to say is suddenly to become free with a liberty which makes speech and silence equally easy. What one says will be something that has probably been said before. One need not trouble about being heard: the thing that is being said has been heard

---

46. This text was published as an introduction to a collection of photographs with accompanying quotations in *Silence in Heaven: A Book of the Monastic Life* (New York: Studio Publications, 1956); the quoted passage is from p. 24; a somewhat shortened and revised version of the essay is found in *Seasons of Celebration* (New York: Farrar, Straus & Giroux, 1965), pp. 204-215.

before. One ceases to depend on being heard, or thought of. And then
suddenly, one realizes that he has spoken, in the past, as if speech and
communication gave him a real existence. Speech has only served us as a
protection against the secret terror of not existing!
Once the illusion is clear, a man is delivered from the necessity to speak in
his own defence, and therefore speaks only for his brother's comfort.[47]

Thus solitude excludes not speech, but the misuse of words to provide a
spurious reassurance of one's own significance, or correctness, or very
existence. To be free is to be liberated from this dependence on the
opinions, even the recognition, of others, and so to be empowered to
speak on their behalf. Such are the roots of any genuine prophecy.

This meditation on the nature of the free man's song is followed by a
consideration of the free man's journey, with its obvious pertinence to the
speaker's situation at the beginning of the final variation:

> The free man does not float
> On the tides of his own expedition
> Nor is he sent on ventures as busy men are,
> Bound to an inexorable result:
> But like the birds or lilies
> He seeks first the Kingdom, without care.   (ll. 209-214)

Here two models of human achievement are rejected as incompatible with
genuine freedom, that of autonomous individualism which glories in its
own independence, and that of external conformism which requires for
success the attainment of some predetermined result. The futility of either
project is evident from the contradictions intrinsic to each: the image of
floating on the tides suggests the degree of dependence involved in the
most independent of expeditions, while the riskiness of the busy men's
"ventures" indicates how precarious and uncertain the achievement of "an
inexorable result" actually is. In comparison with the second we are better
able to see in what sense the speaker is "not sent," while he cannot like the
first simply invent his own path and choose his own destination. The
alternative to both is to seek the Kingdom of God. Here the "sacramental"
teaching of the natural world becomes explicitly related to the message of
the Gospel. As birds and lilies (and "the seed, the salt,/ The snow, the cell,
the drop of rain. . ."), simply by being themselves, help to realize the reign
of God, so the journey to true selfhood and to the Kingdom are one and the
same. This means that the journey is not primarily an external one, for the
kingdom is present insofar as a person is conformed to the will of God, the
image of Christ:

---

47. *Silence in Heaven*, p. 27; this passage is not found in the version published in *Seasons of Celebration*.

> Nor need the free man remember
> Any street or city, or keep campaigns
> In his head, or countries for that matter
> Or any other economy.   (ll. 215-218)

There can be no map which charts a course to the Kingdom, no campaigns (political or military) which can seize it, no economy (both in the etymological sense of "household rules," limited or particular instructions, and in the more common sense of wealth as a goal or source of satisfaction) which provides the key to apprehending it. The Kingdom is the beyond within, and can be reached only by losing the superficial self in order to be found in God.

At this point the final recapitulation begins, and Elias, now inclusive of the speaker, re-emerges as the paradigm of the "free man":

> Under the blunt pine
> Elias becomes his own geography
> (Supposing geography to be necessary at all),
> Elias becomes his own wild bird, with God in the center,
> His own wide field which nobody owns,
> His own pattern, surrounding the Spirit
> By which he is himself surrounded:
> For the free man's road has neither beginning nor end.   (ll. 219-226)

In these climactic lines, which critic George Woodcock considers to be "among the best poetry -- and the most moving -- that Merton ever wrote,"[48] all distinctions between internal and external, between seeker and goal, subject and object, even in a sense between the human and the divine are transcended in a luminous encounter with Reality beyond limitation. While a direct infusion of Oriental wisdom is perhaps unlikely in a poem dating from 1954, a comparison of Elias under the pine with the Buddha under the bo-tree is nevertheless suggestive, for what is described, or rather intimated, here, is surely an experience of enlightenment, in which utter emptiness and destitution suddenly reveals itself as total fullness.[49]

The experience is first of all that of personal unification. Not only is the journey of Elias an interior one, it is a journey taken by being still, for his goal is nothing other than to be who he is. Elias is his own goal, his own way, his own geography.[50] There is nowhere he need go, no time he need wait,

---

48. Woodcock, p. 76.

49. In his discussion of "Elias," which he erroneously assigns to 1949, Woodcock writes, "Merton may already have begun his fruitful meeting of minds with Lao Tzu and Chuang Tzu, for what he says might well have been written by a Taoist poet" (p. 76).

50. The image of geography is important for Merton's poetry from the epigraph to *Early Poems (1940-1942)* (published in 1971): "Geography comes to an end,/ Compass has lost all earthly north,/

for the realization of authentic identity is constrained by no spatial or temporal limitations.[51] But this act of being is in no way exclusive. There is no longer an observer to be distinguished from what is observed, for the self-conscious subject, the empirical self who "has" experiences, has disappeared. Elias simply is, and thereby, with an immediacy ungraspable by reflection, is united to, identified with, all else that is. His "geography" is both nowhere and everywhere: it encompasses all reality, all being, because the transcendent self, the true self, is not found through a process of differentiation but by an existential awareness of unity.[52] Its own being opens out onto and participates in all being in that "deep contemplative awareness of reality" described near the conclusion of "The Inner Experience":

> The contemplative is . . . one who, being perfectly unified in himself, and recollected in the center of his own humility, enters into contact with reality by an immediacy that forgets the division between subject and object. In a certain sense, by losing himself, and by forgetting himself as an ˙ ˙ ˙ object of reflection, he finds himself and all other reality together.[53]

Yet this embrace of being in general is not to be construed merely as an annihilation of uniqueness and specificity. Since each creature has its own inimitable way of expressing the act of being, what is most universal is also, by a mysterious coincidence of opposites, most particular. Thus Elias identifies not only with the landscape in general but with specific elements of that landscape, the "wild bird" and the "wide field," symbols throughout the poem, respectively, of the congruence of inner identity and outward expression and of unity as complementarity (i.e., seed and stone). Linked not only by the assonance/consonance of their adjectives but by

---

Horizons have no meaning/ Nor roads an explanation" (*Collected Poems*, p. 2; these are the first four lines of the final poem of the collection, "Sacred Heart 2," p. 24), to the posthumously published long poem, *The Geography of Lograire* (1969). Particularly interesting for comparison with "Elias" is "Song: Contemplation," from *Figures for an Apocalypse*: II. 30-32 read, "For suddenly we have forgotten your geography,/ Old nature, and your map of prey,/ And know no more the low world scourged with travelling," and the poem concludes with the arrival of the Spirit, not, as in "Elias," to surround and be surrounded, but to seize the poet in His talons (l. 41) and separate him spatially from "the drag of earth" (l. 43) so that he might "Trample the white, appalling stratosphere" (l. 47; *Figures*, p. 41; *Collected Poems*, pp. 158-159).

51. See *Thoughts in Solitude*, p. 96: "The lightning flashes from east to west, illuminating the whole horizon and striking where it pleases and at the same instant the infinite liberty of God flashes in the depths of that man's soul, and he is illumined. At that moment he sees that though he seems to be in the middle of his journey, he has already arrived at the end. For the life of grace on earth is the beginning of the life of glory. Although he is a traveller in time, he has opened his eyes, for a moment, in eternity." See also Merton's statement, "In prayer we discover what we already have. You start where you are and you deepen what you already have, and you realize that you are already there"; quoted by David Steindl-Rast in "Man of Prayer," in *Thomas Merton, Monk: A Monastic Tribute*, ed. Patrick Hart (New York: Sheed & Ward, 1974), p. 90.

52. See "Notes for a Philosophy of Solitude": "His solitude . . . does not set him apart from them in contrast and self-affirmation. It affirms nothing. It is at the same time empty and universal. He is one, not by virtue of separation but by virtue of inner spiritual unity. And this inner unity is at the same time the inner unity of all" (*Disputed Questions*, p. 196).

53. *Cistercian Studies*, 19:4 (1984), pp. 343-344.

the chiastic pattern of their modifiers ("wild" correlates with "nobody owns"; "wide" and "at the center" are both spatial), the paired images recall above all their earlier appearance together in the refrain of the opening variation:

> "Where the fields end
> Thou shalt be My friend.
> Where the bird is gone
> Thou shalt be My son."   (ll. 22-25; 47-50)

In these concluding lines, the questions raised by that quatrain, which are of course questions of "geography," at last receive their answer. Where the fields end, where the bird is gone, is nowhere, the pointless center which opens out on the fathomless abyss of divine love. Elias becomes his own wild bird because he too is centered on God, his own wide field (in which is hidden the treasure of the Kingdom) because to him is given the absolute freedom of absolute dependence on God: this is the essence of the divine friendship, the divine sonship promised earlier. Because the center of the self is not the self but God, to discover one's true center is to pass beyond the self without leaving the self: "If I penetrate to the depths of my own existence and my own present reality, the indefinable 'am' that is myself in its deepest roots, then through this deep center I pass into the infinite 'I Am' which is the very Name of the Almighty."[54]

This then is the "pattern" of mutual indwelling, mutual abiding, which is the most comprehensive expression of Elias' identity and vocation. To be "surrounding the Spirit/ By which he is himself surrounded" suggests first of all the ultimate reason why the journey inward to self and outward to the world is one and the same: being and doing, contemplation and action, lead both from and to "the Spirit [which] fills the world, is all-embracing" (Wisdom 1:7). But it also suggests that the "geography" which Elias "becomes" is finally nothing less than the infinite fullness of the divine Trinity in which he finds himself, which he finds within himself. It is the geography, the pattern, of the great prayer in the Epistle to the Ephesians:

> that he may grant you from his glorious riches to be strengthened with power through his Spirit unto the progress of the inner man; and to have Christ dwelling through faith in your hearts; so that, being rooted and grounded in love, you may be able to comprehend with all the saints what is the breadth and length and height and depth, and to know Christ's love which surpasses knowledge, in order that you may be filled unto all the fullness of God. (Ephesians 3:16-19)[55]

---

54. *Thoughts in Solitude*, p. 70.

55. Merton quotes and comments on this passage as presenting "a full and profound picture of the idea of contemplation that fills the New Testament everywhere" in "The Inner Experience," *Cistercian Studies*, 18:3 (1983), p. 207.

Thus "the free man's road" is God Himself, a beginning without beginning and an endless end, his present ground, his eternal center. This road leads backward to Paradise and forward to the Kingdom, without leaving that spot where "The pathway dies/ And the wilds begin" (ll. 3-4), because finally there is nowhere to go, and no one who is going. The free man, the true self, is one who has disappeared into God, the Alpha and the Omega, the All in All.

In his essay on Merton's Christological thought, George A. Kilcourse writes, "Failure to come to grips critically with Merton's poetic talent scandalously eclipses the essential Merton," and cites Romano Guardini's observation to the effect that "artistic imagination precedes theological reflection by a decade, even a generation."[56] Certainly "Elias" bears out both these observations, in a number of ways. First of all, it marks Merton's return to poetry after composing little or no verse since the late 1940s (his most recent collection, *The Tears of the Blind Lions*, had been published in 1949), and is itself an affirmation of the validity of his art: in the song of the solitary bird Merton presents an image of the contemplative as poet.[57] Secondly, the main focus in the poem, as in Merton's own life, is the search for a deeper and more complete solitude, for that center of quietness where the encounter with self and God might take place. As one of the earliest and finest examples of what George Woodcock calls "poetry of the desert" (as distinguished from "poetry of the choir"),[58] "Elias" bears witness to the increasing thirst for solitude which would lead Merton a decade later into his hermitage. At the same time, the poem reflects the turn toward the world which is so prominent a dimension in Merton's later writings: the judgmental attitude toward secular society which particularly characterized some of the earlier poetry is exorcized during the course of the poem, to be replaced by a vivid sense of the common human condition of brokenness, which evokes not haughty condemnation but personal repentance and universal compassion. Finally, neither solitude nor openness to the world impedes authentic social criticism; rather, they enhance

---

56. George Kilcourse, "Pieces of the Mosaic, Earth: Thomas Merton and the Christ," in Timothy Mulhearn, ed., *Getting It All Together: The Heritage of Thomas Merton* (Wilmington: Michael Glazier, 1984), pp. 102, 103; a generally better edited version of this essay, in *The Message of Thomas Merton*, ed. Patrick Hart (Kalamazoo: Cistercian Publications, 1981), pp. 129-153, does not include the first sentence quoted. Kilcourse concludes his essay, interestingly, by quoting ll. 183-191, 199-204, of "Elias."

57. The shift in attitude toward poetry during this period can be seen by comparing the 1947 version of "Poetry and the Contemplative Life," which concludes that the poet might be required to make a "ruthless and complete sacrifice of his art" (*Figures*, p. 110) for the sake of his contemplative vocation, with the much more positive conclusion of "Poetry and Contemplation: A Reappraisal," published in 1958 (see above, note 17).

58. Woodcock, p. 58.

it. For Merton as for his Elias, there is no contradiction between the contemplative and the prophetic, both of which resonate with human hopes and fears, and both of which are grounded in the discovery of true identity.

While all these elements can be found in Merton's various prose writings of the period, their synthesis in the poem could itself be described as somewhat "prophetic," a prefiguration of the stance of "marginal man" which Merton adopts in the 1960s as the essence of his monastic vocation. "The monastic life has a certain prophetic character about it," Merton will later say, because the true contemplative "is a living witness to the freedom of the sons of God and to the essential difference between that freedom and the spirit of the world," yet this does not set him against the world but rather "is something which the monk *owes to the world.*"[59] What the poem is uniquely able to provide is a look at the *process* of integration, the struggle to discover the underlying unity of the seemingly diverse identities of poet and solitary, prophetic critic and representative human being.

But the significance of "Elias" is not confined to the insights it provides about its author. It must finally be evaluated on its own terms, as a poem. In his subtle and effective use of the Biblical Elias as paradigm for the prophet/contemplative dilemma, in his firm control of the shifting tone and mood, in the complex development of his theme, particularly in the full six-part version of the poem, in the cyclic pattern of the structure, which exemplifies in its own way Eliot's dictum that "the end of all our exploring/ Will be to arrive where we started/ And know the place for the first time,"[60] Merton has fashioned a satisfying and successful work of art which richly repays a careful reading. It may well be that, as a poet, Merton wrote too much and revised too little, as Eliot already commented in the late 1940s,[61] and that "he needed a Pound to cut him to size,"[62] as his friend Daniel Berrigan remarked in reviewing the thousand-plus pages of *The Collected Poems.* But the unevenness and sheer bulk of Merton's output in verse should not lead, as it generally has, to a neglect of his genuine accomplishment in this field. "Elias -- Variations on a Theme" represents an excellent starting point for integrating Merton's poetry into his overall achievement as writer and spiritual guide, and for assessing his contribution to twentieth-century American poetry.

---

59. *Contemplation in a World of Action* (Garden City, New York: Doubleday, 1971), pp. 8-9.

60. T. S. Eliot, "Little Gidding," *Four Quartets,* in *The Complete Poems and Plays, 1909-1950* (New York: Harcourt, Brace & World, 1952), p. 145.

61. See Mott, p. 242.

62. Daniel Berrigan, "The Seventy Times Seventy Seven Storey Mountain," *Cross Currents,* 27:4 (Winter, 1977-1978), p. 393.

THOMAS MERTON'S

UNDERSTANDING:

THE CLARITAS STRATEGY

by **Michael Rukstelis,** C.O.

At the close of Thomas Merton's only published novel *My Argument with the Gestapo*, originally written in 1941 while teaching English at St. Bonaventure University in New York, the narrator says "the only reason for wanting to write [is] Blake's reason."[1] What "Blake's reason" might mean can be evidenced in an examination of Merton's Columbia University thesis, composed in 1938, on this eighteenth-century poet. Accordingly, I want to pay careful attention to some important portions of that thesis entitled "Nature and Art in William Blake: An Essay in Interpretation." A close reading of the thesis will help readers see how Merton's essay is an important source text, on at least two levels, for later Merton works. On one level, the Blake thesis suggests how Merton's own religious perspective eventually came to be shaped by the interpretive decisions he made about art and about the artistic process, as either are related to the mystic or contemplative experience. On another level the thesis reveals the

---

1. Thomas Merton, *My Argument with the Gestapo* (Garden City, New York: Doubleday & Company, 1969), p. 259.

beginnings of a symbolic language for vision, which I call here *the claritas strategy*.[2] The claritas strategy becomes an important context for readers of Merton, because it suggests to some extent how contemplative insights emerged.

That William Blake became for the younger Merton a model of a religious artist, if not a model of a radical prophet, has already been noted by some of Merton's readers.[3] But Merton also acknowledges Blake's influence in his own works like *The Seven Storey Mountain* and others. In his St. Bonaventure lecture notes, for example, Merton frames all his material about Blake's poetry with a parenthetical statement about the poet's life. Blake's life, reasons Merton, was ". . . a vital unity" of "his philosophy, his work, & [sic] his religion . . . . He lived these all in one."[4] Thus in 1941 Merton had a thumbnail sketch of an identity that represented new life in the midst of what he himself characterized as a time of lost innocence and exile: "The sense of exile," Merton would write in *The Secular Journal*, "bleeds in me like a hemorrhage. Always the same wound, whether a sense of sin or of holiness, or of one's own insufficiency, or of spiritual dryness."[5]

An important context to mention at this juncture involves Merton's view of Blake's achievement as a Christian artist: "As an artist, Blake found in art a way of knowing and loving the principle of all Being."[6] As early as 1938, Merton was not only finding a partial model for his own vocation as a Christian writer in Blake, but he was also beginning to see the 'way' of the artist, not as contradictory to, but as complementary with, the religious vocation he had vaguely in mind at the time: "This seizure of intelligible realities without using concepts as a formal means is something analagous

---

2. This analysis of Merton's work follows Stanley Fish's reflections on interpretive or perceptual strategies that a reader brings to a particular text. See Fish's "Interpreting the *Variorum*" in *Is There a Text in This Class?* (Cambridge, Massachusetts: Harvard University Press, 1980), pp. 163-167. I also want to acknowledge the influence of David Bleich's book *Subjective Criticism* (Baltimore & London: Johns Hopkins University Press, 1978), on my thinking during the composition of this essay. See especially his chapter "Epistemological Assumptions in the Study of Response," pp. 97-133.

3. Monica Furlong in *Merton: A Biography* (San Francisco: Harper & Row, 1980) discusses how Merton's reading of Blake profoundly influenced his conversion to Catholicism (see pp. 48-49 and pp. 75-76). Also George Woodcock mentions Blake's influence on Merton's conversion in *Thomas Merton, Monk and Poet: A Critical Study* (New York: Farrar, Straus & Giroux, 1978), pp. 10-12. Ross Labrie in *The Art of Thomas Merton* (Fort Worth: Texas Christian University Press, 1979) mentions Merton's interest in Blake, but he discusses Merton's interest in "the roles of religion and art in relation to the vitality of the whole society" without making any explicit connection to Merton's perception of Blake as a religious artist (see pp. 8-10).

4. Faddish-Siracuse File, Friedsam Memorial Library, St. Bonaventure University, Olean, New York.

5. Thomas Merton, *The Secular Journal of Thomas Merton* (New York: Farrar, Straus & Cudahy, 1959), p. 264.

6. Thomas Merton, "Nature and Art in William Blake: An Essay in Interpretation," in *The Literary Essays of Thomas Merton*, ed. Brother Patrick Hart (New York: New Directions, 1981), p. 430. Further references to the thesis are from this edition of *The Literary Essays* and are referred to in the text as *LE*.

in both the poet and the mystic, but they both operate differently and on different planes" (*LE*, pp. 444-445). As this facet of the thesis is presented in a more distilled form in his Bonaventure lecture notes, the meaning of Blake's reason becomes more explicitly art as a means to mystical union with God. Merton writes: "Everything Blake ever wrote, painted or said is either directly or indirectly concerned with the steps toward achievement of mystical union with God."[7]

Before going on to the thesis it is important to consider some broad concerns that Merton brought with him in writing this interpretive essay. One of these is clearly a need to defend Blake as a Christian poet. Part of the problem Merton has with readers of Blake, most notably J. Middleton Murray's reading, is that they "refuse to interpret Blake as a Christian and continue to seek explanations for everything he said among Gnostics, astrologers, and alchemists" (*LE*, p. 431). The other concern involves Merton's perceptions of Blake's thought about art as "recondite" or obscure (*LE*, p. 391). Since much of the discussion in the second chapter of the thesis touches on the "Imagination," we may assume that this is the particular aesthetic aspect of Blake's art that Merton sees as most in need of clarification. Finally, I want to suggest here that these concerns, which involve both public and private dimensions of Merton as a Christian and a writer, become in the writing situation motives for defense of the imagination as a value in the Christian religious vocation. Because this value appears in need of a clarified meaning that can be viewed (by Merton as well as by others) as having an orthodox meaning for the contemporary Christian, the burden of the thesis becomes deciding what that meaning is. Ultimately, Merton will find meaning for much of Blake's "more recondite" thought about the imagination through a Thomistic interpretive strategy.

Thomas Merton uses one of William Blake's prophetic poems, *The Four Zoas*, as the basis for his investigation into the subject of Blake's thought on the role of the intellect as it pertains to the artist. Merton claims the myth of the fall as central to the meaning and shape of the poetry in the prophetic books. For example, he notices that Blake "always deals with the fall into a violent, tragic conflict of ideas, and the subsequent regeneration into spiritual and intellectual harmony" (*LE*, p. 410). Thus the Blakean poet and his drama are located within a Christian mythic context, which is in turn associated with the tradition of the Christian "mystics" like Augustine. Such a tradition is known for its tendency to view human experience as a struggle

---

7. Faddish-Siracuse File, St. Bonaventure University.

between extreme forces. "This is the drama," says Merton, "which the mystics understand to underly the whole of human life. It is the pattern of the contigent universe" (*LE*, p. 410).

A couple of assumptions inform this world view and need to be briefly addressed. First, matter in the contigent world "is inextricably tied up with the idea of the fall, the expulsion from Eden" (*LE*, p. 426). Urizen is a prototypical father of this fall and creator of our world. He is the eternal whose "self-will . . . causes the fall from intelligibility into the blindness of matter" (*LE*, p. 427). Thus Merton sees Blake connecting matter and materialism with unintelligibility, which is associated with the Blakean hell (Ulro) and evil ("lack of intellect and the impossibility of participating in God's Grace . . . nonexistence") (*LE*, pp. 432-433).

For the sake of "clarification," Merton invokes a more orthodox Christian authority by comparing St. Thomas Aquinas's view of matter to Blake's in order to show "that matter is the principle of change, and change denies intelligibility; and that, therefore, things are intelligible insofar as they are immaterial" (*LE*, p. 426). Because Urizen (i.e. Your Reason)[8] subjects himself only to the empirical, he stands as the principle *par excellence* of ignorance; he cannot ever fully know and love what is eternal in him. Thus, he "represents empiricism and doubt, and also dogmatism, because he is blind to imagination, passion, spirit. Consequently, he cannot really understand life or experience at all" (*LE*, p. 427). Urizen's "eternal" pursuit of material intelligibility becomes expressed in the fallen world as the tyranny of "abstract codes based on mathematical reasoning and materialism" (*LE*, p. 428). And, as usual, such a discussion is closely linked with Merton's own experience at the time. Monica Furlong puts it succinctly:

> What Blake and Maritain between them taught Merton . . . was that art is part of a mystical and contemplative understanding of the world . . . . It came to Merton that, child of his age that he was, he had tried to interpret life in terms of sociological and economic laws, but that these separated from faith and charity became yet another imprisonment.[9]

Another assumption that informs the mystic world view is the belief that real existence is a perfect knowing and loving of God. Intelligence here is closely associated with a subject's experience of transcendent being. So, on one hand, Merton associates Blakean imagery of dogmatism and blindness with the Urizenic quest to control matter, and he calls this quest unintelligible and illustrative of nonexistence. On the other hand, Merton

---

8. S. Foster Damon, *A Blake Dictionary: The Ideas and Symbols of William Blake* (New York: E. P. Dutton & Co., 1971), p. 419.

9. Monica Furlong, p. 75.

links intelligence with what is eternally transcendent. This notion, however, finds expression, not in the Blakean imagery as much as from the Thomistic language he introduces: "Things are intelligible insofar as they are immaterial." What is important for readers to notice is Merton's interpretive decision to link intelligence with transcendence, and to view this as constituting, as he says, "real existence (heaven)" (*LE*, pp. 433). Thus, "What is real, true, beautiful, good is transcendent. This is real existence."[10]

I have already mentioned that Merton chooses to use "the aesthetic ideas of St. Thomas Aquinas . . . as a key to help us unlock some of the more difficult problems in Blake's thought about art" (*LE*, pp. 391, 431). He adopts the Thomist language because it is clear and critical; it will help readers to "see into the depths of Blake's own more recondite thought" (*LE*, p. 391). Yet, while Merton finds meaning for much of Blake's "more recondite thought" about the Imagination through a Thomistic interpretive strategy, he understands St. Thomas within a narrow context. Merton himself acknowledges in the preface to the thesis and in his Columbia notebooks that a close reading of Jacques Maritain's discussion of art as a virtue of the practical intellect in *Art and Scholasticism* provides the basis for his understanding of Thomism.[11]

In the Blake thesis, Merton focuses his attention on the idea of the virtue of the practical intellect. He understands "virtue" in a number of ways. Virtue is seen as an agent of transformation, which, according to Maritain, " 'triumph[s] over the original indetermination of the intellective faculty, . . . [and] raises it in respect of a definite object to a maximum of perfection' " (*LE*, p. 432). Virtue is also seen as an act going on in the artist which is never impaired by the temporal and contigent world: "The work may be imperfect, but the art in the artist is unimpaired" (*LE*, p. 433). As an act (again following Maritain), virtue has also an autonomous quality or a "permanent condition perfecting in the line of its own nature the subect [sic] which it informs" (*LE*, p. 431). Finally, virtue is seen as a conceptual agency by which "the knower and the thing known actually become identified" (*LE*, p. 432). This agency describes the operation of connaturality in the artist.

---

10. *The Literary Essays*, p. 432. It is worth comparing what Merton says in the thesis about the artist and the role of the intellect in art with what he says in *New Seeds of Contemplation* (New York: New Directions, 1961), cf. pp. 290-297. For example, "The world was not made as a prison for fallen spirits who were rejected by God: this is the gnostic error" (p. 290).

11. Columbia "Blake Notebooks," Vol. 2, 127552, Friedsam Memorial Library, St. Bonaventure University, Olean, New York. Besides extensive notetaking on Maritain, Merton also looked at some of St. Thomas Aquinas's *Summa Theologica*. Some of his note headings include: "Art and Nature," "Art and Prudence," "Art and Beauty."

The question for Merton, then, becomes "does [Blake] have any idea of art which would correspond to that of virtue or *habitus*?" (*LE*, p. 432). His answer to the question provides him with the opportunity to apply Thomistic aesthetic strategies to Blake's figure for the Imagination, who is Los. For example, Merton identifies the central act of Los in the Zoas as creating or building forms for the sake of the fallen eternals. Additionally, these forms operate to keep the eternals from falling into non-entity in Urizen's world; through forms Los will eventually lead fallen beings back to eternity: "But Los, imagination, we remember, created forms, builds the City of Art to keep eternals from falling into his [i.e. Urizen's] nonentity (or sin). In the end he leads them back to eternity, truth, real existence (heaven)" (*LE*, p. 433). Thus even though Blake does not know about "habitus," Merton sees built-in parallels between Blake's so-called concept of Imagination and St. Thomas's concept of habitus/virtue.

Merton then links the habitus/virtue idea of St. Thomas with the Blakean vision of Imagination, which is "a special kind of artistic vision necessary" (*LE*, p. 435). He argues that "The man of imagination, the artist, because of the 'virtue' of his art, sees more than his eyes present to him" (*LE*, p. 436). This is so because "the intellect [perceives] through the eye" to "the formal relations of objects to one another" (*LE*, pp. 435). The rationality of the intellect, then, becomes very subjective in that "we perceive the relationships that interest us; as we look at nature, we interpret it" (*LE*, p. 435). Quoting one of Blake's letters, Merton indicates that a ramification of this vision is that nature becomes reorganized by the virtue in the artist: " 'But to the eye of the man of Imagination,' " writes Blake, " 'Nature is Imagination itself' " (*LE*, pp. 436). Such a reorganization or transformation of nature gives the artist the freedom to look "through nature" (*LE*, p. 443) and "into the very essence of things" (*LE*, p. 445). For the Blakean artist, the "perfect portrait of a person will always be that one's 'essential image,' his image as he 'is in God' " (*LE*, p. 435).

In this way the Blakean Imagination converges with the Thomistic idea of the virtue of the artist. In this sense, Imagination operates to reorganize (or create forms for) the natural world in order to reveal the secret image of God, God's essential intelligence, already pre-existing in individual things. More specifically, Merton describes form as "revelation of essence." It is, according to Maritain, the " 'peculiar principle of intelligibility' " (*LE*, p. 443) in each creature, and it is what gives each its own individual character, its "*quidditas*" (*LE*, p. 442). Form, then, operates to determine and complete the "ontological secret" of everything (*LE*, p. 443).

Ultimately, however, Merton holds up claritas, "the glory of form shining through matter," as the condition of form *par excellence* (*LE*, pp. 443). Thus, as a "condition" of form, claritas takes on a central place in his decision about how the form of a thing would "apply" to Blake's aesthetic ideas, especially to Blake's concern for beauty.

Merton claims that beauty for Blake was always distinct and particular to a given thing and thus beauty did "not conform with certain ideal and unchanging types." Merton applies a Thomistic definition of beauty as

> 'a certain excellence or perfection in the proportion of things to the mind,' and this excellence depends upon three conditions: integrity, proportion, and clarity. (*LE*, p. 442; my emphasis)

The language I have underscored recalls an aspect of Merton's earlier discussion of the relationships in nature that are of interest, especially of ontological interest, to the person. On the one hand, this implies the artist's personal participation (intellectually, physically, and appetitively) in and creative use of the "virtue" in him to reveal the secret image of God in the world. On the other hand, the implication seems to be that the subjective rationality of the intellect is regulated by the particular person's own ontological orientation, which is of course integrally bound up with who that person is. I shall develop each of these implications in greater detail during a discussion of a passage from *The Sign of Jonas* later in this essay.

Meanwhile, claritas is an otherly and extra-human condition. It is the condition that best satisfies the intellect's demand not just for intelligibility and light but also for "essential beauty" (*LE*, pp. 443-444). Yet, at the moment in which the artist and the essential beauty of a thing "meet," the artist, as a sensuous being, falls under the influence of the form of a thing that his own virtue as artist has just revealed. As the claritas of some thing's form touches the artist, the artist knows it as beautiful first through the senses and then through the mind (*LE*, p. 443).

Beauty, then, can be said to be connatural to someone because the splendor of form that shines through matter (i.e. claritas) touches the artist first through the senses. In this way the intellect can enjoy and delight in the beauty of a creature or "a thing as it is essentially," "directly and intuitively," and "without using concepts as a formal means" (*LE*, pp. 443, 444). Within the claritas strategy, then, connaturality seems to have not just a transformational agency in the knower's identification with the thing known, but it also uncovers an attitude, cultivated by the artist in the process of doing his art, which deliberately abandons intellectual manipulation.[12]

The formation of the claritas strategy as a strategy for meaning may be briefly summarized in the following way. The virtue of the practical intellect is used as a means of explanation. In other words, it is a way of understanding Blake's "more recondite thought" about the concept of the Imagination. As we have seen, the Thomistic "key" clarifies Blake's obscure thought by providing not just an explanation but a strategy for explanation that satisfies both psychological and intellectual needs of the time: St. Thomas, writes Merton at one point in the thesis, "comes to conclusions which astonish us with their brilliance and yet delight us with their perfect soundness and consonance with our experience and intellectual needs" (*LE*, pp. 446). Meanwhile, in ascribing to the Blakean Imagination the Scholastic meaning of virtue, Merton explains how it is possible for the artist to become free enough to look "through nature" and "into the very essence of things." Such vision depends partially upon the relationships in nature that interest the artist; thus the artistic vision is subjective. However, I have suggested from this point that the artist's subjectivity (as well as the initiatives he takes in making art) is regulated by that person's ontological orientation.[13]

The claritas strategy explains the visionary power of the artist to transform the natural (fallen) world into a place where intuitions about God may be born and grow up. As we shall see, this relationship between a person and a local landscape becomes vital to the creation and development of that visionary power. However, this power of vision has the capacity to conquer and enslave the natural world too. For Merton, the problem is and will remain the perverse use of the artist's imagination. In short, imagination may be manipulated for purposes that, unlike Blake's reason, attempt to seize and possess being for material ends.

One can begin to see how fine a line there is between the artist

---

12. In his thesis, Merton seems interested in Hindu asceticism because it provides a process that best engages his own concern to develop a physical and intellectual program of discipline compatible with his understanding of the artist. Hindu "thinking," then, is used to support his on-going analogy between the mystic intuition and the pure aesthetic experience of the artist, "without the accompaniment of ideation." Furthermore, in his discussion of the role of judgment in art and the necessity of training the intellect to judge, Merton turns his attention briefly to the importance of asceticism as a "sacrifice of immediate physical goods for the good of the spirit, for the success of the work of art." However, Merton's original model of the artist, the Blakean poet, does not lend itself well to this concern. Therefore, Merton appeals to "the artistic process" of the Hindu artist who, "with a strict routine of asceticism and contemplation ... must purge himself of all personal desires." Subsequently, the artist is free enough to visualize "his subject as it is described in a given canonical prescription (mantram); he contemplates this ideal model until he comes to 'reflect' it, becomes identified with it, holds it in view in an act of nondifferentiation, then draws it" (See *LE*, pp. 445. 448). Finally, Merton draws these ideas from his reading of Ananda K. Coomaraswamy's *The Transformation of Nature in Art* (Cambridge: Harvard University Press, 1934).

13. "Ontological" here necessarily involves a holistic view of the person.

figure, Blake's Los, who with his building of forms attempts "to keep eternals from falling into [Urizen's] nonentity (or sin)," and Urizen's own building of forms which entrap and sink being into the oblivion of material intelligibility. The Los figure and the Urizen figure, who represent different uses of the intellect, provide the basis for Merton's understanding of the role of the intellect in the realm of contemplation. The tension that exists between the two uses shows itself throughout his career as a contemplative writer. On the one hand, vision may be obedient to the "Urizenic" demands to structure the world according to its own material needs and preoccupations. On the other hand, when vision is released from those demands it is free to engage a person or people in "God's discovery of us." "We only know Him," writes Merton in *Seeds of Contemplation*, "in so far as we are known by Him, and our contemplation of Him is a participation of His contemplation of Himself. We become contemplatives when God discovers Himself in us."[14] An episode from *The Sign of Jonas*, dated 10 February 1950, will demonstrate how the "claritas strategy" I have just identified surfaces and plays out some of these concerns.

I call this episode from *The Sign of Jonas* the "Hawk and Starlings" passage.[15] In it, Merton is especially interested in how the action of a hawk stands in relation to the experience of the contemplative monk. The hawk's arrival signals for Merton an extraordinary shift in attention from preoccupation to release from preoccupation. The starlings that once filled the pasture and dominated perceived relationships are now dispersed by the hawk. The hawk is presented as symbolic mediator of human and divine encounter by means of the subjective initiative of the artist. This is to say that the claritas strategy demands nothing less from the artist than a rendering of the essential image of the hawk, precisely because it is in the monk's interest (ontologically) to be oriented by such an image. We have such a "portrait" in this passage; and it works not only to reorganize the scene but also to constrain Thomas Merton's review of relationships in the scene, including his own implied relation to that scene.

The features of this episode are like those I shall describe in this essay when I discuss the origins of the "Le Point Vierge" symbol in the Cuban epiphany as it is represented in both *The Secular Journal* and *The Seven Storey Mountain*. In the "Hawk and Starlings" passage there is a sudden awakening, but on this occasion the awakening reflects not a sudden

---

14. Thomas Merton, *Seeds of Contemplation* (Norfolk, Connecticut: New Directions, 1949), p. 32.

15. Thomas Merton, *The Sign of Jonas* (New York: Harcourt, Brace & Co., 1953), pp. 274-275. Further references will be cited in the text and refer only to these pages.

recognition of the "Truth" as in the Cuban epiphany, but rather it reflects an obfuscation. The sudden awareness is of "great excitement" in the pasture, and this excitement is associated with the starlings. Merton describes the birds in consistently exaggerated terms. They are perceived as one body and as filling what would otherwise be a "bare" winter pasture: "And the starlings filled every large and small tree." While the body is identified as one that fills the pasture, its behavior is described in general, almost casual terms. The starlings filled every tree and "shone in the light and sang." When they move to avoid an attack by an eagle, they do so as a "whole cloud of them." When the danger has passed over, "they all alighted on the ground" and continued "moving about and singing for about five minutes." Merton's description, in effect, isolates the birds as one body and characterizes its behavior as amorphous. From such a description, the reader gains an impression of distortion of the scene, the cause of which Merton assigns to the birds themselves. Thus the birds, which fill the pasture with "their" excitement, become a way of talking about a loss of definition, perhaps even of identity.

This loss of definition in the scene is reinforced by observations about other birds and their behavior in relation to the starlings. There are originally three tiers of birds involved in the scene -- buzzards, crows, and an eagle. The buzzards are the farthest away and act only as "observers." Frightened apparently by the great excitement, the crows are in the process of distancing themselves -- ("soaring, very high, keeping out of the way") --from the scene. If a tendency of avoidance is characteristic of the behavior of the buzzards and crows, the eagle's behavior is notable for its imprecision. The eagle is introduced as "flying over the woods" and then observed to have "attacked a tree full of starlings." The attack is unsuccessful and this bird comes "nowhere near" the starlings. Instead the effect of the eagle's attack is to relocate the "cloud" of starlings from the tree to the ground. In other words, the relationship between the one possible predator and the starlings is described in terms that reinforce the starlings' domination of the physical scene.

The starlings' domination of the scene, however, is reversed by the hawk's attack. The hawk's behavior is formulated in terms that suggest what it is, what its nature, or "quidditas," is. Merton isolates two attributes of the hawk: one is the speed of its descent, and the other is the precision of its attack. Furthermore, these two attributes are reviewed and developed through different contexts in the passage. One such context is concerned with the event itself: the hawk's initial appearance. Heretofore the starlings have dominated the scene with their "excitement." The hawk's appearance, on the other hand, is communicated as an event in its dispersal of the starlings: "I saw a scare go into the cloud of birds." The sudden shift in attention from that which had preoccupied attention (i.e. the starlings) to that which releases attention from preoccupation (i.e. the hawk) is associated with an attitude of surprise. In fact, the surprise registered here is rehearsed in language with which readers of Merton are already familiar: "Then, like lightning, it happened." The image of lightning here, just as the image of the thunderclap in the earlier Cuban epiphany, signals a special awareness, which accounts for both the experiential and the ineffable in the event.[16]

The first context closes with a description of the hawk's apparently perfect execution of its hunting act. Imagery that suggests that precision of weaponry enforces a new relationship between the hunter and prey also poses a strong contrast to the eagle's approach. Furthermore, the imagery of precision highlights the two attributes *par excellence* of the hawk: its speed and its exacting aim. Thus, the hawk "shot straight into the middle of the starlings" and "got his talons into the one bird he had nailed."

This imagery of precision is reviewed and developed in further reflection in the passage. Merton rehearses the outcome of the attack --"Then every tree, every field was cleared" -- through the hawk. He characterizes the hawk's identity as unique: "He stayed in the field like a king with the killed bird, and nothing else came near him. He took his time." Such an identity stands by itself in contrast to the domination of the pasture by the starlings. Now, and quite simply, "The hawk, all alone . . . possessed his prey." The language suggests that the hawk is in control of the area, but it also announces an image of balance previously unapparent. For example, the crows, which are "still in sight, but over their wood," and the vultures, newly introduced but seen to be possibly circling "something dead," are described in terms that suggest them to be in their proper places, to be, so to speak, at home. Thus, in this second context, the new relationship enforced between the hunter and prey through the hawk's precise act reorganizes the space of the pasture and constrains Merton's review of relationships in it.

---

16.   Starting with the Cuban epiphany, there are several such moments in Merton's writing career. Generally, these are "beginner's" recognitions, which signal a moment of liberating insight on the one hand, and a change in life direction on the other. See the so-called "Louisville epiphany" in *Conjectures of a Guilty Bystander* and the revelation at Polonnaruwa in *The Asian Journal* (New York: New Directions, 1975), pp. 233-236. See also *New Seeds of Contemplation* where Merton describes the kinds of beginnings a contemplative might have: "The best of these kinds of beginnings is a sudden emptying of the soul in which images vanish, concepts and words are silent, and freedom and clarity suddenly open out with you" (p. 275).

Thomas Merton seems more consciously interested in the relationship he uncovers between the hawk and the contemplative: "I think that hawk is to be studied by saints and contemplatives; because he knows his business."[17] In addition to this interest, however, the apostrophe to the hawk in the final paragraph signals an earlier understanding about the role the intellect plays in the production of beautiful forms. Here again the artist exercises a subjective initiative in choosing relationships in nature that are of special interest to the monk, especially as they direct that person to solitude.

In isolating the hawk's speed and exacting aim, Merton also indicates what is unique about the hawk. In Thomistic terms, he identifies the bird's perfection, the excellence of its nature, while posing it over and against the starlings' amorphous body, which previously overshadowed the pasture scene. These attributes of speed and aim, then, are also conditions of the creature's form; they reveal, furthermore, the hawk's "peculiar principle of intelligibility," its essential image. The physical hawk, then, has become a symbolic object for mediating an understanding of the experience. The hawk, in other words, becomes that which frees the artist to look "through nature" and "into the very essence of things" (*LE*, pp. 443, 445). As mediator of an encounter between human and divine, the flight of the hawk and its hunting skill are a "beautiful thing," and both affect Merton's view of the relationships in the now "cleared" pasture scene. Thus the hawk's appearance gives rise to language that invokes its revealed image, its essential beauty.

But this experience also includes an unacknowledged relationship to the starlings. The scene's sudden shift in consciousness importantly reflects how Merton participates in the death of the "slowest starling." Here his attention shifts from participation in the original acts of domination and relationships of power to participation in an act of powerlessness and death. Thus, while the hawk means death to the "slowest starling," its revealed image also means "death" to the monk and dispersal to the forms he imposes on reality. For the person who is constantly pushed about by undirected energies or who grafts onto the world his own self-preoccupations,

---

17. Readers should note the strong resemblance in diction, theme, and even cadence between Merton's final paragraph in this passage and Gerard Manley Hopkins' poem, "The Windhover." I have Richard Aticks of the University of Central Florida to thank for pointing this out to me. Another more hidden presence in this passage is St. John of the Cross. At an earlier point in *The Sign of Jonas*, Merton writes: "Didn't Saint John of the Cross hide himself in a room up in a church tower where there was a small window through which he could look out at the country?" (p. 109). The hideaway in the "Hawk and Starlings" passage resembles St. John's own hideaway; the view is from a "small window" in the "garden house attic" which looks out over the bare pasture.

what breaks through the intellect's verbal forms is a moment of "love a thousand times more terrible."[18] The hawk's flight was a "terrible" thing because what is understood, precisely by the manipulative intellect, to be breaking through into reality as a fact of experience is God.

The hawk's possession of the bird becomes a kind of icon of God's possession of the monk. This is the moment in which the intellectual encounter with God achieves a private and ecstatic character. This moment is prepared for by Merton's understanding of the role of the intellect as revealing, and not manipulating, the splendor of form shining through matter. In the context of the apophatic way, this aesthetic understanding of the experience is formulated as the artist's apprehending a thing's "onto-logical secret, ... directly and intuitively, ... and without using concepts as a formal means."

This is also a moment in which monastic discipline orients the artist, who has in effect broken away, back towards the lived-in world. The return to the attic is a deliberate and ritualized refusal to remain exclusively in charge of the strategies that might otherwise distort or spiritualize his experience. I want to emphasize this return as disciplined because the monastic attitudes of solitude, poverty, and penitential sacrifice direct the "extreme case" of solitude back towards a communal and public realm of experience: "Now I am going back to the attic and the shovels and the broken window and the trains in the valley and the prayer of Jesus." This return is a psychological necessity and an intellectual discipline if the monk is to avoid a "spurious solitude" and an isolate (or angelic) stance. What emerges here in part, then, in the "Hawk and Starlings" passage is the role of the monk in regulating the visionary experience of the artist.

I am now in a position to make two observations about the claritas strategy and its explanatory function. This interpretive strategy indicates to readers Merton's quiet motive, on the one hand, to return to an original moment of revelation. On the other hand, it reveals his motive to proclaim and develop that revelation to an audience -- in this case, a Christian reading community. The claritas strategy reveals a problem peculiar to Merton. The intellectual problem (i.e. his understanding) or "paradox" that Merton faced comes out of this tension between a yearning to return to a moment of revelation and a need to say what that revelation is.

---

18. Cf. Merton's own language in "The Inner Experience: Prospects and Conclusions (VIII), *Cistercian Studies*, XIX (1984), p. 344: "When he tries to be his own God, and insists on keeping his hands on everything, remembering everything, and controlling everything, he drives himself to ruin. For when man thinks himself powerful, then at every moment he is in desperate need: he is in need of knowledge, strength, control, and he depends on countless instruments."

Furthermore, in Merton's attempt to proclaim the public and communal dimensions of the private revelation to his reading community (and this is especially so in his early writing), his explanation will itself be developed and even enriched, while the original experience of the revelation will tend to be distanced, if not distorted.[19] Perhaps the best way to illustrate what I mean about this developmental and yet distortive tendency in Merton's explanations about revelation, especially as these explanations are surfaced by the claritas strategy, is briefly to look at the origins of what I shall call the "Point Vierge" symbol.

In the spring of 1940, Merton took what probably seemed to him a long deserved vacation. He travelled to Cuba just over a year after completing his Master of Arts thesis on the subject of Blake's thinking about art. This trip to Cuba is recorded in both *The Secular Journal* and in *The Seven Storey Mountain*. In both accounts, he describes a moment of awakening to the presence of God in a church in Havana, in which, says Michael Mott in *The Seven Mountains of Thomas Merton*, "Merton drew close in words to the experience which was beyond words."[20]

There are at least three features that influence Merton's recounting of the epiphany in April 1940 in Havana while attending mass in the Church of San Francisco. The first feature is the initial realization of God's presence during the Consecration. In the *Journal* account this new awareness is expressed by the images of a "thunderclap" ("something went off inside me like a thunderclap") and a "thunderbolt."[21] In the autobiography the special awareness is named differently: "There formed in my mind an awareness, an understanding, a realization."[22] In this account, the image of "thunderclap" again appears to emphasize the experiential impact in the midst of the ineffable: ". . . this awareness: it was so intangible, and yet it struck me like a thunderclap" (*SSM*). The "metaphor" of light is a second feature worth noticing. In both accounts Merton attributes his initial intuition of God's presence in the scene as coming from the "good big shout" of "all those Cuban children." The later account, however, more clearly associates the children's "Creo" with an intellectual action: "There formed in my mind an awareness, an understanding, a realization of what

---

19. By distortion I mean simply "to distort" or "to twist out of a natural, normal, or original shape or condition." See *Webster's Ninth New Collegiate Dictionary* (1983).

20. Michael Mott, *The Seven Mountains of Thomas Merton* (Boston: Houghton Mifflin Co., 1984), p. 151.

21. Thomas Merton, *The Secular Journal*, pp. 76 and 77. Further references will be cited in the text as *SJ* and will refer to pages 76-78 only.

22. Thomas Merton, *The Seven Storey Mountain* (San Diego: Harcourt Brace Jovanovich, 1976), p. 284. Further references will be cited in the text as *SSM* and will refer to pages 284-285 only.

had just taken place on the altar, at the Consecration." The "awareness" becomes expressed in metaphor as a light "a thousand times more bright" than the children's shout had been. Here Merton gives the metaphor special force by frequently characterizing it as dark or blinding, and by displaying the prominence of the intellect's role in receiving the light: it was "as if a sudden and immediate contact had been established between my intellect and the Truth Who was now . . . before me." Finally, the autobiography is emphatic about the discontinuity between light of Truth present to the mind and natural light: "It was a light that was so bright that it had no relation to any visible light and so profound and so intimate that it seemed like a neutralization of every lesser experience" (*SSM*).

The *Secular Journal* entry does not emphasize this dimension of the light metaphor. Although here too the metaphor describes God as beyond the powers of the natural eye or mind to see "anything or [apprehend] anything extraordinary," the light is presented within the context of a public and communal reflection about God working through the church scene. While Merton talks about the certainty that comes from his experience and links it to both an "order of knowledge" and a "strong movement of delight," his focus remains directed towards the children and God's action through them: "All this was caused directly by the great mercy and kindness of God when I heard the voices of the children cry out 'I believe.' " Subsequently, the "certitude of faith" gained here is associated with "the same kind of certitude that millions of Catholics and Jews and Hindus and everybody that believes in God have felt." Thomas Merton is here emphatic about there being "nothing esoteric about such things" as "These movements of God's grace" which are in everybody; they are, in fact, available to all: "They are common to every creature that was ever born with a soul" (*SJ*). Fundamental to this passage is its public and communal view of God working through people, and the light metaphor reflects that view.

There is a third feature influencing Merton's expression of the dark experience of God in the prose. This feature concerns the working of the transcendent light upon the sense and mind of the person who comes in "contact" with God. In *The Seven Storey Mountain*, Merton places emphasis on intuition of God as an intellectual realization, which is compared to a light "a thousand times more bright" than the children's shout of affirmation. Furthermore, the logic of the apophatic way, a logic peculiar to Merton's monastic interests and concerns during the composition of his autobiography, finds expression through his emphasis on the discontinuity between light present to the mind and natural light. Thus, the "sudden and immediate contact . . . established between my intellect and the Truth" is perceived as a light that "was blinding and neutralizing" not just to the physical senses but also to the ability to "see" conceptually: "This awareness . . . disarmed all images, all metaphors, and cut through the whole skein of species and phantasms with which we naturally do our thinking."[23]

While the *Journal's* view is communal and public, the autobiography surrenders this view to a more private and ecstatic focus. The "movement of delight" in the *Journal* "manifest[ed] itself in the Faith of all those children" by means of "the great mercy and kindness of God" (*SJ*). In the later account, the metaphor of light, which shifts attention from the children to the Consecration, becomes emphasized as *the* point of contact between the mind and "the Truth Who was now physically and really and substantially before me on the altar" (*SSM*). This contact is perceived as a new awareness and as such belongs to a transcendent "order of knowledge, yes, but more still to the order of love," as it pertains to the intellect's quest for an encounter with pure being.[24]

Although a private character and ecstatic tone seem to pervade the language of the autobiography, Thomas Merton's new awareness is not wholly intellectual. In his reconstruction of the experience Merton retains important elements of his original experience. For example, the children's "good big shout" still initiates what will later be called the "metaphor [of light] which I am using, long after the fact" (*SSM*). The children remain agents of revelation; they initiate the thunderclap of recognition in both passages through the physical presence of their "loud and strong and clear voices" (*SJ*). And they invoke a spontaneous joy and otherly light in the passage from *The Seven Storey Mountain*: "But that cry, 'Creo en Dios!' It was loud, and bright, and sudden and glad and triumphant; it was a good big shout, that came from all those Cuban children, a joyous affirmation of faith." Importantly, it is the Cuban children who mediate Merton's initial

---

23. Cf. Thomas Merton, *Conjectures of a Guilty Bystander* (New York, Image Books, 1968), p. 158: "At the center of our being is a point . . . which is never at our disposal, from which God disposes of our lives, which is inaccessible to the fantasies of our own mind or the brutalities of our own will."

24. Compare this treatment of the "point of contact" with the image of the "apex of existence" in *Seeds of Contemplation*, pp. 31-33, a book published a year after *The Seven Storey Mountain*. This surprise development in *Seeds* comes when Merton calls attention to God's mission to us in a way that recalls the artist figure of Los and his mission of creating forms to keep eternals from falling into nonentity. In this meditation Merton indicates God's supernatural mission to us is to "come down from heaven to find us." God's initiative then "bridges the infinite distances between Himself and the spirits created to love Him, by supernatural missions of His own Life" (p. 33). Thus the "point of contact" and the "apex of existence" images rehearse, although from different "directions," possible names for, as well as explanations about, new life in God's form: "God utters me like a word containing a thought of Himself" (p. 31).

awareness of God in the autobiography, and not the metaphor of light and contact.

The later interpretation of the experience regards a "contact" between a person's intellect and the Truth of God as paramount. Such an interpretation suggests a development in Merton's understanding about the role of the artist in expressing contemplative intuition. This development is based on, and consistent with, the thesis's concern for how the intellect is used when reconstructing that sudden and immediate encounter with God. In the earlier version the children were more clearly the ordinary, yet otherly, mediators of the sudden revelation; thus, they constrained Merton's initial explanation of the epiphany. However, the metaphor of light gains a more exclusive focus in the later passage, and it, in effect, reforms the original public and communal view of God. In other words, the later version poses a second and more narrowly construed mediator (light/contact) over and against what seems to be an original and naturally expansive mediator (the children). The effect of this new interpretation on the initial account (and surely upon the original intuition) is as much a distortion of the originally expressed insight (as to where God seems located) as it is a development of Merton's explanation about the radically transcendent and unknowable nature of God.

The claritas strategy realizes its fullest explanatory capability in what is known to many as the "Louisville epiphany" in *Conjectures of a Guilty Bystander*. The symbol by which this strategy is realized is *Le Point Vierge*.[25] The symbol integrates into a new interpretive arrangement the more disparate explanations about a sudden and immediate encounter with God, as I have just represented them in the two versions of the Cuban epiphany above. In the Louisville epiphany Merton consciously uses *le point vierge* to describe the moment of revelation. Moreover, *le point vierge* becomes such an important mediator of the epiphany that it, in effect, reorganizes the scene in ways similar to those described in the "Hawk and Starlings" passage.

Le point vierge describes a core of reality which is the shared "center of our being" and which is the hidden "secret beauty" of those people that

---

25. It is important to recognize that this passage from *Conjectures* was written originally in March, 1958, and revised in September, 1965. Michael Mott indicates this chronology in *The Seven Mountains of Thomas Merton* (pp. 311-313). He also notices a pattern similar to that in my discussion of the Cuban epiphany. He describes a "rhetoric of distancing" that occurs in the writing: "Merton talks of coming closer to the crowd at the very time his rhetoric is distancing 'the crowd' as an ever more abstract concept of another writer's imagination" (p. 312). Mott's evaluation is critical of the piece: "Part of the problem is that Merton goes on to see the crowds in Louisville through his reading of the Third of Thomas Traherne's Centuries: 'There is no way of telling people that they are all walking around like the sun' " (p. 312). Obviously at this point in my discussion I find Mott's evaluation, as I hope to show, limited.

Merton sees in the street.[26] On one hand, the symbol recalls the sudden "lightning" realization of the Cuban epiphany in that it is compared to a "spark" or, again, "It is like a pure diamond, blazing with the invisible light of heaven." The light on this occasion, though, is emphatically located in the people he sees walking around like "billions of points of light coming together." On the other hand, his description of the spark as having a transcendent quality reminds us of the earlier understanding of claritas as a condition of form that best satisfies the intellect's need for essential beauty. Consequently, this spark, although integrally bound up with who these people are, is distinguished from them as a "point of nothingness" and as "absolute poverty." Furthermore, it "belongs entirely to God" and "is never at [the] disposal . . . of our own mind or the brutalities of our own will."

Le point vierge clarifies and renews the meaning of the monk's existential loneliness. Moreover, the verge point recasts the religious artist's long-sought-after "vital unity" in terms of the contemplative's solitude and, in turn, interprets solitude. Consequently, this spark of light in part reviews what we saw as the visionary's deliberate refusal to remain exclusively in charge of his created meanings (i.e. the monk's ethos of preferring not to know); and yet the spark also directs the monk towards that which is the basis for his joy and profound solidarity with the people in Louisville: his solitude in God. Thus a special kind of vision again comes into play which describes two related contexts of experience.

The first context comes under the purview of the manipulative intellect and describes the spurious solitude that this use of the intellect creates. Because the Louisville piece turns on the dichotomy between natural seeing and faith seeing, this vision of the people cannot be gained by the ordinary act of seeing or understanding; nor can the person who has this sort of vision "naturally" devise a "program for this seeing." In fact, what sets the monk apart from the people in the street is definitely not an active cultivation of a set of rules for seeing, especially if they are devised as a prescription for belonging to God alone. Merton goes to some lengths to indicate "sixteen or seventeen years" of misunderstanding the monk's identity as "a different species of being, pseudoangels, 'spiritual men,' " which is reinforced by taking vows. The consequence for Merton has been the creation of a dream world "of separateness, of spurious self-isolation in a special world, the world of renunciation and supposed holiness."

---

26. *Conjectures of a Guilty Bystander*, p. 158. Subsequent references to the so-called "Louisville epiphany" will be taken from pp. 156-158.

In the second context, *le point vierge* radically reorganizes the knowledge about what constitutes the realm of the holy. In short, the realm of the holy now involves in a very personal way, the public and communal dimensions in life.[27] This knowledge leads to the realization central to the passage that overwhelms the person who for so long has inhabited the world of "spurious self-isolation." The notion, then, of monastic life as a "separate holy existence" is an illusion created by Merton himself and encouraged, in part, by the existing structures. The knowledge that constitutes the new and unique revelation is that "when I am alone they are not 'they' but my own self. There are no strangers." Moreover, because this knowledge of the holy is placed back into the domain of the "world," it becomes an "understanding" that overwhelms and is "such a relief and such a joy to me that I almost laughed out loud." *Le point vierge* signals this radical reorientation and new found solidarity with people; in addition, the symbol clarifies the difference between the "spurious solitude" of the manipulative intellect and the solitude of vital unity lived by the monk. Ultimately, the loneliness that sets Thomas Merton apart from the people in Louisville becomes, "by a peculiar gift," the solitude that unites him as monk to them: "I was suddenly overwhelmed with the realization that I loved all those people, that they were mine and I theirs, that we could not be alien to one another even though we were total strangers."

In conclusion, I would like to call the reader's attention to the subjective and therefore foundational bases for this essay. The most important decision I made in the process of writing it was to identify as problematic Merton's perception of Blake's theory of art as obscured or "recondite." As Merton develops a new understanding of Blake's Imagination, he addresses and somewhat resolves an even more fundamental question that he has at this time about the relationship between the artist and the mystic.[28] Thus, my attention eventually became ordered by what I (and many other readers of Merton) have determined to have been a conflictual relationship for him. Because I decided I wanted to know more about this relationship, my decision redirected my attention to moments of revelation that I thought "activated" that relationship between artist and mystic and

---

27.   Mircea Eliade, in his discussion "Sacred Space and Making the World Sacred" in *The Sacred and the Profane: The Nature of Religion*, trans. Willard R. Trask (San Diego: Harcourt Brace Jovanovich, 1959) provides a broader anthropological picture for my discussion about the "realm of the holy," by looking at the sundry mythical symbols that describe sacred space and the creation of such space.

28.   Cf. Merton's thesis in *The Literary Essays*: "This seizure of intelligible realities without using concepts as a formal means is something analogous in both the poet and the mystic, but they both operate differently and on different planes" (pp. 444-445).

which best described it.[29] However my attention is initially ordered, the meanings I make come out of my own personal situation; the explanations I create are motivated by demands inherent to my lived situation.[30] In order to suggest how this may be so, I must provide some brief biographical information about myself.

I live in a small city in South Carolina. I live in a Roman Catholic religious community called an Oratory, among sixteen other men, about half of whom are ordained priests, and half of whom are lay members. I am a lay member of the Congregation. In Oratorian communities, there is no canonical prescription for vows such as stability, poverty, or chastity as in a traditional monastic community like Merton's. Although priests who live in the community have priestly vows, lay members live there "voluntarily." John Henry Cardinal Newman, who became an Oratorian after his conversion to Catholicism, describes Oratorian community simply as "nothing more or less than" a group of "secular priests [and lay members] living together, without vows. . ."[31]

I have lived in this Congregation for less than two years, and during this time one of the basic questions with which I have lived is whether I want and/or need to live and commit myself to a celibate lifestyle *and* in this particular community. I have asked this question from at least two points of view. I have asked it from a social or public point of view because I have become more sensitive to the serious questions many people in my own tradition ask about the role of celibacy in "religious life." Moreover, I am sensitive to the people in my region of the country who are suspicious of the value of celibacy. The second point of view is more personal: I have noticed that my own conception of what constitutes community is altered when I acknowledge the possibility of celibacy as part of my lifestyle.

My contention here is that the interpretive strategy I formulated in the course of this essay reflects some of my outstanding interests and concerns in a newly organized and acknowledged way. My analysis of

---

29. Cf. David Bleich in *Subjective Criticism* and his discussion of "the nature of our investigation of, or understanding of, language" in his chapter, "Motivational Character of Language and Symbol Formation," pp. 38-67. Among other things, his discussion indicates that when one's assumption is that "What a person *wants to know* determines explanatory adequacy," that person discovers himself in a "new epistemological circumstance" (p. 41). Bleich sees this new assumption as a central feature of what he calls "the subjective paradigm."

30. My understanding of motive is influenced by Bleich's formulation: "*A motive is a subjectively regulated cause*" (p. 44). I follow Bleich's use of "motive" especially because I understand my present situation in life not as inevitable but as chosen: "In particular, motivation is necessary as an explanatory principle when we aim to understand deliberate behavior or other human action in which choice figures prominently" (p. 45).

31. Placid Murray, O.S.B., *Newman the Oratorian* (Leominster, Herefordshire, England: Fowler Wright Books, 1980), p. 314.

Merton's thesis leads me to two key interpretive conclusions. Put together, these conclusions may be summarized in the following way. Artistic vision reorganizes the natural world in a way that reconstitutes space in which being can behave. Consequently, a person is able to review old meanings (i.e. Blake's more recondite concept of the Imagination) of words. Furthermore, as one develops new explanations or meanings in that reorganized space or scene (i.e. Merton's praise of the Hawk's essential beauty), attention preoccupied with other personally created "forms" is released.

These two conclusions form the basis for what I call the claritas strategy. However, the claritas strategy is not something objectively "there" in the texts which have been examined. Rather this interpretive strategy is created by my own interests and concerns on the occasions in which I respond to a text. In other words, my own lived situation bears decisively on the *kind* of attention I direct towards a particular text. In this way, the claritas strategy emerges out of my on-going interaction with certain passages written by Thomas Merton.

I have already suggested how the claritas strategy helped me to evaluate and clarify the meaning of solitude in the Louisville passage. The basic insight is that knowledge about what constitutes the realm of the holy, as Merton's attention is directed by the *point vierge* symbol, now involves him in a more personal way in the public and communal dimensions of life. In addition, such an explanation partially satisfies a demand inherent to my situation for developing my intuition about celibacy as a way of finding closeness or intimacy with people in different public situations.

My contention is that the interpretive strategy I have formulated out of my reading of Merton had made this demand noticeable.[32] As a result, I was able to clarify an on-going (and at times problematic) perception of myself as a man who chooses to be celibate. Moreover, the claritas strategy becomes a key interpretive context for, because it calls attention to, "new" meanings to problematic perceptions of a word or value as I know either in my situation.[33] This interpretive context may clarify, but it also reorients me in a "new" way to my community. The implication of the claritas strategy is that I now have a way to gain knowledge about, as well as a more complex understanding for, a value to which I am daily committed.

---

32. Cf. Fish, "Interpreting the *Variorum*," pp. 166-167: "In short, what is noticed is what has been *made* noticeable, not by a clear and undistorting glass, but by an interpretive strategy" (p. 166).

33. Bleich sees interpretation as "not a decoding or an analytical process . . . [but rather] a synthesis of new meanings based on the assumption that the old shared meanings of words and works are not in question, but that the *present perception* of these meanings have created the experiential circumstance for resymbolization" (p. 95). I share this assumption with Bleich. In addition, Bleich's term "resymbolization" coincides with my use of "interpretive conclusions."

Considerable Dance.

FROM PROPHECY TO PARODY:

THOMAS MERTON'S

CABLES TO THE ACE

by **David D. Cooper**

During the 1960s, Thomas Merton was perhaps best known, especially among post-Vatican II Catholics, for his efforts to fashion a viable Christian humanism in a post-Christian era of religious reform.[1] At a time too of great social upheaval and personal unrest, many readers turned to Merton's writings on the curative possibilities of contemplation, a timely and natural outgrowth of Merton's own monastic experience.[2] Merton's new humanism and his claims for the therapeutic potential of solitude shared two things in common. Each were responses to alienation as the distinguishing feature of life in advanced technological civilization. And each was forged from the crucible of critical social theories which sought, through rigorous dissent, to revitalize that civilization with humanist reforms.

---

1. Merton's major essays on Christian humanism have been collected in *Love and Living*, ed. Naomi Burton Stone and Brother Patrick Hart (New York: Farrar, Straus & Giroux, 1979), pp. 133-232.

2. See, e.g., "Notes for a Philosophy of Solitude" in *Disputed Questions* (New York: Farrar, Straus & Cudahy, 1960), pp. 170-207; "Creative Silence" in *Love and Living*, pp. 38-45; and "Rain and the Rhinoceros" in *Raids on the Unspeakable* (New York: New Directions, 1966), pp. 9-23.

Nowhere are those common elements more pronounced than in Merton's late poetry, especially *Cables to the Ace*, his radical experiment with the language of alienation and its implications for a new poetry -- an anti-poetry -- of pure signs. The new poetry that began to appear in the mid-60s, that is to say, entirely abrogates traditional symbolism in favor of *indicative signs*. Its distinguishing hallmark is Merton's wholesale renunciation of conventional syntactical patterns of meaning and inherited standards of poetic truth, which help account for the opacity and, at times, the utter abstruseness of his later poetry and its abrupt departure from any of his previous work. Merton's anti-poetics suggests generally, then, that he believed a poetry stripped of the efficacy of symbolic language was a poetry essentially of unmeaning, a poetry of denatured tropes parroting the banality of the contemporary mind. Merton's new humanism was the response of a committed humanist outraged by the dehumanizing effects of mass culture. Similarly, his new poetry was the reaction of a poet angered by what Merton once described as "the spasmodic upheaval of language" reflected in mass culture modes of discourse.

This issue of Merton's anti-poetics has been widely discussed in Merton scholarship,[3] and it is difficult to pin down a consensus among literary critics, some of whom have gone to extraordinary lengths to unslip the Gordian knot of *Cables to the Ace*.[4] It may well be, in the final analysis, that Merton's purpose in *Cables* was only to frustrate critical good sense and create a post-modern paean to unmeaning whose sole aim was to dislocate decoding efforts. A curious spectre haunts *Cables*. Might it be a repository of jokes where Merton pokes fun at literary scholars who seem bent, as he once said of Joyce studies, on pursuing "an academic treasure hunt which [Joyce] took far less seriously than they?" In any event, in the following discussion of Merton's late poetics we will try to avoid springing the playful traps strewn especially throughout *Cables*, choosing instead a safer, less problematic course: namely, that Merton's denatured anti-poetics was his way of entering, as a poet, into the consciousness of alienated man and mimicking his style of speech -- his way, he himself remarked, of declaring war on dehumanizing modes of contemporary discourse which exacerbate human alienation. Like Merton's radical humanism, his new poetry is, above all, a poetry of dissent.

---

3. See Ross Labrie, *The Art of Thomas Merton* (Fort Worth: Texas Christian University Press, 1979), pp. 134-147; Sister Therese Lentfoehr, *Words and Silence: On the Poetry of Thomas Merton* (New York: New Directions, 1979), pp. 97-114; and George Woodcock, *Thomas Merton, Monk and Poet: A Critical Study* (New York: Farrar, Straus & Giroux, 1978), pp. 173ff.

4. See, e.g., Luke Flaherty, "Thomas Merton's *Cables to the Ace*: A Critical Study," *Renascence* 24:1 (Autumn 1971): pp. 3-32.

2.   One thing is certain: any discussion of Merton's anti-poems cannot be separated from his continuing interest in critical social theory. Among important direct influences and models -- such poets as Merton's friends Robert Lax[5] and the Chilean anti-poet Nicanor Parra[6] -- Merton also needed a firm theoretical and philosophical basis for his experiments with a new poetry. He found that substratum in the writings of Herbert Marcuse whose model of a one-dimensional society merged into a perfect partnership with other writers who had previously shaped Merton's radical humanism, including Marx, Dietrich Bonhoeffer, Albert Camus, and Erich Fromm.

Marcuse's social critique, set forth in *One-Dimensional Man*, uncovered serious deficiencies in modern industrial society which he felt had led to an advanced state of human alienation. By way of quick overview, Marcuse argued that contemporary society was so dominated by the technological processes of production/distribution/consumption that it had succumbed, in effect, to a technological totalitarianism. A society under the domination of its technology not only determines the occupations, skills, and attitudes of workers necessary to sustain its technological apparatus, but, according to Marcuse, it must also control and define the needs and aspirations of its workers. Technological totalitarianism -- defined by Marcuse as "a non-terroristic economic-technical coordination which operates through the manipulation of needs by vested interests"[7] --effectively obliterates any distinctions between private and public life and individual and societal needs, thus creating a "one-dimensional society" comprised of one-dimensional persons. When economic and technological contigencies prevail, such things as individuality, dissent, and nonconformity lose their critical function -- indeed, Marcuse claimed, they become socially useless.

With its emphasis on repression and subjugation of individual needs, Marcuse's model of the one-dimensional society carries profoundly antihumanistic consequences. He insisted that the prevailing societal forces of process, technique, and operation subvert the economic, political, and intellectual freedom of individuals. Individual needs, he stressed, collapse under the tyranny of vested collective interests, the kinds of interests "which

---

5.   See especially Thomas Merton and Robert Lax, *A Catch of Anti-Letters* (Kansas City: Sheed, Andrews & McMeel, 1978).

6.   See Merton's translations in *Poems and Antipoems*, ed. Miller Williams (New York: New Directions, 1966).

7.   *One-Dimensional Man: Studies in the Ideology of Advanced Industrial Society* (Boston: Beacon Press, 1964), p. 3. Further references appear in the text.

perpetuate toil, aggressiveness, misery, and injustice." "The more rational, productive, technical, and total the repressive administration of society becomes," Marcuse concludes, "the more unimaginable the means and ways by which the administered individuals might break their servitude and seize their own liberation" (pp. 6-7).

Of particular interest to Marcuse, and more germane to his influence over Merton's new poetics, was the way in which one-dimensional behavior and thought are expressed in modern modes of communication.[8] Discourse in a one-dimensional society, Marcuse considered, must reflect the same repressive and totalitarian characteristics as the economic and political forces which manipulate individual needs in order to sustain the collective technological agenda. The language of one-dimensional man, Marcuse claimed, testifies then to those societal forces responsible for his repression. Thus, language in a one-dimensional society has yielded to a progressive "functionalization" which repells non-conformist and idiosyncratic elements from the patterns and movements of speech. One-dimensional language is dominated by "operationalism;" it is the language of "technological reasoning" which rigorously promotes positive thinking and action, a language "that orders and organizes, that induces people to do, to buy, and to accept." Moreover, Marcuse argued, this functional language stifles "transcendent, critical notions;" it disables such rhetorical elements as "symbols of reflection, abstraction, development, contradiction." Above all, by devaluating transcendence, dissension, contradiction, critical reflection, etc., functional discourse *"militates against a development of meaning,"* Marcuse writes, because "it does not search for but establishes and imposes truth and falsehood."

Marcuse examined the concrete manifestations of one-dimensional discourse in such areas as contemporary patterns of syntax and usage, historical writing, political language, and advertising copy. He summarizes:

> Abridgment of the concept in fixed images; arrested development in self-validating, hypnotic formulas; immunity against contradiction; identification of the thing (and of the person) with its function -- these tendencies reveal the one-dimensional mind in the language that it speaks. (pp. 96-97)

And he concludes:

> In and for the society, this organization of functional discourse is of vital importance; it serves as a vehicle of coordination and subordination. The unified, functional language is an irreconcilably anti-critical and anti-

---

8. See especially "The Closing of the Universe of Discourse," *Ibid*, pp. 84-120.

dialectical language. In it, operational and behavioral rationality absorbs the transcendent, negative, oppositional elements of Reason. (p. 103)

3.   Turning now to Merton, ample evidence -- stated explicitly or otherwise implied -- suggests that he interpreted Marcuse's functional discourse as the language of alienated man. In *Zen and the Birds of Appetite*, for example, Merton announces his complete agreement with Marcuse's critique of one-dimensional thinking and discourse "in which," Merton writes, "the very rationality and exactitude of technological society and its various justifications, add up to one more total mystification."[9] Consider further Merton's essay "Symbolism: Communication or Communion?", a wide-ranging series of reflections and commentary on the fate of symbolism in technological society. Although Merton does not cite *One-Dimensional Man* directly, the essay resonates with Marcuse's ideas. It may be appropriate to argue, then, that Merton used Marcuse's insights into the functionalization of modern language as a springboard to discuss its spiritual ramifications. If, as Marcuse claimed, modern language had succumbed to sheer operationalism, Merton argued, by extension, that the functionalization of discourse had been accompanied by a gradual *dysfunctionalization* of symbolic language. And it followed for Merton that this erosion of the power of the symbol and the deterioration in the modern person's capacity to respond to symbolic language are "alarming symptoms of spiritual decay."

Merton attributes the degradation of symbolic language in scientific and technological society to "an incapacity to distinguish between the *symbol* and the *indicative sign*." The preeminent function of the sign, Merton explains, is to communicate practical and factual information. The symbol, in contrast, has no utilitarian value whatsoever; it does not convey information or *explain*. Given then the overwhelming premium set on function, operation, and process in modern mass culture, as Marcuse had argued, the nonutilitarian symbol is drained of its efficacy and routed from the language of mass-man.

Useless as a means of communication, Merton comments on the higher purpose achieved by the symbol, "the purpose of going beyond practicality and purpose, beyond cause and effect."[10] He stresses the trans-

---

9. Thomas Merton, *Zen and the Birds of Appetite* (New York: New Directions, 1968), pp. 139-140.
10. *Love and Living*, p. 67. Hereafter referred to in the text as *L&L*.

cendent function of symbolism, its role as a vehicle of union and synthesis, and its power to awaken "spiritual resonances" that evoke a deeper awareness "of the inner meaning of life and of reality itself." Symbols mobilize and animate vital resources of creativity and spirituality. Merton draws on the power of symbolic language itself in an effort to approximate the function and purpose of symbolism. "A true symbol takes us to the center of [a] circle, not to another point on the circumference. A true symbol points to the very heart of being, not to an incident in the flow of becoming" (*L&L*, pp. 54-55).

> The symbol [Merton writes] awakens awareness, or restores it. Therefore, it aims not at communication but at communion. Communion is the awareness of participation in an ontological or religious reality: in the mystery of being, of human love, of redemptive mystery, of contemplative truth.
>
> The purpose of the symbol, if it can be said to have a "purpose," is not to increase the quantity of our knowledge and information but to deepen and enrich the *quality* of life itself by bringing man into communion with the mysterious sources of vitality and meaning, of creativity, love, and truth, to which he cannot have direct access by means of science and technique. (*L&L*, p. 68)
>
> The vital role of the symbol [then] is precisely this: to express and encourage man's acceptance of his own center, his own ontological roots in a mystery of being that transcends his individual ego. (*L&L*, p. 65)

As Merton positions his discussion of symbolism's transcendent values into the context of modern technological culture -- a context clearly indentifiable as Marcuse's one-dimensional society -- Merton's commentary pivots sharply into critique and lament. One-dimensional society, after all, obliterates the distinction between public and private existence; therefore, it bars contact with those ontological roots of which symbols aim to evoke awareness. Modes of modern communication, which Marcuse showed to be dominated by utilitarian processes, effectively cripple the higher function of symbolism to transcend, as Merton argued, practicality and cause and effect. The operational rationality of modern discourse -- a central premise of Marcuse's critique -- absorbs and denies transcendent vocabularies. In one-dimensional society, the symbol as a vehicle of communion, in short, surrenders to a discourse of signs with its sole purpose of identifying facts and conveying information.

Merton also acknowledges, at least implicitly, Marcuse's claims for the totalitarian character of functional language, a language that, as Marcuse says, serves only to induce people "to do, to buy, and to accept." Elsewhere -- for example in Merton's "War and the Crisis of Language," a far sharper protest against denatured contemporary prose than his jeremiad on the degradation of symbolism -- Merton cites many examples in modern usage which illustrate the breakdown of communication into deception. By analyzing advertising copy, political jargon, and even religious language, Merton parallels Marcuse's argument that such modes of discourse reveal a language of "power," "self-enclosed finality," and "totalist dictatorship" in action. This is a language, Merton argues, of final utterance and hypnotic formulation in which "the insatiable appetite for the tautological, the definitive, the *final*"[11] defies contradiction and dissent and, as Marcuse stressed, militates against the development of meaning, what Merton prefers to call "the contamination of reason . . . by inherent ambiguity." Merton selects examples especially from military terminology -- such as "kill ratio," "pacification," "free zone," "liberation" -- which reflect precisely those characteristics of operationalism that Marcuse claimed preclude the genuine development of meaning. Such terms are, first and foremost, rooted in cliche. They exemplify what Marcuse described as the abridgment of concepts in fixed images: that is, they oversimplify, compress, and economize content to the point of utterly obscuring underlying concepts. This is the kind of terminology, as Merton would say, that contaminates reason through ambiguity. Specifically, Merton explains, a "free zone" is an area where anything that moves can be assumed to be the enemy and shot. He cites the case of an army major who explained the shelling of a South Vietnamese village as "liberation;" "it became necessary," the major reports, "to destroy the town in order to save it." More recent examples would include the CIA's manual for anti-Sandinista rebels in Nicaragua which urges "the selective use of violence" against government officials (assassination) and proposes the "elimination" of a popular Contra supporter in order to create a "martyr" for the cause (disloyalty and murder).

This is, by and large, a discourse of gross deception, evasion, euphemism. It is a business-like and antiseptic sort of terminology in which clinical certainty successfully masks sinister connotations. Such terms seem immune to contradiction in their masterful and unsentimental justifications of the otherwise ugly strategies of war. Although the above examples are drawn from military jargon, their distinguishing features, as Marcuse and Merton show, extend to all manner of linguistic forms in one-dimensional society. What unifies the range of discourse in such a society is the will to power which dictates ethically neutral patterns of speech. As Merton

---

11. Thomas Merton, *The Nonviolent Alternative*, ed. Gordon Zahn (New York: Farrar, Straus & Giroux, 1980), p. 238. Hereafter referred to in the text as *NVA*.

explains, the logic of power speaks the language of power, "a language that is all the more pervasive because it is proud of being ethically illiterate and because it accepts, as realistic, the basic irrationality of its own tactics" (*NVA*, p. 241). It is, above all, a language inherently dehumanizing and contemptuous of fundamental human values and needs -- a discourse, Merton writes, "of double-talk, tautology, ambiguous cliche, self-righteous and doctrinaire pomposity, and pseudo-scientific jargon that mask a total callousness and moral insensitivity, indeed a basic contempt for man" (*NVA*, p. 246).

Returning to Merton's discussion of the degradation of symbolism, the dynamics of his argument reduce to a basic conflict between Marcuse's totalitarian functional discourse and Merton's own interpretation of the purpose of symbolism, between a language which indoctrinates truth and falsehood and a language which promotes the search for truth. Drawing on a line from *Cables to the Ace*, at stake, Merton maintains, is nothing less than the survival of symbolic language in "a culture of bare-faced literal commands." Sounding a note of serious alarm, Merton questions that survival as long as the modern person, he suggests, remains "cut off from any reality except that of his own processes . . . and that of the extraordinary new world of his machines." "When man is reduced to his empirical self and confined within its limits, he is, so to speak, excluded from himself, cut off from his own roots, condemned to . . . a wilderness of externals . . . [where] there can be no living symbols" (*L&L*, p. 65).

Not willing to conclude his reflections on the dysfunctionalization of symbolic language on such a pessimistic note, Merton calls on artists and poets -- "the ones most aware of the disastrous situation [and] for that very reason the closest to despair" -- to restore vitality to the corrupt and degenerate sense of symbolism and check the process which continues to devalue symbolic language in technological society. He calls for a renewal of wisdom that, like his new humanism, "must be more than a return to the past, however glorious. We need a wisdom appropriate to our own predicament," a wisdom that recognizes and cooperates with the "spiritual and creative vitality" of symbolism and refuses, above all, any complicity with the logic and language of power. "One thing is certain," he notes finally, "if the contemplative . . . and the poet . . . forsake [that] wisdom and join in the triumphant, empty-headed crowing of advertising men and engineers of opinion, then there is nothing left in store for us but total madness" (*L&L*, p. 79).

4. That last comment is somewhat perplexing, especially in light of *Cables to the Ace* in which Merton, contrary to his own advice to fellow poets, eschews symbolic language. By extrapolating modes of mass culture discourse into a new poetry devoid of symbolism, the practicing poet of *Cables* sounds as if he is compromising the essayist of "Symbolism: Communication or Communion?". At least it may appear as though Merton fails to heed his own counsel because *Cables*, while by no means an exercise in "total madness," is nonetheless an anti-poetry that shuns the vitality and wisdom of traditional symbolism; it is a poetry that prefers instead to join in what Merton elsewhere condemns as empty-headed crowing along the road to lunacy. Any hints of conflict, however, between Merton's advice to other poets and his own practice of anti-poetry should not be construed as such clear evidence of cross-purposes or contradictions. After all, by mimicking the discourse of ad-men and engineers of opinion in *Cables* Merton is, in effect, condemning that discourse. Besides, Merton's approach to the fundamental issue of language, and especially the fate and the practice of poetry in contemporary society, is complicated by a separation of perspectives, by two distinct personae with separate obligations.

As a priest, for example, Merton viewed the degradation of symbolism in technological society as evidence of spiritual decay. This is the voice, then, that issues apocalyptic warning signals in "Symbolism: Communication or Communion?". This is the persona that elsewhere calls on contemporary poets to liberate themselves from society's "coercive or seductive pressures" and assesses the poet's responsibility as "a moral obligation to maintain his own freedom and his own truth."[12] It is as a priest that Merton addresses a gathering of Latin American poets whom he urges "to remain united against . . . falsehoods, against all power that poisons man, and subjects him to the mystifications of bureaucracy, commerce and the police state." Modern poets must seek their liberation, he further intones, by renouncing "tutelage to established political systems or cultural structures" and their "impurity of language and spirit . . . ."[13] As a spiritual counselor, Merton defines the poet in such homilies as these, in short, as a prophet who restores a spiritual vision to reality and the future.

But as a practicing poet, Merton seemed more interested in parody than prophecy. As a poet himself, in other words, Merton viewed the degradation of symbolism in technological society as opening up new

---

12. "Answers on Art and Freedom" in *Raids on the Unspeakable*, pp. 170-171.
13. "Message to Poets," *Ibid.*, pp. 155-159.

possibilities for an innovative poetics: a radically experimental, post-modern anti-poetry notable for its lack of any moral fervor or prophetic spirit, a poetry that does not resist "the mystifications of bureaucracy, commerce and the police state" but rather submits to such mystifications. Both the poet and the priest recognized, as Merton -- echoing Marcuse -- says in *Zen and the Birds of Appetite*, that "Western culture . . . [had] reached the climax of entire totalitarian rationality of organization and of complete absurdity and self-contradiction" (p. 140). The priest resisted that recognition because it raised the specter of a modern ethos alien to his spiritual traditions. But the poet, especially of *Cables to the Ace*, accepted it and sought after an aesthetic appropriate to what Marcuse had defined essentially as a one-dimensional society distinguished by one-dimensional thought and behavior. If, when speaking as a priest, Merton urged other poets to liberate themselves from that ethos, as a poet he entered it and began experimenting with the kind of poetry, as he notes in a review of Roland Barthes' *Writing Degree Zero*, "which reminds the reader not to get lost . . . in false complicities with the message or the emotion, not to get swept away by illusions of inner meaning, a slice of life, a cosmic celebration, or an eschatological vision."[14] This is a poetry -- an *anti-poetry* -- that does just the opposite of what traditional poetry, empowered by symbolism, should do. Anti-poetry does not bring the reader "into communion with . . . mysterious sources of vitality and meaning, of creativity, love, and truth." Merton defines the purpose of anti-poetry and the role of the anti-poet most succinctly in an entry in *The Asian Journal*: "The anti-poet 'suggests' a tertiary meaning which is *not* 'creative' and 'original' but a deliberate ironic feedback of cliche, a further referential meaning, alluding, by its tone, banality, etc., to a *customary and abused context*, that of an impoverished and routine sensibility, and of the 'mass-mind,' the stereotyped creation of quantitative response by 'mass-culture.' "[15] The anti-poet abandons all conventional postures and approaches because "he can no longer trust the honesty of his customary dialogue with the rest of society." He is cut off from public discourse in a culture of specialization and separation where, as the poet Wendell Berry has more recently suggested, "the old union of beauty, goodness, and truth is broken." The anti-poet must then surrender "all charismatic exaltation, all aspiration to

---

14.   *The Literary Essays of Thomas Merton*, ed. Brother Patrick Hart (New York: New Directions, 1981), p. 142. Hereafter referred to in the text as *LE*.

15.   *The Asian Journal of Thomas Merton*, ed. Naomi Burton, Brother Patrick Hart and James Laughlin (New York: New Directions, 1975), p. 286.

power, all *numen*, all that would seem to give him some ascendancy over the reader" (*LE*, p. 145).

In a manner of speaking, then, the anti-poet declares himself poet laureate of Marcuse's one-dimensional society. "Marcuse," Merton acknowledges in *The Asian Journal*, "has shown how mass culture tends to be anticulture --to stifle creative work by the sheer volume of what is 'produced,' or reproduced. In which case, poetry . . . must start with an awareness of this contradiction and *use* it -- as anti-poetry -- which freely draws on the material of superabundant nonsense at its disposal . . . and feed [it] back . . . into the mass consumption of pseudo-culture" (p. 118).

5.   So the following discussion of entries selected from *Cables to the Ace* builds on the fundamental proposition that Merton's radical aesthetic of the anti-poem incorporates many elements of Marcuse's "functional discourse" in one-dimensional society.[16] As indicated earlier, however, any effort to give a comprehensive and unified reading of *Cables* is bound to be frustrated by its apparently purposeful uncenteredness and its anything-goes free-wheeling pitch. Many things tumble together in disarray. While melancholic (as in Cable 12, for example), it is at times utterly comic, as when a midget suddenly pops out in Cable 27 and cries: "Hats off! Hats off to the human condition!" In a Prologue which is bullying to the point of insult, Merton sets the stage for an aggressiveness that also surfaces in many Cables, the same sort of aggression that heated much of Merton's social criticism and prompted him once to confess to a certain petulancy rooted in egotism. Some Cables are grossly, though playfully nonsensical, while in others the babble gives way to esoteric utterance, pensive and wise (Cables 37 and 38). One may wonder too why Merton saw fit to include some of the love poems he wrote for a nurse in Louisville: for example Cable 78, "Harmonies of Excess,"[17] where a serene lyricism seems so discordant and compromised as it jostles against the opposite moods of its neighboring entries. All of this makes for a disorienting reading experience, a disruptive, automatic, random conjoining of disparate elements -- "mosaics," Merton called them, or "Familiar Liturgies of Misunderstanding" -- where poetry and anti-poetry, verse and prose blocks fire, so to speak, in cylinders oddly

---

16.   Selections are taken from *The Collected Poems of Thomas Merton* (New York: New Directions, 1977), pp. 393-454.

17.   These so-called "love poems" have been collected in *Eighteen Poems* (New York: New Directions, 1986).

out of time. Nonetheless, we can at least identify a major leitmotif that trails through *Cables to the Ace*: it can be read profitably as a sustained Marcusian meditation on the dysfunctionalization of symbolic language in technological society, a sort of anti-poetry *qua* social criticism.

In Cables 1 and 2, for example, Merton immediately pits the quantitative function of signs against the qualitative values of the symbol and judges the outcome. "Cables" -- as in *telegraphic* cables -- are themselves signs because their purpose is to convey information, to communicate not commune. In Cables 1 and 2, then, messages skip across the page like electric pulses -- short syntactical bursts punctuated by stops -- "played and sung" by one-dimensional societies ill-fated by a totalist technocracy.

> 1.
> Edifying cables can be made musical if played and sung by full-armed societies doomed to an electric war. A heavy imperturbable beat. No indication where to stop. No messages to decode. Cables are never causes. Noises are never values. With the unending vroom vroom vroom of the guitars we will all learn a new kind of obstinacy, together with massive lessons of irony and refusal. We assist once again at the marriage of heaven and hell.

> 2.
> A seer interprets the ministry of the stars, the broken gear of a bird. He tests the quality of stone lights, ashen fruits of a fire's forgotten service. He registers their clarity with each new lurch into suspicion. He does not regret for he does not know. He plots the nativity of the pole star, but it neither sets nor rises. Snow melts on the surface of the young brown river, and there are two lids: the petals of sleep. The sayings of the saints are put away in air-conditioned archives.

"Cables are never causes. Noises are never values." The higher critical functions of causation and value judgment are drowned out here by the hypnotic "heavy imperturbable beat" of Cable (sign) language and absorbed into the omnipresent white noise of vrooming guitars, captured elsewhere, in Cable 77, in a better image as "the copyrighted tornado/ Of sheer sound." The seer in Cable 2 speaks a different language. He interprets and tests and registers clarity. His knowledge derives from intuition. His plotting of the origin of a star does not follow the precise mathematical procedures of astronomy. He exercises higher order cognitive and intellectual faculties, in other words, which Marcuse claims are essentially those of the non-conformist. But the fate of Merton's non-conformist poet-seer in a world where there are "no messages to decode" is hinted at by the nature of the objects upon which the seer trains his intuitive powers. Those objects are metallic and strangely funereal: "the broken gear of a bird," "stone lights" and "ashen fruits," the kinds of objects which might clutter a sterile, even irradiated landscape. The potential symbolic value of a bird or of lights and fruits is negated anyway by the adjectives which modify them. The ultimate fate of the seer is indeed sealed when Merton negotiates a final non-sequitur leap: "The sayings of the saints are put away in air-conditioned archives."

Merton arrives at a similar judgment in Cable 5 where the form of commentary first changes from prose blocks to verse.

> Gem notes
> Of the examiner
> Or terminal declarations:
>
> The Directors
> Have engineered a surprise
> You will not easily discover:

The speech -- the "Notes" -- of the examiner in these lines is that language of self-enclosed finality -- or "terminal declaration" -- which Marcuse identifies as the chief characteristic of totalitarian discourse. It is the speech of directors and dictators and those "engineers of opinion" whom Merton had previously ostracized in his essay on the degradation of symbolism. Their surprise is not only hard to discover but, once discovered, it quickly slips away.

> Come shyly to the main question
> There is dishonor in these wires
> You will first hesitate then repeat
> Then sing louder
> To the drivers
> Of ironic mechanisms
> As they map your political void

Functional discourse dehumanizes; there is dishonor in the language of cables and electric wires. But even if the "you" addressed in the stanza hesitates through faint recognition, he still seems doomed to a hypnotic speech of drives and mechanisms. Cut off from participation in a deeper ontological reality, he enters a landscape of his own emptiness where the directors happily survey his "political void." And among the "many original/ Side effects" of residence in that wasteland of mechanisms, that ethos of operationalism, is that "Each nominal conceit/ Will be shot down by an electric eye" and "Events are finally obscure forever." Symbol and metaphor, along with the critical self-reflection and indeed the very evidence of history itself -- those things Marcuse identifies, in short, as "transcendent functions" -- are stifled and incapacitated until

> You wake and wonder
> Whose case history you composed

As your confessions are filed
In the dialect
Of bureaux and electrons.

Merton had previously defined the purpose of symbolic language as awakening awareness or restoring it; he characterized the symbol as a vehicle of self-discovery. But here functional and operational modes of speech prevail -- "the dialect," that is to say, "Of bureaux and electrons" -- so the case history of self-awareness, arrived at through modes of self-reflection such as confession, becomes little more than fodder for the filing cabinet, like those sayings of the saints shelved away in hermetic archives. Little wonder that Merton immediately follows in Cable 6 with Caliban's curse, quoted from Shakespeare's *The Tempest*: "The red plague rid you/ For learning me your language!"

Throughout these early entries Merton establishes clear links between his own Cables and those various features that Marcuse identifies as preeminent hallmarks of functional discourse in advanced technological society. In the Cables which follow Merton continues to expand those linkages by further developing the controlling image of electricity, an especially ironic choice in light of Merton's own death by accidental electrocution. Electricity is exquisitely organized power transmitted through networks of highly organized circuits, cables, conduits. It is a perfect image for the coordination of functional energy, and Merton uses it to portray a social environment, as Marcuse might say, entirely dominated by its technological apparatus, a social order wired-in to process and technique. Merton traces patterns of electrical flow from the specific to the global -- from "academies of electrical renown" to "the electric village" and "the electric world" and finally to an "electric universe." Ultimately the "electric cosmos" itself comes to resemble a macrocosmic circuit board where everything -- commerce, industry, agriculture, politics, education, metaphysics, religion as well as all modes of human discourse -- flows through "imitable wires," "everlasting carbon vines," and "electric walks." Time itself marches in the electronic parade, for even "the next ice-age [is programmed] from end to end."

Technological totalitarianism -- the politics of Merton's electric village -- must insulate itself, as Marcuse further reasoned, against any non-conformist or idiosyncratic elements which might challenge the organization and control of vested collective interests. It stands to reason that errant pulses or surges are to Merton's electric ethos what dissent, non-conformity, and individuality are to Marcuse's one-dimensional society. Following the metaphor, an electric cosmos must be glitch-proof and protected against anything that threatens to blow a fuse or trip a circuit.

In a further allusion to the operational and behavioral rationality that Marcuse claimed necessarily governed one-dimensional thought and behavior, Merton devotes Cable 19 to a vignette depicting a man wired to a rat's brain in the laboratory of a behavioral scientist. It is a morbid presentation of human behavior shaped and controlled by the mechanisms of pleasure and punishment. "Split second doses of motivation/ Keep you in stitches," Merton writes, and human ecstasies are triggered by rats pushing "pleasure buttons." This is a claustrophobic nightmare that effectively underscores Marcuse's contention that "the more total the repressive administration of society becomes, the more unimaginable the means and ways by which the administered individuals might break their servitude and seize their open liberation." In fact, portraits of such "administered individuals" appear frequently throughout *Cables*. Merton uses the behavioral scenario, for example, in Cable 52 where strictly controlled and ordered human behavior is likened to the robotic activity of an ant, obediently carrying out "his appointed task" and mindlessly following "his appointed round/ In the technical circuit." Or consider the businessman in Cable 50 whose entire being is shaped by the pleasures of "Cracking new money." He worships "truth-telling twenties/ And fifties that understand," and he offers a prayer to "the cunning dollar": "Make me numb/ And advertise/ My buzzing feedbacking/ Business-making mind." His consciousness and conscience and spirit owe allegience to a cult of commerce that provides for all his values, aspirations, and needs. "The dollar . . . tells me no lie/ . . . [it] knows and loves me/ And is my intimate all-looking doctor." Like this disciple of commerce, all of Merton's portraits of administered, alienated individuals reflect operational minds in action: minds that define objectives -- pleasure, wealth -- and identify means -- conformity, commerce -- while betraying an astonishing ineptness in such things as ethical calculation, moral reasoning, and critical self-reflection.

Rats, ants, robotic businessmen -- these, as Merton would no doubt prefer to say, are anti-portraits of human beings reduced to ciphers by the cult of order and organization. These are persons dehumanized, alienated, stripped of their individuality, just like the woman in Cable 43 who is transformed into an empty caricature of the ideal Woman by the ad-man -- the shaman of one dimensional society -- who sells her a new face. Here again the operational mind springs into action: a mind that defines an objective (beauty) and identifies a means (cosmetics) without the slightest

pause for or interest in any authentic self-awareness. Here is a ritual seduc-
tion, an esoteric initiation into the cult of eternal youth, a baptism in
cosmetics full of magic and mysterious charms. "Let us cool your bitter
sweet charm," chants the ad-man, "with incense and verse." He conjures a
"rich pigment," "a new glaze of ours . . ."

> . . . to melt away
> Stubborn little worries known as lines
> To restore with magic lanolin our flawless picture of
> YOU
> Yes you, our own pity-making sweet charade of oils

This is only one entry among many others in *Cables* where Merton
parodies the popular genre of Madison Avenue. Like Marcuse, Merton was
fascinated by the language of advertisement, especially its incantory and
charismatic power, as Marcuse said, to induce people to do, to buy, to
accept. Incidentally, while working on *Cables*, Merton received regular
consignments of ad-copy which he requested from his friends. "I would
much appreciate good, gaudy, noisy *ad* material," he mentioned to W. H.
Ferry, noting "how conscious [I am] of the wacky material there is to exploit
in ads." (Apparently Merton had his limits. After receiving a bundle of such
ads, he quickly returned notice: ". . . Enough! . . . Am still retching. Weak
stomach, getting old . . . Old gut won't take it. This will be quite enough to
produce the long poetic retch I was planning."[18]) As he said in "War and the
Crisis of Language," it is "the vocation of the poet -- or the anti-poet -- *not*
to be deaf to [advertisements] but to apply his ear to their corrupt charms."
Among such consignments of ad material, and perhaps as a prototype for
the cosmetics ad that he parodies in Cable 43, Merton cites in that essay the
example of an Arpege hair spray advertisement culled from *The New
Yorker*:

> A delicate-as-air-spray
> Your hair takes on a shimmer and sheen that's wonderfully young.
> You seem to spray new life and bounce right into it.

He celebrates this hair spray verse as a "masterpiece" of anti-poetry that
stands "inviolate in its own victorious rejection of meaning." Like the
lanolin magic of Cable 43, Arpege "is endowed with a finality so inviolable
that it is beyond debate and beyond reason . . . at once totally trivial and
totally definitive." That "it has nothing to do with anything real" seems of
little consequence or concern. And like the "flawless picture of YOU"
conjured in Merton's own ad parody, Arpege "is so magic that it not only

---

18. *The Hidden Ground of Love: The Letters of Thomas Merton on Religious Experience and Social
Concerns*, ed. William H. Shannon (New York: Farrar, Straus & Giroux, 1985), p. 229.

makes you smell good, it 'coifs' you with a new and unassailable identity."
By applying his ear to the charm of ad copy in *Cables*, Merton not only
parodies its linguistic features but he enters into the mentality of salesman-
ship and what he firmly believed to be its consciousness of moral illiteracy.
That, as Merton said, is the duty of the anti-poet: to "feedback" for mass
culture consumption a language that testifies to the impoverished and
dehumanized sensibility of the mass mind.

That sensibility, moreover, is so vulnerable to the persuasive and
hypnotic power of manipulation, as Marcuse argues, that its higher order
intellectual skills are crippled. Such cognitive functions as abstraction,
conceptualization, synthesis, demonstration, and critique atrophy when
operational logic (designation, identification, assertion, imitation, etc.)
dominates consciousness and modes of thought. If modes of discourse
reflect modes of thought, it follows that language itself becomes what
Marcuse calls a "closed language" that "does not demonstrate and explain
-- it communicates decision, dictum, command" (p. 101).

Much of the abstruseness and the frankly annoying incoherence of
Cables, then, might well be the result of Merton's implementing a
Marcusian-like "closed language" and capitalizing especially on the disruption of meaning inevitable in a language closed to higher order cognitive functions. The anti-poet not only "feeds back" an impoverished sensibility, he taps the rich resources of "superabundant nonsense" at his
disposal, as Merton notes in *The Asian Journal* with direct reference to
Marcuse, and returns it too back into mass culture circulation. Throughout
Cables Merton often taps into that reservoir; he borrows popular modes of
discourse and parodies their formal structures while simultaneously dis-
rupting and disjointing patterns of meaning.

For example, by culling terminology common to manufacturing and
industry -- the accepted and standard jargon of commerce -- Merton
assembles such terms into a syntactical cackle in Cable 25: "Elastic programs
to draft nonspecialist energy and rotate funds to speedup intake of output." In addition to ad copy, similarly farcical constructions are used to
satirize business memoranda (Cable 26), academic discourse (Cable 33),
gossip columns (Cable 41), even cut lines for newspaper photographs
(Cable 70): "Clean-cut pirate meets and befriends priceless stolen owl. . ."
The ultimate dismembering of semantics occurs in Cable 48, a ludicrous
burlesque of a newscast. It is sufficient to quote only the first stanza:

> Children of large nervous furs
> Will grow more pale this morning

> In king populations
> Where today drug leaders
> Will promote an ever increasing traffic
> Of irritant colors
> Signs of this evident group
> Are said to be almost local

Here are typical references to time and place: this morning, today, local. And Merton selects stock verbs which are common to any news broadcast: "promote," "are said to be." But the factual certainty one expects from a newscast is derailed by the passive voice. Besides, time, place and action are mediated by nonsensical constructions. Absurd adverb and adjective clauses, random modifiers, and non-sequitur transitions sabotage logical semantic relationships until meaning is so disrupted that the broadcast collapses into an inane babble, into "a copyrighted tornado/ Of sheer sound."

Let us consider finally Cable 30 where all of these previously discussed elements fuse together into a distinctly Orwellian meditation on the utter banality of an utterly ordinary day: the day, we might say, of a typical one-dimensional citizen in a typical one-dimensional society. During this day, events are strung together by a chain reaction of signals, and people go about their activities as if switched on and off by terminals in a grid. The functional discourse of signs and its potential to dehumanize; the controlling image of electricity; totalitarianism, operationalism, automatization; the parody of ad copy; and the broken syntax of nonsense -- all of these are indiscriminately conjoined to depict the narcosis of human routine in an environment cluttered with signs. Morning begins with the ubiquitous sounds of sizzling bacon and perking coffee ("the chatter of meats" and the "Nine o'clock boil"), which in turn trigger an exodus of crowds and traffic into high rise buildings topped with flashing neon signs -- "An electric goat's head/ Turns and smiles/ Turns and smiles" -- which in turn switch on a counter-exodus back through "Names Omens Tunnels" to "Night sanctuaries/ Imaginary refuge/ Full of flowers" and "The solemn twittering of news," until the entire day disappears into a vortex of ultimate unmeaning as

> The iron voice in the next apartment
> Cries NOW
> And you flush the toilet.

Cable 30 is probably one of the purest examples of anti-poetry in Cables to the Ace. It is composed entirely of signs, like the literal blinking tautology of that absurd flashing neon goat's head. The crowds that shuffle along "in cotton mist/ And Chloroform" are composed of entirely alienated indi- viduals bereft of ontological roots, so the poem itself is stripped of symbolic language. Cable 30 refuses any participation in an ontological or religious reality of which, as Merton claimed, symbols evoke awareness. There is no "mystery of being, of human love, of redemptive mystery, of contemplative truth" in Cable 30's "energy of motors." Even the pitiful clergyman in the anti-poem joins the mindless march as he "goes by/ With a placard/ 'You can still win'." Christian confidence in salavation -- The Good News -- is just another message, another billboard ad in this ethos of signals and signs.

THE PATTERN IN THOMAS MERTON'S

CABLES TO THE ACE

by **Gail Ramshaw**

The tradition of the American epic poem, evident in the works of Walt Whitman, Ezra Pound, Hart Crane, and William Carlos Williams, is also seen in the major poems of Thomas Merton. Since *The Geography of Lograire* is an incomplete posthumous publication and is thus difficult to discuss definitively, Merton's 1968 poem, *Cables to the Ace*, provides the better opportunity for such form criticism.[1] Typically in the American epic poem the protagonist-poet, usually standing within a specific geography, juxtaposes his art to the American experience within a lengthy series of sections which may range from self-contained poems to newspaper quotations. One task which form criticism brings to the genre of the American epic poem is the search for the pattern within the form. Is there a logic to the ordering of the sections beyond the sequence of publication? If so, what is the logic? If not, does the lack imply artistic deficiency? The following study will demonstrate both Merton's process of composition in the writing of *Cables to the Ace* and the pattern which exists within the

---

1. Thomas Merton, *Cables to the Ace* (New York: New Directions, 1968). Subsequent references to this edition will be cited in the text.

Editor's Note: This essay is a revised version of a paper given at the "Thomas Merton Consultation," *American Academy of Religion* Annual Meeting, New York, 15-18 November 1979.

completed poem. For, in this case, the genre of the American epic poem has a pattern: a dialogue between the noise of the world and the voice of myth is patterned into a widening gyre with three focal points, the prayerful lyrics of sections 7, 45, and 80.

We must begin by admitting that if any pattern exists in *Cables*, it is, at first, next to invisible. The poem is comprised of an epigraph, a prologue, an introduction, 88 sections, an epilogue, and a curious final phrase. No outline or table of contents is published or has been found among Merton's papers. Of the critics who have discussed this work, none has noted any order to the sections.[2] One study calls the poem "a mosaic of prose and poetry."[3] The word "cables" in Merton's title implies the plural: many poems. The subtitle repeats the plural in "Familiar Liturgies." In the prologue (p. 1) Merton uses the plural in calling his poems "Horatian Odes" and "mosaics." Until the final typescript the poem was entitled *Edifying Cables*, this title also supporting a hypothesis that the poem is a collection of poems, the order of publication being no more, but no less arbitrary, than that in any collection of poems. In writing to Jacques Maritain of this work, Merton uses the plural verb: *"The Edifying Cables* are finished. . ."[4] Found among Merton's papers was a stray piece of paper which describes the poem:

> Edifying Cables
> On the surface the poetic statement was toneless, and now discordant, deliberately illogical, tentative and crude. Below the surface lies something more deadly: a subliminal irony, a savage elaboration of the absurd. This is far from the dry alienated complaint of Eliot's "Hollow Men." It is rather an active involvement in contemporary absurdity, a Zen-like zest in the ring of hollowness inside the experience of the sixties.[5]

Here also the word "illogical" suggests a composition without grand design.

But literary critics are seldom contented with the poet's own analysis, and so we shall test the assumption that the poem is constructed without inherent logic. It is not clear in Merton's comment whether the piece is illogical only "on the surface." One way to trace the logic of the poem is to

---

2. Luke Flaherty, "Thomas Merton's *Cables to the Ace*: A Critical Study," *Renascence* 24 (1971), pp. 3-32; Victor A. Kramer, *Thomas Merton* (Boston: Twayne, 1984), pp. 127-135; Walter Sutton, "Thomas Merton and the American Epic Tradition: The Last Poems," *Contemporary Literature* 14 (1973), pp. 49-57; and George Woodcock, *Thomas Merton, Monk and Poet: A Critical Study* (New York: Farrar, Straus & Giroux, 1978), pp. 173-176.

3. Ross Labrie, *The Art of Thomas Merton* (Fort Worth: Texas Christian University Press, 1979), p. 138.

4. Thomas Merton to Jacques Maritain, 18 November 1966, Thomas Merton Studies Center, Bellarmine College.

5. Thomas Merton, "Comment concerning *Edifying Cables*," Thomas Merton Studies Center, Bellarmine College.

discover the logic of its composition. Somewhere in the process of composition, whether in the original writing or in a subsequent reordering, the poet might give evidence of the work's pattern. We will trace the composition of *Cables to the Ace* through the following stages: its antecedents in stories and correspondence, Holographic Notebook # 15, sequences of extra poems, and three typescripts.[6]

We begin before the poem's beginning, in the short story entitled "Martin's Predicament, or Atlas Watches Every Evening."[7] By playing with the myth of Atlas, Merton focuses on "imperatives," modern society's substitution of impersonal commands for personal communication. Noise obliterates voice. To discipline Atlas, whose movements are causing world chaos, the protagonist Martin becomes an autocrat:

> We must have imperatives. And in fact we have them. I may humbly say that I am a man of imperatives. I am jokingly referred to as "Mr. Imperative." He stands up and begins to dictate telegrams: *Plan complete protection and worldwide total control remaining flexible while matching research with cosmic needs* NOW . . . . ("MP," p. 119)

Martin, the modern man, regards himself as an imperative: "That's why I regard myself as global imperative number one" ("MP," p. 121).

This same image of imperatives is found in Merton's correspondence with Robert Lax. Included with a letter of 24 February 1965 is a "Book of Proverbs," of which the following is an excerpt:

1. I will tell you what you can do ask me if you do not understand what I just said
2. One thing you can do be a manufacturer who makes appliances
3. Be a Man-u-fac-tu-rer
4. Be a manufac
5. Make appliances sell them for a high price
6. I will tell you about industry make appliances
7. Make appliances that *move*
8. Ask me if you do not understand what is move
9. First get the facts
10. Do not understand
   . . . .
32. Apply this to the facts and see what happens
33. Wear dermal gloves in bed.
34. Here is an appliance that will terrorize mothers
35. And fight the impossible
36. Man-u-fac-ture: wear it on your head.

---

6. The unpublished works were organized for this study and are on file at the Thomas Merton Studies Center, Bellarmine College.

7. Thomas Merton, "Martin's Predicament, or Atlas Watches Every Evening," in *Raids on the Unspeakable* (New York: New Directions, 1966). Hereafter referred to in the text as "MP."

37. Wear dermal gloves on your head every morning.
38. Beat it here come the mothers[8]

In a later letter to Lax, Merton uses the theme of imperatives to criticize the censorship imposed upon him at the monastery:

> Dear Russ and Bill.
> Well you are probably wondering why I haven't written from the camp for so long. I'll tell you about it. The camp has been on fire for months. It all started in the flypaper factory where I was chief in charge of Trappist fly paper a communist front organization numbering millions. I'll tell you about the millions some other time. The fire began in the *imperatives* section.
> Let me tell you about our imperatives section. Just a moment. Let me tell you about it. The best way to tell you is to tell you our product. We make imperatives. They are like fly paper. A simple imperative is "Stay on the flypaper Jack or just try to get off anyway" that is one of our more simple imperatives. I make millions. Each imperative is a communist front. Behind the flypaper is a communist fly who is not on paper. He is classified.
> (*CAL*, pp. 60-61).

In examining Merton's Holographic Notebook # 15,[9] one sees why the Atlas story and the Lax correspondence are so significant. On the notebook's cover is written in Merton's hand, "Notes for Poems -- Cables for an Ace and unpublished Aug. 1965," and in this notebook are dozens of entries -- poems, quotations, comments -- 52 of which become sections in *Cables*, most having undergone few alterations from notebook to publication. The notebook begins with the several poems which eventually become sections 66, 67, and 69 of the poem and which develop the theme of society's imperatives. The abrasiveness of society's imperatives is followed by six poems describing the poet's hope for love and order. However, with an illogic which becomes a regular feature of Merton's construction of the poem, this unit at the opening of the notebook is broken up in the final *Cables*, so that the order becomes sections 66, 67, 69, 76, 11, 7, 8, 9, and 12.

Throughout the remainder of this working notebook some poems merely follow the previous poem consecutively, with no links between adjacent poems evident; other poems grow out of the previous poem, extend its theme, or comment upon it. In either case, sometimes the order of composition is retained in the published work, but more often it is not. For example: the title of poem 14 in the notebook, "To sons: not to be

---

8. Thomas Merton and Robert Lax, *A Catch of Anti-Letters* (Kansas City: Sheed, Andrews & McMeel, 1978), pp. 58-59. Hereafter referred to in the text as *CAL*.

9. Thomas Merton, *Holographic Notebook # 15*, Thomas Merton Studies Center, Bellarmine College. This notebook was formerly numbered 75 in initial processing by Tommie O'Callaghan.

numb," is echoed in poem 15 as the poet begs for money to "Make me numb." Yet these adjacent poems become sections 20a and 50 of the published work. Poems 24 and 25 in the notebook, lyrical dreams in which the poet merges with nature to achieve salvation, are separated as sections 10 and 72 in the final version. *Cables* retains only two small groupings in their original sequence: poems 1 to 3 become sections 66 to 69, and poems 6 to 8 become sections 7 to 9. This scrambling obscures any units which the writer originally framed. The notebook's several dominant themes -- society's imperatives, the possibility of natural harmony, the breakdown in human communication -- recur without design and suggest no organization other than the writer's varied moods. We hasten to add that even this critical treatment of the notebook, with its numbering of poems for discussion, exaggerates the order within the notebook, implying more pattern than actually exists.

In the earliest extant typescript of *Cables to the Ace*, the shape of sections 1 through 32 is evident, but the second half of the final work is not yet represented. This first group of twenty poems appears to be a random selection of individual pieces with no cohesive structure or unified purpose. The second typescript, dated September 1966, entitled *Edifying Cables or Home Liturgies of Misunderstanding*, adds twelve poems which begin to shape the end of the work. A significant omission is the imperatives section, despite the presence of the imperatives at the beginning of the notebook. *Edifying Cables* is an unsatisfactory work, too long for its random form and its lack of pattern.

A typed sequence of seventeen poems entitled "A Canto from Edifying Cables" contains material not found in the notebook. Most of this sequence becomes sections 53 through 61 of the final work. There is a second typed group of twenty-five poems which Merton filed with the typescripts of *Cables*. This group bears no title, characteristic paper, or pagination; some poems were in the notebook, none in *Edifying Cables*, but nineteen become part of *Cables to the Ace*. Still other such sequences of poems exist.

In the second draft of *Edifying Cables*, the title changes to *Edifying Cables and Other Poems*, suggesting a book of independent poems. This second rendering of *Edifying Cables* is nearly identical to the published work. Section 19 was the last addition to the work, as evidenced by Merton's numbering of 20a and 20b, to avoid renumbering the whole manuscript. Sections 62 through 69, which include the original imperatives section, do not yet appear in the manuscript.

A second notable difference between the last version of *Edifying Cables* and the published *Cables to the Ace* is the earlier manuscript's absence of Zen. It has been theorized that "transcendence through Zen" is a major structural technique in *Cables* and that the poem revolves around the reflection of Zen and mysticism in sections 37, 38, 39, 62, 80, 82, 84, and 86.[10] However, sections 80 and 82 deal with Christianity more than with mysticism, and every other one of these sections was not in the manuscript until after August 1967, appearing only in the published version. It is unlikely that, if Zen were a central theme of the poem, all those sections dealing specifically with Zen would enter the manuscript at the "eleventh hour."

And so through correspondence and notebooks to typescripts and sequences one searches in frustration for an outline of the completed work. On the contrary, the evidence suggests that where intelligible logic or ironic contrast dictated the order of composition, that order is purposefully discarded as the poem takes final shape. It would seem as if the poem's last three words, "Pourrait etre continue" (p. 60), "is being able to be continued," implies that the poem has no conclusion, only an ending, and that had Merton chosen to add more sections to his work, no aesthetic principle or poetic logic would have deterred him. One might judge that, like William Carlos Williams' *Paterson*, the poem ends, not because the poem brings about its own conclusion, but because the poet stopped writing.

Perhaps. But before the case for pattern is closed, let us allow the poem itself to testify. We must hear the poem repeatedly and so discover the patterns which, whether Merton intended or not, hold the ninety sections into an artistic unit which only by heeding the inherent pattern would be able to be continued. Merton told the monastery's novices that *Cables to the Ace* was composed like a symphony in different movements.[11] In a symphony there is something which keeps all its movements in and keeps other movements out. Such a patterning in form is hinted at in the epigraph from Alain Robbe-Grillet (title page), stating that "the questioning of the world in which we find ourselves cannot be done except by form, and not by a vague social or political anecdote."

Of the ninety sections in *Cables to the Ace*, exactly half, forty-five sections, are written in prose, and the other half in poetry. The sections

---

10. Luke Flaherty, "Thomas Merton's *Cables to the Ace*: A Critical Study," p. 26.
11. Thomas Merton, "Father Louis Talks," Tape # 245B, Thomas Merton Studies Center, Bellarmine College.

include brazen satire, percussive declamation, gentle observation, romantic lyrics, urgent imperatives, straight narratives, and quotations of one sort or another. Most of the sections participate in some way in a contest of oratory in which the noise of the world is pitted against the voice of myth. The poem is like a double fugue, in which two contrasting themes are developed both in isolation from and in relationship to one another. Prayer versus protest, mystic confronting machine, lyric and static: the poet conducts a dialogue with chaos. The dialogue is laid out in three widening gyres. The three prayerful lyrics -- section 7, "Weep, weep," section 45, "Anatole Anatole," and section 80, "Slowly slowly" -- each marks the conclusion of one cycle and in varying degrees allows or forbids the return of the noise of the world. This pattern will be examined in more detail in the later parts of this essay.

The conflict between the world and the poet is contained even in the title. "Cables" suggests society's brazen speech, its telegrams of social disintegration. In section 1 and 4 cables fail to alleviate social confusion:

> Edifying cables can be made musical if played and sung by full armed societies doomed to an electric war. . . Cables are never causes. (p. 2)

> "Put the whole family out into the hall." (Plato) Now they are outside receiving those hard cosmic cables without interceptions. (p. 3)

Cables are also electrical connections, symbols of impersonal communication:

> They improve their imitable wire
> To discover where speech
> Is trying to go. (p. 10)

> Found fifty persons all with wires in the pleasure center
> They were being moved by rats. (p. 14)

Only in section 87 is "cables" positive: "By the cables of orioles/ I am about to build my nest" (p. 60). However, the epilogue reinforces the negative imagery as the radio blasts out the noise of its cables.

The title states that the cables are sent to the Ace. "Ace" is the expert pilot, the excellent competitor, the social critic, the sensitive perceiver with the unifying poetic vision. In section 87 the poet concludes, "As I walk away from the poem/ Hiding the ace of freedoms" (p. 60). The figure of the ace is variously the uncommitted observer; the impersonal judge; the detached mystic; and the poet who must cope with society's cables. To restate the tension Merton adds a second title, *Familiar Liturgies of Misunderstanding*. A liturgy must be familiar in order to unite the individuals to the given order. Merton contends that the society's liturgies promote not healing but only misunderstanding. The title concedes that the voices of society are dominant, for in the end the liturgies of misunderstanding drown out the poet's attempts at prayer.

The first cycle of the poem is short, seven sections long. In sections 1 to 6 the poem speaks the noise of the world. Society is "doomed to an electric war," obsessed with the "vroom vroom of the guitars," "a heavy imperturbable beat." No indication where to stop. No messages to decode. Cables are never causes. Noises are never values" (p. 2). Section 1 joins Blake in attempting to marry heaven and hell by juxtaposing the vision of renewal with the clamor of society. In section 2 (p. 2) the seer is reduced to the scientist. The healing possible through the saints has been put into cold storage by a mechanized society bent only on individual comfort. Section 3 (p. 3) records the failure of language. Words create "more and more smoke" to surround the poet. "Some of the better informed have declared war on language." In section 4 (p. 3) Pláto's idealism yields to an epistemology in which knowledge beclouds and irritates. Section 5 (pp. 3-4) claims that eventually the manipulated individual submits to the controlling Directors. The "ironic mechanisms" have succeeded, the "electric eye" has won. Section 6 (p. 4), quoting Caliban, summarizes the theme of the failure of language. However, Caliban is evil in and of himself; he has not been corrupted by his environment, but has spoken discord into idyllic surroundings. Neither Caliban nor the poet can blame social disintegration on "society."

Section 7 (p. 5) is the poet's first attempt at a plea for order. "Original Sin" commemorates Father's Day, recalling prayer to the Father and the interferences of human sin and satirizing the anthropological view of epistemology. The gentle "Weep, weep, little day," reminiscent of Blake's lyrics, looks to the Father, to the bones of the past, to the ape-like origins of humanity, and to the halting emergences of language, vainly hoping in these ancestral traces to find the father who can erase the sin. In the last stanza history itself weeps as the primates beat with the words and with the bones. Primordial history offers not the forgiving father, but rather a creature more destructive and inarticulate than its human descendant. Each stanza of the lyric ends with a short, punctuated dimeter, cutting off the longer lines with the aborted finality expressive of the failure in this search for roots.

After this lyrical plea, this failed prayer, the poem continues with its second cycle in which the world's noise dominates the dialogue. In some sections brazen satire mocks prevalent social values. Special emphasis is placed on the failure of language to create and sustain human community. Several sections present Zen as an alternative to chaos, but the meeting of the opposites is only curious, hardly climactic. Another failure is the attempt to find a wholesome peace in natural beauty and in mythic intention. A minor theme in the French surrealistic section is the death of the gods in the modern age.

Merton's search for mythic systems which can hold society together can be seen in the short section 20a (p. 16):

> To daughters: to study history.
>
> Finn, Finn
> Tribal and double
> Wide awake rocks
> The fatal craft
> Cutlash Finn
> To kill time
> Before and aft --
> Er he sinks his fin
> Again in his
> Own Wake.

This short poem, an impressive condensation of Western roots, is dedicated to the daughters, to those who bear the next generation. They are to "study history," to remember their encompassing historical past, their "tribal and double." The verse recalls the incantation of the witches in *Macbeth*: "Double, double, toil and trouble:/ Fire burn and cauldron bubble." In Shakespeare's incantation the witches use past and present evil to conjure up future evil. Merton, a compatriot of witches, urges the daughters to remember the generation of evil in Shakespeare's ruthless tragedy. The name Finn recalls Huckleberry Finn, the adolescent pioneer who travels down the great American river to discover his past, present, and future and so provides a contrast between the human comedy of Mark Twain's masterpiece and the "wool of bat and tongue of dog" of Macbeth's witches. "Finn" also denotes James Joyce's epic *Finnegans Wake*, a collage of western myth and civilization. In its circular composition of languages, literature, and history, *Finnegans Wake* links the details of modern life to the archetypes; thus this novel exemplifies the possibility of healing which the daughters can discover in history.

The third line, "Wide awake rocks," calls to mind Scylla and Charybdis, the crashing rocks between which Ulysses and his ship must journey. The past is not only the silent Mississippi, gently carrying Huck's raft, but also the crushing blow of the angry sea. If Finn is crushed by these rocks, not only he as a cultural hero dies; history, the sense of past time, dies with him: "To kill time/ Before and aft." In these churning waters of time Finn now becomes a fish. He is both less and more than human, part animal, but also in part Christ, represented in Christian iconography as the fish that the Greek acronym suggests. The fate of Finn, who did not study history, is to "sink his fin/ Again in his/ Own Wake."

The Finn-fish recalls Christ who must embrace his own death in order to conquer the evil of history. These lines again suggest Joyce's novel: to attend one's own wake is to immerse oneself in the cultural wake, both the trail of the ship of life and the visit to the casket, the life and death journey of the mythical heroes. By living within the cultural wake, one prepares for the horror of one's own. "Again... Wake" repeats the allusion to Joyce's work which commemorates all of sleep, just as Ulysses who travels between the rocks commemorates all of wakefulness.

In less than thirty words Merton has shown the daughters how to study history by remembering and heeding Greek myth, British tragedy, American adventure, Irish folklore, Joyce's comedy, and Christian symbolism. In ten short lines these diverse mythic systems are brought together into one pattern, and the chaos of historical amnesia is challenged by the power of the voice of myth.

The context of oratory continues until Caliban and his chaos reenters in section 44. Just as the plea of section 7 is preceded by Caliban in section 6, so section 45 follows Caliban in section 44. Section 45, the precise center of the work, "Prayer to Saint Anatole," marks the close of the second and wider cycle. It has been suggested that St. Anatole is a reference to Anatolius, 230-282 A.D., a Laodicean bishop with a reputation for wide knowledge in the sciences.[12] Merton may also be playing on the Greek noun *anatole*, a significant word in the New Testament's accounts of the Messiah's birth. The word is variously translated east, rising, branch, and Messiah, and so in one word provides, through a pun, the entire myth of the Messiah as a branch arising from the east. Merton's lyric, by looking to science, air travel, and air warfare as a possible savior, recalls both a scientific bishop and a search for the Messiah in the sky.

"Anatole Anatole" (p. 31) begins like ancient church collects with a statement of the human condition. Jets streaming across the sky separate the poet from the saint. Not the Spirit's flame but "the chemical flame" inspires this prayer: the fire enlightening this plea is the burning bomb damage, the music is "electric lyres" and "fatal recorders." The central

---

12. Luke Flaherty, "Mystery and Unity as Anagogical Vision in Thomas Merton's *Cables to the Ace*," Master's Thesis, University of Louisville (1969), p. 68.

section of *Cables*, a letter to a saint, is itself a cable to an ace: yet in the midst of the cultural warfare the communication is unsuccessful.

The third and final cycle in the poem comprises the second half of the work and culminates in section 80, the poem's only effective prayer. A dozen of these forty-five sections convey the same worldly noise which has pervaded the first half of the work. Some sections have given way to a defeated sense of loss. Merton satirizes the distorted values and language of the media in his newscast (section 48) and in "Dramas of the Evening" (section 70). The imperatives of society, which we first met in the Atlas story, take up sections 67 and 69. Again a natural order is evoked, the romantic aesthetic recalled, Zen and mysticism attempted; even the Christian mystics Eckhart, Ruysbroeck, and Theresa of the Heart offer their voices to the dialogue.

The climax of the third cycle is the most eloquent section of the work, section 80 (p. 55). The Christian paradox of life within death lies in the image of Christ walking through the garden: the garden of Eden, the garden of Gethsemani, the Easter garden. Christ comes "through the ruins," the wrecked cities." and the frightened disciple, who in meeting Christ sees "only the harvest moon," has chosen natural cycles as his symbol. The first three stanzas begin "Slowly slowly," recalling the "Weep, weep" of section 7 and the "Anatole Anatole" of section 45. The stanzas are filled with the falling rhythm of trochees: slowly, garden, speaking, sacred, branches, cornfields, harvest, murmur. The wait for the eschaton is apparent: Christ comes only slowly. The poem's last stanza responds to the frustrated petition of section 7, which sees historical humanity for the bones that they are, and ends, "Weep little history." Section 80 answers the previous faltering prayer in this way:

> The disciple will awaken
> When he knows history
> But slowly slowly
> The Lord of History
> Weeps into the fire.

The small-h history of human knowledge is contrasted with the capital-H History of the realm of God. Salvation comes not in cultural heroes but in a weeping Lord, whose voice speaks from within the noise, who will put out the fire in the ruins with his tears. This penitence brings nearly to an end the babble of society's cables. The disciples will awaken when the ability to balance life and death is realized.

The final nine sections present the artistic dilemma in personal terms. The prayer has steadied the poet: the poet tries now to retain that stability in light of the world's chaotic forces. There is little noise here in the end, only musings on peace. In the last section the poet "shuts down its trance" (p. 60), and the epilogue concludes the poem with the radio blaring out its nonsensical slang and toothpaste ads. Even though the last plea was heard, even though the Lord of History has been summoned, the ace must still hear the cables, for the noise remains.

One can hardly suggest that *Cables to the Ace* is a structural masterpiece. Merton never made explicit any logic for the ordering of his ninety sections. However, the evidence of the poem makes us admit the power of the lyrical pleas, "Weep, weep," "Anatole Anatole," and "Slowly slowly," and one cannot dispute that the placement of these lyrics and of the poems around them creates a pattern of three cycles, always widening out into the noise of the world. Thus while the work is not flawless in construction nor are individual sections perfect in word selection, the poem is a powerful statement of the twentieth-century myth maker, an epic of the American poet, a sustained experience of the dialogue between the noise of the world and the voice of myth, and it remains a major piece of Merton's poetic legacy.

MERTON'S JOURNEY

FROM *SEEDS* TO *NEW SEEDS*

by **Ruth Fox**, O.S.B.

In 1949, just eight years after entering the Cistercian Order, Thomas Merton authored a book on contemplative life and prayer called *Seeds of Contemplation*. In the introduction he called it a "collection of notes and personal reflections . . . that came to mind at odd moments and were put down on paper when there was time, without order and without any special sequence."[1] Addressed not only to monks, but to all Christians, the book covers topics concerned with living the Christian life, especially the life of prayer. Just twelve years later, in 1961, Merton issued a revised edition of this book, *New Seeds of Contemplation*. His purpose was "not simply to make a larger book out of a small one, but to say many new things that could profitably be added to the old."[2] By comparing these two books we can determine what "new things" Merton added and thus gain some insight into the evolution of his spiritual theology in the intervening years.[3]

---

1. Thomas Merton, *Seeds of Contemplation* (Norfolk, Connecticut: New Directions, 1949), pp. 13-14.

2. Thomas Merton, *New Seeds of Contemplation* (New York: New Directions, 1961), p. ix.

3. After the first draft of this study was completed a much more thorough textual comparison was published by Donald Grayston, *Thomas Merton: The Development of a Spiritual Theologian*, Toronto Studies in Theology 20 (Lewiston, New York: Edwin Mellen Press, 1985). Grayston's detailed textual analysis supports my thesis. Grayston used not only the two popular versions of *Seeds* and *New Seeds* but also the typescript for each of these volumes and also a little known revised edition of *Seeds* (Norfolk: New Directions, 1949) which appeared nine months after the original. Subsequent references to this study are referred to in the text as "Grayston."

Before examining some of the textual changes in the later book, we will review a number of the significant events of Merton's life between 1949 and 1961 that influenced these changes.[4]

Biographical Background

On May 26, 1949, the same year that *Seeds of Contemplation* was published, Merton was ordained to the priesthood. This event which he eagerly anticipated was followed by a period of depression and spells of scrupulosity when saying Mass. He struggled with boredom in choir, insomnia, longing for solitude, and an inability to write creatively. In November he was asked to teach a class to the scholastics and novices, which added to an already heavy schedule. It is not surprising that he succumbed to flu in the community epidemic in the spring of 1950. In September he was admitted to the hospital in Louisville with sinusitis, and again in November for a nose operation and stomach and chest problems that were treated by rest. Whether it was the medical attention, the rest, or the opportunity for contacts outside the cloister, Merton experienced an inner renewal and peace, and, as well, the return of his writing ability.

He was named Master of Scholastics in the spring of 1951, with the responsibility of teaching and guiding some forty young men preparing to be choir monks. He enjoyed the classes, the spiritual counselling, and the association with these enthusiastic men who, by and large, loved and admired him. Gradually the pressure of his duties again conflicted with his desire for solitude and his irrepressible need to write. "He felt under continual tension and began increasingly to think that he was not called to the communal conventual life but to something far less structured, which, while keeping him away from the distractions of 'the world,' would allow him more liberty for private prayer and contemplation" (Furlong, p. 203). He began thinking seriously of transferring to the Carthusian or Camaldolese Orders where he could be more of a hermit.

Early in the 1950s he was informed that his journal *The Sign of Jonas* was being withheld from publication by the Abbot General of the Cistercian Order because, as a journal, it was not "in the tradition." But Merton's publisher and friend, Robert Giroux, wrote to Jacques Maritain who in turn

---

4. The events in Merton's life from 1949 to 1961 as given here are taken from his journal *The Sign of Jonas* (New York: Harcourt, Brace & Company, 1953) and from two biographies: Monica Furlong, *Merton: A Biography* (San Francisco: Harper & Row, 1980) and Michael Mott, *The Seven Mountains of Thomas Merton* (Boston: Houghton Mifflin Company, 1984), subsequently referred to in the text as "Furlong" or "Mott."

apparently influenced the Abbot General to change his mind. "But it left a scar on Merton -- there would be worse scars from censorship to follow -- and may have influenced his desire to leave the Trappists" (Furlong, p. 204).

He was also angered by an Official Visitor of the Cistercian Order who condemned the "hermit mentality" which he found at Gethsemani, and who told the community they could not walk in the forest outside the enclosure. Merton's abbot, James Fox, tried to calm Merton after the Visitation by naming him Chief Ranger of the woods, so that he, at least, could legitimately "patrol" the forest.[5] The exact sequence of events which followed is difficult to trace from the various sources, but, about this time, Merton wrote to Rome for permission to transfer to another Order, while at the same time Dom James asked Rome to deny the petition (Mott, p. 297). The Abbot General became involved in the process, and placed a five year ban on Merton's writing in the hope that that would lessen the tension of which he complained. In the meantime the Kentucky State Forestry Department built a fire watchtower on a ridge near the Abbey. Merton immediately spotted it and asked the abbot for permission to be the Fire Warden and to make the tower a hermitage of sorts. The abbot obtained permission from the Abbot General who agreed, "but with this condition, that Fr. Louis be 100% hermit -- that is, not be a cenobite in the morning and a hermit only in the afternoon" (Fox, p. 150).

Then a strange turn of events occurred. Three days after this permission was made known to Merton, he came to Dom James and volunteered to take the vacated position of Novice Master. The abbot was pleased to appoint him to this important position, but with two conditions, "one, that you'll keep the job for three years, and two, that you'll give no conferences on becoming hermits" (Fox, p. 151).[6] The abbot kept him in this position for ten years (1955-1965), at which time Merton resigned to take up the hermit life officially at Gethsemani. It is ironic that this monk -- whose writings were questioned by superiors and censors of the Order, who was in the process of requesting a transfer to another Order, who manifested neurotic symptoms of illness at times, who was carrying on a fight with his superiors to become a hermit in a cenobitic tradition -- should be appointed, at his

---

5.   James Fox, "The Spiritual Son," in *Thomas Merton/ Monk: A Monastic Tribute,* ed. Patrick Hart (Garden City, New York: Doubleday & Company), 1974, pp. 147-149. Subsequent references in the text are referred to as "Fox."

6.   Mott comments, "Dom James was astonished. He had worked hard to get Father Louis what he said he wanted. To the abbot this was a major failure of nerve on Merton's part. Having almost attained the solitude he had been talking about for at least seven years, Merton backed off." (Mott, p. 287).

own request, Novice Master, the one who would teach, guide, and form the future members of the community. Merton energetically assumed the duties of Novice Master, and even decided to give up writing in order to devote more time to the novices. But, in spite of his resolve and the five-year ban, he could not refrain from writing, and so journals, essays, lectures, translations, and poetry continued to flow. In the midst of this, Merton still had periods of depression and hankerings after more solitude.

In the summer of 1956, Merton was allowed to attend a conference at Collegeville, Minnesota, where he had a disastrous confrontation with a psychoanalyst, Dr. Gregory Zilboorg. In the presence of Merton's abbot, he accused Merton of being pathological, adding "You want a hermitage in Times Square with a large sign over it saying 'HERMIT'." It was perhaps the most damaging ten minutes of Merton's monastic life and left both him and his abbot lingeringly suspicious that he was mentally unbalanced and unfit for the hermit life (Mott, p. 297).

Through much of the fifties, Merton continually seemed to maneuver to become a hermit at Gethsemani or elsewhere with Dom James sabotaging each initiative, and Merton subsequently repenting and resolving to be obedient. An involved and dangerous game developed between the two men with a lack of mutual trust, and yet "there survived beyond all this a mutual respect and even a deep, if guarded and sorely bruised, affection" (Mott, pp. 278, 283). Finally, in 1960, an ecumenical center was built on the Abbey grounds, and Merton was granted permission to use it as a place of solitude.

Out of these varied experiences and struggles several books emerged and *New Seeds of Contemplation* appeared in 1961. It is easier to understand and appreciate the additions and changes made by Merton in his revision when we know something of the personal challenges he faced. I will now examine these more carefully, as we compare *New Seeds of Contemplation* with *Seeds of Contemplation*.[7] In each section, after noting the changes made by Merton, I will recount some biographical material from his other concurrent writings that relate to the topic under discussion. Finally, I will attempt to interpret, where possible, the ways in which Merton moved from *Seeds* to *New Seeds*.

---

7.   References to *Seeds of Contemplation* and *New Seeds of Contemplation* will hereafter be cited in the text as *Seeds* or *S* and *New Seeds* or *NS*.

Contemplation

When one compares *Seeds* and *New Seeds*, one's first observation is that the latter book is longer by nearly one hundred pages. Although there are thirty-nine chapters compared to twenty-seven in the first book, there are really only three chapters of completely new material, two at the beginning and one at the end. Most of the other additions are excursions into topics that were only lightly treated in the first book. The two new chapters at the begining are an attempt at a fuller description of contemplation, even though Merton says contemplation is

> beyond explanation, beyond discourse, beyond dialogue, beyond our own self. (*NS*, p. 2)
> Contemplation is the highest expression of man's intellectual and spiritual life. It is that life itself, fully awake, fully active, fully aware that it is alive. It is spiritual wonder, . . . a sudden gift of awareness, an awakening to the Real within all that is real. A vivid awareness of infinite Being at the roots of our own limited being. (*NS*, pp. 1, 3)

It can be compared to a spiritual vision, yet it is not vision because it is beyond seeing, and cannot be grasped in images, or even in words or concepts. It reaches out to an experience of God, an awareness of an "existential contact" with God. It is God answering God's own call to us.

Somewhat at a loss for words and concepts, Merton continues in the second chapter of *New Seeds* with a negative approach: what contemplation is not. But even this approach is insufficient.

> The only way to get rid of misconceptions about contemplation is to experience it. One who does not actually know, in his own life, the nature of this breakthrough and this awakening to a new level of reality cannot help being misled by most of the things that are said about it. For contemplation cannot be taught. (*NS*, p. 6)

Perhaps that is why Merton could not treat contemplation as thoroughly in the first book; he had become a Catholic only eleven years before, and had been a monk for only seven years. It is amazing that he had as much depth and knowledge of prayer as he did. Or was *Seeds* mostly a synthesis of what he had read in the works of John of the Cross and Bernard of Clairvaux, both of whom he mentioned in his introduction? Was it only after twelve more years that he was able to speak more directly from his own experience of contemplation?

> Contemplation can never be the object of our calculated ambition. It is not something we can plan to obtain with our practical reason. . . . It is not we who choose to awaken ourselves, but God who chooses to awaken us. (*NS*, p. 10)

The topic of contemplation appears in many of his works during the years between *Seeds* and *New Seeds*. *The Ascent to Truth* (1951) is a treatment of mysticism with special emphasis on contemplative prayer according to St. John of the Cross. *Bread in the Wilderness* (1953) has a chapter on "Contemplation in the Liturgy." *No Man is an Island* (1955) treats of silence and solitude as the climate for contemplation, and *Thoughts in Solitude* (1958) expands on that theme. That Merton studied St. Bernard's spiritual theology is evidenced in a book published post-humously, but containing essays written between 1948 and 1954, titled *Thomas Merton on Saint Bernard*.[8]

True Self and False Self

In *Seeds* Merton introduces a concept that reappears several times in *New Seeds* -- the contrast between the true self and the false self. This concept is intimately connected with the experience of contemplative prayer, for if contemplation is defined only in terms of feelings and reactions, it is being situated where it cannot be found, in the superficial consciousness of the false self.

> Contemplation is not and cannot be a function of this external self. There is an irreducible opposition between the deep transcendent self that awakens only in contemplation, and the superficial external self which we commonly identify with the first person singular. (*NS*, pp. 6-7)

This "I" that observes itself and talks about itself is not the true "I" which is united to God in Christ. The outer "I" is a mask, a temporal disguise for the hidden self which is eternal.

Merton continues his elucidation of the false and true self in Chapter Four of *New Seeds* in the context of what was originally Chapter One in *Seeds*, "Everything That Is, Is Holy." He retains the thesis that the saints love everyone and everything because they love God, but he begins the chapter with a new passage on detachment from self.

> There is no evil in anything created by God, nor can anything of His become an obstacle to our union with Him. The obstacle is in our "self," that is to say in the tenacious need to maintain our separate, external, egotistic will. (*NS*, p. 21)

This false self becomes a god which both uses created things for its own glory and yet calls them unholy because only the ego of the false self is

---

8. A thorough exposition of Merton's thought on contemplation as it developed through the years is presented in John J. Higgins, *Thomas Merton on Prayer* (New York: Doubleday & Company, 1971).

holy. The enjoyment of creation is seen as sinful, and the false self cultivates feelings of guilt which make it feel pious. It cannot be said that the false self is located in the body, because the body is holy -- the temple of God. Neither the body nor the soul is the whole self because the two cannot be divided. "If the two are separated from one another, there is no longer a person, there is no longer a living, subsisting reality made in the image and likeness of God" (NS, p. 27).

That Merton grew to understand a distinction between selfhood, which is basically good, and the false self can be seen in two sentences from Seeds which he revised for the later book:

Seeds	New Seeds
The only true joy on earth is to escape from the prison of our selfhood. (p. 22)	The only true joy on earth is to escape from the prison of our own false self. (p. 25)
....	....
To worship ourselves is to worship nothing. (p. 23)	To worship our false selves is to worship nothing. (p. 26)

He continues this distinction in the next chapter discussing the need to be true to one's nature and identity in God. "We are at liberty to be real, or to be unreal. We may be true or false, the choice is ours. We may wear now one mask and now another, and never, if we so desire, appear with our own true face" (NS, p. 32). Because we are free, we share with God the creation of our own identity. But there is a temptation to play with masks; in fact, Merton claims, "I was born in a mask" (NS, p. 33). He continues with material from Seeds where he had originally introduced this concept: "Everyone of us is shadowed by an illusory person: a false self" (S, p. 28), which is not known by God because it tries to exist outside the realm of God's will and love, and it is here that sin originates.

Merton draws further distinctions on the "selves" in Chapter Thirty-eight on "Pure Love" where he added four pages to his original material.

> If there is an awareness of myself as separate from God when I pray, then I am not yet in the fullness of contemplation. As long as there is an "I" aware of itself, we remain in the realm of multiplicity, activity, incompleteness, striving and desire. The true inner self, the true indestructible and immortal person, the true "I" who answers to a new and secret name known only to himself and to God, does not "have" anything, even "contemplation."   (NS, p. 279)

But this true self remains hidden and appears to be as nothing, to be unreal, while the illusory self appears to be real. But this outer self is only "a shadow, a garment that is cast off and consumed by decay" (NS, p. 280).

Perhaps fearful that he had been too severe and negative with the illusory or false self, Merton offers a corrective in the last chapter of *New Seeds*.

> Yet we must not deal in too negative a fashion even with the "external self." This self is not by nature evil, and the fact that it is unsubstantial is not to be imputed to it as some kind of crime. It is afflicted with metaphysical poverty: but all that is poor deserves mercy. So too our outward self: as long as it does not isolate itself in a lie, it is blessed by the mercy and the love of Christ. (*NS*, p. 295)

Merton's thoughts on the true self and the false self could possibly have had their origin in his study of St. Bernard, who speaks of the "false nature."[9] Perhaps his own growth in self understanding and his guidance of the scholastics and novices also provided some of the background for his distinction of the "selves." He wrote in his journal in 1951,

> I have become very different from what I used to be. The man who began this journal is dead, just as the man who finished *The Seven Storey Mountain* when this journal began was also dead . . . . Thus I stand on the threshold of a new existence. The one who is going to be most fully formed by the new scholastics is the Master of Scholastics.[10]

Mercy and Compassion

One of the interesting and revealing changes made by Merton in *New Seeds* is a new emphasis on the "mercy" of God. There are two passages of about a page and a half each added to two chapters from *Seeds*. In the chapter "Pray for Your Own Discovery" from the earlier book, Merton writes that God utters the Divine Word in us, and if we are true to that word, we shall be full of God's actuality and find God in ourselves. "We become contemplatives when God discovers Himself in us" (*S*, p. 32). In this context Merton expands his thoughts on mercy in *New Seeds*.

> When I consent to the will and the mercy of God as it "comes" to me in the events of life, appealing to my inner self and awakening my faith, I break through the superficial exterior appearances that form my routine vision of the world and of my own self, and I find myself in the presence of hidden majesty. (*NS*, p. 41)

This mercy of God is revealed and shared with us so that we are filled with God's glory and become more our true selves.

---

9. *Thomas Merton on Saint Bernard*, Cistercian Studies, Series 9 (Kalamazoo: Cistercian Publications, 1980), pp. 181-188.

10. Thomas Merton, *The Sign of Jonas*, pp. 328, 330. Hereafter referred to in the text as *SJ*.

> This is the "mercy of God" revealed to us by the secret missions in which
> he gives himself to us, and awakens our identity as sons and heirs of his
> kingdom . . . . In the revelation of mercy and majesty we come to an
> obscure intuition of our own personal secret, our true identity. (*NS,* p. 42)

Thus God's mercy and our true identity are interrelated.

In the chapter "The Moral Theology of the Devil" from *Seeds*
Merton claims that the devil wants us to believe that all created things,
including people, are evil, and that God wills evil and suffering. The devil
encourages meditation on sin, especially the sin of others. Sin is pleasure,
and pleasure is sin. Since pleasure is inescapable, no one can avoid sin
either; so the concept of sin becomes irrelevant and meaningless. In *New
Seeds* Merton expands on the devil's moral theology. In the devil's system,
hell was the first thing created, and those who follow this system are
obsessed with hell and evil. Multiplying laws and rules, they insist on
punishment as the fulfillment of law.

> The law must devour everything, even God. Such is this theology of
> punishment, hatred and revenge. He who would live by such a dogma
> must rejoice in his punishment . . . . The Law must triumph. There must be
> no mercy. This is the chief mark of the theology of hell, for in hell there is
> everything but mercy. That is why God Himself is absent from hell. Mercy
> is the manifestation of His presence. (*NS,* p. 91)

There are at least five other passages in *New Seeds* where material
was changed from the original version, in order to stress God's mercy.

Seeds	*New Seeds*
The saint knows nothing but the love and the mercy of God and he is on earth to bring that love and that mercy to all men. (p. 21)	The saint knows the mercy of God. He knows that his own mission on earth is to bring that mercy to all men. (p. 25)
From then on our life becomes a series of choices between the fiction of our false-self, whom we feed with the illusions of passion and selfish appetite, and our true identity in the peace of God. (p. 34)	. . . and our loving consent to the purely gratuitous mercy of God. (p. 41)
Let my tongue taste no bread that does not strengthen me to praise your glory. (p. 35)	. . . to praise your great mercy. (p. 44)

. . . and we are able to find out who He is from the experience of His own selflessness reflected in our purified wills. (p. 56)	. . . from the experience of His mercy, liberating us from the prison of self-concern. (p. 78)
In order to know and love God as He is, we must have God dwelling in us in a new and special way. (p. 33)	. . . in a new way, not only in His creative power but in His mercy, not only in His greatness but in His littleness, by which He empties Himself and comes down to us to be empty in our emptiness, and so fill us in His fullness. (p. 40)

A reader of Merton can only conjecture why these additions and changes were made in favor of "mercy." During the years when he was struggling with a frustrated desire to be a hermit, when his writing was censored and banned, when he felt misunderstood by his abbot, did he come to experience more fully his own need for the mercy of God? Did he realize that he could not earn his own peace of soul, that all he could do was to open his arms to receive God's undeserved gift of mercy?

As early as 1950 he wrote in his journal about his severe inner struggle.

> When the summer of my ordination ended, I found myself face to face with a mystery that was beginning to manifest itself in the depths of my soul and to move me with terror. Do not ask me what it was. I might apologize for it and call it "suffering." The word is not adequate because it suggests physical pain. That is not at all what I mean. It was a sort of slow, submarine earthquake which produced strange commotions on the visible, psychological surface of my life. (*SJ*, p. 230)

In looking back at that experience he could see that the cloud lifted on its own the following year. From it he discovered that a vocation to be a solitary "is a vocation to fear, to helplessness, to isolation in the invisible God" (*SJ*, p. 231).

A later book, *No Man is an Island* (1955), contains a chapter on "Mercy," which would seem to reflect Merton's own experiences.

> Only the man who has had to face despair is really convinced that he needs mercy . . . . It is better to find God on the threshold of despair than to risk our lives in a complacency that has never felt the need of forgiveness.[11]

One can hardly discuss the mercy of God without realizing that when mercy is received, one must in turn be willing to give it to others. Mercy arises

---

11. Thomas Merton, *No Man is an Island* (New York: Harcourt, Brace & Company, 1955), p. 21. Hereafter referred to in the text as *NM*.

from a sense of compassion for the other. Merton relates mercy and compassion to solitude, for it is solitude that teaches the saints

> to bring the good out of others by compassion, mercy, and pardon. A man becomes a saint not by conviction that he is better than sinners but by the realization that he is one of them, and that all together need the mercy of God. (*NS*, p. 57)

Merton strongly believes that compassion and mercy must arise out of solitude; in fact, "the only justification for a life of deliberate solitude is the conviction that it will help you to love not only God but other men" (*S*, p. 52). Solitude is a gift given for the sake of the whole body of Christ; it gives a "clarity of compassion." Compassion and mercy are not optional virtues for a solitary.

> But I cannot treat other men as men unless I have compassion for them. I must have at least enough compassion to realize that when they suffer they feel somewhat as I do when I suffer. And if for some reason I do not spontaneously feel this kind of sympathy for others, then it is God's will that I do what I can to learn how . . . . Contemplation is out of the question for anyone who does not try to cultivate compassion for other men. (*NS*, p. 77)

Through the experience of depression and despair, Merton came to know the mercy and compassion of God, and knowing it, he recognized the obligation of sharing it with others.

Solitude and the World

The chapter on "Solitude" in *Seeds* undergoes some changes in thought and is expanded into two chapters in *New Seeds*. Merton retains the core of the original version which emphasizes that true solitude is more internal than external. "The truest solitude is not something outside you, not an absence of men or of sound around you: it is an abyss opening up in the center of your own soul" (*S*, p. 59).

But he speaks more strongly in *New Seeds* about the necessity of exterior solitude. He claims that those who say "only solitude of the heart really matters" (*NS*, p. 90) have never experienced real solitude. He also makes a plea for quiet, dark churches where people can retreat to enjoy the silent presence of God, a place where they can descend into the quiet places of their heart to worship God in secret. Then he takes an unusually ironic tone to criticize "men dedicated to God" who restlessly run away from interior solitude.

They do everything they can to escape it. What is worse, they try to draw everyone else into activities as senseless and as devouring as their own. They are great promoters of useless work. They love to organize meetings and banquets and conferences and lectures. They print circulars, write letters, talk for hours on the telephone in order that they may gather a hundred people together in a large room where they will all fill the air with smoke and make a great deal of noise and roar at one another and clap their hands and stagger home at last patting one another on the back with the assurance that they have all done great things to spread the kingdom of God. (*NS*, p. 83)

One wonders if Merton was taking a jab at his own activities of the past ten years, especially because of the reference to writing circulars and letters, and to the ecumenical meetings which he had initiated at Gethsemani. It was mainly through his efforts that an ecumenical center was constructed on the Abbey grounds in 1960, the year before the book was published. Or were there other monks at the Abbey who Merton thought were not appreciating their solitude enough? That Merton's attitude toward the world and its place in a life of solitude was changing can best be illustrated by comparing passages from the two books.

Seeds	*New Seeds*
Do not read their newspapers, if you can help it. Be glad if you can keep beyond the reach of their radios. Do not bother with their unearthly songs or their intolerable concerns for the way their bodies look and feel. (p. 60)	Be glad if you can keep beyond the reach of their radios. Do not bother with their unearthly songs. Do not read their advertisements. (p. 84).
Do not smoke their cigarettes or drink the things they drink or share their preoccupation with different kinds of food. Do not complicate your life by looking at the pictures in their magazines. (p. 61)	Expanded into two pages of comment. (pp. 84-86)

Since Merton omits his earlier prohibition against reading newspapers, we can surmise that he was reading them, though perhaps on only a limited scale. He makes a comment in his journal *Conjectures of a Guilty Bystander* that "by exception, I was able to read the papers" while a patient in a Louisville hospital.[12] Though this note was written in 1962, it is probably safe to assume that he read the papers on his previous hospital stays.

---

12.   Thomas Merton, *Conjectures of a Guilty Bystander* (New York: Doubleday & Company, 1966), p. 264. Hereafter referred to in the text as *CGB*. \

For a one sentence prohibition of drinking and smoking in *Seeds* he substitutes a two page discourse on self-discipline. He now admits that contemplatives do not necessarily have to give up smoking and drinking altogether, but they should keep such desires under control. In these areas a serious contemplative would practice self-denial. "In general it can be said that no contemplative life is possible without ascetic self-discipline" (*NS*, p. 86).

By the time of *New Seeds*, television had become a commonplace in the world, but Merton admits, "I am certainly no judge of television, since I have never watched it" (*NS*, p. 86). However, judging from what he heard from his friends, he called it "degraded, meretricious, and absurd, . . . a completely inert subjection to vulgar images" (*NS*, p. 86). This seems to be a rather severe judgment to make from hearsay. In spite of his disdain for television, he does not prohibit its use, but says it should be used only with extreme care and discrimination.

In another passage he moves from the idea of escaping from the world to the concept of compassion for those who live in the world.

Seeds	*New Seeds*
But if you have to live in a city . . . accept it as the love of God and as a seed of solitude planted in your soul, and be glad of this suffering: for it will keep you alive to the next opportunity to escape from them and be alone in the healing silence of recollection and in the untroubled presence of God. (p. 61)	But if you have to live in a city . . . accept it as the love of God and as a seed of solitude planted in your soul. If you are appalled by those things, you will keep your appetite for the healing silence of recollection. But meanwhile -- keep your sense of compassion for the men who have forgotten the very concept of solitude. (p. 87)

Living in the city is no longer called a suffering, and one who lives there does not have to run for escape. Compassion is substituted for condescension. In a later chapter a short passage indicates another change in attitude toward the world. In discussing the role of feelings and emotional states in prayer, Merton warns that explosions of good feeling may be more natural than supernatural, and are certainly not to be taken necessarily as signs of spiritual advancement. But since they may have good natural effects, they are not harmful either.

Seeds	*New Seeds*
. . . a couple of glasses of wine or a good swim -- and monks neither drink wine, (in America) nor do they swim. (p. 162)	. . . a couple of glasses of champagne or a good swim. (p. 246)

Note that Merton no longer claims that monks do not drink or swim!

That Merton had a special love for solitude is seen not only in *Seeds* and *New Seeds*, but can also be detected in his other writings that were published between these two books. Two chapters on solitude and silence appeared in *No Man is an Island* (1955). In a completely new book on the topic, *Thoughts in Solitude* (1958), he wrote that he now was able to "enjoy special opportunities for solitude and meditation."[13] He also admitted, "when solitude was a problem, I had no solitude. When it ceased to be a problem I found I already possessed it, and could have possessed it all along" (*TS*, p. 85). In the book *Disputed Questions* (1960), he included a chapter on the philosophy of solitude -- a chapter which had trouble getting by the censors of the Order.[14]

Even though there was no significant change in Merton's thoughts on solitude, we do find his attitude changing toward the world and its relation to solitude. Some specific changes seen in *New Seeds* were noted above, but we can also detect the progression of those changes in other works written between 1949 and 1961.

In his journal *The Sign of Jonas* Merton wrote in 1951 that one of his problems on entering the monastery was that he had a false solution for his relationship to the world.

> The false solution went like this: the whole world of which the war is a characteristic expression, is evil. It has therefore to be first ridiculed, then spat upon, and at last formally rejected with a curse. Actually, I have come to the monastery to find my place in the world, and if I fail to find this place in the world I will be wasting my time in the monastery. (*SJ*, p. 322)

In *No Man is an Island* (1955) he seems to vacillate in his attitude, as though he cannot make up his mind about the relationship of the contemplative to the world. "We cannot become saints merely by trying to run away from material things. To have a spiritual life is to have a life that is spiritual in all its wholeness" (*NM*, p. 98). In a later passage he continues in a different vein and seems to contradict his previous stand.

> The essence of the monastic vocation is precisely this leaving of the world and all its desires and ambitions and concerns in order to live not only for God, but by Him and in Him, not for a few years, but forever. The one thing that most truly makes a monk what he is, is this irrevocable break with the world and all that is in it, in order to seek God in solitude.
>
> (*NM*, p. 144)

---

13. Thomas Merton, *Thoughts in Solitude* (New York: Farrar, Straus & Cudahy, 1958), p. 11. Hereafter referred to in the text as *TS*.

14. See Therese Lentfoehr, "The Solitary" in *Thomas Merton/ Monk: A Monastic Tribute*, ed. Patrick Hart (Garden City, New York: Doubleday & Company, 1976), pp. 70-74, for quotations from Merton's letters indicating a problem with censors.

Finally, a few pages later, he comes round to his original pact with the world. "And then they will come to realize something of their mission to embrace the whole world in a spiritual affection that is not limited in time or space (*NM*, p. 155). A couple of years later, in *The Silent Life* (1957), he is more specific on what he means by the "world," and this clears up some of his previous ambiguity.

> The meaning of the monk's flight from the world is precisely to be sought in the fact that the "world" (in the sense in which it is condemned by Christ) is the society of those who live exclusively for themselves. To leave the "world" then is to leave oneself first of all and begin to live for others.[15]

In this passage we see quite a significant change. An experience that Merton had in Louisville in 1958 was a confirmation of his new way of perceiving the world. He wrote about it in *Conjectures of a Guilty Bystander*.

> In Louisville . . . I was suddenly overwhelmed with the realization that I loved all those people, that they were mine and I theirs, that we could not be alien to one another even though we were total strangers . . . . The conception of "separation from the world" that we have in the monastery too easily presents itself as a complete illusion. (*CGB*, p. 156)

Later in the same journal he continued his reflections on the world and what it means.

> I think the question of "turning to the world" is in fact a question of being patient with the unprepossessing surface of it, in order to break through to the deep goodness that is underneath. But to my way of thinking, "the world" is precisely the dehumanized surface. (*CGB*, p. 257)[16]

The insight Merton had on the street corner in Louisville had a great impact on his view of the world and its relationship to solitude. He had come a long way from *Seeds* to *New Seeds* -- from separation to embracing.

Monastic Virtues

Some of the topics treated differently by Merton in *New Seeds* are what might be called "monastic virtues": poverty, study, and humility. In Chapter Thirty-five on "Renunciation" we find in *New Seeds* an added emphasis on the importance of contemplatives' accepting some degree of poverty. Although they need some security and the essentials of life in

---

15.   Thomas Merton, *The Silent Life* (New York: Farrar, Straus & Giroux, 1957), p. 8.

16.   See also Elena Malits, *The Solitary Explorer: Thomas Merton's Transforming Journey* (San Francisco: Harper & Row, 1980), p. 39.

order to pray, they should not require the satisfaction of every bodily and psychological need. They must be able to identify with the poor by actually experiencing some of the risks of poverty. However, destitution is not a virtue either, and prayer may be impossible if one must struggle just to survive.

> And though it may be good for a monastery to be poor, the average monk will not prosper spiritually in a house where the poverty is really so desperate that everything else has to be sacrificed to manual labor and material cares. (*NS*, p. 253)

Merton continues with a paragraph from *Seeds* saying that an uneducated brother who does manual labor may be more of a contemplative than a scholarly priest. But in *New Seeds* he adds several paragraphs defending education and intellectual pursuits. He condemns a kind of pride that is sometimes found in contemplatives -- a pride in being unlearned. Contemplation should be based on a sound theology.

> We must not separate intellectual study of divinely revealed truth and contemplative experience of that truth as if they could never have anything to do with one another . . . . Unless they are united, there is no fervor, no life and no spiritual value in theology, no substance, no meaning and no sure orientation in the contemplative life. (*NS*, pp. 254-255)

Was Merton perhaps defensive of his own intellectual curiosity and desire for learning? He had earlier begun reaching out to philosophies and theologies beyond the Roman Catholic tradition. Was he being criticized in the community for his study and extensive reading? Had he come to the awareness in his own life of a need for a broader base in theology to support his deepening experience of contemplation? In journal passages written during the intervening years in *Conjectures of a Guilty Bystander*, we find that Merton makes several entries with references to readings he has done in the ecumenical sphere, with such theologians as Barth, Bonhoeffer, and J. A. T. Robinson, as well as the much admired Gandhi.

Another observation is given on humility and sanctity. The saints are humble because they are themselves in God's sight. Not trying to imitate the holiness of others, they work out their own salvation by being true to themselves. Merton then adds a few paragraphs caricaturing the false holy person -- the one who conforms to the expectations of others, and thus satisfies the community.

> It makes them all feel that they are "right," that they are in the right way, and that God is "satisfied" with their collective way of life. Therefore nothing needs to be changed. But anyone who opposes this situation is wrong. The sanctity of the "saint" is there to justify the complete elimination of those who are "unholy" -- that is, those who do not conform.
>
> (*NS*, p. 102)

Merton was one of those not conformning to the typical mold of the Cistercian saint. He was a popular author, had friends with whom he exchanged letters, and desired to be a hermit. One wonders if there were "saints" in his community who were trying to eliminate, or at least discredit, him. In this context, Merton inserts a paragraph on art, which seems almost out of place.

> So too in art, or literature. The "best" poets are those who happen to succeed in a way that flatters our current prejudice about what constitutes good poetry. We are very exacting about the standards that they have set up, and we cannot even consider a poet who writes in some other slightly different way, whose idiom is not quite the same. (*NS*, p. 102)

Merton was not considered one of the "best" poets by the critics and other poets. When he heard that T. S. Eliot said he wrote too much and revised too little, and was only a "hit or miss" poet, he was devastated and threatened to stop writing poetry (Mott, p. 242). One can detect in Merton a sensitivity to criticism, and even some alienation because he was a non-conformist, a truly unique poet and contemplative, one that did not fit the established mold.

Relationships and Theological Clarifications

Some of the most eloquent additions to *New Seeds* are passages on the feelings of hatred, resentment, and fear. In the chapter "A Body of Broken Bones" four sentences on hatred from *Seeds* are expanded into three pages where Merton offers a psychologically enlightened analysis of hatred. We are born into isolation, loneliness, and insufficiency, and insofar as we feel unworthy and lonely we hate ourselves. This self-hatred results either in self punishment -- which does not cure the sense of unworthiness -- or in projection of the hatred onto others because they are unworthy. The one who hates others is blind to the unworthiness in self, but condemns it in others. This can lead to a nauseating hate of everything and everyone -- for there is no one who is worthy. What is the remedy for this tormenting sense of unworthiness that lies at the root of hate?

> The beginning of the fight against hatred, the basic Christian answer to hatred is not the commandment to love, but what must necessarily come before in order to make the commandment bearable and comprehensible. It is a prior commandment, *to believe*. The root of Christian love is not the will to love, but *the faith that one is loved*. The faith that one is loved *by God*. (*NS*, p. 75)

The discovery that worthiness is irrelevant to God's mercy will deliver a person from the bondage of hate to true liberation of spirit. Bondage of the spirit may also be the result of resentment -- another emotion that Merton treats in *New Seeds*. Resentment arises when one has to live in "servile dependence upon a system, an organization, a society, or a person that one despises or hates" (*NS*, p. 109). Unable to escape this dependence, a person survives only by seeming to approve the oppressing agent or system, and then one hates oneself for succumbing. But rather than admit this pretense, a person claims that someone else has taken away their freedom.

> But as long as you pretend to live in pure autonomy, as your own master, without even a god to rule you, you will inevitably live as the servant of another man or as the alienated member of an organization. Paradoxically it is the acceptance of God that makes you free and delivers you from human tyranny, for when you serve Him you are no longer permitted to alienate your spirit in human servitude. (*NS*, p. 110)

Another feeling related to hatred and resentment is fear, a topic Merton expanded from two pages in the first book to eight in *New Seeds*. He sees fear as being a cause of war. "At the root of all war is fear: not so much the fear men have of one another as the fear they have of *everything*. It is not merely that they do not trust one another; they do not even trust themselves" (*NS*, p. 112). Hatred of self which is not consciously faced becomes hatred of others. Evil not recognized in self is projected onto others. Then, by violence if necessary, one tries to get rid of the evil ultimately by annihilating the others who are at fault.

> We have to destroy something or someone. By that time we have created for ourselves a suitable enemy, a scapegoat in whom we have invested all the evil in the world. He is the cause of every wrong. He is the fomentor of all conflict. If he can only be destroyed, conflict will cease, evil will be done with, there will be no more war. (*NS*, p. 114)

Thus the truth is bypassed that all of us are more or less wrong, that all must work together for peace. Merton remarks about the irony of postmarking mail with the stamp "pray for peace" and then spending billions of dollars on nuclear weapons. It is a mocking of God -- like drinking poison while praying for health. True peace must begin with love. "If you love peace, then hate injustice, hate tyranny, hate greed -- but hate these things *in yourself*, not in another" (*NS*, p. 122).

These expanded reflections on the feelings of hatred, resentment, and fear -- all dealing with human relationships -- would seem to be the fruit of Merton's additional years of community living since *Seeds*. It is quite well known that there were personal conflicts between Merton and Abbot

James Fox. Merton's private journals reveal some of his struggles with his Abbot over such issues as reception of visitors, confidentiality of written correspondence, censorship, the desire for a hermitage, and threats to transfer to another Order. The journal entries reveal feelings of mistrust and even rebellion in his relationship with the Abbot.[17] There is no doubt that such conflicts provided Merton with the opportunity to analyze the complex world of emotions. In the 1950s Merton also became more sensitive to the importance of social relationships and world peace. In 1960 he devoted the book *Disputed Questions* to that topic. The theme of the various essays is "the relation of the *person* to the *social organization* . . . . Every ethical problem of our day -- especially the problem of war -- is to be traced back to this root question."[18] In the years after *New Seeds* (not covered in this essay), Merton's writings turned more and more to the ethical questions of society.

As we have seen, omitted material in a revision of a work may be as indicative of a change or evolution in thought as added material. There are omissions in *New Seeds* which indicate a change in Merton's attitude toward the content and style of prayer. That contemplatives must reach out to other people was recognized by Merton even in *Seeds*. They cannot remain in their own enclosed, sanitized space because the perfection of the contemplative life is to be found in shared love. While admitting this, he still expresses a fear that thoughts about other persons could be a distraction in prayer -- a fear that later disappears.

Seeds	*New Seeds*
The silence of contemplation is deep and rich and endless society, not only with God but with men. Yet perhaps for the time being it is better to forget about it because it might upset our imagination. For if we remembered individuals and thought of them in our contemplation, that would tend to withdraw us from God and therefore from spiritual union with them. (p. 49)	. . . The contemplative is not isolated in himself, but liberated from his external and egotistic self by humility and purity of heart -- therefore there is no longer any serious obstacle to simple and humble love of other men. (p. 66)

The revision indicates that other people are no longer considered obstacles

---

17. See Mott for several journal entries, pp. 340-342.
18. Thomas Merton, *Disputed Questions* (New York: Farrar, Straus & Cudahy, 1960), p. viii.

and distractions in prayer, but an integral part of prayer.

Merton's attitude also changed toward other religious traditions. In *Seeds* he is not yet open to the East; in fact, he claims absolute superiority for the Roman Catholic tradition.

Seeds	*New Seeds*
What one of you can enter into himself and find the God who utters him? If, like the mystics of the Orient, you succeed in emptying your mind of every thought and every desire,... yet you will not find God. (p. 31)	What one of you can enter into himself and find the God who utters him? If you succeed in emptying your mind of every thought and every desire,... yet you will not find God. (p. 39)

The negative references to the "mystics of the Orient" and the implied judgment on the spirituality give way to Merton's increased knowledge and interest in the religions and philosophies of the East. This is evidenced in a similar omission in the chapter on "Tradition and Revolution." He attempts to explain and defend the notion of Church dogma and tradition as a foundation for contemplation.

Seeds	*New Seeds*
For outside the *magisterium* directly guided by the Spirit of God we find no such contemplation and no such union with Him -- only the void of nirvana or the feeble intellectual light of Platonic idealism, or the sensual dreams of the Sufi. But the first step to contemplation is faith; and faith begins with an assent to Christ teaching through His Church. (p. 87)	[Omitted] But the first step, etc. (p. 146)

Merton is on the way not only to respect the religious thought and prayer of the East, but to learn from it. In the period just preceding the publication of *New Seeds* he was "coming under the influence of Zen ... He found himself attracted to the meta-synthetic and intuitive perspectives of Zen, to its delicacy and grace, and to the opportunities that it gave him to encounter Asian contemplatives" (Grayston, p. 169). In journal material from the late 1950s and early 1960s, published in *Conjectures of a Guilty Bystander*, he wrote that truth is not found by refusing to look outside one's own self or tradition.

> If I affirm myself as a Catholic merely by denying all that is Muslim, Jewish, Protestant, Hindu, Buddhist, etc., in the end I will find that there is not much left for me to affirm as a Catholic; and certainly no breath of the Spirit with which to affirm it. (*CGB,* p. 144)

Although it is beyond the scope of this essay, Merton will come eventually to the point in his life where he identifies strongly with much of the spirituality of the Orient, and even seeks to incorporate aspects of it in his own life.

Other theological clarifications are also made in *New Seeds.* In Chapter Twenty-one on "The Mystery of Christ," he focuses on the place of Christ in contemplative prayer. Faith in Christ is the source of contemplation; the humanity of Christ is the entry way into the experience of God.

> For the man Christ *is* the Word of God, even though His human nature is not His divine nature. The two are united in One Person, and are One Person so that the Man Christ is God. If you have discovered some kind of contemplation that gives you only one without the other you are a heretic. (*S,* p. 92)

In *New Seeds* the last sentence is omitted and replaced by two pages of exposition on the Nestorian heresy. There is a danger of separating the humanity and divinity of Christ in prayer, so that the contemplative relates to the human or divine nature of Christ, rather than with the person of Christ. "To love Him merely as a *nature* would be like loving a human friend for his money or his conviviality. We do not love Christ for what He has but for *Who He is*" (*NS,* p. 153). Merton also revised a passage in *Seeds* where he was guilty of such a separation himself.

Seeds	New Seeds
Yet at the same time the mere name of Jesus or the indistinct, unanalyzed notion of Christ is enough to keep their faith fully occupied in a simple awareness of Him Who is really present in our souls by His Divinity. (p. 93)	. . . Who is really present in our souls by the gift of His personal love and by His Divine Mission. (p. 155)

Four pages on Mary in *Seeds* were expanded into nine in *New Seeds,* mostly to explain the Catholic concept of devotion to her. Merton emphasized that Mary's role is completely dependent on and related to Christ's. That he had been over zealous in the first edition can be recognized in some of his changes.

Seeds	*New Seeds*
We believe that hers was the most perfect sanctity outside the sanctity of God. (p. 100)	We believe that hers was the perfect sanctity outside the sanctity of Christ her Son, Who is God. (p. 167)
. . . .	. . . .
And all our sanctity depends on her will, on her pleasure. (p. 103)	And all our sanctity depends on her maternal love. (p. 173)

In his ecumenical outreaches, perhaps Merton realized that many people misunderstood the Roman Catholic's love for Mary, so he attempts to clarify it. Hardly anything significant appears in print by Merton about mariology after *New Seeds*.

Conclusion

By comparing *Seeds* with *New Seeds* we have been able to trace some of the most significant changes that occurred in Merton's thought from 1949 to 1961. Were the changes and developments only a normal process of spiritual growth, or were they indicative of a more profound conversion? That question cannot be objectively answered because any judgment made is based on the subjective experience of the one making it. But the process can be summarized as Donald Grayston writes: "Having fled from the world in anger, self-reproach and confusion, he had returned to it in love and compassion" (Grayston, p. 182).

Most of us have observed in contemporary spiritual writers, and in ourselves, a similar development of theology. However, there is this significant difference -- Merton's new and evolving insights traced here were all pre-Vatican II. And that would seem to be very important, perhaps more significant than the changes themselves. Following Vatican II most Catholics expressed a greater compassion and openness to the world, pursued an interest in traditions other than Roman Catholic, and made applications of psychology to spirituality. But not many can claim, as Merton could, that this development preceded Vatican II. Perhaps we could say that some of Merton's "Seeds" blossomed in Vatican II, and are even now bearing fruit, probably beyond what even he could have envisioned.

LIGHTS ACROSS THE RIDGE:

Thomas Merton & Henry David Thoreau

by **John Albert**, O.C.S.O.

Introduction

In a journal entry dated December 6, 1950, later included in *The Sign of Jonas*, young Father Louis Merton, O.C.S.O. (1915-1968) wrote of reading "beautiful pages on morning and being awake" in *Walden*, by Henry David Thoreau (1817-1865). Merton copied out this line, giving it his own emphasis: "I went to the woods because I wished *to live deliberately, to front only the essential facts of life, and see if I could not learn what it had to teach and not, when I came to die, to discover that I had not lived.*" Thoreau -- comments Merton -- adds "mystery" here: "Nor did I wish to practice resignation unless it was necessary." Merton supposed Thoreau to mean he did not intend to be resigned to anything like a compromise with life.[1]

On July 16, 1965, Thomas Merton formally began life as a hermit, his cinder-block cabin on a wooded hillside opposite the monastery having become as significant for him as the slat-board

---

* Preliminary Note: This essay is the result of the editorial work and encouragement of five persons to whom I extend my thanks. Sister Mary Alice Lawhead, O.S.B., of St. Meinrad College, Indiana, served so graciously as research assistant and second reader for my thesis written in 1970 on Thoreau's theory of dissent. She continues to enliven my Merton-Thoreau studies. Brother Patrick Hart, O.C.S.O., and Dr. Robert E. Daggy read the account of my stay in Merton's hermitage in its earlier form. Both men have been supportive of my Merton efforts in our meetings and in their continued correspondence. Drs. Dewey and Victor Kramer are responsible for the "literary map" that showed in an analytical way what I had done intuitively, as well as for numerous corrections and suggestions that have strengthened the structure and form of this work. Finally, I thank my abbot, Armand Veilleux, O.C.S.O., and my community for allowing me to acquire the Merton and Thoreau source material used in this study. Brother Mark Dohle, O.C.S.O., in particular contributed a much-needed perspective during the long weeks of redacting and typing this manuscript: his kindness and his humor kept me moving.

1. Thomas Merton, *The Sign of Jonas* (New York: Harcout, Brace & Company, 1953), p. 316. Hereafter referred to in the text as *SJ*.

and plaster hut on Walden Pond had been for Henry David Thoreau. "I am accused of living in the woods like Thoreau instead of living in the desert like St. John the Baptist," Merton wrote in *Day of a Stranger*. "All I can answer is that I am not living 'like anybody.' Or 'unlike anybody.' We all live somehow or other, and that's that. It is a compelling necessity for me to be free to embrace the necessity of my own nature . . . . I live in the woods as a reminder that I am free not to be a number. There is, in fact, a choice."[2]

In the following essay, I propose to present an account of my stay in Merton's hermitage in early 1984 during my first (and at the time of this writing only) journey from my monastery since my entrance into Trappist life in 1974. Here, I give not only details of my days and nights spent there, and descriptions of Merton's hermitage itself, but also develop the connection between Merton and Thoreau through an exploration of Merton's hermitage, not only as the material place of significance it surely is for all persons privileged to stay there, but as "metaphysical space" and "sacred place" -- that is, as region of the mind, heart and spirit wherein Merton, Thoreau and I finally met.

I will allow Thoreau and Merton to emerge through the narrative of my text in a manner that shows their dynamic personal development and the changing configuration of their thought and feelings. Diverse as their thinking was, both pondered the same fundamental questions: What is it that forms the bond of the human family? What are the native rights of the person over against his or her moral obligations and civil duties? What is the place of the human creature in Nature?

Merton and Thoreau lived in eras of tremendous discontinuous change and hammered out on the anvils of their consciences a practical moral philosophy of dissent from all social and spiritual rigidity in favor of the history, needs and struggle of each human person. Thoreau in his own time and Merton in ours have both been described as creatures of a froward and intractable nature when measured against the standards of their neighbors. Both chose to live differently and paid the price of their convictions. They abhorred political and theological intolerance (no matter how intolerant of others they at times may have been) and constantly sought to clarify the distinction between unity and uniformity; moral responsibility and social conformity; personal definition and corporate identity.

Unique as their personal stances were Thoreau and Merton did not speak out in isolation: they knew they were living links in a tradition and they did all in their power to preserve it. For a proper understanding of their thoughts on dissent, we must look to the theoretical underpinnings of concepts and ideas which found expression in their writings. Intellectual influences on Thoreau and Merton were extremely wide and varied and in this essay I examine the tenets of classical philosophers and modern European social analysts who shaped our understanding of conscience, natural law and the social contract and to those dissenters who inherited and reshaped these theories into a specific American radicalism. Abolitionism and the civil rights movement informed the opinions of Thoreau and Merton and both in turn influenced their times. Joined with these Western forces is the influence of the Orient, and I therefore present glimpses of Thoreau and Merton in relation to the wisdom of the East as well.

The contents of this essay have been given their particular form based on two sets of literary figures which are distributed through the ten sections, each of which is integrated with the others in a movement of ideas and images. From natural geography the "journey," the "finding," and the "return" are borrowed, and to these figures accommodated meanings are added. Thus, there is a rhythm in parts 1., Seeking the "Sacred Place," and 10., "The Return," when I write of my intellectual search and the desires of my heart. Parts 2., A Dwelling of

---

2. Thomas Merton, *Day of a Stranger*; edited with an introduction by Robert E. Daggy (Salt Lake City: Gibbs M. Smith, 1981), pp. 31, 33. Hereafter referred to in the text as *DS*.

"Kindred Spirits," and 9., "Disarming the Heart," also balance: I describe finding the place of solitude and peace and the movement from alienation to world community. Parts 3., The "Abode of Conscience" and 4., Action According to a "Higher Law" also go together and treat of inner space -- the human conscience and action according to principle -- human integrity. These theoretical sections are connected with parts 7., Preserving the "Tradition of Dissent," and 8., The Nature of "American Radicalism," which demonstrate the origin and development of our nation's radical political tradition and how this tradition is one of direct social action.

Parts 5., "Voices and Lights" in the Night, and 6., Facing "East," also balance and are the centerpiece structurally and in content. Here the images borrowed from geography are retained but shift to give way to symbols borrowed from astronomy and developing technology. We see the natural lights of sun, moon and stars; the lights of candle, wood-burning stove and oil lamp; the lights of the electric utilities nearby in the hermitage, and far away in the distant farm houses across the dark Kentucky valleys, plus the flashing lights of planes passing in the night. If we hear voices of Nature and imagination, we also see some of the "intellectual lights" of our Western tradition and the "enlightened" masters of the East. And, hopefully, we also see new lights of insight into the meaning of who we are. Ultimately, light serves as metaphor for Merton and Thoreau, shining brilliantly through life and beyond death.

A further concentration on these natural and allegorical images reveals a pattern. This opening up of the narrative, and parts 1. and 2., represent dawn and daytime. Parts 3. and 4., evening. In parts 5. and 6., night -- the descent into self -- and new morning meet. In parts 7. and 8., new day -- representing also new life -- arises and gives way to night in part 9. In part 10. the narrative closes, yet it is open-ended: we remain in night, with the new day in expectation. This imagery can be extended to include the nature of our own times, poised as we all are in hope for a better world brought about by our hard work in cooperation with the grace of the Risen Christ.

As it has evolved, this essay demonstrates the literary method employed by Henry Thoreau and Thomas Merton. For them short notes quickly scribbled on scraps of paper or in a pocket notebook (spontaneous recording) are extended into fuller, reworked passages in a permanent journal (reflective rewriting). Paragraphs can be expanded and restructured into complete essays which combine original material with material from further reading on a pertinent subject. Personal details may be edited out in favor of a greater "objectivity;" facts are added for clarity and color. Often such reworked and expanded material formed the basis for lectures. Finally, completed essays were enlarged into books -- including the journal *genre* -- or as one of a series of collected essays in book form. For both Thoreau and Merton, the journal form itself became supremely important. Toward the end of his life, Thoreau's journal was his primary work. Toward the end of *his* life, Thomas Merton established a literary trust to assure the publication of his writings, including journal accounts.

Returning to favorite Thoreau and Merton texts, I have found refreshment of spirit and new insights in familiar territory. Staying in Merton's hermitage was both a confirmation of my appreciation for him, and an occasion of challenge. In my account I have moved from notes jotted and rewritten there into a full essay incorporating theoretical material researched and written many years ago. Thoreau and Merton have informed my conscience these many years. As I marched against the Vietnam War on November 15, 1969 and April 24, 1971 in Washington, D. C., and against racism in Forsyth County, Georgia, on January 24, 1987, I carried in my pocket writings by both men. This essay is presented as an expression of gratitude by a second-generation Merton student who came of college age in the 1960s. For young people coming to awareness in the 1980s, I hope it is an invitation to look to their past as well as toward their future.

★ ★ ★ ★ ★

1.   Seeking the "Sacred Place"

I pass, wet-footed, through meadows made into marsh by rains lasting since early morning. From the circle of knobs thick with cedar pines and sycamores configurations of steam shimmer in the intensifying sunlight. A white tuft cloud plume hovers above trees that conceal Thomas Merton's hermitage, dove above nest of peace, image of my aspirations for this stay. I ascend the packed dirt path along the hedge row my mind a minstrel singing memories of first visit here, twelve years ago, with seminary friends and John Howard Griffin. But heart serves a wiser guide, creates gaps in reactions, backtracks joyous emotions, stalks present feelings. I am alone now. I walk the perimeter of the hermitage building, getting my bearings, appreciating the grace of being allowed to be here again. I sit on the concrete porch a long while.

Religious persons from primitive times to the present have connected the spiritual journey in the interior of their hearts with the outward journey to "holy places." Sinai, Mecca, the Garden of Lumbini are revered by Jews, Moslems, and Buddhists. The land where Jesus lived and died, places particularly associated with Mary, the homes of specially loved saints immediately come to our minds as Christians. Sacred places, yes, and famous. Others -- less well-known -- are cherished by us all. As external signs of interior values, sacred places -- big and small -- have unending depths of meaning for us.

In Japan, the training of the young Zen monks begins with a journey, the *angya* (literally: "going on foot"), the external pilgrimage that symbolizes his inner spiritual search. The bamboo bonnet; the silk-covered box on his back holding a robe, a book or two, a writing pad and brush; his rice-paper umbrella; the wooden clog-sandals -- all are still to be seen in this age of planes and trains as the novice visits shrines and monasteries throughout the land, seeking the master who hopefully will bring him to enlightenment.

In Russian Orthodoxy, the spiritual pilgrimage has been beautifully portrayed in the book entitled *The Way of the Pilgrim*. We feel that we are travelling with the pilgrim, not only as he makes his way from village to village, but reciting with him ever deeper in our own depths the ancient Jesus Prayer: "Lord Jesus Christ, Son of God, have mercy on me, a sinner!"

In the Western tradition of Benedictine monasticism, the vow of stability to a monk's monastery replaced the spiritual journey. St. Benedict (living in an unstable society and all too aware of the dangers of wanderlust), wrote about bad monks -- the *gyrovagues* (Greek: *guros* = circle + Latin: *vagari* = to wander) -- who roamed from place to place, a rule unto themselves, a menace to others. Modern Trappist life, a branch of Benedictine monasticism, still maintains this tradition of stability. Normally a man will visit other monasteries and spiritual centers in search of the appropriate place for him before he enters a community. After he enters, he accepts the realities of separation from loved ones, the regularity and austerity of staying in his monastery year after year.

For Thomas Merton, the Abbey of Our Lady of Gethsemani in Kentucky became the holy place of his inner pilgrimage when he entered the Trappist community on December 10, 1941, at the age of twenty-six. Born in France; reared partly in England and partly in America; a traveler throughout Europe; a student at Columbia; a professor at St. Bonaventure's; a pilgrim to the shrine of Our Lady of Cobre in Cuba -- Merton had sought himself and God in many places. At Gethsemani, he confronted both and, for the next twenty-seven years, labored in that understanding. In his monastery and particularly in the Abbey church, young Merton found his external sanctuary, his "sacred place." But as he progressed as a monk, Merton desired and sought ever greater solitude and release from the restrictions of institutional religious life. In one of his later essays, "Is 'The World' a Problem?" Merton wrote: ". . . due to a book I wrote thirty years ago [*The Seven Storey Mountain*], I have become a sort of stereotype of the world-denying contemplative -- the man who spurned New York, spat on Chicago, and tromped on Louisville, heading for the woods with Thoreau in one pocket, John of the Cross in another, and holding the Bible open to the Apocalypse. This personal stereotype is probably my own fault, and it is something I have to try to demolish on occasion."[3]

Having grown to a greater inner freedom as a monk, it was here in his hermitage that Merton found his deepest physical and spiritual center. "I exist under trees. I walk in the woods out of necessity," he wrote in *Day of a Stranger*. "I am both a prisoner and an escaped prisoner. I cannot tell you why, born in France, my journey ended here in Kentucky. I have considered going further, but it is not practical. It makes no difference. Do I have a 'day?' Do I spend my 'day' in a 'place?' I know there are trees here. I know there are birds here . . . . I share this particular place with them: we form an ecological balance. This harmony gives the idea of 'place' a new configuration" (*DS*, p. 33).

---

3. "Is 'The World' a Problem?" *Katallagete* 5:1 (Spring 1974), p. 28.

No monk is really under a prison sentence. While his "incarceration" is positive and self-imposed, the monk nonetheless inclines his heart to the admonition of Sacred Scripture, remembering those in prison (of whatever sort of confinement that might be) as though in prison with them, keeping in thought and prayer all ill-treated persons as if he were to share their fate (Hebrews 13:3). From his hermitage, as he descended deeper into the mystery of his own contemplative vocation, Merton became ever more sensitive to the plight of all human persons in our post-technological age and he looked to other religious traditions -- Hinduism, Buddhism, Sufism, the Cargo Cults of New Guinea, the Ghost Dance of the American Indians --to help him articulate his own struggle as a brother in the human family.

Merton's great need to communicate with others -- coupled with his growing celebrity -- were undercurrents that made his hermitage existence less and less possible. Merton had made a few trips within the United States after his entrance into Gethsemani Abbey: with his abbot to explore property for a foundation in Ohio; to Saint John's Abbey in Minnesota for a psychiatry workshop; to New York City to meet with Zen scholar D. T. Suzuki. Following the election of a new abbot in 1968, Merton was given permission to travel to Washington, D. C.; to explore hermitage sites in New Mexico, California and Alaska. Still a monk of Gethsemani, he had hoped to find his desired solitude in a more remote place while maintaining contact with friends through his Abbey in Kentucky. As one of the most informed and acknowledged Catholic authorities on the contemplative experience -- East and West -- Merton was invited to attend the international Benedictine-sponosred monastic symposium in Bangkok, Thailand in 1968.

Thus, for Merton, the spiritual journey of the heart and the outward journey to holy places became a reality once again. For him it was the fulfillment of a dream: to meet real Oriental masters in their own monasteries, to dialogue with them about Krishna, Buddha and Christ, to learn as much as he could from them as their own spiritual traditions eroded in the onslaught of post-modernism.

Shortly after giving his talk at the Bangkok conference he was attending, Merton was killed by accidental electrocution and/or heart failure. The date was the same as his entrance into Gethsemani: December 10th. His spiritual journey closed in a cyclic pattern. He had arrived at last at his true and final home. He was now complete.

Merton's 1960s hermitage meetings with honored guests -- famous and unknown -- were of vast importance to him. Merton was a renegade who fought for the woods as his refuge: first, walks beyond the retention wall were permitted; then came periods of watch in the hill-top fire tower; later, the hermitage could be used for specific intervals; and here, Merton was "at home" at last, his forays into the woods as unknown land ("raids on the unspeakable," he called them) having ended. Even though Merton --during the last year of his life -- considered more isolated sites (even as far away as Hawaii, Scotland and Nicaragua), in his final journey, this his hermitage at Gethsemani in the woods of Kentucky was a tether to his past. I enter it now and bolt the door.

2. A Dwelling of "Kindred Spirits"

Henry Thoreau once said there is no sight so beautiful as mud on a man's boots. I spend time de-beautifying my boots, making them less Thoreauvian. The wonderful sensation of donning warmed socks! My boots cook well on the wood-burning stove. Wet corduroys and blue zippered-jacket dry in the bedroom. I put on new grey trousers. Checking the leather pouches carried criss-cross around my shoulders, I find all needed items have been removed. On the desk: Thoreau's *A Yankee in Canada* and other writings; *Zen Dust* by Isshu Miura and Ruth Fuller Sasaki; Merton's *Raids on the Unspeakable* and *Day of a Stranger*; my compact black leather *New American Bible* and red leather-bound *Grail Psalter*. Everything is in order.

I spend time paging through thirty-two different Merton books (from *The Seven Storey Mountain* to *Cables to the Ace*); twenty-five monographs; and the loose sheets of paper which fill the corner shelf-cabinet. I am here now. Still the guns of Fort Knox boom. I feel the sorrow of Merton's not being here. This place of peace is his.

Though I lived just eighteen miles from here as a seminary student at Saint Mary's College from 1966 to 1969, I never tried to meet Merton. I felt he would want to be left alone. Already, I guess, I sensed my own contemplative vocation and valued Merton's solitude. I read his books in those days, hard-back first editions of *The Seven Storey Mountain, The Waters of Siloe, The Ascent to Truth, The Sign of Jonas*. I saw Merton here at Gethsemani in a hallway once during one of our seminary bus trips, slipping into a guesthouse room, almost undetected. He paused to look at me. Perhaps at that time I knew myself too little really to say anything to him, but a personal connection had been made. There were other -- indirect -- connections.

Teaching at Saint Mary's was Father Daniel Walsh. It was to Dan, then a layman teaching the philosophy of Saint Thomas Aquinas at Columbia, that young Thomas Merton first seriously confided his desire to become a Roman Catholic. Gradually Merton would learn from Dan about the Trappists and Gethsemani Abbey in Kentucky. Years later, Merton brought Dan to Kentucky as philosophy instructor at the Trappist Abbey and the local Catholic colleges. Under Merton's influence, Dan Walsh eventually embraced the priesthood while I was at Saint Mary's. In class Dan would read Merton's letters as they arrived from Asia, and one day in December of 1968 he tearfully broke the news to us that Merton had just died. And it was Dan who first pointed out to me Merton's grave at Gethsemani.

Later, from 1969 to 1973, as a seminary student attending Saint Meinrad College and School of Theology not far from Gethsemani in Indiana, I read Merton's later books. Writing my bachelor's thesis in philosophy on Thoreau's "theory of dissent," and struggling with social issues of that time, I read: *New Seeds of Contemplation* and *Faith and Violence*, *Conjectures of a Guilty Bystander*, *Zen and the Birds of Appetite*, *Cables to the Ace*, *The Geography of Lograire* and John Howard Griffin's *A Hidden Wholeness* and Edward Rice's *The Man in the Sycamore Tree*.

There were further visits here to Gethsemani, and it was John Howard Griffin -- working on the official biography of Merton at the time --who first welcomed friends and me here to the hermitage in January of 1972. Gradually, as my own contemplative vocation emerged, Merton was with me, with *Mystics and Zen Masters*, *Raids on the Unspeakable*, *Contemplation in a World of Action* and *Day of a Stranger*. And Merton's portrayals of Our Lady of the Holy Ghost Abbey, Conyers, Georgia in *The Waters of Siloe* and *Gethsemani Magnificat* figured in my vocational discernment.

At Conyers, I found many other connections with Merton. Holy Spirit -- as her first daughterhouse -- enjoys a living spiritual heritage with Gethsemani. Many of our "founders" were already seniors when young Thomas Merton entered the Trappists, one Conyers monk welcoming him first as retreatant and finally "for life;" all somehow adding to the spirit that made the monastery so attractive to him. They would watch the short monk in tennis shoes on his way to the room where he labored at the archives and his books. Merton can be seen in the photographs of 1944, embracing his brothers departing for the foundation in Georgia. Other members of our community met Merton along their way, one as a young man with whom Merton spoke in a Cuban marketplace (and later wrote about in *The Seven*

Storey Mountain); another as a junior monk under Merton's guidance in his formative years before coming to Georgia. The impact of Merton is still felt in our lives.

"Great persons are not soon learned," wrote Thoreau in his journal on Friday, 25 March 1842, "not even their outlines, but they change like the mountains and the horizon as we ride along."[4] In a letter to a friend written that same month and year, Thoreau said: "For we are not what we are, nor do we treat or esteem each other for such, but for what we are capable of being."[5]

Some of Thomas Merton's 1968 journal fragments -- read by him into a dictaphone machine -- were published after his death as *Woods, Shore, Desert*. On the cover of this book naturalist Annie Dillard is quoted as saying: "This is a welcome addition to the Merton canon. It's one of the world's truly interesting journals . . . it shows Merton in his best and truest role as a writer."[6] Whatever the full context of her remarks, Annie Dillard's statement about Merton's best and truest role is debatable. I wonder if people who are not monks or nuns can appreciate Merton as he was best and truest: as monk. Or, perhaps, Annie Dillard is correct, and Merton was more writer than monk. Or equally both? But our best and truest role is to be who we are. Merton was -- without doubt -- Merton!

In *Nature, Grace and Religious Development*, a book which Merton may have read, Barry McLaughlin makes this assessment which is to the point: "the conflict is heightened by the individual's realization that in attaining professional competence he cuts himself off to a certain extent from the religious organization, achieving prestige in an outside group that knows nothing of his other role. At the same time his professional achievements often cannot be accurately evaluated by superiors and other members of his religious community."[7] Merton, for his part, writes in *Woods, Shore, Desert*: "A happening. Presence and witness but also speaking of the unfamiliar . . . speaking of something new to which you might not

4.   Henry David Thoreau, *Journal: Volume I: 1837-1844*, edited by Elizabeth Hall Witherell et al. (Princeton: Princeton University Press, 1981), p. 390. Hereafter referred to in the text as *J*.

5.   *The Correspondence of Henry David Thoreau*, edited by Walter Harding and Carl Bode (Westport, Connecticut: Greenwood Press, 1974), p. 62. Thoreau's letter to Mrs. Lucy Brown was written at Concord on 2 March 1842.

6.   Thomas Merton, *Woods, Shore, Desert* (Santa Fe: Museum of New Mexico Press, 1983). Hereafter referred to in the text as *WSD*.

7.   Barry McLaughlin, *Nature, Grace and Religious Development* (New York: Paulist Press, 1964), p. 60.

yet have access. An experiment in openness. Problems. Too much conformity to roles. Is it just a matter of brushing up the roles and adjusting the roles? A role is not necessarily a vocation. One can be alienated by role filling" (WSD, p. 5).

In every highly developed and dehumanizing society, monks and hermits have joined outlaws and fugitives on the fringe -- all equally rebellious though perhaps for quite distinct reasons. Robbers-become-monks, and the sometimes shady movements back and forth between the sub-cultures (recall the legendary friendship of Robin Hood and Friar Tuck), are all part of monastic lore.[8] Though it had been a consistently examined problem throughout his writings, Merton focused on human alienation and the vocation of the monk (as poet) in a particularly marked manner in his efforts as a hermit-author. Merton gathered around him a host of spiritual witnesses who shadow through and shine in these later writings. He felt they shared with him a common participation in loss and yearning, sorrow and human aspiration. They reminded him to be not too quick to throw off the negative impulses he discovered within himself, for whatever reason.

How could Merton not be attracted to Thoreau, who once wrote: "If you have nothing to say let me have your silence, for that is good and fertile."[9]

3. The "Abode of Conscience"

Henry David Thoreau's refusal to pay the poll tax in protest against our country's war with Mexico (and his subsequent night in jail as a result); his protest against Massachusetts slave laws and assistance to black fugitives; his defense of Captain John Brown; even his two-year stint at Walden Pond are now part of our common history. Even Thoreau himself is now

---

8. I have given extensive treatment to the theme of Merton as "outlaw" in "Ace of Songs -- Ace of Freedoms: Thomas Merton and Bob Dylan," American Benedictine Review 37:1 (March 1986), pp. 67-95 and 37:2 (June 1986), pp. 143-159. For a presentation of the ancient monastic spirituality of "prisoner for Christ" with references to Merton, see "In the Heart of Christ: The Monk, The Outcast, The Prisoner," Hospitality 5:2 (February 1986), pp. 4-7 and 5:3 (March-April 1986), pp. 8, 12. See also "The Monastery: Freedom in the Love of God," Hospitality 5:9 (November 1986), pp. 7-9.

9. This quotation is from Thoreau's previously unpublished pre-1845 manuscript Reform and the Reformers included in the Princeton Edition; see Reform Papers, edited by Wendell Glick (Princeton: Princeton University Press, 1973), p. 190. Hereafter referred to in the text as RP. I have drawn the connection between Merton and Thoreau in four previously published essays: "Inauguration of Prayer House," Theology Activities Organization Newsletter, Saint Meinrad School of Theology (Fall 1971), p. 2; "The Contemplative Witness of Henry David Thoreau," Monastic Exchange 8:3 (Fall 1976), pp. 7-14; "Mind Guards against the White Knight: Thomas Merton and Bob Dylan," Merton Seasonal 9:3 (Autumn 1984), pp. 4-10; and "Thomas Merton's Journey Home," Georgia Bulletin 22:43 (6 December 1984), p. 5.

regarded by many as an authentic guardian and transmitter of the true "American Spirit." Why?

In the opening pages of his essay *On the Duty of Civil Disobedience*, Thoreau answers this question: "The only obligation which I have a right to assume is to do at any time what I think right."[10] But here Thoreau is not speaking of mere personal opinion in disregard of the thinking of others. What he is doing is setting forth his first principle for action: obedience to the dictates of his conscience.

Conscience -- from the Latin *conscientia* and the Greek *synidesis* -- is the practical judgment of reason upon an individual act as good and to be performed, or as evil to be avoided. The term is applied to: 1) the intellect as the faculty of forming judgments about right and wrong individual acts; 2) the process of reasoning that the intellect goes through to reach such a judgment; 3) the judgment itself which is the conclusion of this reasoning process. Conscience is not a particular doing of something, but rather a mode of being which protects the integrity of the human person and safeguards the unity of our existence. For the ancient Stoics (Thoreau first studied them during his years at Harvard), conscience was the root of the independence of the human person.

The development of conscience comes about under the influence of morally significant impressions drawn from our human environment together with our own life-experience. It begins with the adoption of external patterns of moral and civil conduct from others (legal conscience) and progresses to the point where an independent position is adopted as a personal response to these adopted codes. Conscience brings to our mind the objective moral norm in its relation to a decision to be made in a particular situation. Since the judgment of conscience is the judgment of the intellect -- and the intellect can err, either by adopting false premises or by drawing an illogical conclusion -- conscience can be correct or erroneous. Conscience can be erroneous in not conforming to objective or universal good or evil -- judging a thing to be good that is objectively evil, or a thing to be evil that is objectively good. The human will seeks only the good (what is perceived as right and correct and profitable), and for this reason a certain conscience may make an erroneous judgment, but a certain conscience is never false.

---

10. *Reform Papers*, p. 65. Thoreau's prolonged meditation on his July 1846 arrest was delivered as a lecture on 26 January 1848. First published as *Resistance to Civil Government* by Elizabeth Peabody in *Aesthetic Papers* on 14 May 1849, Thoreau's most famous essay has circulated in our time under the title I have given.

The moral value of an act is measured exclusively according to the judgment of conscience arrived at after due consideration of all involved circumstances. In a situation where a concrete decision must be made, conscience cannot be dispensed with or replaced by opinions or direction from an external course. In other words, ultimately we stand alone. The judgment of conscience is the definitive norm for our individual decision, but it does not thereby become a general norm for people faced with similar decisions. Both Merton and Thoreau were quick to declare that they proposed their own life-choices to no one else as a moral imperative.[11] Thoreau's doctrine of social reform was best summed up in Chapter Two of *Walden*, "Where I Lived, And What I Lived For": "In the midst of this chopping sea of civilized life, such are the clouds and storms and quick-sands and thousand-and-one items to be allowed for, that a man has to live . . . simplify, simplify."[12]

Thoreau demanded for all men and women the freedom to follow unique life styles, lives shaped by their own free choices. Thoreau recognized the mystery of "otherness" in human life. His wisdom was to allow himself and others to be themselves, but he required "the best self" from all. "A man must serve another and a better use than any he can consciously render," he wrote in *Reform and Reformers* (*RP*, p. 190). Though he could say: "For an impenetrable shield, stand inside yourself,"[13] Thoreau was by no means a recluse, certainly no hater of humankind. He did not advise total withdrawal from society, but rather lifting it up by means of self-discipline and a life lived in harmony with Nature. In August 1850, he wrote to a friend: "Our thoughts are the epochs in our lives: all else is but a journal of the winds that blew while we were here."[14] Henry David Thoreau was a man of thought, and a thoughtful man. His life is a testimony to the capabilities of the human person, the intellectual and spiritual powers given to us by God to realize our own self-worth, and to help others to do

---

11. My sources for this treatment of the complex subject of the human conscience are: Austin Fagothey, *Right and Reason: Ethics in Theory and Practice* (St. Louis: C. V. Mosley Company, 1967), p. 35; Rudolf Hofman, "Conscience," *Sacramentum Mundi: An Encyclopedia of Theology* (1968), 1:411-414; John L. McKenzie, S.J., "Conscience," *Dictionary of the Bible* (Milwaukee: Bruce, 1965), p. 147. Through Merton I was led to Dietrich Bonhoeffer (1906-1945). See Bonhoeffer's *Ethics*, edited by Eberhard Bethge (New York: Macmillan, 1955), pp. 64-70, 242-248, for his final writings on conscience.

12. Henry David Thoreau, *Walden*, edited by J. Lyndon Shanley (Princeton: Princeton University Press, 1971), p. 91. Hereafter referred to in the text as *W*.

13. This quote is from Thoreau's 1840 essay "The Service," *Reform Papers*, p. 7. For Thoreau's developing ideas concerning inner strength, see Robert D. Richardson, *Henry Thoreau: A Life of the Mind* (Berkeley: University of California Press, 1986), pp. 54-57, 104-106.

14. Letter to Harrison Gray Otis Blake written at Concord 9 August 1950. In *Correspondence*, p. 265. Thoreau is reporting on his trip to Fire Island where he had gone in July to recover the remains of Margaret Fuller, victim of a sea disaster.

the same.

In comparing the basic asceticism in *Walden* with that of Saint John of the Cross -- in a journal entry dated 8 December 1950 (again, included in *The Sign of Jonas*) -- Thomas Merton saw agreement on the fundamental idea, not "of course on the means or technique" except to some extent. Merton's lines which immediately follow show us his inner identification with Thoreau. Those words are: "Ascesis of solitude. Simplification of life. The separation of reality from illusion" (*SJ*, pp. 16-17).

In his "Notes for a Philosophy of Solitude" (a much-reworked redaction was published in *Disputed Questions* in 1960), Merton connected with Thoreau once again. " . . . though I am treating of the traditional concept of the *monachos*, or solitary," commented Merton, "I am deliberately discarding everything that can conjure up the artificial image of the monk in a cowl, dwelling in a medieval cloister." Merton continued: "In this way I intend obviously, not to disparage or to reject the monastic institution, but to set aside all its accidentals and externals, so that they will not interfere with my view of what seems to me to be deepest and most essential." "But by that same token," Merton added, "the 'solitary' of these pages is never necessarily a 'monk' (juridically) at all. He may well be a layman, and of the sort most remote from cloistered life, like Thoreau or Emily Dickinson."[15]

Later, in *Conjectures of a Guilty Bystander* (1966), Merton praised Thoreau's "idleness" as "an incomparable gift" and its fruits as "blessings that America has never really learned to appreciate." Merton concluded: " . . . Thoreau proffered his gift nevertheless, though it was not asked for, and he knew it would be neglected. Then he went his way, without following the advice of his neighbors. He took the fork in the road."[16]

By the time he had come to write "Rain and the Rhinoceros" (which was included in *Raids on the Unspeakable* in 1966), Merton's identification with Thoreau was fixed. Here Merton says: "Thoreau sat in *his* cabin and criticized the railways. I sit in mine and wonder about a world that has, well, progressed." "I must read *Walden* again," Merton continues, "and see if Thoreau already guessed that he was part of what he thought he could escape. But it is not a matter of 'escaping.' It is not even a matter of protesting very audibly." Merton then resigned himself to the obvious fact: "Technology is here, even in the cabin. True, the utility lines are not here yet, and so G. E. is not here yet either. When the utilities and G. E. enter my

---

15. *Disputed Questions* (New York: Farrar, Straus & Cudahy, 1960), Merton's note, p. 177.
16. *Conjectures of a Guilty Bystander* (Garden City, New York: Doubleday & Company, 1966), p. 227.

cabin arm in arm it will be nobody's fault but my own. I admit it. I am not kidding anybody, even myself. I will suffer their bluff and patronizing complacencies in silence. I will let them think they know what I am doing here."[17]

4. Action According to a "Higher Law"

Thomas Merton struggled with the problem of human knowledge of "good" and "evil" and he aligned himself with Henry David Thoreau in an attempt to understand "civil law" and "civil rights." In his essay "Events and Pseudo-Events: Letter to a Southern Churchman" (published in *Faith and Violence* in 1968),[18] Merton wrote that the contemplative will concern himself with the same problems as other people, "but he will try to get to the spiritual and metaphysical roots of these problems -- not by analysis but by simplicity." This, of course, as Merton admitted, "is no easy task."

In the *Politics*, Aristotle long ago declared: "Man is by nature a political animal." Characteristic of our human nature, we crave companionship, and are not capable ourselves of supplying even our own most basic needs. Our ability to speak -- whether with words or signs -- indicates that we are meant to communicate with each other, and progress is the mark of our human cooperation toward the further development of human goals and the fulfillment of our aspirations as persons. In the essay, cited above, Merton declared: " . . . I cannot claim that I have discovered anything worth saying. Yet since I have been asked to say something, I will at least hazard a few conjectures" (*FV*, pp. 146-147). Thomas Merton and Henry Thoreau fought to preserve the integrity of the human conscience, not as isolated individuals, but as persons struggling to be responsible to the societies in which they lived. Having already examined conscience as the base of their respective spiritualities, let us look for what might be some "metaphysical roots" of the political actions of Merton and Thoreau. To do this we will consider the nature of the social bond and the nature of civil law in relationship to "Natural Law."

For Saint Thomas Aquinas (c. 1225-1274) -- since God is the Author of human life -- all political power comes from Him. But, for Thomas, the

---

17. *Raids on the Unspeakable* (New York: New Directions, 1966), pp. 12-13. Hereafter referred to in the text as *R*.

18. *Faith and Violence: Christian Teaching and Christian Practice* (Notre Dame, Indiana: University of Notre Dame Press, 1968), pp. 146-147. Hereafter referred to in the text as *FV*.

constitutional form of this political power -- or "authority" -- resides in the people and is determined by them: e.g. monarchy, aristocracy, democracy, and so on. The exercise or actual enjoyment of political authority, in the United States of America, for instance, is conferred or withdrawn by us, the American people. We transmit to our "governors" the authority with which they govern us.

Upholders of the "divine right of kings" contended that the sovereign received his or her power directly from God, and that the people were in no way the cause of this power. They held that the people were morally bound in all instances to obey the king or queen as ordained minister of God. In opposition to this theory of divine right, political theorists upheld, in the Age of Enlightenment, the notion of the "sovereignty of the people," contending that political power was given to the people directly by God without recourse to the monarch.

According to the political philosophy of Thomas Hobbes (1588-1679), who published his masterwork *Leviathan* in 1651, human persons are necessarily engaged in an incessant struggle for power over others, and every person naturally shuns what is deemed evil. Ultimately, each person must choose to be ruled (and sovereignty must be unified and absolute) or to be free (and with liberty comes anarchy). For Hobbes, the only means by which persons could avoid immediate destruction and provide for themselves a fitting life style was to recognize and accept the sovereignty of a power greater than themselves: in the surrender of personal rights they found security and comfort.

In building his political philosophy, John Locke (1632-1704) started with the concept of a state of nature in which persons live as equal but separate units forming an enduring union or society. Each unit (person) recognizes limitations of his or her own will, "especially the two limitations of a right of property, vested in his [or her] fellow-units, and of a right of punishment of transgressors of natural law, vested in each and all." Locke claimed this right of property because each person has property in his or her person, and therefore in his or her labor and the things into which that person injects labor. In the state of nature in which persons are judges in their own cases, imperfections ensure: partial judgments; inadequate force for the execution of judgments; variety in judgments passed by different persons in similar cases. Therefore, remedies are needed: a judicature to administer law impartially; an executive to enforce decisions of the judicature; and a legislature to lay down a uniform rule of judgment. Locke believed that the people become a corporate body through their own association (social contract) and may appoint a trustee government with which it makes no contract, which it may dismiss for breach of trust on its own interpretation of the nature of that trust.

Thus, for Locke, each person is morally bound to cooperate for a common good. In *The Second Treatise of Government* (1690) Locke declared that a person can justly kill a thief who threatens only property, even without endangering the owner's life. Locke systematically segregated sacred things from secular things, allowing freedom of conscience in religion after carefully barring it from interference in secular society. Locke made conscience a safeguard for property by defining it as an interior articulation of externally posited rules rather than of personal conviction. Locke ushered in a new social order in which persons communicated on the basis of posited rights, having exchanged certain rights enjoyed in nature (e.g. the punishment of criminals) for security guaranteed in the social order (i.e. the right to maintain private property).

French political philosopher Jean-Jacques Rosseau (1712-1778) agreed with Thomas Hobbes that sovereignty must be absolute, but he rejected the Englishman's "either/ or" conclusion. Rousseau solved the dilemma between freedom and government by resolving that human persons can be both ruled and free if they rule themselves. Thus, for Rousseau, a person is free if that person rules himself or herself; a people can be free if it retains sovereignty over itself and enacts its own laws which it is obliged to obey. Unlike John Locke, Rousseau contended that final sovereignty is found not in the individual or even in a body of individuals. The sovereignty of which he speaks is a single "moral person," and the final form this sovereignty takes is the "general will" of that moral person. Rousseau regarded each person as surrendering himself or herself to no other person, but alienating all individual rights to the whole community. But he was by no means an environmental determinist; he argued for ethical truth known through human intuition and maintained a belief in a God who stood above all pain, pleasure and material self-interest.

Though differing from Merton and Thoreau in status and experience, Rousseau, of the European political philosophers -- with his Swiss "rusticity," utopian village near Neuchatel, and his love of solitude -- is closest to them as kindred spirit. He was an idealist who evolved in response to the demands of practical realism. Though probably never influencing the development of their thought directly, he has had tremendous impact on the social climate of the nineteenth and twentieth centuries. Further comment on him helps our understanding of Merton and Thoreau.

In *Discourse on the Sciences and the Arts* (begun in 1749) and *Discourse on the Origin of Inequality* (1755), Rousseau wrote that the arts of civilized societies served only "to cast garlands of flowers over the chains men bore." The sciences did not save but brought moral ruin. Progress was an illusion: what appeared to be advance was retrogression. Modern civilization left people neither happier nor more virtuous. Happiness belonged to the human person's life in a state of nature. Virtue was possible in a simple society, where men and women and children lived austere and frugal lives. Greater sophistication brought with it greater corruption, and greater abundance brought greater laxity. In the mountain village near Neuchatel, Rousseau found "real democracy" -- a simple form of culture in a small state where persons lived as equals in a face-to-face society, knowing everyone else yet being self-sufficient. Here he found no need for reformers; democracy already existed: the problem was to keep it. Progressive, liberal ideas -- such as centralization, national parliament, merger of independent groups, and universal suffrage -- were seen by Rousseau as not only unnecessary, but as actual threats to the existing order. At this point he saw conservatism as the defense of freedom. He thought of the "state of nature" as one of innocence. In it, the human person was distinguished from the beasts by the faculty of self-improvement and by his or her only moral quality: compassion or sympathy. In the state of nature the human person lived in self-harmony. It was when he or she became sociable -- for help against natural disasters or in hunting -- that a person became wicked. These bondings and associations sharpened feelings of sympathy, which increased care and the sense of obligation.

Cultivation of the earth and enclosure of land gave rise to the idea of private property, and this gave rise to greed. People became aware of inequality of possessions, talents, skills, fortunes and destinies in life. Wealth brought slavery; power brought conflict; society brought war. Laws were enacted to combat disorder and restore tranquility. Violence threatened the lives of the poor. The rich became doubly endangered: violence threatened not only their lives but their property. The laws of civil society gave the poor new fetters and the rich new powers. All of this destroyed natural liberty forever; fixed the law of property and inequality for all time; transformed shrewd usurpation into settled right; and -- to benefit a few ambitious persons -- subjected all humankind thenceforth to labor, servitude and wretchedness.

By the time Rousseau came to write *The Social Contract* in 1762, he realized the effect of the establishment of political societies was more than the institutionalization and increase of inequalities. His reading of Hobbes and Locke helped him come to see that everything in the real world of his time was radically connected with politics, and that whatever was done about it, no nation would be other than what the nature of its government made it, a proposition not unlike that of St. Thomas Aquinas. Rousseau struggled throughout his remaining years to reconcile his inner conflicts. He was reprimanded for his love of solitude by his sometime friend Denis Diderot with the words: "Only the bad man lives alone." But Rousseau --for all his troubles -- maintained his probity to the end. He concluded *The Confessions* (1770): "I have told the truth. If anyone knows anything contrary to what I have here recorded, though he prove it a thousand times, his knowledge is a lie and an imposture; and if he refuses to investigate and inquire into it during my lifetime he is no lover of justice or of truth."

There is -- as Thoreau and Merton knew well -- a close and integral connection between the contracts of society with its government and what is known as "Natural Law," whether in the formulations of Aquinas, Hobbes, Locke, or Rousseau or other social theorists. Having looked at the abstract notions of the past that inevitably formed the political heritage bequeathed to Merton and Thoreau, let us look at some contemporary notions of "Higher Law" and "Civil Law" at this point in our reflection on the lives of the Concord and Gethsemani hermits.

As human persons, we seek concrete norms which will serve us in our effort at self-realization and self-fulfillment. We have the ability -- by the use of our reason reflecting on our nature -- to distinguish moral good from moral evil. Our intelligence points to the existence of a natural law, prior to all posited human legislation. This capacity for moral knowledge holds us responsible for our actions. Natural law comprises the realm of moral obligation which can be determined as a standard for moral behavior and enforced as civil law. The basis of it in the human person, and the knowability of it, give natural law its universal validity and make it the criterion of all legislation, both religious (e.g. *The Code of Canon Law* of the Roman Catholic Church) and civil (e.g. *The Constitution* of the United States of America).

Civil law -- based on reason -- for the common good is promulgated by the person or persons charged with the care of the community. Law as ordinance is a mandate imposing civil and moral obligations. A law is always from public authority, and lasts until it is repealed, as opposed to a personal order which ceases at the death of either party. To be reasonable, a law must be consistent with itself and with other laws, without conflicting obligations being imposed on those under its authority. A law must be just -- respecting existing rights guaranteed by higher laws -- and burdens (responsibilities for its enforcement) must be distributed equally. A law -- to be just -- must be enforceable for all and all must be able to enact it, and the common good must be maintained as the desired end without needless restrictions of liberty.

Keeping in mind the lifestyles Thoreau and Merton had chosen, and a full awareness of the religious freedom we enjoy in the United States, we can see that natural law and civil law guarantee and preserve the rights of each one of us due us as human persons. We are equally entitled to live happily, to pursue a desired end in life, to exercise our rights in freedom. However, the reality of "rights" coincides with the reality of "duties." Each one of us has a moral and civil obligation to preserve the rights of others as human persons. The human person always retains his or her rights, even though these may not be exercised -- either through voluntary choice (as in the case of Thoreau's refusal to vote and Merton's choice of monastic restrictions) or denial of the exercise of personal freedom (as in the case of the civil rights struggle wherein Merton linked Thoreau with Martin Luther King, Jr.). Even though we may not exercise all our rights, we as human persons are bound at all times to fulfill our duties.

Moral law (natural law and the ethical teachings of religion) direct us as free beings to act towards our ends -- our goals, our common good -- by imposing obligations on our free will. These obligations or duties or "oughtness" are called "moral necesiity." Moral laws can be broken by us who are bound to them, but moral necessity means that they "ought not" be broken.

Laws of society must be obeyed. There exists the necessity of maintaining civil order so that the rights and the peace and security of the state can be preserved. But the freedom to criticize, to persuade, to protest, and to assemble peaceably are essential to effective government and are rights of the individual person (and groups of persons within society) which must be safeguarded. And, finally, it is only when we have obeyed the laws of society scrupulously that we are in a position to judge which particular laws are good and just, which unjust and iniquitous. Only then can we -- if necessary according to our understanding of moral law -- disobey civil laws in well-defined circumstances.[19]

---

19. This synthesis of social theories is based on numerous sources. See: Earnest Barker (ed.), *Social Contract: Essays by Locke, Hume and Rousseau* (New York: Oxford University Press, 1962), pp. viii, xii-xiii,

In "Events and Pseudo-Events: Letter to a Southern Churchman," Merton wrote that the monastic life does not necessarily imply a total refusal to have anything to do with the world. Such a refusal would, in any case, be illusory. It would deceive no one but the monk himself. It is not possible, contended Merton, for anyone however isolated from the world, to say: "I will no longer concern myself with the affairs of the world." We cannot help being implicated; we can be guilty by default. But the monastic and contemplative life does certainly imply a very special perspective, a viewpoint which others do not share, the viewpoint of one who is not directly engaged in the struggles and controversies of the world.
Merton continued:

> Now it seems to me that if a monk is permitted to be detached from these struggles over particular interests, it is only in order that he may give more thought to the interests of all, to the whole question of the reconciliation of all men with one another in Christ. One is permitted, it seems to me, to stand back from parochial and partisan concerns, if one can thereby hope to get a better view of the whole problem and mystery of man.
>
> (*FV*, pp. 146-147)

In "Rain and the Rhinoceros," Merton wrote that the solitary, far from enclosing himself in himself, becomes every man. "Thus the solitary," continues Merton, "cannot survive unless he is capable of loving everyone, without concern for the fact that he is likely to be regarded by all of them as a traitor" (*R*, pp. 18, 22).

---

xix-xx, xxx, xxxiv; Fagothey, *Right and Reason*, pp. 106-107, 276-277, 279, 284-285; Johannes Grundel, "Natural Law," *Sacramentum Mundi*, 4: 157-163; Yves Simon, *A General Theory of Authority* (Notre Dame: University of Notre Dame Press, 1962), Appendix: "On the Meaning of Civil Disobedience"; F. J. Thonnard, *A Short History of Philosophy*; translated by Edward A. Maziarz (New York: Desclee Company, 1956), p. 245.

Concerning Thomas Hobbes, see: *Leviathan*; ed. with an introd. by C. B. MacPherson (New York: Penguin Books, 1968), pp. 39-40; Staughton Lynd, *Intellectual Origins of American Radicalism* (New York: Vintage Books, 1968), pp. 23, 109, 145.

For primary sources on John Locke, see: *The Second Treatise of Government*; ed. with an introd. by Thomas P. Peardon (New York: Liberal Arts Press, 1952); *Two Tracts on Government*; ed. by Philip Abrams (Cambridge: Cambridge University Press, 1967). See also: John Dunn, *The Political Thought of John Locke* (Cambridge: Cambridge University Press, 1969); and Barker, *Social Contract*, pp. xix-xx; Lynd, *Intellectual Origins*, pp. 23, 43, 79.

Sources for the life and doctrine of Jean-Jacques Rousseau are: *The Confessions of Jean-Jacques Rousseau*; translated with an introd. by J. M. Cohen (New York: Penguin Books, 1953), p. 13; *The Social Contract*; translated and inrtroduced by Maurice Cranston (New York: Penguin Books, 1968), pp. 16-21, 24; and Barker, *Social Contract*, pp. xiii, xxx, xxxiv; Lynd, *Intellectual Origins*, pp. 33-34. See also: *On the Social Contract, with Geneva Manuscript and Political Economy*; ed. by Roger D. Masters; translated by Judith R. Masters (New York: St. Martin's Press, 1978); Alfred Cobba, *Rousseau and the Modern State* (Hamden: Archon Books, 1961); Mario Einaudi, *The Early Rousseau* (Ithaca, New York: Cornell University Press, 1967); John . Hall, *Rousseau: An Introduction to His Political Philosophy* (Cambridge, Massachusetts: Schenkman Publishing Company, 1973); and Paul Merril Spurlin, *Rousseau in America -- 1760-1809* (University, Alabama: University of Alabama Press, 1969).

For an appreciation of Rousseau the solitary in connection with Merton and Thoreau, see: *The Reveries of the Solitary Walker*; translated with preface, notes and an interpretative essay by Charles E. Butterworth (New York: Harper Colophon Books, 1982. For the text of our American law, see: *The Constitution of the United States with Case Summaries*; ed. by Edward Conrad Smith (New York: Harper Perennial Library, 1972). On the evolution of Thoreau's and Merton's political philosophy, see my essays cited in notes 8 and 9 above.

5. *"Voices and Lights" in the Night*

In a journal entry dated 19 February 1855, Thoreau wrote: "If you wish to know how I think, you must endeavor to put yourself in my place. If you wish me to speak as if I were you, that is another affair."[20] I have explored the far-stretched parameters of Thoreau's mind and the geography of his Concord pond -- all in imagination! And I have endeavored to put myself in Merton's place too, first across the vast ranges of his writings, now through my actual presence here in his Kentucky hermitage. Rarified thinkers as they were, and men ever struggling to know and obey the higher law of their conscience, both Merton and Thoreau had their bodies grounded in the earth.

Here in the front room the axe, peuter candlestick and oil lamp -- all could have come from the Walden cabin -- remind me of the days Thoreau and Merton needed them as implements of existence, symbols of their survival in the wilderness. This cinder-block house teaches me how non-abstract Merton's hermitage years were. Merton -- like Thoreau -- knew that the person who keeps one foot in heaven and one foot on earth will be torn asunder. Thoreau and Merton were not angels but men who married Nature as their bride, and as gifted poets left us the legacy of their wonder.

The sun is passing, the wind is up. My ears ring with the whistle of the distant invisible train -- Thoreau's locomotive skirting Walden Pond? As he predicted they would in his musings on Thoreau in his Concord hut and the realities of his own situation in modern life, "progress" and G. E. have come to Merton's hermitage. Some conveniences came at Merton's own initiative, others later on. The Coleman stove for warmth and cooking oatmeal is gone. Now there is electric power and a Capital Rangette with two burners; a Munsey oven; a refrigerator; an Arvin plug-in heater. There is a full bathroom with sink, shower, toilet, mirror and heat to take away any worry about fending against the elements -- no snakes or "black widows" to fear here. There is also running water, cold and hot. And a chapel. Ancient Zen practice meets modern technology in Merton's bamboo and paper

---

20. *The Journal of Henry David Thoreau*; edited by Bradford Torrey and Francis H. Allen; with a foreword by Walter Harding; in fourteen volumes bound as two: Volumes I-VII (1837-October 1855); Volumes VIII-XIV (November 1855-1861) (New York: Dover Publications, 1962), VIII: p. 197. Until the completion of the Princeton Edition this reprint of the 1906 edition of Thoreau's journals remains the standard source. For handier selected editions, see: *The Heart of Thoreau's Journal*; edited by Odell Shepard (New York: Dover Publications, 1961); and *H. D. Thoreau: A Writer's Journal*; selected and edited with an introd. by Laurence Stapleton (New York: Dover Publications, 1960).

umbrella; opening it ever-so-gently I find a tag:

    Bangasa   Designed by John Reynolds   Made in Japan.

As a hermit, Merton was fond of his kinship with 6th century recluse Philoxenos of Syria, as he tells us in "Rain and the Rhinoceros." Philoxenus once wrote: " . . . it is not he who has many possessions that is rich, but he who has no needs." Merton comments: "Obviously, we shall always have *some* needs. But only he who has the simplest and most natural needs can be considered to be without needs, since the only needs he has are real ones, and the real ones are not hard to fulfill if one is a free man" (*R*, p. 23).

The images and appointments of the cabin reflect this spirit. In the front room, a carved crucifix near the door, a photograph of Merton by John Howard Griffin on the wall near a window, Merton's dormitory cell card: **N. LUDOVICUS 127**. Nearby, an icon of Our Lady and Child. Another icon (Annunciation) on the mantle of the fireplace and a macrame wall-hanging. I miss the Japanese scroll calendar pictured in *A Hidden Wholeness*.[21] The bookshelf and cabinet have been moved to make way for the wood-burning stove and heat-vent to the bedroom. The furniture is attractive, heavy, Shaker-like and functional (some made by artist-friend Victor Hammer): a slant-top desk; a long bench with lift-top now used for tools; a wide sitting-bench against the east window. In the kitchen a framed print dated in script, July 3, 1854, done through a medium, who told the printer to write: "Your Tree is the Tree of Life." Near the bedroom door a Papal Blessing parchment: "*Beatissimo Padre Eremita Thomas Merton . . . Ex Aedibus Vaticanus, die 3-XII-1966.*" In the bedroom, two chairs, a huge trunk (treasure chest type) with blankets, a wooden night stand, a closet with old-style Gothic vestments. On one wall a painting, floral. On the floor I find a framed Japanese Madonna and Child painted on silk. I put it on the night stand near the bed. On the north wall, near the window, an icon of the Dormition of Mary.

A miniature oil painting on wood, abstract but in icon style, which Merton used to keep on the fireplace mantel (you can see it also in the Griffin photographs),[22] now hangs near the chapel door. Holding it closer

---

21. John Howard Griffin, *A Hidden Wholeness: The Visual World of Thomas Merton* (Boston: Houghton Mifflin Company, 1970), pp. 77, 109.

22. *Ibid.*, pp. 30, 43. For other hermitage views besides those found in this book, see: Thomas Merton, *Day of a Stranger*; edited by Robert E. Daggy (Salt Lake City: Gibbs M. Smith, 1981) and Edward Rice, *The Man in the Sycamore Tree: The Good Times and Hard Life of Thomas Merton* (Garden City, New York:

with my hands I see the stark forms are human figures, five, wide, tall, with tiny bead heads and slender feet. In the background, right, is a suggestion of a Byzantine church, with domes and cross. The colors may have been brighter once. Green, streaks of red, black and shades of yellow-gold. Church Fathers? Holy Doctors? How did Merton identify with these forms?

★ ★

The valleys fill with mist, cloaking the silos of the distant farms, as night comes in. The Abbey bells announce Vespers. I recite *Psalm* 139: "O Lord, you have probed me and you know me . . . ." I reminisce. I ponder. I reflect. I pray. I project toward the tomorrow of my decisions. I fast from familiar fellowship and take a meal of cheese and fruit and bread and tea. I sit with my thoughts and the firelight, the jewels that slowly sparkle from distant hills. The pop and hiss of the embers, the sound of my own breathing. The eerie bark of dog and sound of deer. An owl's hoot punctuates the night. All of us together in an envelope of silence.

I imagine Merton's voice as I read these lines from *Day of a Stranger*:

> One might say I have decided to marry the silence of the forest. The sweet dark warmth of the whole world will have to be my wife. Out of the heart of that dark warmth comes the secret that is heard only in silence, but it is the root of all the secrets that are whispered by all the lovers in their beds all over the world. So perhaps I have an obligation to preserve the stillness, the silence, the poverty, the virginal point of pure nothingess which is at the center of all other loves. I attempt to cultivate this plant without comment in the middle of the night and water it with psalms and prophecies in silence. It becomes the most rare of all the trees in the garden, at once the primordial tree, the *axis mundi*, the cosmic axle, and the Cross."
>
> (*D*, p. 49)[23]

I feel the quick deepening within myself. The death of leaving the known, the loved, the symbolic, the holy in my own monastery and the Abbey here. The promise of resurrection is buried in new life experiences. Little deaths. Not so little deaths lived in our lives! Again, I hear Merton speaking in the night here in his hermitage: "A light appears, and in the light an icon. There is now in the large darkness a small room of radiance with psalms in it . . . . In the formlessness of night and silence a word then pronounces itself: Mercy" (*D*, p. 43).

Doubleday & Company, 1970), pp. 82-88. Rice's photographs show us the hermitage before the chapel and bathroom were added. For replicas of Thoreau's cabin and images associated with him, see: *The Annotated Walden*; edited with an introd. by Philip Van Doren Stern (New York: Bramhall House, 1970) and William Howarth, "Thoreau: Following the Tracks of a Different Man," *National Geographic* 159: 3 (March 1981), pp. 349-386.

23. Compare *Walden*, pp. 131-134.

I speak to myself. I try to fashion with words a communicable meaning: "Zero," "coming to myself," "nothing happening, just me." Merton drew the veil for others but spoke of his real self only indirectly, Christ in his heart his true religiosity. We come home to ourselves and the house is empty. We cannot convey this "nothing happening" feeling. It is positive and replete with life and purpose. It is pure being. It is repose. Our nest is nowhere and everywhere. We need not even be "Zero" for others. That takes care of itself if we are "Zero" with ourselves. No barriers in between. Openness. Fullness. Completeness.

The hoot owl clamored to be heard long ago. A glimpse of moonlight through the trees. "How good is the Lord to all, compassionate to all his creatures" (*Psalm* 144: 9).

6.   Facing "East"

I awake as the Lauds bell rings. I open the day still cast in darkness with *Psalm* 31: " . . . the joy of being forgiven." I recite the "Lord's Prayer." My mind roves . . . I read *Song of Songs*, 6: 7; *Psalm* 16; *John* 1: 1-15. A theme of love and protection in the spiritual night. "Even in the night my heart exhorts me." I belong to the One who loves me more that I can love Him. In Him is my light and life in the darkness and death of weakness and sin.

Three deer cross the meadow. Vast bolts of unravelling grey-blue fog. Cloth of clouds embossed with green pine-tree pattern. The hoot owl has gone away. The trees advance one by one from their night-time hiding. Light plays on power lines, paints Fujis on the horizon.

Greeting the dawn with *pranayamas* from the porch. Attempting to see what Merton saw, looking for what he saw by first looking to the phenomenon of clouds and mist, of crows and jet planes, of lights across the ridge, the anagogy of movement of lights across the shore of *samsara* and *nirvana*.

★ ★

"I cannot tell you what I am more than a ray of the summer's sun," wrote Thoreau in his Journal on 26 February 1841. "What I am, I am, and say not. Being is the great explainer" (*J*, p. 273).

Thoreau pioneered Western society's study of the East one hundred years before Merton began his explorations of Oriental cultures and religions. Like Merton's, Thoreau's was no mere academic interest. Thoreau, as

Merton after him, looked to the East not only outside of himself, but within. That integral harmony of being Merton described in his hermitage writings was depicted by Thoreau in his first published book -- *A Week on the Concord and Merrimack Rivers* (both travelogue and allegory as it is) --through a quote from a "Hindoo sage." The rendering Thoreau gives is this: "As a dancer having exhibited herself to the spectator, desists from the dance, so does Nature desist, having manifested herself to soul ————. Nothing, in my opinion, is more gentle than Nature; once aware of having been seen, she does not again expose herself to the gaze of soul."[24]

In *Walden* -- his second and only other book published in his lifetime -- Thoreau looks at this integral harmony from the perspective of the divine. Here, quoting from a "Hindoo philosopher," Thoreau wrote: " . . . soul, from the circumstances in which it is placed, mistakes its own character, until the truth is revealed to it by some holy teacher, and then it knows itself to be *Brahme*" (*W*, p. 96).

All of *A Week on the Concord and Merrimack Rivers, Walden*, the accounts of his journeys, his critical essays and his voluminous journals, can be seen as Thoreau's attempt -- like that of Merton himself -- to rearticulate in his own experience the ancient wisdom of the East. Thoreau looked back at the past, and asked himself the question: "Who is writing better Vedas?" (*J*, p. 313).[25] How well Thoreau succeeded, each reader of *Walden* (for instance) must judge on Thoreau's own words. In his chapter on "Solitude," Thoreau wrote:

> This is a delicious evening, when the whole body is one sense, and imbibes delight through every pore. I go and come with a strange liberty in Nature, a part of herself. As I walk along the stony shore of the pond in my shirt sleeves, though it is cool as well as cloudy and windy, and I see nothing special to attract me, all the elements are unusually congenial to me. The bullfrogs trump to usher in the night, and the note of the whipporwill is borne on the rippling wind from over the water. Sympathy with the fluttering alder and poplar leaves almost takes away my breath; yet, like the lake, my serenity is rippled but not ruffled . . . . There can be no very black melancholy to him who lives in the midst of Nature and has his senses still. (*W*, p. 129)[26]

---

24. *A Week on the Concord and Merrimack Rivers*; edited by Carl F. Hovde et alii (Princeton, New Jersey: Princeton University Press, 1980), pp. 382-383.

25. This entry was dated Monday, 7 June 1841. On 23 March 1842, Thoreau wrote: "In my brain is the sanscrit which contains the history of primitive times. The Vedas and their Angas are not so ancient as my serenest comptemplations" (*Ibid.*, p. 387).

26. In the "Monday" chapter of his *A Week on the Concord and Merrimack Rivers*, Thoreau had already written: " . . . for the senses that is furthest from us which addresses the greater depth within us. It teaches us again and again to trust the remotest and finest as the divinest instinct, and makes a dream our only real experience" (*loc. cit.*, pp. 174-175). See also my essay: "Two Studies in Chuang Tzu: Thomas Meron and Oscar Wilde," *Merton Seasonal* 12: 1 (Winter 1987), pp. 5-14.

★ ★

A rifle shot cracks the silence! A hunter in the woods?

★ ★

Full breakfast of whole-wheat bread, cheese, my first hard-boiled egg since coming to Gethsemani, with a sprinkling of salt and pepper, a banana and instant coffee.

★ ★

Overhead, an Army helipcopter. I wave from the porch. Other human persons are inside, each waves back to me from his own secret solitude. Over in the distance a jet shoots straight upward, its streamer trailing down below the sun.

★ ★

I sit and read *Zen Dust*, full as it is with *koans* and stories of the Buddhist patriarchs.

Zen Master Fa-Tsang (Hozo, 643-712) said: "Because sentient beings are deluded they think they should discard the illusory and enter the real. But once enlightenment is attained, the illusory is itself the real. There is no other real to enter." Fa-Tsang propounded the Zen doctrine of the mutual and unhindered interpenetration of all existence with each other (known as "Indra's Net") and set up in the center of a meditation hall a Buddha-image illumined by a torch, and so arranged ten mirrors around it that they were all facing one another. Each of the mirrors was then seen to reflect not only the central image but the reflection in each of the other mirrors and the reflection of the reflections *ad infinitum*.[27]

Who saw this? Does it relate to the Christian doctrine of the Mystical Body of Christ? Where do you find Him? Who is the image? Who is the torch? Who the mirrors? As I stand on this porch of Merton's solitude perceiving the phenomena as phenomenal, am I connected to him or anyone else? When the monk prays alone where is he? The guns are still. It is too early for war games, but where are the soldiers? Perhaps it is their hour of prayer. On my *rakusu* (prayer robe) I wear a tiny silver cross, gift from a friend who is a military chaplain. The "unhindered mutual

---

27.   Isshu Miura and Ruth Fuller Sasaki, *Zen Dust: The History of the Koan and Koan Study in Rinzai (Lin-chi) Zen* (New York: Harcourt, Brace & World, 1966), pp. 181, 183. Merton commented on this book in "The Zen Koan," included in *Mystics and Zen Masters* (New York: Farrar, Straus & Giroux, 1967), pp. 235-254. Hereafter referred to in the text as *ZD*.

interpenetration" of all reality. I am united to my Community in Georgia though no one there knows precisely where I am at this moment, nor do I know where each of them is. "That they All may be One." Our prayer could be: "That we realize our Oneness."

★ ★

Two wild dogs pass in front of the wooden cross and wagon wheel. I hear the logs crackle, the steam from the tea water like a steady motor, the scratch of my pen across the page. The Abbey bells ring, reminder to the hermit of his community, an invitation to unite heart with hearts, perhaps prayer with prayers. Ta-hui Tsung-kao (1089-1163) was honored by Emperor Hsiao-tsung in 1158 who with his own hand wrote three characters describing Ta-hui's temple. Translated into English they say: "Hermitage of Marvelous Joy." This is my feeling in being here, the creatures passing, the solitude, the reading, the writing, the movement of the sun. In the year of his death Hui-neng (Eno, 638-713) gave a sermon to his disciples ending with this exquisite verse which epitomizes his teaching: "The soil of mind embraces every kind of seed; with the falling of the universal rain, one and all put forth sprouts. When the flower of sudden awakening bursts into bloom, the fruit of enlightenment ripens of itself" (ZD, pp. 165, 169).

Here the fruit of enlightenment is no enlightenment, or enlightenment in the true sense. Nothing is happening. Or, rather, everything is happening quietly of itself. No special sensations, no extraordinary phenomena, only waking and sleeping, reading a lot and eating a little, watching the sun and hearing the birds and the bells and the water pipes thumping. Am I here? Yes, just me. No Thoreau or Merton, no Suzuki or Hui-neng. Just copying words, putting blue on white.

Hung-chih Cheng-chueh (1091-1157), who taught in China during the founding and flowering of Citeaux in France, told his disciples: "If you have even a little Buddhist theory, then all kinds of concepts, illusions, and mixed-up thoughts will be produced in profusion. The koan is manifest right here before you. Penetrate it to the root; penetrate it to the source" (ZD, p. 172). This is the essence of all true growth, spiritual, psychological: emotional self-awareness, making the hidden known, the obscure clear, the easy difficult and the difficult easy through practice. This was the mind of the early Cistercians as well. This is our task, difficult and painful, freeing and joyful. Certainly, I feel, it was Merton's right effort here.

7. Preserving the "Tradition of Dissent"

In reflecting on non-violence in his essay "Non-Violence and the Christian Conscience," Thomas Merton wrote:

> Those who have read a little on the subject may perhaps associate the origins of non violence with Tolstoy, Thoreau, the Quakers. All this is, to a Catholic, religiously odd. As for those who have never heard of Tolstoy, Thoreau and the Quakers, they know non-violence as something invented by Negroes (Gandhi was, of course, a "Negro"). They include it in the category of underworld activities which whites get into when they associate too intimately with Negroes. From there on, the shape the myth takes depends on your own regional outlook. If you are from the North, non-violence rates as something odd and irrational if not actually sinister, like smoking marihuana. If you are from the South, it is classed in the same sociological hell as all the other suspect activities in which Negroes and whites intermingle socially (exception made, of course, for lynching which is perfectly respectable, and in no way tainted with non-violence).
>
> Here we come to the heart of the myth. While non-violence is regarded as somehow sinister, vicious and evil, violence has manifold acceptable forms in which it is not only tolerated but approved by American society. (FV, p. 34)[28]

Thomas Merton found in the person of Martin Luther King, Jr. a non-violent spirit as similar as the one he found in Henry David Thoreau. In *Letter from Birmingham Jail* (16 April 1963), King wrote:

> Human progress never rolls in on wheels of inevitability; it comes through the tireless efforts of men willing to be co-workers with God, and without this hard work, time itself becomes an ally of the forces of stagnation. We must use time creatively, in the knowledge that the time is always ripe to do right.

In this now famous letter, King also lamented that too many church people had become more cautious than courageous and remained silent "behind the anesthetizing security of stained-glass windows,"[29] a terrible image, even today, when contrasted with the shattered stained-glass windows of

---

28. Mohandas K. Gandhi (1869-1948) became a subject of study for me, under Merton's influence, in association with Thoreau. Merton wrote in "Gandhi and the One-Eyed Giant": "It was through his acquaintance with writers like Tolstoy and Thoreau, and then his reading of the New Testament, that Gandhi rediscovered his own tradition and his Hindu dharma (religion, duty)." See *Gandhi on Non-Violence* (New York: New Directions, 1965), p. 4. For Gandhi's doctrine, see: *An Autobiography: The Story of My Experience with Truth* (Boston: Beacon Press, 1957); *Non Violent Resistance (Satyagraha)* (New York: Schachin Books, 1961); and Haridas Muzumdar, *Gandhi Versus the Empire* (New York: Universal Publishing Co., 1932).

For the religious and political thought of Tolstoy (1828-1910), see: Leo Tolstoy, *On Civil Disobedience and Non-Violence* (New York: Bergman Publishers, 1967) and Ernest J. Simmons, *Introduction to Tolstoy's Writings* (Chicago: University of Chicago Press, 1969).

29. *Why We Can't Wait* (New York: New American Library/ Signet Books, 1964), pp. 86, 90. King (1929-1968) was a student of both Gandhi and Thoreau. For the books published in his lifetime, see: *Stride Toward Freedom* (New York: Harper & Row, 1958); *Strength to Love* (Philadelphia: Fortress Press, 1963); *Conscience for Change: Massey Lectures, 7th Series* (Toronto: Canadian Broadcasting Corporation, 1967); and *Where Do We Go from Here: Chaos or Community?* (Boston: Beacon Press, 1968).

the bombed Black Baptist church where four little girls were slain by racists as they worshipped. King did not waver from his non-violent stance. For him, love was the deliberately cultivated motive for all right action, and this he described in his Nobel Foundation Lecture (given 11 December 1964 at Oslo University), as the "supreme unifying principle of life . . . the key that unlocks the door which leads to ultimate reality."[30]

In "Religion and Race in the United States," Merton wrote that in the Negro Christian non-violent movement, under the leadership of Martin Luther King, the *kairos*, the "providential time," met with a courageous and enlightened response. For Merton, this movement was one of the most positive and successful expressions of Christian social action that had been seen anywhere in the twentieth century. Merton concluded: "It is certainly the greatest example of Christian faith in action in the social history of the United States" (*FV*, pp. 130-131).[31]

Merton was certainly accurate in his linking of King with Thoreau. King -- like Merton himself -- felt that he was in direct line as dissenter with Thoreau, and he attempted to bring Thoreau's doctrine into our century. By looking outside of themselves and their environment, both Merton and King were like Thoreau, who wrote in the chapter "Reading" in *Walden*: "I aspire to be acquainted with wiser men than this our Concord soil has produced, whose names are hardly known here" (*W*, pp. 107). In the concluding chapter of his account of his life in the woods, Thoreau gave the underlying intention of all his intellectual endeavors: "Rather than love, than money, than fame, give me truth" (*W*, p. 330).

Thomas Merton, as we know, was extremely proud of his American citizenship when he obtained it. His later struggles with our nation's policies toward armaments and the Vietnamese War were expressions of disillusionment and pained conscience. King rooted his practice of non-violent civil disobedience in the American Constitution and its subsequent Amendments, guaranteeing as they do fundamental civil rights. Both Merton and King found in Thoreau, not an anarchist, but an authentic American citizen. For a fuller understanding of their appreciation of Thoreau, and

---

30. Nobel Foundation Lecture, Oslo University, 11 December 1964. See also: Martin Luther King, "Love, Law and Civil Disobedience" in *The Social Rebel in American Literature*; edited by Robert Woodward and James Clark (New York: Odyssey Press, 1968).

31. On 20 January 1968, Merton wrote to June Yungblut in Atlanta concerning a possible meeting at the Abbey of Gethsemani with King, Vincent Harding and others involved in the civil rights movement [Michael Mott, *The Seven Mountains of Thomas Merton* (Boston: Houghton Mifflin, 1984), p. 511]. For a critical response to media's distortion of King into an innocuous "dreamer," see: Vincent Harding, "Re-Calling the Inconvenient Hero: Reflections on the Last Years of Martin Luther King, Jr.," *Union Seminary Quarterly Review* 40: 4 (1986), pp. 53-68. For a discussion of King in relation to Thoreau, see: William Stuart Nelson, "Thoreau and the Current Non-Violent Struggle for Integration," *Thoreau Society Bulletin*, Bulletin No. 88 (Summer 1964).

our knowledge of him, we can look back beyond him to influences -- direct and indirect.

In "Life Without Principle," published in October 1863 seventeen months after his death, Thoreau wrote:

> To speak impartially, the best men that I know are not serene, a world in themselves. For the most part, they dwell in forms, and flatter and study effect only more finely than the rest. We select granite for the underpinning of our houses and barns; we build fences of stone; but we do not ourselves rest on an underpinning of granitic truth, the lowest primitive rock. Our sills are rotten. What stuff is the man made of who is not coexistent in our thought with the purest and subtilest truth?"
>
> (*RP*, p. 168).[32]

Henry Thoreau did not leave behind a formulated, sytematized philosophy. He drew from many sources -- East and West -- and did not tie himself to any one particular school of thought, including the Christianity (or christianities) of Concord. As a "transcendentalist," as a "Utopian," Thoreau was a theorist, but he realized in his own life the duties incumbent upon him, and clearly fulfilled them as a man of concern for others. Thoreau's greatest witness -- perhaps -- lies in the manner in which he lived out age-old human convictions and human values. F. O. Matthiessen wrote of him: "What others were preaching he proved on his pulses, and when the implications of a doctrine were thus found to be true, he set himself to live them."[33]

In the fourth of seven versions of *Walden* drafted over a period of eight years, Thoreau wrote: "It was on the morning of the 4th of July 1845 that I put a few articles of furniture some of which I had made myself into a hayrigging which I had hired, drove down to the woods, put my things in their places, & commenced housekeeping" (*W*, p. 361). Thoreau intentionally began his stay at Walden Pond on 4 July 1845 -- he was not quite twenty-eight years old (he was born on 12 July) -- as a "personal declaration of independence." His arrest and overnight stay in Concord jail (on 23 or 24 July 1846) for non-payment of the poll tax was once again a conscientious act of principle based on his belief in higher laws concerning the human person.

As a young poet, Thoreau succinctly expressed the doctrine of personalism in the following poem:

---

32. From 1854 to 1860, Thoreau frequently delivered his essay as a lecture under such titles as "Getting a Living," "The Connection between Man's Employment and His Higher Life," and "What Shall It Profit?" (Textual Introduction, pp. 369ff).

33. *American Renaissance: Art and Expression in the Age of Emerson and Whitman* (London: Oxford University Press, 1968), p. 80.

My life more civil is and free
Than any civil polity.
Ye princes keep your realms
And circumscribed power
Not wide as are my dreams
Nor rich as is this hour . . .

What can he give which I have not?
What can ye take which I have got?
Can ye defend the dangerless?
Can ye inherit nakedness?
To all three wants time's ear is deaf.

Penurious states lend no relief
Out of their pelf --
But a free soul -- thank God --
Can help itself . . .
The life that I aspire to live
No man proposeth me --
No trade upon the street
Wears its emblazonry.[34]

Amos Bronson Alcott (1799-1888) once said of Thoreau: "This man is the independent of independents -- is, indeed, the sole signer of the Declaration, and a Revolution in himself -- a more than '76 -- having got beyond the signing to the doing of it fully."[35] As a practical social scientist, Thoreau worked not only with what *might* be the human condition but also with what actually obtained in reality. He recognized that he was not left to do merely what he wanted but rather was enabled by the demands of human society to do what he *ought*. Like Hobbes, Locke and Rousseau, Thoreau wrestled with the fundamentally vexing problems of human existence: freedom to live and liberty in action; the might of power and the right of truth; self-government and social restraints; conscience and civil law. For Thoreau -- as we have seen --the ultimate criterion for action was doing at all times what in his conscience he felt to be right and he was willing to pay for his convictions with his life.

Thoreau's life, future and "sacred honor" were not risked for light or transient causes. Like Thomas Jefferson and Benjamin Franklin before him, like all human beings, Thoreau was more disposed to suffer, while evils were sufferable, than to right himself by abolishing the forms of civil and church government to which he was accustomed. Thoreau was a prudent

---

34. Quoted in *Familiar Letters of Henry David Thoreau*; edited by F. B. Sanborn (Boston: Houghton Mifflin, 1894), p. 235. See also Sanborn's *The Life of Henry David Thoreau* (Boston: Houghton Mifflin, 1917).

35. Quoted in *American Renaissance*, p. 79. For the "Orphic Sayings" and other selections from Alcott, see: Perry Miller (ed.), *The American Transcendentalists* (New York: Doubleday & Company, 1957), pp. 85-92. Hereafter referred to in the text as *AT*.

man -- we can be sure -- and when he spoke out against the established order in lecture and essay, he was fighting, not only for his own but for the equality, inalienable rights, life, liberty and happiness of all persons.[36]

In his essay on the moral duty of resisting unjust government, Thoreau wrote:

> Action from principle, -- the perception and the performance of right, --changes things and relations; it is essentially revolutionary, and does not consist wholly with any thing which was. It not only divides states and churches, it divides families; aye, it divides the *individual*, separating the diabolical in him from the divine. (*RP*, p. 72)

In linking himself with the *Declaration of Independence*, Thoreau not only forged a bond with Hobbes, Locke and Rousseau, but significantly also identified himself with a tradition of British dissent inherited from James Burgh, Richard Price, Joseph Priestley and Thomas Paine. An examination of this tradition of dissent can help us better appreciate Thoreau's impact on Merton, for these writers clearly laid the ground for America's unique philosophy of revolution[37].

James Burgh's three-volume *Political Disquisitions* (1774) had an enormous influence on ordinary people besides its effect on other theorists and prominent people in English and American society. His earlier *Dignity of Human Nature* (1754) was still highly enough regarded eighty years later for Thoreau to borrow it from the Harvard Library.[38] Thoreau read Burgh's thesis that "self-evident truth" is not collected or deduced but intuitively perceived. For Burgh, this proposition held for all truth, moral truth being no less certain than mathematical truth.

In *Review of the Principal Question and Difficulties in Morals* (1758), Richard Price posed the problem of moral right and wrong, good and evil, and how they are perceived. With Burgh, Price concluded that there was an objectivity in truth based on inner intuition: the human person can intuitively tell that an action is good or evil in much the same sense that he or she can perceive that an object is a certain color or of sour or sweet taste. Price

---

36. Obviously these are terms from the *Declaration of Independence*. In his essay on civil disobedience Thoreau revealed his universal concern: " . . . when a sixth of the population of a nation which has undertaken to be the refuge of liberty are slaves, and a whole country is unjustly overrun and conquered by a foreign army [a reference to the Mexican War], and subjected to military law, I think that it is not too soon for honest men to rebel and revolutionize. What makes this duty the more urgent is the fact that the country so overrun is not our own, but ours is the invading army" (*Reform Papers*, p. 67).

37. Staughton Lynd, *Intellectual Origins of American Radicalism*, p. 4. Hereafter referred to in the text as *IO*.

38. Thoreau entered Harvard in 1833 at age sixteen. He signed Burgh's book out in 1834.

wrote of moral truth as an inner light and an interior function of the human intellect. Applying his respect for the human person to politics, Price, in *Discourse on the Love of Our Country* (1789), proposed a concept of world citizenship in which love of one's country does not imply superiority of one's own nation.

In 1765, Joseph Priestley published *Remarks on a Code of Education, Proposed by Dr. Brown* in answer to the Anglican minister's pamphlet concerning civil liberties. Brown believed that any natural desire which might be inconsistent with the "general Weal" is to be given up as a voluntary tax, paid in exchange for the "higher, more lasting" benefits of social life. Here he expressed the idea of natural rights as property which can be alienated in exchange for an equivalent return. For him, conscience should be guided by whatever religion the state prescribes. A free state was not a state in which manners and principles are propounded. Priestley went beyond the critiques of both Burgh and Brown, calling for a change in society by more freedom for the individual. Priestley insisted that human beings can and must free themselves from their oppressive circumstances: we cannot be freed by external powers. For him, every person retains and can never be deprived of natural rights, and every true government is founded upon the freedom of human persons from external restraints and all things imposed upon persons without their consent. Thus, in Priestley's words: "Political liberty . . . consists in the power the members of the state reserve to themselves, of arriving at the public offices, or, at least, of having votes in the nomination of those who will them." For him "civil liberty" was that power over their actions which members of a state reserve to themselves which their offices must not infringe (*IO*, pp. 24, 27-28, 48-54).

Thomas Paine (1737-1809) -- coming to America after thirty-seven years of life in England -- quickly became a significant exemplar of progressive, radical thought. In 1776 (about the same time that Price's *Observations on the Nature of Civil Liberty* was published in London), Paine's *Common Sense* appeared in Philadelphia. No appeal for independence had an influence remotely comparable to Paine's tract, and it quickly sold almost 150,000 copies. The immediate counter-attack of numerous Loyalists proved Paine's power. *Common Sense* blames government -- not property -- for world problems.

> A government of our own is our natural right; and when a man seriously reflects on the precariousness of human affairs, he will become convinced, that it is infinitely wiser and safer to form a constitution of our own in a cool, deliberate manner, while we have it in our power, than to trust such an interesting event to time and chance. . . . O ye that love mankind!

Ye that dare oppose not only the tyranny but the tyrant, stand forth! Every
spot of the old world is overrun with oppression. Freedom hath been
hunted round the globe. Asia and Africa have long expelled her. Europe
regards her like a stranger and England hath given her warning to depart.
O receive the fugitive, and prepare in time an asylum for mankind.

Paine spoke of a "sense" in each human person which lies dormant and,
unless excited to action, will descend with that person to the grave. He
contended that government ought to bring forward this sense in regular
operation to the capacity with which it appears in revolution. In his work
Agrarian Justice, Paine claimed that poverty and property did not exist in
the natural state in which God created man, signifying the end of the theory
of "possessive individualism." Paine regarded government as the basis of
society, but a revolution in the economic system is the necessary com-
panion of revolution in the governmental system. Writing to Thomas Jefferson in 1788, Paine listed as "natural rights" only those most closely akin to
conscience which the individual could exercise unaided: thinking, speaking, forming and giving opinions.

Paine's egalitarian thought found its fullest expression in *Rights of
Man* (1791/ 1792), his response to Edmund Burke's *Reflections on the
Revolution in France*. From 1750 through the French Revolution dissenters
on both sides of the Atlantic poured forth pamphlets and books expound-
ing a common doctrine of natural law, made by God, evident to each
human person. American revolutionaries needed a moral philosophy to
justify such seditious actions as the Boston Tea Party and turned to the
European radical philosophers for help in the intellectual articulation of
their principles and convictions. Not until the argument shifted substantially away from English rights and over to natural justice in the Colonies did
Price and Priestley influence American minds. Thomas Paine brought to the
Colonies the most forceful expression of radical political thought and
carried back to France the new philosophy of revolution forged in the
white heat of the American Revolution. Rooted as it is in European theories
of dissent, the "American radical tradition" bears its own unique character
based on efforts to make a life for all better than the existing one through
high ideals put into daily practice.[39] Let us now look at how this American

---

39.   Quoted in *Great Issues in American History: A Documentary Record*; edited by Richard Hofstadter
(New York: Vintage Books, 1958), pp. 53, 61. See also *Intellectual Origins*, pp. 25, 54, 76. For a good source on
Thomas Paine, see: *Rights of Man*; edited with an introd. by Henry Collins (New York: Penguin Books, 1969).
An intriguing connection is formed when we think of Paine's appearance in the radical art of Bob Dylan
(1941-   ) who so much influenced Merton in the 1960s. I have written about Dylan and the "Tom Paine
Award," received shortly after the death of John F. Kennedy in 1963, in "Ace of Songs -- Ace of Freedoms:
Thomas Merton and Bob Dylan," Part 1, p. 85.

radical tradition -- later exemplified by Henry Thoreau and Thomas Merton -- was preserved by Quakers and Abolitionists in the nineteenth century.

8. The Nature of "American Radicalism"

History tells us of the great influence of Thomas Jefferson, John Adams and Benjamin Franklin in the formation of an American political philosophy supportive of the revolutionary overthrow of England's control in the destiny of our nation; and in the articulation of an indigenous American "radicalism," the *Declaration of Independence* and the *Constitution* becoming the textual sources and roots of our philosophy of dissent. The 1976 and 1987 second-century anniversaries celebrated by the United States -- no matter what form these festivities took --demonstrated the power of the political theories inherent in these documents to endure.

There emerged, from the ideologies described above, a tradition of responding to social crisis through social change, the resolution of conflict through direct action in the social order based on whatever vision or idea of what constituted a "better way of life" might be held by dissenting citizens. In the nineteenth century, the Abolitionists picked up this tradition from Paine and Jefferson: that is, the contention that those freedoms associated with the mind are absolute and inalienable. Against schools, churches, and the United States government itself, the Abolitionists hurled the theory that free discussion (freedom of speech) was not something obtained from human convention and human concession, but a "birthright . . . as old as our being, and a part of the original man."

Revolutionaries of the Abolitionist Movement, unlike revolutionaries of 1776, confronted, not an arbitrary king and the laws of a foreign Parliament, but the laws of their own republican government. The reality of this conflict was compounded for Americans, paradoxically, because the organized power of the community -- the reigning government -- purported to be the least intrusive of any on earth: it was non-aristocratic and democratic. The presidency of Andrew Jackson, for example, claimed to champion the cause of the "common folk," who -- at least in theory -- were all able to fulfill their socio-political desires and personal talents (*IO*, p. 120; *AT*, p. 288).

The early American Quakers were effective agents in the transfer of radical political thought into direct radical social action in their own times. Just as the Dissenters' insistence on freedom of conscience was the backbone of eighteenth-century radicalism, the Quakers' life style extolled the ideas at the heart of radical abolitionism. In 1790, a group of Quakers submitted two petitions to the First Congress against slavery, arguing that the Constitution required the blessings of liberty to be administered "without distinction of color, to all descriptions of people" and for a restoration of liberty to those who, alone in a free land, "were degraded into perpetual bondage and groaning in servile subjection."

The Quaker concept of the "inner light" grafted neatly onto the Dissenters' belief in freedom of conscience and expounded the Abolitionist idea of individual perfectibility. By the 1830s, what might be called Philo-Quakerism pervaded the North, providing intellectual sustenance for the anti-slavery movement. The idea of inner light was closely connected with the idea of immediate emancipation, for immediate emancipation "seemed mainly to imply a direct, intuitive consciousness of the sinfulness of slavery, and a sincere personal commitment to work for its abolition." Quakerism provided American Abolitionists not only with a program for emancipation but with a systematic discussion of civil disobedience in the works of Jonathan Dymond. Dymond recommended a system of resistance clearly noticeable to the law makers and causing those in authority to become weary of enforcing an abhorrent and disregarded law. His argument for non-violent resistance laid the path for the radical activities of William Lloyd Garrison (1805-1879).

In the Abolitionist newspaper, *The Liberator* (1 January 1831), Garrison presented his case against slavery. His words are worth quoting:

> I am aware, that many object to the severity of my language, but is there not cause for severity? I will be as harsh as truth, and as uncompromising as justice. On this subject, I do not wish to think, or speak, or write, with moderation. No! No! Tell a man whose house is on fire to give a moderate alarm; tell him to moderately rescue his wife from the hands of the ravisher; tell the mother to gradually extricate her babe from the fire into which it has fallen; -- but urge me not to use moderation in a cause like the present. I am in earnest -- I will not equivocate -- I will not excuse -- I will not retreat a single inch -- and I will be heard. The apathy of the people is enough to make every statue leap from its pedestal, and to hasten the resurrection of the dead.

Garrison declared that he would not obey laws requiring him to return fugitive slaves or in any way require his cooperation with an "unjust" system. He proposed that Abolitionists submit to taxation, which is involuntary, but should decline the voluntary acts of voting and holding public office. Garrison believed that the Abolitionist Movement, more than any other movement, entrusted the people with the management of their own

cause and invited Negroes, workingmen, women, and all foreign suppor-
ters to join in a world fellowship. In introducing the eighth volume of *The
Liberator* in December of 1837, he announced his concern for peace with a
"government of brute-force," as well as freeing slaves. In 1838, he joined in
the formation of the New England Non-Resistance Society, which pledged
itself to non-participation in all wars, to voluntary self-exclusion from all
political offices which might oblige the office holder to use violence, and to
abstention from voting to prevent misuse of power by elected officials (*IO*,
pp. 103, 108-109, 139).[40] Garrison's strategy was expounded by Wendell
Phillips (1811-1884) who spoke at the Concord Lyceum six times during
Thoreau's years of active involvement as member and curator. In "Wendell
Phillips Before Concord Lyceum" (dated 5 March 1845), Thoreau wrote of
Phillips as a "clean," "erect," and "consistent" man not responsible for
slavery, "the hypocrisy and superstition of the church, nor the timidity and
selfishness of the state; nor for the indifference and willing ignorance of
any" (*RP*, pp. 59-60; 303-307).

Despite its localized New England context and its relative lack of
philosophical sophistication, Thoreau's doctrine of civil dissent is histori-
cally linked with the larger protest against the established order of the age
in which he lived. Certainly, there are like elements of rhetoric, style and
content in Thoreau's work.[41] On 26 January 1848, at the Concord Lyceum,
Thoreau delivered his essay on civil disobedience, under the title "Resistance to Civil Government." The impact of Garrison is evident in Thoreau's
words.

> Must the citizen ever for a moment, or in the least degree, resign his
> conscience to the legislator? Why has every man a conscience, then? . . . .
> How does it become a man to behave toward this American government
> today? I answer, that he cannot without disgrace be associated with it. I
> cannot for an instant recognize that political organization as my govern-
> ment which is the slave's government also . . . . Unjust laws exist: shall we
> be content to obey them or shall we endeavor to amend them, and obey
> them until we have succeeded, or shall we trangress them at once? . . . if
> the injustice is part of the necessary friction of the machine of govern-
> ment, let it go, let it go; perchance it will wear smooth -- certainly the
> machine will wear out. If the injustice has a spring, or a pulley, or a rope, or

---

40. For Garrison's comments in *The Liberator*, see *Great Issues in American History*, p. 322. For a
comprehensive treatment of these issues with appropriate texts from the seventeenth century to the 1960s,
see: *Nonviolence in America: A Documentary History* (Indianapolis: Bobbs-Merrill Company, 1966).

41. For the fullest account of Thoreau's life and work, see: Walter Harding, *The Days of Henry Thoreau*;
rev. ed. (Princeton: Princeton University Press, 1982). See also: *Henry David Thoreau: Studies and Commen-
taries*; edited by Walter Harding, George Brenner and Paul A. Doyle (Rutherford, New Jersey: Fairleigh
Dickinson University Press, 1972) and Walter Harding & Michael Meyer, *The New Thoreau Reader* (New
York: New York University Press, 1980).

> a crank, exclusively for itself, then perhaps you may consider whether the remedy will not be worse than the evil; but if it is of such a nature that it requires you to be the agent of injustice to another, then I say, break the law. Let your life be a counter friction to stop the machine.

But, we know very well, the revolution Thoreau pleaded for was non-violent and spiritual, fought primarily in the heart of each person. Speaking of the fundamental option between complicity with an unjust government and revolution, Thoreau added these words in the course of his lecture:

> If the alternative is to keep all just men in prison, or give up war and slavery, the State will not hesitate which way to choose. If a thousand men were not to pay their tax-bills this year, that would not be a violent and bloody measure, as it would be to pay them, and enable the State to commit violence and shed innocent blood ... If the tax-gatherer, or any other public officer, asks me, as one has done, "But what shall I do?" my answer is, "If you really wish to do anything, resign your office." When the subject has refused allegiance, then the revolution is accomplished.
>
> (*RP*, pp. 65, 67, 72, 73, 76, 77)

On 16 June 1854, Thoreau wrote: "The remembrance of the baseness of politicians spoils my walks. My thoughts are murder to the State; I endeavor in vain to observe nature; my thoughts involuntarily go plotting against the State. I trust that all men will conspire."[42] After meeting insurrectionist John Brown during his visit to Concord in 1857, Thoreau championed Brown's cause and became the first man in the North to plea for Brown's stance as a worthy example of a noble man "dying for a principle."[43] But Thoreau's real appraisal of human life and his balanced perspective was summed up by himself in the opening paragraphs of his essay on civil disobedience, where he wrote: "To speak practically and as a citizen, unlike those who call themselves no-government men, I ask for, not at once no government, but at once a better government" (*RP*, p. 64).[44] We can be sure that Thomas Merton would concur with this opinion.

---

42. *Journal* (Dover Edition), Vol. 6, p. 358 (Vol. 1, p. 756).

43. Thoreau expressed himself as an "abolitionist" in "Slavery in Massachusetts" (4 July 1854); "A Plea for Captain John Brown (lecture; first printed version 1860); "Martyrdom of John Brown" (2 December 1859); and "The Last Days of John Brown" (4 July 1860); see: *Reform Papers*, pp. 91ff.; 111ff.; 139ff.; 145ff; (Textual Introductions), pp. 331ff.; 341ff.; 355ff.; 363ff.

44. Thoreau speaks of Benjamin Franklin in this essay. For a discussion of the motto -- "That government is best which governs least" -- with regard to Thoreau and Thomas Jefferson see: (Textual Notes), p. 322. Thoreau refuted what he considered the principle of moral expediency in William Paley's "Duty of Submission to Civil Government Explained" -- that is, taking the easier way out of a civil difficulty or opting for the safer path of conduct -- but by no means was he an anarchist who favored violence as an end in itself. (See the text of his essay, pp. 67-68 and the critical notes, pp. 323-324.)

9. *"Disarming the Heart"*

Half-way up the dirt road ascent there is a view of the Abbey of Gethsemani, left, and Merton's cinder-block hermitage, right, in perfect linear balance, in tension, a visual line from one end of the horizon to the other, two scales hinged at an invisible center, both kept level by the other. How much they need each other, the *cenobium* and the hermitage, the community and the solitary monk. Gethsemani needed Thomas Merton. Merton needed Gethsemani. We need our particular communities and our families, and we need to go apart to rest and pray, at least for a little while now and then.

In September 1850, Thoreau made an excursion to Quebec with his friend William Ellery Channing. In the account of the journey which he called *A Yankee in Canada*, Thoreau wrote of the *coureurs de risques*, "the runners of risks" and the *coureurs de bois*, "runners of the woods" -- Canadians possessed a roving spirit of adventure which carried them farther, in exposure to hardship and danger, than ever the New England colonist went, leading them not to clear and colonize the wilderness, but to "range over it" (*de courir les bois*). The energies of the youth were spent this way, to the detriment of a militia to fight Indians and the English. Thoreau contrasts this with the *censitaires* who built on narrow stretches of land, all adjacent, along the rivers. The government had to compel emigration in their regard to bring the estates under cultivation, leaving the owners of the *"terre"* now less reluctant "to leave the paternal roof; than formerly, "removing beyond the sight of the parish spire, or the sound of the parish bell."[45] Perhaps the monastic experiment is a balancing in the tension between the *censitaires* on the nearby settled *"terre,"* and the *coureurs de risques*, within each Order, within each Community, within each monk himself. In his Canadian adventure, as in everything else, Thoreau was alert, attentive, responsive to his environment. He said he found the Falls of St. Anne "by guess and by compass . . . at their discretion." Speaking of his arrival and first impressions of Quebec City, he recalled: " . . . we endeavored to realize that now . . . we were taking a walk in

---

45. The Princeton Edition of Thoreau's travel writings has not yet been published. I am citing from *A Yankee in Canada* (Montreal: Harvest House, 1961), pp. 58-59. Hereafter referred to in the text as *YC*. Three portions of a projected five-part publication of this essay appeared in *Putnam's Magazine*, starting in January 1853 before Thoreau removed the manuscript due to the editor's censoring of certain passages. The essay was first published in full text with miscellaneous papers in 1866 after Thoreau's death under the title *A Yankee in Canada, with Anti-Slavery and Reform Papers (A New Thoreau Handbook)*, pp. 46-48; this source gives the trip length as twelve-and-a-half days. Thoreau appears anti-Catholic in this essay, as well as anti-British, but his railings as always were against dehumanizing institutions not persons; wherever he found sincerity he always gave respect.

Canada . . . which a few days before had seemed almost as far off as England and France." He continued: "Well, I thought to myself, here I am in a foeign country; let me have my eyes about me, and take it all in" (YC, pp. 70, 44-45). By our own intuition, with the advice of a spiritual guide, we attempt to find our way to God. Do not Thoreau's words articulate my own arrival and stay here? I sense the special grace that brought me here and I endeavor to realize the meaning of my walking in Merton's path. "Connections," Merton would call all these.

★　★

I disconnect the big push broom handle and carry it as a walking staff and as a protection against dogs. Birds chatter at each other across the lawn as I stand by the board fence in front of the hermitage. A tree split, by lightning or decay, has been pieced together with iron rods, the work of some gentle healing hands ministering as to human limbs. Climbing the rickety ladder behind the house I see the flat tar roof and shiny metal lightning rods, sharp like punji sticks. The tool shed is about the size of Thoreau's cabin at Walden, but I make no attempt at accurate judgment. It is more the feeling of the place that draws the parallel. Saws and pitch-forks and crucifix all suspended together; Louisville phone directories and twigs to kindle the fire stacked along the floor -- cozy place for snakes and mice. Standing on the wall of stones (built 2' high and winding about 40' behind the hermitage) I hear the woodpecker and railroad whistles, the ubiquitous crow, the whishing car.

★　★

Taking a foot-path once walked with friends twelve years ago, I retrace our steps, find the stone cross, and make my way down to the road, thick with mud and puddles to be jumped. The monastery and out-buildings loom high to my left. I turn right at the logging trail, a swath gashed across the hillside. The wood-cutters are thinning the forest to help the young trees grow, but I am filled only with a sense of desolation and destruction. Felled limbs all around. Deep ruts cut here and there. Half trees hanging from those still standing. Immense trees saw-scarred or fallen. Stacks of logs and trunks of every length, awaiting their burning.

Trellises of pine and sabers of cedar cross above me as I pass, my nostrils tingling with the scent of wood-chips and mucky leaves and fungus all mushed together. The shock of car light cast along the path, its glass and metal casing catching the sun like a diamond brooch against a cape of suede. Vast shadow across the sun! A vulture hawk glides low over my head, slick and glimmering against the sky. Higher up into the hillside the path narrows. Packed thick with crisp leaves, it becomes more solid under foot, finally, steadily, bringing me back, directly behind the hermitage.

In writing *A Yankee in Canada*, Thoreau was as anti-war as in his essay on civil disobedience. The guns of the citadel of Quebec, he concluded, were faithfully kept dusted by officials, in accordance with the motto: "In time of peace prepare for war," and he lamented: " . . . but I saw no preparation for peace: she was plainly an uninvited guest." For him the guns and fortress carried their beholder back to the Middle Ages, to the siege of Jerusalem, to the time of St. Joan of Arc, and to the days of the buccaneers. Comparing it to a Lombard gun seen in the armory, Thoreau judged the whole citadel a fit object for the museums for the curious:

> Such works do not consist with the development of the intellect. Huge stone structures of all kinds, both in their erection and by their influence when erected, rather oppress than liberate the mind. They are tombs for the souls of men, as frequently for their bodies also. The sentinel with his musket beside a man with his umbrella is spectral. (YC, pp. 97, 99-100).

What would Thoreau say of our immense Trappist monasteries, especially those in the Orient and Third World countries, symbols of a culture and ethos so foreign to their own? Our Abbot General Dom Ambrose Southey has raised a similar observation, from the perspective of poverty. Merton the hermit gazed upon his own abbey and wrote:

> Over there is the monastery, bugging with windows, humming with action. The long yellow side of the monastery faces the sun on a sharp rise with fruit trees and beehives. This is without question one of the least interesting buildings on the face of the earth. However, in spite of the most earnest efforts to deprive it of all character and keep it ugly, it is surpassed in this respect by the vast majority of other monasteries. It is so completely plain that it ends, in spite of itself, by being at least simple. A lamentable failure of religious architecture -- to come so close to non-entity and yet not fully succeed! I climb sweating into the novitiate, and put down my water bottle on the center floor. The bell is ringing. I have duties, obligations, since here I am a monk. When I have accomplished these, I return to the woods where I am nobody. (D, pp. 55, 57.

Thoreau visited Canada during a period of relative peace in the United States: the war with Mexico was over and the Civil War had not yet begun. For him, the military in Quebec symbolized the presence of the oppressive government of England from which his own country had long been free. Ironically, he spoke in this instance in favor of the American government over against what he perceived as an aristocratic feudal-like power foreign to the ways of the New World. The America he knew allowed for "manliness," "originality," "independence" and for the most part left him alone (YC, pp. 105-106).

Thoreau continued his walking tour and his critique: "A fortified town is like a man cased in the heavy armor of antiquity, with a horse-load of broad-swords and small arms slung to him, endeavoring to go about his business. Or is this an indispensable machinery for the good government of the country?" History proved to Thoreau the uselessness of such battle preparation, and the folly of the garrison. Wolfe sailed by it with impunity, and took the town of Quebec without experiencing any hindrance in the least from the fortifications. "They were only the bone for which the parties fought," commented Thoreau. The sentinel keeps his watch for another hostile Wolfe; or some persevering Arnold about to issue from the wilderness; some Malay or Japanese, perchance, coming around by the northwest coast, to assault the citadel: "Why I should as soon expect to find the sentinels still relieving one another on the walls of Niniveh, which have so long been buried to the world! What a troublesome thing a wall is! I thought it was to defend me, and not I it. Of course, if they had no wall they would not need to have sentinels" (YC, pp. 100-102). Gandhi reiterated this theme with similar metaphor when he said that he who has no treasures to steal has no need of guards to protect them. Thoreau and Gandhi and Merton sought to remove the metaphysical wall, each in his own way. The inner way, the way of working on oneself. Destructing the inner fortifications. Removing the bricks one by one. Where does that leave us? We all begin and end in the same place. We all share a common vulnerability.

On 19 February 1841, Thoreau wrote: "We seem but to linger in manhood to tell the dreams of our childhood, and they vanish out of memory ere we learn the language" (J, p. 269). The more we study Thoreau, the more we realize his own flexibility, his power to change. Some may choose to judge him unstable and contradictory. Like the rest of men, perhaps he was. But he had a sense of proportion in things natural, human and divine. He was a man of his times and he knew it. The Walden experiment was neither the strict isolation presumed nor the book the simple

product of his two year stay. Thoreau and his writings evolved. Consistently opposed to government interference in individual's rights, he nonetheless supported government policies protecting common lands, mountains and rivers from human despoilment. He turned the tools of his advantage, being himself an advanced pencil maker and self-appointed community surveyor. The Yankee from Concord got to Canada on the Fitchburg railroad and Burlington steamboat. In his last years he ventured as far as Minnesota in search of health and Indian culture, no mean feat in his day, even by rail and water-wheel.

★ ★

Merton himself was a transcendentalist and could identify with Thoreau on principle, his own practice equally divergent from the idealized image of hermits in ancient Egypt or medieval France. Both entered into their chosen reclusions in the same month on days of personal significance, Thoreau writing his own "declaration of independence" with his July 4th actions, Merton professing his spirituality of darkness and light, *todo y nada*, with John of the Cross and Teresa large and small under the patronage of Our Lady of Carmel one hundred and twenty years later. Merton's cabin, in his time, was primitive enough, and the thought of the not-healthy middle-aged monk using logs to warm himself and the woods to relieve nature remind us of his seriousness. Merton, like Thoreau, wanted and welcomed guests, most of them anyway. There were many days in the Abbey and trips to nearby towns. As monk-author his peace of heart was sometimes disturbed by loss of manuscripts in the mail and publication delays.

From this cabin in the Kentucky woods Merton mocked the passengers of an overhead plane downing their "timeless cocktails" and slammed the 3:30 A. M. SAC bomber with unbending invective in a flash of sarcasm: "[loaded with] strong medicine . . . strong enough to burn all these woods and stretch our hours of fun into eternities" (D, pp. 14, 29). But Merton the Gethsemani hermit got to the West Coast and the Orient on jet flights. And Merton the Trappist pacifist came back a corpse transported from Thailand by the armed forces on a military plane used in the Vietnam War. Greatest irony of all -- the man who eschewed machinery and modern devices delivered the last talk of his life before movie cameras and died from the electricity of a floor fan!

★ ★

10.   "The Return"

Henry David Thoreau left us tender, even exquisite lines describing his own sense of the fragility of life and human impermanence. In "*Sic Vita*," a poem of his younger years, he wrote:

> I am a parcel of vain strivings tied
> By a chance bond together
> Dangling this way and that, their links
> Were made so loose and wide,
> Methinks,
> For milder weather.[46]

Like Merton in his own lifetime, Thoreau had the reward of peace to a high degree already in this world. Yet, like Merton, he knew the depths of human longing. In his mid-thirties, Thoreau confided to his journal: "I pine for one to whom I can speak my *first thoughts* . . . . I know of no one to whom I can be transparent instinctively."[47] Five years before his death on 6 May 1862, he wrote these lines in his journal: "That aching of the breast, the grandest pain that man endures, which no ether can assuage . . . If the teeth ache they can be pulled. If the heart aches, what then? Shall we pluck it out?"[48]

★   ★

Night is setting in. Darkness is coming on. I stop. I sit in Merton's chapel. Nothing else is happening. I am not being carried away by any other current. I pray Vespers, using texts as they come to hand. *Psalm* 11 -- images of war and peace, solitude and social involvement with evil, images of destruction, associations with the SAC plane: "He rains upon the wicked fiery coals and brimstone; a burning blast is their allotted cup." But this destiny is our own choice and our own doing if it be done. We take refuge in the Lord. We seek our own peace with ourselves and each other. *Psalm* 13 -- "How long, O Lord? Will you utterly forget me? How long will you hide your face from me? How long shall I harbor sorrow in my soul, grief in my heart day after day?" Tonight, sitting in joyfulness of heart, I reach out in spirit to prisoners in their confinement and the lonely in their unwanted isolation, and wish for them this place, this clear cold night, this stillness.

---

46.   Thoreau quoted this poem in the Friday section of his first book; see *A Week on the Concord and Merrimack Rivers*, p. 383.

47.   Quoted by William Howarth in *The Book of Concord: Thoreau's Life as a Writer* (New York: Penguin Books, 1982), p. 79.

48.   The entry was dated 23 February 1857; *Journal* (Dover Edition), Vol. 9, pp. 177, 278 (Vol. 2, pp. 1121, 1122).

The psalm concludes: " . . . let me sing of the Lord, 'He has been good to me'!" And the desert text of *Hosea*, the promise of restitution to full union in love and mercy. What punishment for our sinfulness: "I will espouse you to me forever; I will espouse you in right and in justice, in love and in mercy; I will espouse you in fidelity, and you shall know the Lord." While the whole of this hermitage and its surroundings were for Merton a hallowed place of prayer, we can imagine him here, in this little chapel, in special union with Our Lord in the Eucharist, in the undisturbed hours of the night, before and after the SAC plane's passing. The loneliness and inner restlessness he later expressed in the Asian journal[49] were elements in his encounters with Christ here in this room. And Merton, to his core, was a priest of the Eucharist. Concluding Number 87 of *Cables to the Ace* he wrote: "I am about to build my nest in the misdirected and unpaid express as I walk away from this poem, hiding the ace of freedoms."[50]

A senior monk who knew Thomas Merton well once told me: "Ah, that was Louie. Always hiding 'the Ace of Freedoms' -- like Christ!" Merton felt he had to pretend not to be religious, sometimes putting on a rough and bravado air, so as not to lose what he really was, killing the "Ace of Freedoms" to help him live secretly in his heart. This is what I feel about Merton from this room, perhaps of all in the hermitage the least changed since he left. The west wall holds the black metal tabernacle painted with pale gold sun-burst face on the door, and red splotches on the side.

On this wall also hangs the ceramic crucifix made by Ernesto Cardenal while he was a member of this community, and five icons. The triptych above the tabernacle was sent to Merton as a gift by scholar Marco Pallis. The Madonna and Child icon, from Mount Athos, was sent by artist and designer Robert Rambusch.[51] Two others, Elias in his fiery chariot and Rublev's Trinity, were made by Brother Columban at Saint Meinrad. I do not know the source of the fifth icon -- Elias in his cave -- the title paper pasted on the back is printed in German.

On the floor there are three rugs from Christ in the Desert Monastery, Abiquiu, New Mexico, one larger in Indian maze-patterned border of black, gray and white, the center tan. The smaller ones are variegated in color and criss-crossed geometric patterns. In the far corner of the room, left, a small table, covered with a blue woven cloth, holds the extinguished

---

49. *The Asian Journal of Thomas Merton*; edited by Naomi Burton Stone, Brother Patrick Hart and James Laughlin (New York: New Directions, 1973), pp. 103, 148, 184.

50. *Cables to the Ace* (New York: New Directions, 1968), p. 60. Hereafter referred to in the text as C.

51. Brother Patrick Hart -- Merton's onetime secretary -- clarified these details for me in a letter dated 5 June 1985.

vigil lamp below the empty tabernacle and an oblong box with objects of great personal value to Merton. It contains eight relics in gold and silver filigree cases and a rough beaded prayer-rope, all carried by him to Asia and returned here after his death. This is verified by a note written by Merton's Abbot and pasted on the back of the box. We can thus learn Merton's favorite saints: Charbelus (hermit), Peter Damascene, E.C.D.; Nicholas of Flora; Therese of the Child Jesus; Bruno (Carthusian); Romuald (Camoldolese); Thomas of Canterbury (bishop, martyr); Bede (Confessor, Doctor, historian). In the corner, right, is a small table with *lectionary* and *sacramentary* of the New Rite, cruets, a bookstand, matches and tapers. The small altar in the center of the small room is of cedar. The bottom part itself a cabinet with chalice, linens and other items for the Holy Sacrifice. Economy of space is observed. On the altar, two brass candlesticks, square, with small flanges. An old desk lamp rests on the altar for use by the celebrant. A black cover protects the altar cloth. Overhead, ceiling lights. Two chairs and a prie-dieu complete the room.

★ ★

The wind howls. The roof beams creak. I think of Merton and Thoreau, lights across the ridge of death. I think of Christ: " . . . *lumen ad revelationis gentium.*" I challenge the hermitage darkness with electricity, wrap myself against the cold and step into the black night. I return, all around me now more perceptible, the full moon to my back and wild dogs baying in the distant woods. The hoot owl is silent. Water gleams in mud ruts. I hop here and there to keep my dry feet clean. Like stars, lights from far away farm houses silhouette the sight line. A bell rings, unseen guide.

Turning the curve of the foot path, my shadow stretched before me, I gasp at the immense luminescence of the Abbey. Lit with lanterns, it is a British man-of-war anchored in a foreign harbor. Or perhaps some Whistler or Monet instant reprint. The sky above and ahead of me a tunnel of black with silver shining through and fading, a vast canvas thrashed by El Greco with his enormous brush. Branches like black snakes strike at my imagination. I turn and cross the causeway, find my way along the bulk of the great retaining wall. Pavement is smooth to booted feet, steady, sure. Landmarks from Merton's "Fire Watch, July 4, 1952" (*Sign of Jonas*) -- the sheet-tin steeple, the old novitiate and infirmary -- have vanished. Tonight, Nature has transformed Merton's "lamentable failure of religious architecture," has softened rough edges, mollified the bleakness of line and form. I go inside, along empty corridors. The *preau*, sterile, cold, hard by daylight, tonight like water. Lights from rooms and lamps along its concrete paths flicker and sparkle, like Japanese lanterns or luminarillas around a hacienda somewhere in Santa Fe, in the movement of clouds and shadows. No need to wear my hood up. I allow the breeze to sooth my face, toussle my hair.

The flit of light casts Sesshu patterns on the wood-block floor as I step into the Abbey church. At last I sit in this deep, great whale of Father Louis. I listen to my own necessity. I want to build a tabernacle over these sacred days here. Then, a familiar voice in the night. Gethsemani's Jonas whispers back to me: *"But birds fly uncorrected across burnt lands. The surest home is pointless"* (C, p. 60).

THE MERTON PHENOMENON

IN 1987:

A Bibliographic Survey

by **Robert E. Daggy**

Brother Patrick Hart has written in the foreword to a new book on Merton: "As the twentieth anniversary of Thomas Merton's death is commemorated, we are once again confronted with the mystery of this monk whose life and work continue to have considerable impact on both religious and secular society. How does one account for this phenomenon?"[1] This essay attempts, not so much to explain the phenomenon (or rather that part of it connected with continuing publication of material *by* and *about* Merton), as to report on it, focusing on materials published from late 1986 through 1987. It was a middling year in Merton publication, not exactly quiet, but not so overwhelming as some years have been. Several important items appeared, much of the work dealing with familiar Merton studies "themes": silence, solitude, self, and what I like to

---

1. Anne E. Carr, *A Search for Wisdom and Spirit: Thomas Merton's Theology of Self*; foreword by Brother Patrick Hart (Notre Dame, Indiana: Notre Dame University Press, 1988), p. vii.

call the "phenomenon" writings, those which seek to introduce Merton to a new audience (frequently one previously unfamiliar with him) or to provide a short, basic overview of the Merton career.[2] One of the better of these phenomenon articles to appear in 1987 is Bonnie Bowman Thurston's "Thomas Merton: Symbol of a Century," *Vision Quest* 1:4 (Winter 1987), pp. 1-2. Significantly, perhaps, this article was written for a Disciples of Christ publication and in short and snappy fashion, Thurston gives an overview of Merton which shows, in part, why he has been important to the twentieth century. She says:

> His life demonstrates that new insights do not necessarily need to conform to old ones. Merton's life shows that ideas about any subject can be outgrown or worn out. When a theory is no longer serviceable, when it causes discomfort or no longer fits, it can be discarded from the intellectual and theological wardrobe. Merton suggests that to cling to an outgrown idea is to refuse to mature, to choose emotional and intellectual discomfort, to distort the nature of reality.

In "Thomas Merton's 'Bluejeans' Spirituality," *Holy Cross* 8:3 (Autumn 1986), Fr. Bernard Van Waes, O.H.C. introduces Merton to those who receive the newsletter from the Anglican (Episcopal) monastery at West Park, New York. He says:

> Like many prophetic figures, it is possible that his greatest influence is yet to be evaluated. I would like to remember him as a man who was profoundly rooted in the great tradition of Christian prayer and spirituality common to East and West alike, and whose clarity and insight energized the contemporary search for meaning in ordering and interpreting our world. It is a "bluejeans"/ everyman spirituality not restricted to an elite or religious audience, but for all.

Also in this category (in Roman Catholic publications) were Mary Fidelia Chmiel's three-part "Merton: Symbol of True Conversion" in *Pittsburgh Catholic*; Mary de Lourdes Muench's quite brief "Merton, on Fire" in *Sisters Today* (June/ July 1987); and Portia Webster's "Thomas Merton: A Man for All Generations," *Living Prayer* 20:1 (January/ February 1987). The last is an account of Webster's experiences with Merton during his visit to Our Lady of the Redwoods in California before he left for Asia. She says, in reference to Merton's conferences: "[He] radiated a deep and profound respect for the dignity of each person present . . . for the unique quality that

---

2. These essays and articles usually have titles or sub-titles which point to the "phenomenon" aspect: "Conscience of an Era;" "He Summed Up an Era;" "Moving toward Sainthood;" "Our Man for All Seasons;" "Phenomenon [!] and Poet;" "Spiritual Guide for the '80s;" "Man for All Times;" "Columbus of the Human Spirit;" "Pathfinder;" "Explorer of Inner Space;" etc.

was the singular essence of any person, thing or idea." Her article provoked the only response in a "Letter to the Editor" of any during this time period. Myriam Dardenne of Redwoods wrote (printed in the July/ August 1987 issue of *Living Prayer*) that she felt some of the events were presented out of context and that she wished to "dissociate [herself] from the view of Redwoods and Mother Myriam" in the article.

These "phenomenon writings" show that Merton's impact continues as does the simple fact that most of his major books remain in print, in paperback editions for the most part it is true, but in print.[3] Some have appeared in *facsimile reprints*. In late 1986, Unicorn Press published, at $6.00, a reprint edition of *Cables to the Ace*, thus bringing that volume of poetry back into print in individual edition. New Directions issued a facsimile reprint of the 1949 edition of *Seeds of Contemplation* at $18.95, making available that original work without the additions and emendations contained in *New Seeds of Contemplation*. Both reproduce, fairly faithfully, the look of the original editions. *Seeds of Contemplation*, and its redaction *New Seeds*, continue to provoke interest and Mitch Finley, a writer who seems ubiquitous in this period, discusses *New Seeds* in his book, *Catholic Spiritual Classics: Introductions to Twelve Classics of Christian Spirituality* (Kansas City: Sheed & Ward, 1987), pp. 64-69. Finley notes:

> If there is one word that might be used to describe the spirit of Thomas Merton's *New Seeds of Contemplation*, that word might be "iconoclastic." It's a word that refers to the ancient practice of idol smashing. To be an iconoclast is to shatter false gods. Merton does this with regard to romanticized notions of contemplation, ideas of God, and ideas of spirituality which by-pass relationships with other people.

Equally impressive -- some would say amazing -- is that the majority of the more than forty books written *about* Merton remain in-print and available. Doubleday re-issued a paperback edition [$4.95] of Raymond H. Bailey's *Thomas Merton on Mysticism*, first published in 1975. Bailey did not revise this relatively early study of Merton and a major weakness in re-issue is that it fails to confront or discuss the serial publication of *The Inner*

---

3. Notable exceptions are Merton's two early hagiographies, *Exile Ends in Glory* and *What Are These Wounds?*, which he rated "Bad" and "Awful" respectively in his evaluation of his own books. Individual volumes of poetry, following the publication of *The Collected Poems of Thomas Merton* in 1977, are mostly unavailable. Four of the more than twenty books compiled and edited after his death in 1968 have gone out-of-print at the time of this writing: *A Catch of Anti-Letters/ Thomas Merton and Robert Lax* (1978); *Day of a Stranger* (1981); *The Geography of Holiness: The Photography of Thomas Merton*, edited by Deba Prasad Patnaik (1980); and *Introductions East and West: The Foreign Prefaces of Thomas Merton*, edited by Robert E. Daggy (1981). Limited editions -- such as *Early Poems/ 1940-42* (1971); *Eighteen Poems* (1986 - 250 copies); *Hagia Sophia* (1978 - 50 copies); *Letters from Tom*, edited by W. H. Ferry (1984 - 500 copies); and *Boris Pasternak/ Thomas Merton, Six Letters* (1973 - 150 copies) -- are expensive and largely unavailable.

Experience in *Cistercian Studies* or intervening scholarship on this work. On the other hand, Farrar, Straus & Giroux has published a revised edition of William H. Shannon's *Thomas Merton's Dark Path* (omitting the original subtitle: *The Inner Experience of a Contemplative*) [$8.95] which, of course, discusses the writing and development of *The Inner Experience*. The revision consists of the addition of a sixteen page "Prologue: Six Years Later." *The Inner Experience*, now available in off-print format, was discussed by Mitch Finley in a review-essay for popular consumption, "Contemplation on the Brink," *National Catholic Reporter* 23:26 (24 April 1987), pp. 9-10. Finley concludes: "[*The Inner Experience*] is one of the most important studies of the contemplative spirit to appear in the second half of the 20th century." Finley also did a review-essay of four recent studies, "Four Profiles of the Many-Sided Thomas Merton," in *Our Sunday Visitor* 75:39 (25 January 1987), p. 7. He covers Patrick Hart's "trilogy" of essay collections: *Thomas Merton/ Monk: A Monastic Tribute* [enlarged edition]; *The Message of Thomas Merton*; and *The Legacy of Thomas Merton*. He also discusses Victor A. Kramer's *Thomas Merton*, first published in 1984 as part of Twayne's United States Authors Series. This latter book went quickly out-of-print, but has been revised, altered and re-published by Cistercian Publications under the title, *Thomas Merton: Monk and Artist* [$14.95].

Previously unpublished Merton material appeared during the year. Though published in mid-1986, Merton's *Eighteen Poems*, a compilation of poetry written to and for the student nurse in 1966, aroused perhaps the most interest in 1987 -- an interest picqued even more by the fact that most people were unable to obtain or own the book. 250 copies, at $200 each, were issued by New Directions. This "discreet" publication was printed in a handsome, boxed edition by Yolla Bolly Press of California. Anthony T. Padovano commented in *The Merton Seasonal*:

> The poems are love poems by Merton, two years before his death, to a woman he loved and who, it seems, enriched his life. The story of the relationship has been told before, enigmatically and passionately . . . . How shall we receive these poems and the love they bring us? Our response may be hesitant as we balance the individual's right to one's own life and charism with the claims of communities and commitments to define us in ways we do not always choose. As we answer this question, we reveal our understanding of God and religious life, of human love and of creation itself. Merton invites us to rejoice with him. Are we receptive to the invitation?[4]

---

4. Anthony T. Padovano, "Eighteen Poems: A Commentary," *Merton Seasonal* 11:4 (Autumn 1986), pp. 14-15.

Though interest in the "nurse incident" continues to attract attention (the other two "biggies" always seem to be the circumstances of Merton's death in Bangkok and his relationship with Dom James Fox) and though this incident has been covered sufficiently, it would seem, by Michael Mott, John Howard Griffin, and most recently Basil Pennington, interest has not extended to Merton *and* women in general. Little has been done on this topic though several, most notably Bonnie Bowman Thurston, are doing preliminary work in the area. For this reason, long-time writer on Merton, Thomas P. McDonnell, makes a significant contribution with his "Thomas Merton and the Feminine Principle," *Vortex* 1:2 (Fall 1987), pp. 10, 29-30. Certainly not exhaustive, it does point the way to lines of inquiry which might shed light on the total Merton experience in its discussion of Merton's mother, Rosemary Ruether, the nurse, and some other women.

When *The Asian Journal of Thomas Merton* was edited from his journals and published, the editors decided to begin with his flight east on 15 October 1968. He had, however, left the Abbey of Gethsemani several weeks before and had spent the period from 17 September to 2 October in Alaska. He left, as usual, two different journal accounts of his time in Alaska and I have edited these into a version published in limited edition by Turkey Press of Isla Vista, California. Called *The Alaskan Journal of Thomas Merton*, it also includes an appendix of surviving letters and postcards written by Merton while in Alaska. New Directions will publish a trade edition in 1989 which will be called *Thomas Merton in Alaska* and which will contain the journal, the letters, as well as the conferences which Merton gave in Alaska. The limited edition is reviewed in this volume by Lawrence S. Cunningham. I conclude my "Introduction" with the statement:

> It is clear that Merton liked Alaska, that he thought about the possibilities of living there, or at least thought about it *while* he was there. This part of the trip doubtless helped prepare him, a man unused to travel for more than twenty years, for the more arduous and longer Asian stint. We shall, of course, never know, since he died in Bangkok, whether Merton would ever have become a "monk of Gethsemani" in Alaska. He did say: "If I am to be a hermit in the U. S., Alaska is probably the place for it." Parts of Alaska definitely appealed to him. When Lake Aleknagik "spoke" to him and he answered, "Is this it?" he did not know that it would not be it, that a different destiny lay ahead. But his brief experience in Alaska was a positive and enjoyable one. After it, the monk of Gethsemani was off to California and Asia convinced that Alaska would provide "ideal solitude" in the United States.

Interest in Merton's journals is reflected in at least three publications. The current fascination for journal-keeping may, in fact, provide a partial explanation for the "phenomenon" of continuing interest in Merton since so much of his writing, so much of his exploration of himself, was in journal form. Doubleday has attempted to capitalize on both these interests -- journal-keeping and Merton -- in a boxed, slickly produced publication called *Keeping a Spiritual Journal with Thomas Merton* [$14.95]. The best news about this publication -- it is not really a book as such -- is that it marks a return to Merton editing by his own editor, Naomi Burton Stone. Each page contains at the top a Merton quotation enclosed in a green box -- all too often with a great deal of unnecessary and jarring "white space." Several lines are marked off for each day so a person may keep "journal entries." No specific dates are given so that the publication might be used in any year. Unfortunately, and contrary to Merton's practice, each day is allotted six or seven lines (is Sunday really more a seven-line day than any other?) which can be frustrating if one has more to write and equally frustrating if one has less. Merton's practice was to record what he had to record regardless of length, but the approach here gives *Keeping a Spiritual Journal with Thomas Merton* a canned, commercial and gimmicky feel which gets in the way of Stone's careful and judicious selection of quotations. She cannot be faulted for the book's format perhaps, but she can be commended for citing her sources -- the reader is given the source and page number for each quotation and can thus pursue further reading if prompted by the short quotation. Other "quotation books," such as Thomas P. McDonnell's *Blaze of Recognition* (*Through the Year with Thomas Merton* in paperback), have not pinpointed sources as Stone has and she has thus provided the reader with a much better introduction and guide to pursuing further reading in Merton's books. The publication is reviewed in this volume by Sister Mary Luke Tobin.

Two "essays" dealt with Merton's *Asian Journal*: John Howard Griffin's "Thomas Merton's Last Journal," *Vortex* 1:2 (Fall 1987), pp. 1, 4-5, 29 and Irving Sussman's "The Last Words of Thomas Merton," *Way* 43:3 (May-June 1987), pp. 2-14. The former is a reprinting (without that being made clear) of Griffin's original review of *The Asian Journal* which appeared under the title "The Last Words of Thomas Merton" in *National Catholic Reporter* in 1973. It is an interesting review, as reviews go, but I question its reprinting in this form, even with the title change. I think, as I have for some time, that Griffin would be better served by the publication of a carefully edited volume of his writings on Merton, rather than by these piecemeal publications which add little to the Griffin canon and call on the reader or scholar to go to many different sources in order to view Griffin's writings on Merton as a whole. Sussman's essay is not really about Merton's last words (unless one considers the whole of the bulky *Asian Journal* his "last words"), but is actually a precis of the journal held together by lengthy quotes. As so often occurs when reading those who write about Merton, the reader would do better to go to the Merton source itself. I am reminded of a remark by Francine du Plessix Gray in a review she wrote several years ago: "[The] only valuable passages are the extensive quotes from Merton's own work."[5] Gray herself has included a piece on Merton written several years ago, "Thomas Merton: Man and Monk," in the collection of her "Selected Nonfiction," *Adam & Eve and the City* (New York: Simon & Schuster, 1987). Another of the "phenomenon writings" (originally a review-essay), it was (and is) Gray's attempt to explain Merton's impact in the twentieth century.[6]

In the interview in this volume, Matthew Kelty, O.C.S.O., explains, in part, why Merton taped so many of his lectures to the novices at Gethsemani. Over six hundred of these talks/lectures/conferences are housed at the Thomas Merton Studies Center. A new series of MERTON TAPES has been edited by Clarence Thomson from the Master Tapes at the Center and published by Credence Cassettes, a division of the *National Catholic Reporter*. For those who were unable or who never got around to acquiring any of the tapes published some years ago by Electronic Paperbacks, this new series has nineteen tapes, over 90% of which are previously unpublished. The series includes eight cassettes (16 talks) on PRAYER; one on ART & BEAUTY; three on RAINER MARIA RILKE; two on WILLIAM FAULKNER; two on EARLY CHRISTIAN SPIRITUALITY; and three on MONASTIC SPIRITUALITY. Each cassette tape sells for $7.95.

Several books in translation were reprinted and two new translations of Merton appeared in Poland: *Contemplative Prayer [Modlitwa Kontemplacyjna]*, translated into Polish by Miroslaw Dybowski and published by W Drodze; and a volume of selected poems [*Wybor Wierszy*], edited by Jerzy Illg, published by Znak, with translations by a dozen Polish poets including Nobel Laureate Czeslaw Milosz.

---

5. Francine du Plessix Gray, "The Ordeal of Thomas Merton," *New York Times Book Review* (19 October 1980), p. 30.

6. Originally published in *The New Republic* 180:21 (26 May 1979), pp. 23, 26, 28-30, it was a review-essay on four recently published books: Merton's *Love and Living*; edited by Naomi Burton Stone and Brother Patrick Hart (New York: Farrar, Straus & Giroux, 1979); *A Catch of Anti-Letters/ Thomas Merton and Robert Lax* (Kansas City: Sheed, Andrews & McMeel, 1978); George Woodcock, *Thomas Merton: Monk and Poet* (New York: Farrar, Straus & Giroux, 1978); and Gerald S. Twomey, *Thomas Merton: Prophet in the Belly of a Paradox* (New York: Paulist Press, 1978).

Cistercian Studies continued its serialization of Merton's "St. Aelred of Rievaulx," edited by Brother Patrick Hart, with the third instalment in the first issue of 1987. The second and third numbers contained scholarly articles by William H. Shannon and Walter E. Conn. Shannon's "Thomas Merton and the Quest for Self-Identity" (22:2, pp. 172-189) continues the theme of the search for self which has played through much of his writing on Merton.[7] Conn's "Merton's Religious Development: The Monastic Years" (22:3, pp. 262-289) is a re-working of a chapter from his *Christian Conversion: A Developmental Interpretation of Autonomy and Surrender* (New York/ Mahwah: Paulist Press, 1986). The book is reviewed in this issue by Dewey Weiss Kramer.

The Merton Seasonal of Bellarmine College, heretofore the only publication devoted to Merton and his concerns, appeared quarterly and contained some unpublished Merton material. The Winter issue (12:1) contained a letter from Merton to poet James Edmund Magner who had visited the Abbey of Gethsemani in 1968 during a period of intense personal stress. Merton concluded his letter of counsel and advice with: " . . . unlimited trust is the only sane root of all the rest of it. If one can't trust then it is mad to turn the other cheek . . . etc. And if one can't trust one can only pray to be able to until eventually one becomes able." The Spring issue (12:2) featured Patrick O'Connell's "Sunken Islands: Two and One-Fifth Unpublished Merton Poems," an exciting discussion of his discovery of unpublished Merton material. The "one-fifth" was a section from "Elias: Variations on a Theme" which was inadvertently omitted in final publication, apparently without even Merton himself noticing the omission. The other two -- "The Sting of Conscience (Letter to Graham Greene)" and "Thoughts in an Airliner" -- remained unpublished for different reasons, both involving Merton's editor, Naomi Burton Stone. This article is an example of the "detective work" which can often make scholarship such fun, for the writer and the reader. O'Connell adds a significant portion to the meandering and bewildering maze of Merton's publication history. His contributions to textual analysis, including the one on "Elias" in this volume, point to an area of Merton scholarship relatively untouched by Merton scholars (more on this later from George Kilcourse). He also wrote another article in this period -- " 'Is the World a Problem?': Merton, Rahner and Clark on the Diaspora Church," *American Benedictine Review* 37:4

7. See, for example, "Thomas Merton and the Discovery of the Real Self," *Cistercian Studies* 13 (1978), pp. 298-308; reprinted in *The Message of Thomas Merton*; edited by Brother Patrick Hart (Kalamazoo: Cistercian Publications, 1981), pp. 192-203.

(December 1986, pp. 349-369 -- which discusses Merton in relation to two other twentieth-century figures and follows a line of scholarship which occurs frequently in Merton studies: the comparison (I call them "the comparative articles") of Merton with another significant person or persons.

Such comparisons are useful for understanding Merton's thoughts in relation to another person or for adding perspective, but, more often than not, they have helped us understand relationships within his own life, and, thus, our understanding of the Merton "journey." The Summer issue of *The Merton Seasonal* (12:3) was dedicated to Dom James Fox, O.C.S.O. (1896-1987), Merton's abbot for twenty years, who died Good Friday at the Abbey of Gethsemani. In addition to comments and reflections on Dom James by Brother Patrick Hart and Father Matthew Kelty, there was my "Dom James and 'Good Father Louis': A Reminiscence," a compilation of published and unpublished material by Dom James on Merton and his relationship with him.

Brother John Albert, O.C.S.O., of the Trappist monastery at Conyers, Georgia, contributed two "comparative articles": the first, "Two Studies in Chuang Tzu: Thomas Merton and Oscar Wilde," (12:1, pp. 5-14) pairs Merton with someone who, at first glance, would appear a strange bedfellow, but Brother John demonstrates the relevance of his comparison by showing how these two, who had more in common than one might expect, played, in their different periods, a significant role in explicating Chuang Tzu and Taoism to the West. Merton's role is further demonstrated in *Eastern Spirituality in America: Selected Writings*; edited by Robert S. Ellwood (New York/ Mahwah: Paulist Press, 1987) -- a volume in the "Sources of American Spirituality Series" -- by the inclusion of excerpts from *The Way of Chuang Tzu* in the section on Taoism. Ellwood quotes Michael Mott as saying "the model for Merton of the hidden life was Chuang Tzu" and points to Merton's influence: "There is unfortunately little work available on Taoism or Taoist influence in America. On Merton, on the other hand, a vast literature can be found" (p. 196). Brother John's other contribution to *The Merton Seasonal* -- in the "International Issue" (12:4) which announces the formation of THE INTERNATIONAL THOMAS MERTON SOCIETY (about which, more later) -- is "Thomas Merton and the Dalai Lama: A Special Friendship Remembered" (pp. 19-23), a reflection on that friendship stimulated by Brother John's own personal encounter with His Holiness during his 1987 visit to the United States.

The Kentucky Review, edited by James D. Birchfield, devoted its

Summer issue to "A Thomas Merton Symposium" with a collection of some of the best and most readable essays yet done on Merton. Three of these are "comparative articles," examinations of Merton's relationships with three of his Kentucky friends: artist Victor Hammer, folksinger John Jacob Niles, and photographer Ralph Eugene Meatyard. These, as well as Brother John's article on Merton and the Dalai Lama, demonstrate, to borrow John Howard Griffin's words, that many people "knew the quality of his friendship."[8] We can find in these friendships further elucidation of Merton's search for self. David D. Cooper's "Victor Hammer and Thomas Merton: A Friendship *Ad Maiorem Dei Gloriam*" (pp. 5-28) is a careful and thorough examination of the friendship's development even in difficult moments when they disagreed. Their professional collaboration on limited editions of Merton's work is shown through extensive use of the correspondence between Merton and Hammer (and with Hammer's wife, Carolyn). Finally, Cooper shows us Merton's great sorrow at Hammer's death in 1967. He wrote to Carolyn Hammer: "This [bereavement] is somehow different [than others], because there was no one like Victor. Just no one. And for such a loss there are no compensations" (p. 26). This may well be the best thing that Cooper has written on Merton, an essay worthy of the friendship and one which gives the entire issue value.

Christopher Meatyard, son of Merton's friend Gene Meatyard, contributed an article about his father and Merton, "Merton's 'Zen Camera' and Contemplative Photography" (pp. 122-144). He begins his essay: "If Thomas Merton and the photographer Ralph Eugene Meatyard were alive today and someone came up to them and asked if each would write something about the other, Gene and Tom would look at each other, grin, and roll with laughter. They were happy men" (p. 122). The younger Meatyard captures something of that happiness in an essay with more substance than mere anecdote and tribute. His decision to "explore the commitment of Thomas Merton to photography and visual communication" was itself a happy one, one which shows that commitment in relation to a deep friendship. The inclusion of a dozen Meatyard photographs (some of Merton) and a few Merton visuals is a bonus.

Less satisfying perhaps as an exploration of a friendship is Kerstin P. Warner's "'For Me Nothing Has Ever Been the Same:' Composing the Niles-Merton Songs, 1967-1970" (pp. 29-43). Her brief introduction leaves

---

8. See "Thomas Merton: His Friends Remember Him;" edited with an introduction by Jack Wintz, O.F.M., *St. Anthony Messenger* 86:7 (December 1978), p. 39.

the reader wanting to know more about Merton and Niles and their friendship, but her critical catalogue of the twenty-two songs in the "Niles-Merton Cycle" gives the piece value, and her closing quotation (from Niles) from which she took her title -- "It was the most moving musical and creative experience of my entire life .... For me nothing has ever been the same" -- is itself a moving commentary on this friendship.

A different glimpse of a Merton friendship is given by Victor A. Kramer in "Robert Giroux Speaks about Thomas Merton: An Interview from the Thomas Merton Oral History" (pp. 44-58). Kramer has done good service to Merton studies in his collection and transcription of several interviews with people who knew Merton, providing as he puts it "information about Merton which may prove of benefit for scholars who investigate Merton's life and works in the future" (p. 44).[9] Giroux, Columbia friend, editor and eventual publisher, speaks with candor about his relationship with Merton, making no claim to having known him other than as he did. The interview reflects, as Kramer says, "Giroux's own concerns about the judicious use of language." Documentation of yet another enduring Merton friendship came available in 1987 from another source with the publication of George Hendrick's edition of *The Selected Letters of Mark Van Doren* (Baton Rouge: Louisiana State University Press, 1987) [$30.00]. It includes forty letters from Van Doren to Merton (Merton's letters are not included) between 1942 and 1968.[10] Victor Kramer reviews these letters in this volume.

Another interview with Robert Giroux appeared earlier in the year in Columbia University's *Newman Journal*. This special issue was introduced with: "To some, it may seem odd that the terribly modern students at Columbia College, in the thralls of one of the most secular cities in the world, should take interest in a Trappist monk. Yet, this spring we do so because Thomas Merton (CC '38) was more than just a monk, poet, artist and author; he was one of the leading spiritual voices of our age." Drawings, cartoons, photographs and poems drawn from the Sister Therese Lentfoehr Collection of Mertoniana at Columbia are scattered throughout the issue. There is a section, called "Prayer" here, which contains excerpts

---

9. See Victor A. Kramer, *A Thomas Merton Oral History: Transcriptions of Taped Interviews* (Decatur, Georgia: Deweylands Press, 1985) and "A Conversation with Walker Percy about Thomas Merton" in *Conversations with Walker Percy*; edited by Lewis A. Larson and Victor A. Kramer (Jackson: University Press of Mississippi, 1985), pp. 309-320.

10. Merton's letters to Van Doren will lead off the second volume of the Merton correspondence, *The Road to Joy: The Letters of Thomas Merton to New and Old Friends*; selected and edited by Robert E. Daggy. Farrar, Straus & Giroux has scheduled a September 1988 publication date.

from a taped journal sent to Sr. Therese in 1966, but, while it has some interesting observations on prayer, the lack of introduction, commentary or editorial apparatus leaves the piece without context. Articles by Columbia students Luciano Siracusano and Joseph Seyler, in addition to a poem by Merton's friend Robert Lax, are included with the Giroux interview. The interview, in this case, also reflects Giroux's concern for "judicious use of language," but contains more about their experience at Columbia as well as their later "professional" relationship. Another tribute to Merton from Columbia had come in December with Paul Wilkes' "The Transformation of Thomas Merton," *Columbia* 12:3 (December 1986), pp. 32-36. Based primarily on Merton's own account in *The Seven Storey Mountain*, the "teaser" for this article reads: "College has changed the course of many lives, but few as radically as that of Thomas Merton" (p. 33). Wilkes, concludes, fittingly, that "the years at Columbia proved to be among the most crucial in Merton's life" (p. 36).

Wilkes, despite the fact that he tells us little that Merton has not told us himself about those crucial college years, explores territory in Merton's "geography" which has been traversed much less than the later monastic years.[11] Merton lived nearly half his life before he entered the Abbey of Gethsemani, a half crucial indeed in the final story of his search for self, but it is a much less documented period even by Merton himself. Sources for studying this period (or at least the period up to 1931) have gradually come available with the discovery that several hundreds of his father's letters and a few of his mother's have survived in collections at Smith College, the University of Texas at Austin, Yale University, and the private archives of Richard Bassett. Using these sources -- and later materials from the Merton corpus, such as *Eighteen Poems* -- I have attempted to reconstruct the years from 1921 to 1926 in "Birthday Theology: A Reflection on Thomas Merton and the Bermuda Menage," a fifth essay in *The Kentucky Review* "Merton

---

11. Merton gives the fullest account of his childhood and young adult years in *The Seven Storey Mountain* (New York: Harcourt Brace, 1948), but important allusions appear in other writings such as *Conjectures of a Guilty Bystander (1966)*, *Cables to the Ace* (1967), *The Geography of Lograire* (1969), as well as in *Eighteen Poems*. Monica Furlong gets Merton to conversion and into the monastery in the first one-third of *Merton: A Biography* (San Francisco: Harper & Row, 1980). Michael Mott appears, in *The Seven Mountains of Thomas Merton* (Boston: Houghton Mifflin, 1984), to get Merton to conversion in one-sixth of his biography and to Gethsemani in the first one-third, but his use of flash-backs and flash-forwards, beyond confusing the chronology somewhat, makes it difficult to ascertain just how much of the book is devoted to Merton's pre-monastic years. James Forest spends roughly one-half of *Thomas Merton: A Pictorial Biography* (New York: Paulist Press, 1980) getting Merton to Gethsemani, a fact which reflects the half-and-half division of Merton's life. Two books for young people are glosses on *The Seven Storey Mountain* and add little to Merton's account of his early life: David R. Collins, *Thomas Merton: Monk with a Mission* (Cincinnati: St. Anthony Messenger Press, 1981) and Cornelia and Irving Sussman, *Thomas Merton: The Daring Young Man on the Flying Belltower* (New York: Macmillan, 1976).

Symposium" (pp. 62-89). Passages from the first draft of *The Seven Storey Mountain*, deleted from the final published version, which shed light on this five-year period are included.

The final three essays in *The Kentucky Review* explore areas other than Merton's freindships and childhood. In "Thomas Merton as Theologian: An Appreciation" (pp. 90-97), Lawrence S. Cunningham presents a pellucid and persuasive discussion that, to me, dispenses once and for all with the notion that Merton was *not* a theologian. Though he admits that Merton was "not a theologian in any obvious sense of the term," he quotes Evagrius who once wrote "if you are a theologian you pray in truth; if you pray in truth, you are a theologian." Taken in that sense, Cunningham states: "We cannot only justify our essay's title but add, further, that in that sense Thomas Merton was probably the greatest theologian that this country produced in the twentieth century" (p. 91). In assessing Merton as a continuing phenomenon, Cunningham concludes: ". . . The socially relevant clerics of the 1960s are now, at best, footnotes to church history while the irrelevant monk is still an inspiration and a model for those who thirst for that deepened experience of being human" (p. 96).

George A. Kilcourse ventures into relatively uncharted territory which he calls "a *terra incognita*" in " 'The Paradise Ear': Thomas Merton, Poet" (pp. 98-121). The territory is that of Merton's "diverse and lengthy" poetry canon and, while Kilcourse readily and rightly admits that he cannot exhaust the topic in an essay of this length, he does manage to provide one of the best *shorter* overviews of Merton as a poet. In his last paragraph, he says:

> A brief appreciation of Thomas Merton, poet, cannot presume to explore all the dimensions of this multifaceted, talented person; but it can invite both Merton scholars and readers to include more thoughtfully this dimension of the integral Merton in their study. I dare to envision Merton studies venturing beyond the plateau of these nearly twenty years of significant and valuable theological and spiritual investigation. A truly interdisciplinary scrutiny of his mature writings awaits. (p. 119)

The last essay in the book, but by no means the least important as a reference tool for Merton scholars, is William J. Marshall's "The Thomas Merton Collection at the University of Kentucky" (pp. 145-153). He describes in as great detail as possible this small, choice collection which includes, in addition to the Hammer correspondence, Merton's exchanges with Erich Fromm, Daisetz Teitaro Suzuki, and Boris Pasternak. His essay, a valuable one, stands as nearly the only published attempt to survey a major collection of Merton materials.[12]

The "international" aspect of the Merton phenomenon was given recognition in May when a group of representative Merton scholars meeting at the Thomas Merton Studies Center in Louisville, Kentucky, announced the formation of THE INTERNATIONAL THOMAS MERTON SOCIETY (ITMS) to promote understanding and appreciation and to encourage research and study in relation to his work. The first President, William H. Shannon, had been instrumental in organizing "A Thomas Merton Conference" at the University of London which occurred earlier in May. At that conference Canon A. M. Allchin spoke on "Merton the Monk;" Kenneth Leech on "Thomas Merton, Social Activist;" and Shannon on "Merton the Person." Other officers of the ITMS are Robert E. Daggy, Vice-President; Christine M. Bochen, Corresponding Secretary; and Bonnie Bowman Thurston, Recording Secretary-Treasurer. Certainly the Society's formation reflects international interest but so also does the number of people writing and speaking about Merton in various parts of the world. Constant Broos of Rijmenam, Belgium, coordinated the third "Merton-Weekend" held in Belgium. A unique feature of these programs is that they are held in a different Abbey each year. Speakers have included Edward Buysse, Charles Dumont, O.C.S.O., James Forest, and Henri J. M. Nouwen.

In scholarly areas, Antonio Spolverato completed a doctoral dissertation, titled *Thomas Merton: Dalla Filosofia alla Contemplazione*, at the University of Padua. Vietnamese-born Joseph Dat-Tien-Vu, O.P., did a lengthy (250 pages) master's thesis at the Dominican School of Philosophy and Theology in Berkeley, California, which examined the "self" theme and called *The Recovery of Paradise: A Search for the Self according to Thomas Merton*. Thomas A. Del Prete, on the American scene, finished his doctoral dissertation at Harvard University, titled *"The Formation of the Whole Person": An Interpretative Study of Thomas Merton's Ideas on Education*. This area of the Merton experience has been almost unexplored by scholars, but Del Prete reminds us that Merton spent a considerable portion of his life and energies, both before and after his entrance into Gethsemani, engaged in teaching and that his writings of the "formation of the whole person" and "self-discovery" confront basic concepts in

---

12. The only other published account is M. Basil Pennington's "The Merton Collection at Boston College," *Merton Seasonal* 11:1 (Winter 1986), pp. 8-10. The published bibliographies do not locate materials though it may be assumed that unpublished materials listed in Breit/ Daggy, *Thomas Merton: A Comprehensive Bibliography* (New York: Garland, 1986) are part of the collection at Bellarmine College.

education. He concludes his abstract by saying:

Viewed from Merton's contemplative perspective, the meaning of education assumes an existential dimension that encompasses at once person
and community, knowledge and wisdom. It is this depth and breadth
which recommends Merton's understanding of education for special
consideration in modern educational discussion.

Theses in progress include: Fr. Enda Cunningham from Dublin, Ireland, at
the Collegio Teutonico in Vatican City (*Grace as the Self-Communication
of God the Holy Spirit in the Thought of Thomas Merton*); Vivian Ligo of
Belgium at the Katholieke Universiteit Leuven (*The Language of Paradox in
the* Confessions *of Augustine and* The Seven Storey Mountain *of Thomas
Merton*); and Fr. Thumma Gnana Prakash of Nalgonda, India at the
Gregorian University in Rome (*Beams of Love in Transcendency: The
Experience and Thought of Thomas Merton*). One unfortunate circumstance during the year which the ITMS may eventually help to correct by
diffusing information and materials on Merton was the case of Br. Adrian
Magnait who had planned to do a thesis on Merton's philosophy of silence
at the University of Santo Tomas in Manila, The Philippines. He finally
wrote: "By reasons of time constraints and lack of references, I was obliged
to change my topic to that on which our libraries have plenty of reference
materials."

The Autumn issue of *The Merton Seasonal*, in addition to the essay
on the Dalai Lama and Merton by Br. John Albert, featured three other
"international" pieces. Cyrus Lee contributed "Teaching Thomas Merton
in China" (pp. 9-13), an account of his experiences at the Central China
University of Sciences and Technology in Wuhan. He attempted to introduce his students to Merton through a comparative course in American
Literature. Lee concluded:

As a result of my last trip to China, one of the prestigious universities of
China has agreed to sponsor a Sino-American conference (and dialogue)
on "Chinese Humanism and Western Spirituality." It is up to us in the West
now. Merton died in Thailand without ever visiting China. Shall we carry
his message to the Chinese?

A translation of Kurt Remele's "Conversation with Brother Patrick Hart"
(pp. 16-18), originally published in Germany in *Geist und Leben* 60:2
(March-April 1987), explored in part the reasons for Merton's ongoing
popularity. As Remele puts it: "In the German-speaking countries you can
now see some kind of Merton renaissance."[13] Finally, an edited version of

---

13. Remele points for his evidence to the re-issue of *The Seven Storey Mountain* (*Der Berg der sieben
Stufen*, Koln: Benziger, 1985) and the new translations of *Contemplation in a World of Action* (*Im Einklang*

an interview with Australian actor Richard Moir, aired by the Australian Broadcasting Corporation on 26 May 1987, and titled "Grains of Sand" (a reference to a Bob Dylan song), recounts the influence Merton has had on a well-known television and film personality. When asked how Merton's ideas have affected him, Moir responded: "I read a piece of Merton every day and I write it down and I just attempt to allow it to sink in. It's a sense of awe at everything."

A consistent theme in Merton's writings, naturally, and in work about him has been that of solitude. *Parabola* included an adaptation from *The Wisdom of the Desert*, titled "The Solitary Ones," in their Spring issue and it is clear that what Merton himself had to say about solitude still attracts readers. *Vision Quest*, in addition to the Thurston "phenomenon article," reprinted Dorothy LeBeau's "The Solitary Life of Thomas Merton" (1:4, Winter 1987, pp. 3-6), an essay which appeared originally in *Cistercian Studies* 20:4 (1985), pp. 332-337. Colman McCarthy's "In Search of Solitude," *New Age Journal* 3:3 (May-June 1987): pp. 38-39, 55, 61, 64) basically reported that Trappist monasteries "have become retreats for secular reflection," but discussed Merton and acknowledged the influence of "this life-enhancing priest and writer." Addresses of twelve Trappist monasteries who welcome visitors, which McCarthy calls "The Haunts of Ancient Peace," are given for those who might want to experience moments of quiet and solitude.

Two books *about* Merton, vastly different in scope and content, appeared in this period. The first, Brother Patrick Hart's *Thomas Merton: First and Last Memories*, was published in a limited edition of 250 copies by Necessity Press in Bardstown, Kentucky. Just twenty-two pages long with only ten pages of actual text, it is, with Jim Cantrell's fine drawings, a lovely book, lovely to see and hold, but hardly a full-fledged study of Merton. Rather, and this was its only intention, Brother Patrick Hart, in combining two short essays, has given us a flashing glimpse of two moments with Merton, a reminiscence that stands as it is, simple and telling without explanation or explication.[14] The book is reviewed in this volume by Karl A. Plank.

---

mit sich und der Welt, Zurich: Herder, 1986); *Thomas Merton on Peace (Gewaltlosigkeit: Eine Alternative*, Koln: Benziger, 1986); and Monica Furlong's *Merton: A Biography (Alles, was ein Mensch sucht: Thomas Merton, ein examplarisches Leben*, Freiburg: Herder, 1982). In addition to his interview was Johannes Werner's "Auf der Schwelle zum Schweigen, Annaeherungen an den Dichter Thomas Merton," *Erbe und Auftrag* 63 (October 1987), pp. 362-370.

14. "First Memories" was published as "He Loved the Woods and All Growing Things" in "Thomas Merton: His Friends Remember Him;" edited by Jack Wintz, O.F.M., *St. Anthony Messenger* 86:7

The other book, M. Basil Pennington's *Thomas Merton, Brother Monk: The Quest for True Freedom*, is a much more ambitious and over-reaching production. Pennington originally projected a "monastic biography" and what he presents us gives us, as Walter H. Capps put it, "a rare opportunity to approach Merton from within the monastery." He sums up the content and structure, indeed the purpose, of the book by saying:

> First of all there was Tom's quest for basic human freedom, which he exploited and abused. Then came his quest for the freedom of the faith and the fuller freedom of the monastic life. Within that life he continued to seek, finding a freedom to be open to all reality. He went on to seek the freedom of the eremitical life. In all of this he was seeking the freedom of final integration, which prepared him to enter into the ultimate freedom of the Kingdom of Heaven.

Though not a full-blown biography as such, it is certainly an important "biographical study" of Merton's years in the monastery. It is reviewed in this volume by a third "brother monk," Fr. John Eudes Bamberger, Abbot of Our Lady of the Genesee.

1987, though activity and publication continued apace, was thus not one of the busier years in Merton studies in the sense that production was not so massive as in other years. It was not, perhaps, a year in which a great amount of distinguished material was published, but it was a year which saw *The Alaskan Journal*, the fine essays in *The Kentucky Review* Symposium, Basil Pennington's biographical study, Tom Del Prete's dissertation, and the formation of THE INTERNATIONAL THOMAS MERTON SOCIETY. So it was certainly a year which saw significant additions to the general body and direction of Merton studies, a year in which the Merton phenomenon certainly continued.

(December 1978), p. 36. "Last Memories," originally "Last Mass in the Hermitage," has had a fuller publication history: *Cistercian Studies* 4 (1969), pp. 302-304; *Continuum* 7 (Winter-Spring 1969), pp. 213-215; *Monastic Exchange* (Summer 1969), pp. 85-86; *New Book Review* (October 1969), pp. 3-4; and in translation into German in *Seckauer Hefte* 32:3 (1969), pp. 97-98.

REVIEWS

KEEPING A SPIRITUAL JOURNAL WITH THOMAS MERTON:
A Personal Book of Days
Selected and Edited by Naomi Burton Stone
Photographs by Catherine Hopkins
Garden City, New York: Doubleday and Company, 1987
Unpaged -- $14.95

Reviewed by **Mary Luke Tobin**, S.L.

One of the entries in this newest offering from the writings of
Thomas Merton is a selection Merton himself cherished from an early
Christian writer. I quote it here to set a mood for savoring many delightful
gems, mostly from the pen of Merton himself. " 'Not to run from one
thought to the next,' says Theophane the Recluse, 'but to give each one
time to settle in the heart.' " Allowing the thoughts in this journal to settle in
the heart will be the pleasant task of the reflective reader.

The book's arrangement itself is pleasing. Each page begins with a
carefully chosen quote from among the wide variety of Merton's works
tapped for a selection. Also, each page has space for writing one's personal
reflections beneath the quote. One can use the book year after year since
the entries are not dated as in a calendar, but are divided according to days
of the week. "Week One, Sunday," for example, heads the first page. All
the sources are listed, and easily located in the front of the book.

The task of selecting more than a hundred choice passages from such
a prolific writer as Thomas Merton is understandably difficult. Merton's
range of interests was incredibly diverse. My own preferences would lean
toward setting six or seven themes and grouping quotations around them.
But that arrangement would perhaps lose something of the rich variety
which the book manifests.

It is gratifying to note that many selections are taken from Merton's
letters, as published in *The Hidden Ground of Love* (the first volume of his

selected letters). These quotes may be unfamiliar to many readers, and hence may entice a reader to a fuller acquaintance with the letters. Selections appear from a wide variety of Merton's works, including early and late publications. One beautiful quote, generously shared by the editor of the volume, Naomi Burton Stone, follows: "Don't worry about what kind of Catholic you will be . . . . What God wants is your heart."

I am happy to see that several selections appear from a little known work of Merton's, *Opening the Bible*. For example, Merton reminds us that "the prophets themselves protested in God's name, against the perversion of the word of God in the interests of sectarianism, nationalism, power, politics." And again: "There is nothing comfortable about the Bible . . . . Have we ceased to question the book and be questioned by it?" And "All through the Bible we find the groundwork of a theology of liberation and resistance, even in the historical situation of the Jews and of the first Christians."

The following are some selections which are appealing to this reviewer. Each reader, of course, will flag his or her special choices.

On Trust in God: Certainly we know all will be well, but the ways in which God makes it well are apt to be difficult for us.

On Environment: The same type of absurd logic that drives us to nuclear adventures is driving us to spray thousands of acres with something that does not effectively eliminate the insect we are getting at, but does eliminate the birds that otherwise would eat the insect we don't like. Very important.

On Inner Change: God takes our whole life, and transforms it from within, and leaves it exteriorly what it is: ordinary.

On Being a Christian: The first obligation of the Christian is to maintain one's freedom from all superstition, all blind taboos, and religious formalities.

On Relationships: You can see the beauty of Christ in each individual person, in that which is most each one's, most human, most personal to him or her, in things which an ascetic might advise you most sternly to get rid of.

On World Change: For the world to be changed, we ourselves must begin to change it. We must step forth and make a new kind of history. The change begins within ourselves.

On War: The great peril of the cold war is the progressive deadening of conscience.

On Prayer: We do not pray in order to receive just any answer;
it must be God's answer.
Never was a deeply honest and simple life of prayer
more necessary. It is about all there is left. But
people don't trust God either.
My prayer is then a kind of praise rising up out of
the center of Nothing and Silence.
The first essential step of a true life of prayer is
freedom.

I expect this book to enjoy wide readership. Journal-keeping is a
popular device today for many serious pilgrims in the search for spiritual
growth. This book provides a means, not only for shaping one's daily
reflection and for readjusting one's resolves from month to month, but also
for meeting the challenge of Merton's profound thinking. The book will be
much quoted.

In Merton's last years he enjoyed recording many of his ruminations
on tape. Sometimes he would read a few lines of his own poetry, sometimes
a revision of them, sometimes a favorite passage from his reading. On one
of these tapes, Merton reflects that it might be better to allow varied rich,
provocative thoughts to stand on their own as a sort of mosaic rather than
weaving them into a contrived whole. A new understanding might then
emerge from the very mosaic itself. In this book indeed one can create
one's own mosaic; the unplanned-for personal insights derived from such a
process await us all.

THE ALASKAN JOURNAL OF THOMAS MERTON

Edited with an Introduction by Robert E. Daggy
Isla Vista, California: Turkey Press, 1987
88 pages -- Limited Edition [140 copies]* -- $175.00

Reviewed by **Lawrence S. Cunningham**

1968 was a year of travel for Thomas Merton. Besides the now famous
Asian journey there were two other major trips: one in the Spring to

---

* New Directions will issue a trade paperback edition of *The Alaskan Journal* in 1989, approximately one
year after the publication of the limited edition.

California and New Mexico and the other, actually a prelude to the Asian trip, to Alaska (and New Mexico and California again). Merton, an indefatigable journal keeper, kept notebooks during all of these excursions. The first California/ New Mexico trip resulted in a journal which Merton himself edited after his return to Gethsemani. It was published (with photographs which Merton took) long after his death: *Woods, Shore, Desert* (Santa Fe: Museum of New Mexico Press, 1982). After his death the "working notebooks" that Merton kept during his Asian journey were carefully edited by Naomi Burton, Patrick Hart and James Laughlin: *The Asian Journal of Thomas Merton* (New York: New Directions, 1973). Now, nearly twenty years after his death, we have the Alaskan journal which consists of writing that Merton did in the period between 17 September, when he flew to Anchorage via Chicago to 3 October, when he arrived at Santa Barbara readying himself for the flight East.

What distinguishes *The Alaskan Journal* from the other two journals which have appeared in print is that this is a faithful transcription and integration of two actual working notebooks without editing of the entries themselves by Merton or Daggy. From a purely technical point of view, then, *The Alaskan Journal* provides us with an intimate glimpse of Merton as he wrote without the intrusion of later reflection or subsequent polishing. Such a glimpse, of course, brings with it a certain fragmentary quality which can be, at worst, obscure, but, at best, aphoristic. One must be prepared for an observation about a Poor Clare monastery in Chicago juxtaposed with a fragmentary sentence about a multiple murder in Cleveland gleaned, one supposes, from a newspaper account, read while en route.

For some kind of context I reread the earlier *Woods, Shore, Desert* and the later *Asian Journal* since they frame this journal. What kind of impression does one gain from a perusal of these journals in general and the Alaskan one in particular? What struck me first and foremost was the alertness of Merton's eye and ear. He notes the tameness of grafitti in the Anchorage Airport's men's room and jots down a snatch of conversation between two stewardesses: "When her eyelashes began to fall out I . . . (inaudible)" "Real ones?" "Yes!" But banal moments like those are mingled with the poet's eye. Thus, for example, a sharp reflection on a volcanic mountain, first seen at a distance ("handsome and noble") and then, with the plane approaching it, a sharper view: "A brute of a dirty busted mountain that has exploded too often. A bear of a mountain. A dog mountain with steam curling up out of the snow crater."

Merton's capacity to *see* is all over these pages and nowhere more acute than when he looked at the world around him. The woods of Alaska were "deep in wet grass, fern, rotten fallen trees, big leaved thorn scrub, yellowing birch, stunted firs, aspen." The directional lights at San Francisco's airport strike him as beautiful -- something akin to a concrete poem: XAMN RNWY BFR XING. As one reads those close observations it becomes very clear why Merton took to photography so creatively. He had a capacity to see what Hopkins called the "dearest freshness" of the world. Merton had that peculiarly poetic (and contemplative) power to look afresh at that which is part of the common view. The hasty jottings of this journal note scattered oil drums, the color, names, and condition of the fishing boats, the snow on the head of a nail, the shape of mountains, and the slant of the rain. To read those terse observations is a necessary prelude to an appreciation of his best photographs which were close-up studies of the shapes of nature or simple things on the porch of his hermitage.

Amid those observations, his own reflections on the suitability of various Alaskan sites for a hermitage, his gratitude for the hospitality of the Alaskan clergy and religious, his letters back to Gethsemani and elsewhere (sixteen are appended to the journal), there was the reading, always the reading: from Hermann Hesse to the Tibetan Book of the Dead, from the Orthodox theologian and philosopher Vladimir Lossky to snatches from the Psalms. To that we must add the conferences to contemplative sisters and his celebrations of the liturgy. In brief: the seventeen days of the Alaskan journey were a replication of life in his Kentucky hermitage. And that life was one of intense activity both literary and religious. One gets the sense that, in the final analysis, the kind of life Merton lived was the same irrespective of place. He was a person who hated to waste time yet, as he once wrote in a poem fragment, learning how to waste time perfectly was a talent no person had mastered completely.

There was, obviously, no anchored solitude in his brief stay in Alaska. The journal is an almost breathless catalog of trips, conferences, visits to possible sites for a hermitage, and letters to the monastery requesting books to be sent to this or that person. In the background of that was the anticipation of the journey to Asia. Yet, and the point deserves emphasis, there was Merton the hermit who affirmed his desire for greater solitude either in Alaska or, perhaps, in Asia. It is also worth noting that he firmly stated his being a "monk of Gethsemani." That was possible because he understood his monastic stability to be there even if, after the Asian journey, he would live elsewhere. Thus, those who insist that by 1968

Merton was ready to leave the monastery are correct only in a very limited sense. As his journals of that year make clear, he may well have left the monastery physically for a different eremitical site but he would still have considered himself (and quite rightly) a monk of Gethsemani. Whether that hermitage would have been in Alaska is open to question. He saw the immense possibilities in that vast land and was convinced that many people lived there out of a thirst for solitude but, as he wrote Abbot Flavian Burns, he could make no decision until he returned from Asia. He had to struggle, especially in those later years of his life, with "leaving behind the renunciations of yesterdays and yet [being] in continuity with all my yesterdays." This short journal shows no resolution of such deeply personal challenges but it does reinforce my own deep conviction that whatever the changes that might have happened to him, Merton was deeply and irrevocably a monk. Indeed, not to understand him as a monk, is not to understand him at all.

Apart from the intrinsic worth of a beautiful book as aesthetic artifact is there merit in this hasty notebook of less than a month's making? The obvious answer is that any source that helps us get a fuller picture of a person so complex and important has immense value. With the California/ New Mexico and Asian journals this notebook gives us an intimate look at Merton in the final year of his fecund life as a monk-writer. There is a deeper reason for a claim to be made for this book. Merton was almost always the autobiographer. His immense claim on the imagination of people rests in his capacity to refract the world through the firm center of his own contemplative experience and his yearning for a deepening of that experience. In a sense, all of the journals now published (and those, like *A Vow of Conversation*, yet to come) are necessary resources to read in tandem with the Michael Mott biography to get closer to the authentic persona of this modern spiritual master.

We learn from Merton not doctrine or systematic teaching but a way of being and seeing. Many are not (or better: I am not) anxious to live in Alaska or to read Hesse or the Tibetan *Book of the Dead*. But I would like to live a life which has, at its center, the presence of God and I would like to learn how to look at the quotidian world around me with freshness and wonder. Thomas Merton's writings, especially those which reflect a certain spontaneity, remind me (and, I suspect, many others) how much I miss about myself, others, and the world around us. That is a precious lesson.

Robert E. Daggy edited this volume and supplied an informative introduction. David D. Cooper, a noted Merton scholar, wrote the preface for this edition which sets just the right tone for reading it. The book, in a limited edition, is published by Harry and Sandra Reese at their Turkey Press in Isla Vista, California. It is a beautiful tribute to Thomas Merton and they are all to be congratulated. New Directions will publish a trade edition which will also include the conferences that Merton gave while he was in Alaska.

M. Basil Pennington, O.C.S.O.
THOMAS MERTON, BROTHER MONK:
The Quest for True Freedom
San Francisco: Harper & Row, 1987
xvii, 205 pages   -- $15.95

Reviewed by **John Eudes Bamberger**, O.C.S.O.

When Michael Mott's biography, *The Seven Mountains of Thomas Merton*, was published in 1984 it was read in the refectory at Genesee Abbey. One of the brothers, who had been a member of the Gethsemani community during Merton's last fifteen years there, remarked to me that he had no idea that all those doings detailed in the biography were occurring. Rather, he knew Fr. Louis Merton as one of the monks, living a quiet and regular life and doing his work peacefully as novice-master, then living as a hermit. The Merton he knew did not seem to be described in this biography: his monastic life somehow seemed to disappear behind all the events and contacts depicted in such wealth of detail in the story of his life.

Though I was aware of many of those details, I too felt that somehow a major aspect of the life that Fr. Louis had led in the monastery over so many years had largely proved elusive. Perhaps anyone who has shared life with another, who made up a part of one's daily life for any protracted period of time, would inevitably feel some such incompleteness in any account, even as expert a one as that provided by Mott. Though Fr. M. Basil Pennington never lived with Fr. Louis in community and had but little personal contact with him, he too felt that the monastic dimension of Merton's life had not as yet been adequately treated in any of the biographies, even that of Mott which, in so many respects is a highly competent and readable work. Rather than attempt the daunting task, however, of presenting the full account of Fr. Louis' monastic life and experience Pennington informs his readers that he will only attempt "to fill in some of the lacunae which will enable us to see Thomas Merton more integrally, more fully in context, more deeply." In particular, he focuses on Merton's quest for true freedom, seeking to present Merton's understanding of it and the particulars of his growth in freedom.

Thus this work does not claim to be a biography of Thomas Merton, but rather a study of his life from the point of view of freedom, with a particular attention to his monastic experience in his own community of Gethsemani. As such, it makes a useful contribution to the growing body of material dealing with Merton's life and work.

One of the very real contributions of this work is the use it makes of certain of Merton's writings that have been little utilized in other studies. Even though much of the corpus of Merton's work has been published since his death in 1968, there still remain vast quantities of unpublished and little utilized material. This includes not only some portions of journals, original manuscripts of various works that have been published in highly edited versions, but also some thousands of letters and many of his personal notes used for classes at Gethsemani. In addition to this written body of Mertoniana there are hundreds of taped conferences that remain unedited. Without laying claim to having mined all this material, Fr. Basil does make good use of a significant portion of it and, as he does so quite effectively, illustrates its importance for presenting the daily life of Fr. Louis in its monastic setting.

Here we touch upon what is perhaps a major contribution of this study, namely, its pointing up the need for access to these unpublished materials and their thorough utilization for properly assessing the monastic experience of Thomas Merton, and, secondly, the continuing lack of adequate knowledge and assessment of the daily context of Merton's life as a monk. The present work certainly advances this knowledge and helps the reader to realize more vividly its place in Merton's personal development and thought at various points. One need not agree fully with every explanation and assessment made by the author to profit from his presentation of material and his stress on the importance of the whole question of freedom in Merton's work and life. I believe, too, that this work succeeds, as it sets out to do, in making the reader more conscious of his or her own freedom, of the call to realize it in life, whether lived in the cloister or in the world.

For one thing, Fr. Basil captures something of the sense of freedom and spontaneity that Fr. Louis so largely embodied in his daily life. Even when he was living conscientiously according to the old usages before they had been adapted to the post-Vatican II Church and the modern world, he managed to bring a light touch to life and to evince a spirit of liberty that served to build morale. This was the result not only of his temperament and lively sense of humor, but was also a witness to a strongly held view about monastic life -- it is meant to reveal something of the joy and activity of the Risen Savior and of His Spirit. There was, we felt in the community at that time, an earnestness of purpose even in Merton's lightness of spirit. Various pages of this book rightly set forth this characteristic quite clearly. For instance, Fr. Basil refrains from predicting what Fr. Louis would have done or might have become had he not met the sudden death that overtook him in Bangkok, pointing out that surprise and unpredictability had their role in a special way in his life and that his character displayed surprising attitudes that caused surprise to others.

Fr. Basil seeks to show that there was a kind of unity in Merton's life and experience which is not sufficiently brought out by earlier studies on him. While there are limits to any such demonstration, of course, seeing that even the simplest and dullest of us remains mysterious in so many ways, this study does help one to appreciate better the focus of unity which made Merton's life a whole.

In one or two relationships, however, the attempt to demonstrate this unity does not do full justice to the facts. In the relation of Fr. Louis with his abbot, Dom James Fox, there is acknowledgment in passing of some of the positive elements, but the abbot's relation to his monk is presented largely as a foil to bring out the ways in which Fr. Louis was led to assert and cultivate his freedom. This picture is not altogether false, but it is vastly oversimplified and obviously not sympathetic to the abbot. At this stage of our knowledge about the abbot and community of Gethsemani, anybody who describes in some detail this whole issue of Merton's relation to his superiors, and especially his abbot, would be working with incomplete data. What is needed is a serious study of the community of Gethsemani during these years, as well as a biography of Dom James. Meantime, it might be pointed out that some of the evidence indicates considerable magnanimity on Dom James' part, and Fr. Louis himself came to appreciate that side of his abbot. Not too many relationships would survive the kind of criticism that Merton made to a reporter about his abbot once it got into print; Dom James read it and chose to overlook it and later Merton came to see that he had gone too far. After reading the very blunt critical remarks Merton made in a note to the abbot which Fr. Basil cites, one becomes aware that there were two freedoms involved in their relationships, not one. Only a very free person, such as Dom James Fox, whatever his psychological limits, could have maintained an ongoing and in many ways fruitful relationship with Fr. Louis. So far, too little has been said about the great humility that it required to be Merton's superior for so long.

The other place where the author appears to go too far in presenting Fr. Louis in a favorable light is in justifying his dealings with the student nurse. Michael Mott first presented the data on this relationship and Fr. Basil acknowledges that he bases his interpretation on Mott's account, but takes considerable pains to evaluate the incident in a more positive way. Not everyone who reads both accounts will be persuaded by Fr. Basil's view. It is not an indication, I believe, that one has too rigid a view of what is included under the rubric of "monk" to consider initiating overtures to someone else's fiancee incompatible with that vocation. This does not mean that good cannot come of it in the end, seeing that, due to Merton's great courage and profound faith, he was able to fight his way back to an authentic way of life, as Mott puts it, after a period of compromise. I believe it quite understandable that Fr. Louis got involved in this relationship: I also believe it admirable that he was eventually to work his way back to a new and fuller commitment to his vocation as a monk and that, as a result of what he had experienced, he became a more compassionate and integral human being. But Mott's account, based on the evidence, will suggest to some readers, at least, that there was something inauthentic from the start.

Some of the best pages in this work deal with the place of the Greek Fathers in Fr. Louis' life and, specifically, with their role in stimulating his appreciation of creation as a way to God. "Theoria Physike" led Merton to a deeper involvement with the created world precisely as revealing in contemplation the presence and activity of God in His world. Merton's greater concern for politics and for other aspects of creation is rooted, in part, in his meditation on this teaching of the Greek Fathers.

In summary, Fr. Basil Pennington has made a very real contribution to our understanding of Merton's life and work. He does achieve, I believe, what he set out to do -- to help us hear Merton and his prophetic message. His book also shows us there remains more to do before we shall be adequately informed of Merton's life as a monk and just what it meant in the concreteness of daily life for him and his community as he lived out his adult years at Gethsemani. I think it not the least merit of this book to have made it plain that we do not yet understand very adequately the life of his community during his years at Gethsemani, nor the life of Dom James Fox, his abbot for most of his monastic years. Perhaps there is no such thing as a definitive biography of any person; certainly there are reasons to think there will never be one of Merton. But this study adds to our knowledge and appreciation of him and that makes it worth reading.

Brother Patrick Hart, O.C.S.O.
THOMAS MERTON: FIRST AND LAST MEMORIES
Illustrations by Jim Cantrell
Bardstown, Kentucky: Necessity Press, 1986
Unpaged -- Limited Edition [250 copies] -- $35.00

Reviewed by **Karl A. Plank**

Memory gives rise to presence. A curator of lived moments, memory gathers scattered fragments of experience and bids them abide within the story of their happening. Recollection seeks narrative and therein imparts to remembered bits and pieces a new power and wholeness. Following its own course, time's passing would weaken our tie to the precious instants of former days; freighted encounters, once vital and immediate, grow dull and lose their living relation to each other and to those selves who had been arrested by the wonder of meeting. This threat memory combats, not by restoring a lost time, but by piecing from its scraps a present story within which the past continues to claim us. What time denies, the remembered story enables: an enduring link to our personal history, the presence of time past.

The past does not become present in its entirety. Memory selects. We remember not the sum of our lives, but those portions which identify us: the moments of profundity and simplicity, emptiness and fullness, within which we have glimpsed some aspect of who we are. Whether they recall the novelty of an extraordinary event, or an unsought-for grace in the rhythm of daily life, these memories furnish the fabric of our self-understanding. They claim us with fear and promise; but it is we who claim them in the stories we tell. The choice to narrate is a choice to affirm, to host the presence of memory.

From the blur of stuck-together days, first and last memories protrude as spurs of unusual clarity. Unburdened by worn expectation a first encounter refreshens with the prospect of newness or challenges with the uncertainty of meetings as yet undisclosed. Beginnings interrupt our tedious routine and invite recollection when their time has past, for to remember a beginning is to begin again and to know the presence of promise. So, too, do last encounters loom large in our memory. We approach them with a trusting ease of the familiar, but unknowing all the same. Only another day can attest the finality of a last meeting and on that day we look back with a deeper awareness of preciousness. The last memory yields the presence of love.

Thomas Merton: First and Last Memories testifies to the presence of memory as, within its pages, Brother Patrick Hart tells the story of a novice's early venture with Merton and of their final meeting some seventeen years later. Simple and direct, Brother Patrick's recollections provide an uncluttered glimpse, not of Merton himself as much as of a world he shared at these brief moments in time. A spring day and muddy earth witness Merton and a half dozen choir novices making pilgrimage to the woods to plant loblolly pine seedlings. A cool September morning in 1968 finds Merton sharing the Hermitage dawn with three who have come to bless his journey, only to be blessed in return.

Memoir is not biography. *First and Last Memories* does not intend to satisfy a reader's fascination with the life of Merton, but to affirm a life remembered. As a celebrant of that life, Brother Patrick protects its silences, trusting what comes to expression in his memories to speak sufficiently for itself. This it does with plain eloquence, and more. These glimpses, cherished in their own right, do not point finally to Merton, but to the gracious realities he embodied and made available to others. Here we find, as in a sacrament, the discovery of the holy in ordinary things: the promise of loblolly pines, the precious goodness of eating together, and the nurturing love of friendship caught in the intimacy of snapshots and the exchange of farewells. *First and Last Memories* remembers Thomas Merton but, throughout, it gives presence to the nearness of God in a human life.

Such memories must be preserved with care. Where expressed, they deserve the integrity of craftmanship that protects against their trivialization or easy commerce. The purity of Brother Patrick's prose, the apt illustrations by Jim Cantrell, and the true, hand-crafted production of Bardstown's Necessity Press (operated by Jeannette Cantrell) combine to mark *Thomas Merton: First and Last Memories* as a worthy bearer of presence. In the richness of its simplicity, this volume stands as an icon of the realities narrated on its pages. Wherever grace freights our common world, may we respond with gratitude.

Walter E. Conn
CHRISTIAN CONVERSION:
A Developmental Interpretation of Autonomy and Surrender
New York / Mahwah: Paulist Press, 1986
347 pages -- $12.95

Reviewed by **Dewey Weiss Kramer**

Conversion is a popular topic today and books on the subject easily find a reading public. Walter E. Conn's interest in this subject, however, is more substantial. Though related to the topicality of the subject, it derives from this topic's importance to prominent contemporary theologians who recognize conversion as crucial for a right appreciation of the concrete experiential dimension of a life of faith. Conn, professor of Religious Studies at Villanova University and editor of *Horizons*, Journal of the College Theology Society, agrees with Bernard Lonergan, his former teacher and a major presence in this volume, that "reflection upon conversion can provide an appropriate foundation for a contemporary empirical theology." With this book, Conn wishes to contribute to such a theology, one which shifts the focus away from a preoccupation with individual acts to a more Biblically-oriented concern with the pattern and direction of a person's whole moral life. His method is to clear up the ambiguity which surrounds the term "conversion."

Conn undertakes the task by analyzing the human person's capacity for such conversion. His analysis requires, in turn, that he study the human person her/himself, especially in the value-decision dimension which western culture has traditionally referred to by the metaphor of "conscience." Conscience, as Conn understands it, is the radical drive for self-transcendence, the reality drive for understanding, truth, value, love.

The author develops his interpretation of conscience by drawing on the work of five leading scholars of developmental psychology -- Erik Erikson, Jean Piaget, Lawrence Kohlberg, James Fowler and Robert Kegan. From a critical synthesis of their research and feelings, he comes to a theory of the self as a conscious subject developing cognitively, affectively, and morally toward a goal of self-transcendence. After presenting a pattern of personal development, Conn then focuses on conversion, defined as a structural -- as opposed to one of content -- transformation of conscience, a radical re-orientation of the self's goal from the personal toward the dimensions of truth, value, love.

The moral, cognitive, and affective dimensions of this shift in orientation, Conn discovers, coincide with the major moments or stages or developments of human growth as articulated by developmental psychology. Conversions are thus the conscious counterpart of unconscious stage transitions or crisis resolutions.

The book's detailed incorporation of psychological paradigms and terminology presents difficulties for the person unversed in that discipline, but such paradigms make an integral point. It demonstrates that personal and moral maturity and spiritual development are constitutively interdependent. Indeed, the most advanced stages of the primarily secular psychological paradigms raise questions of at least implicitly religious content. For example, as Kohlberg says, only the person who has fully realized and attempted to lead a life of fully human autonomy can truly experience the utter moral impotence constitutive of human existence; and it is precisely this impotence which forces the personal subject to seek meaning beyond the human.

This material comprises chapters one through four of the work. In chapter five Conn examines the moral dimension of "Christian" conversion, i.e. the specific character which the three conversions or shifts in orientation to truth, to value, to love assume when they take place within the symbolic context of the Christian story; and in chapter six he examines conversion's "religious" dimension. Conn's definitions of these two last-named conversions do not correspond to ordinary usage, and one sees here especially clearly his stated objective of "redoing" conversion. He understands "Christian" (moral) conversion as only the beginning of an ever more profound journey into the mystery of God's love -- the journey of "religious" conversion. Lonergan provides him with his understanding of "religious" conversion as "other-worldly falling in love" or "being grasped by ultimate concern" or "total and permanent self-surrender."

These two final chapters use as a kind of laboratory the example of Thomas Merton, drawing on his writings as documentation. The choice of Merton is fortuitous and not surprising, since Merton himself was keenly conscious of constituting a model for others, a fact expressed clearly in his journals. He wished to share the fruits of his questioning and answering with those he would never know personally. In order to get a hold on himself and his journey, Merton found it imperative to discover the right metaphors. The fact, noted by Conn, that Merton the writer helped Merton the monk toward wholeness (conversion) helps account for the facility with which Merton can serve as an illustration of Conn's theses; and his attention to Merton's symbolic pattern of understanding produces an insightful interpretation of the psychological/spiritual significance of the monk-writer's language. Merton's 1938-41 conversion, described in *The Seven Storey Mountain*, is interpreted here as a moral conversion, whereas the writings and life after 1941 are used to illustrate the distinctively religious dimension of conversion.

Conn's subject matter -- morality, authentic selfhood as realized in the personal/psychological and spiritual dimensions; authentic existence defined in terms of going beyond the limited, egocentric self to a loving embrace of others; the work's extensive use of and reference to other disciplines such as philosophy, literary criticism, theory of creativity; and finally the impetus it can provide to apply the patterns he works out to other artist-Christians (Simone Weil, Reinhold Schneider, Flannery O'Connor, for instance) -- all would justify the volume's being reviewed in an Annual such as this one devoted to interconnections among religion, culture, and social concerns. Its inclusion here is, of course, specifically mandated by Conn's use of Merton as his major demonstration of theory applied to a concrete life.

His presentation of Merton casts more light on the book's painstakingly detailed study of patterns of personal and spiritual growth than do his theoretical formulations on the figure of Merton. This is hardly surprising. Starting with the monk himself, the phenomenon of Thomas Merton has been copiously and frequently analyzed. Conn's emphases inevitably repeat well-known facts and facets -- the journey motif, the tension between monk and artist, the dichotomy of the false and true self, the role of metaphor as way to self-understanding. This is not to deprecate Conn's study of Merton, however. Such insights bear repeating and Conn's probing of his works in chronological order for their developmental clues is helpful. His focus on the false self/ true self theme is especially valuable.

At one point Conn notes in referring to the theories of William James, E. D. Starbuck and V. B. Gillespie that their theories seem almost to have been formulated with Merton in mind. One might make a similar quip about this study, especially in the context of Merton's false and true self problematic. It was in the true self/ false self distinction, incipient in *The Seven Storey Mountain* but first expressed clearly in *Seeds of Contemplation*, that Merton found, in Conn's terminology, the apt metaphor for articulating the transformational pattern of his discovery of God through discovering himself. And this Mertonian metaphor, as will become obvious to the careful reader of Conn's volume, is reflected in the book's own thesis of the self's progress from immaturity, through successive stages, toward authentic selfhood.

This metaphor also constitutes the major focus of the final chapter as illustration of the dimension of the radically religious conversion. Conn traces the development of Merton's concern from *Seeds of Contemplation* to *New Seeds of Contemplation*. He then examines "The Inner Experience" (serialized in *Cistercian Studies* and now available in reprints), drawing again on the formulations of Lonergan's analysis of religious conversion as the personal subject's radical drive for self-transcendence, seeing the true self most fully realized in its surrendering its claim to autonomy in God's love.

Other late Merton works reveal additional dimensions of true religious conversion: the turning toward the universal as reflected in *Conjectures of a Guilty Bystander* and his stance on nuclear armament, the final stages of self-transcendence and universal integration in his work with Zen and the experiences and writings during the Asian journey.

Is this a work which will lead readers to ponder their own position in the continuum of conversion, or will it be treated as a source for studying others? If the latter, it is meant for the theologian; if the former, it is for those serious about their own developmental journey. But a caveat is in order -- it is hard going. The psychological and theological apparatus could easily overwhelm those not well-versed in those disciplines. Still, Conn dedicates it to the memory of his father who "showed him the heart of Christian conversion." It might therefore be assumed that Conn *is* throwing out a challenge to readers to progress in their own faith development.

The author helps as much as is possible. The volume is admirably structured. Chapters begin and end with clear statements of purpose and summaries, sub-sections do the same. There are copious notes which actually amount to an annotated bibliography of the several interconnected topics touched upon in the main body of the work. A careful reading of both text and notes offers insightful summations of the thought of major scholars in various areas such as theology and literature, with bibliographical references able to direct the interested reader toward new lines of inquiry. And finally, Conn's appropriation of secular developmental psychology to examine what has traditionally been considered a theological problem offers supprt for Merton's own discovery (using William Blake's terminology) that a merely natural explanation is ultimately an insufficient basis for authentic selfhood.

THE SELECTED LETTERS OF MARK VAN DOREN

Edited with an Introduction by George Hendrick
Foreword by Dorothy Van Doren
Baton Rouge & London: Louisiana State University Press, 1987
xi,280 pages -- $30.00

Reviewed by **Victor A. Kramer**

I

Mark Van Doren was a writer, poet, teacher, scholar and friend to numerous persons; and he was so over a long period of time. His energy, reflected throughout these letters, was enormous and he was the kind of person who could do many different kinds of things quite well. He lived from 1894 to 1972, and from the earliest moments in his career -- for which we have records -- he was involved in an active life of the mind and pursuit of a dual career as teacher and writer which was, as well, combined with a family life to which he was devoted. His relationships to many writers could be charted at great length, and thus there would be many ways in which an overview of this volume could be organized. Van Doren's active work with other writers such as Allen Tate or John Gould Fletcher would be one way. Van Doren's management of his own various writing projects would be another important pattern to observe. Finally, his relationships with his students such as John Berryman, Robert Lax, and Thomas Merton would be a significant set of patterns which could be observed. The beauty of this book is that its letters, arranged chronologically and with good footnotes, provide the necessary material for future readers to investigate all of these patterns. Reading the book with Van Doren's relationship to Merton in mind one is constantly aware of two things: it was, indeed, fortunate that Merton had Van Doren as his teacher at Columbia; also, Van Doren's tremendous energy and diverse interests *must* have served as a model for Merton himself whose career in some ways seems to reflect Van Doren's, but also surpasses it.

Mark Van Doren is the type of teacher-poet that an earlier age could produce precisely because narrow specialization was neither cultivated nor desired. Van Doren loved to teach and to write and his letters demonstrate how he could juggle these different responsibilities, while at the same time he had little respect for "scholars." A late letter to John Berryman (6-18-71) makes his point quite clear: "Scholarshit is for those with shovels, whereas you're a man of the pen, the wing, the flying horse . . . (p. 267). There is no surprise that the most significant extended conversation reflected in these letters is with Allen Tate, also a man of letters, and someone who was apparently somewhat reluctant to make any easy accommodations with the academic departments of literature.

While Van Doren was early associated with Columbia University, it was clear that his distance was maintained so that he would always retain sufficient energy for his own writing. This fact could be the subject of an extended inquiry about Van Doren's life, loves, and literary interests. It could, as well, be seen as a paradigm which Thomas Merton seems to have absorbed and which allowed Merton to appear to be, in a sense, almost two persons. After 1941, always a monk, Merton never ceased to be a writer, poet, manipulator of words. He must have sensed that this was a combination of talents which his teacher Van Doren possessed. In Van Doren's life and letters the rhythm is an alternation between Falls Village, Connecticut, and the city of New York. In Merton's life it became increasingly a matter of alternation between contemplative patterns as an *isolato* and the realization that the monk had a responsibility to assist those in a more active life. This is also Van Doren's pattern and accomplishment. In both men an almost fierce independence is reflected.

Van Doren saved all of Merton's letters to him and these are preserved in the Columbia University Library. Brought together, the two sets of letters would make a valuable volume. The practical decision of editing selected letters, by both Merton (in a projected five volume series) and Van Doren here, will make scholars work a bit harder, but from Merton's earliest Joycean fun in letters to Van Doren in 1939 to his final letters in 1968, so full of expectation about the coming trip to Asia, the evidence clearly exists to demonstrate that this friendship thrived.* Such interchange assisted Merton to continue to develop his own understanding of the nature of his vocation.

It was to Van Doren that Merton sent many unpublished manuscripts in 1941 before he went to Gethsemani, and it is in the Columbia University Library that the autograph copy of the Poem "Letter to My Friends," the first poem written by Merton at Gethsemani, exists. It was through Van Doren's contact with James Laughlin of New Directions that the poems which Merton had composed before he became a monk were published in the volume *Thirty Poems* (1944). But here, too, the story is complicated. Robert Lax, also a student, friend and correspondent, was in frequent touch with Van Doren, and it was the two of them who collaborated on the project of seeing their friend Merton's poems into print. Van Doren, then, was a facilitator. In February of 1944 he wrote to Laughlin, and by March 10 of that year was "delighted" that Laughlin had written to say he liked what he had read and would publish a book of Merton's poetry.

Of course, the friendship with Merton deepened; the advice and reading continued. The second letter to Merton included in this selection is dated 12 August 1945, and it has to do with the text for *A Man in the Divided Sea*, Merton's second volume of poems. We also know from other correspondence in the Columbia Library that Van Doren kept close contact with others, such as Lax, about Merton. A letter (addressed to "Dear Claudio") from Lax to Van Doren, written on 28 December 1943 after Lax's first visit to Merton, provides, for example, a beautiful picture of the Abbey of Gethsemani from Lax's point of view.

II

In these letters, then, we have the record of Van Doren providing compliments to many different correspondents about their many different kinds of projects. This is what he did -- over the years -- for Berryman, Lax, and Merton. Thus Van Doren is not afraid to write:

---

* Editors' Note: Merton's letters to Van Doren will be the opening section in *The Road to Joy: The Letters of Thomas Merton to New and Old Friends*, selected and edited by Robert E. Daggy, scheduled for publication by Farrar, Straus & Giroux in September 1988.

> Your new poems are very rich -- sometimes too rich, I think, for the thin
> blood outside those walls. I mean, the phrasing runs too often in parallels,
> and admits too many epithets; result, a tincture of monotony. If that is
> heathen criticism let it pass.
>
> Substantially the poems are powerful. The *Duns Scotus* is the best, I
> think, though the whole last series of Figures I like perhaps as well. Do you
> want me to do anything in particular with the MSS.? I suppose Bob Lax has
> copies. I'll keep these, of course, and read them many good times again,
> unless you direct me to send them forth soon. (pp. 180-181)

Van Doren's relationship with Merton was a continuing one. A poem
included in a letter in 1947, for example, is received with gratitude and
enthusiasm. It is, Van Doren insisted, "one of your richest and best" (p. 182).
Two years later the poem appeared in *The Tears of the Blind Lions*. This
continuing exchange between the two writers must have been a source of
encouragement for Merton. When *Figures for an Apocalypse* was published in 1948, Merton could only have been heartened by the words
prompted by his essay which was appended to the book, words about
Merton's doubts concerning poetry and contemplation:

> . . . I hadn't seen the note on contemplation. These two places in the
> book got all my attention at first, and still do in a degree, along with the
> address to Lax and Rice. Nothing has ever touched me more deeply than
> the problem you pose on page 110, and somehow solve on page 111.
>
> I agree, if I may, that the good of other souls justifies a refusal to sacrifice
> the poet's art. But I see and respect the problem, and because you are
> involved in it -- well, that is the immediate reason that I am moved.
>
> Thank you and your superiors for letting this book exist. It is wonderful
> everywhere. (p. 183)

Van Doren remained the teacher-critic for Merton; encouraging,
nudging, suggesting, and as is the case with all good teachers, he loved to
learn from his students. This is one of the most obvious facts reflected
throughout these letters. Van Doren could, and did, sustain correspondence with Tate, and Donald Davidson, and Robert Frost. But Lax and
Berryman, Merton and Allen Ginsberg were the regular recipients of his
correspondence. To Ginsberg in 1948 he writes: "The only thing I have ever
been aware of wanting to do in poetry is this: to give something that exists
outside myself, and this includes ideas, a form in words resembling its own
in something else" (pp. 184-185). To give something permanent form by
making a poem was clearly a driving ambition of Van Doren's, yet to help
others to give form to their personal visions was another of Van Doren's
gifts. It is almost as if Van Doren seemed to realize that mere teaching was
too ephemeral. To his own son he could write of the academic life as being
almost too secure: "One gets to be thought of as nothing but a teacher"

(p. 195). But to write, to give form, and to see how life and form work together, that is a mystery to which *both* Merton and Van Doren apparently could keep returning.

Of the 25 letters in this volume by Van Doren to Merton only five, interestingly, were written between 1941 and 1953. Twenty were written during the period from 1953 to 1968. The frequency of exchange picks up and also the nature of the friendship deepens. When Van Doren writes his own *Autobiography*, he writes to Merton to ask to quote some Merton lines; when Merton's *Selected Poems* is assembled, it is Van Doren who writes the introduction. These poets loved each other. In 1956 Van Doren could send a poem dedicated to Merton, written after a 1954 visit to Kentucky and Gethsemani:

> In our fat times a monk:
> I had not thought to see one;
> Nor, even with my poor lean concerns,
> Even to be one.
>
> No. But in Kentucky,
> Midway of sweet hills,
> When housewives swept their porches, and March light
> Lapped window sills,
> He, once my merry friend,
> Came to the stone door
> And the only difference in his smiling was,
> It sorrowed more. (p. 211)

Such love, such encouragement, is the core of the continuing relationship of these men. Visits, editorial assistance, receiving an award *in absentia* for Merton at Columbia all seemed to strengthen the relationship.

III

During the last years of Merton's life (when he was no longer Novice Master and when more and more books flowed from his pen) when perhaps one would expect fewer letters from Van Doren because he was getting fairly old by then, the letters continued to flow rapidly. Compliments, enthusiasms, excitement inform these letters:

> Look here, young man, you're going to talk yourself out of Gethsemani. I don't really mean this, but how come you know so much about the so-called world and Them who think they run it, and in a measure do? *Letter to an Innocent Bystander* lifted my white hair; so did *A Signed Confession* and -- yes -- *Prometheus*, not to speak of *Original Child Bomb*. My question is of course rhetorical, and does not wait for an answer. If any

is to be given, it will be given by men, and will run this way: It vastly comforts men that you feel wrath and fall to raging. Let there be even more of that, and from Gethsemani, where you never forget what is true even though almost everybody else does.

The Behavior of Titans, I'm feebly saying, is a terrific book, for the aforesaid reasons as well as others. For instance, Herakleitos, and the Atlas in its best form. I had seen others, but this must have been what you most deeply intended. Atlas as you do him is done to stay -- just read page 25 again and see if this isn't true -- and the fatman is so funny that he isn't funny. Meanwhile I keep hearing that dim bell.

As for the desert fathers, I like them even better in this new book. They are funny in the sweetest possible way. They help me at last to see what wit is. It is what one utters when one has truth by the whip end, but doesn't know how to spell whip. (pp. 230-231)

The last years of Merton's life were the most productive. Thus it is not surprising that he would have sent copies of his books to his old friend and teacher during those years. What is surprising is the fact that Van Doren could keep making such insightful comments:

Emblems of a Season of Fury has been going off daily, nightly, by my chair in the living room -- pop, roar, hiss, bang, fire, fire, fire. It is like one of those Vesuvius Fountains we used to have on the Fourth of July -- always more smoke, more fire, more better. It is a wonderful, wrathful, and sweet work. I wish it were going off everywhere, and maybe it is. Much of it of course I knew before, but that didn't matter; or rather, it was all to the good, for thereby your rage was more entirely summed up. (pp. 242-243).

In another letter, also in 1964, Van Doren says to Merton: "Your last letter (not owed; letters aren't owed, any more than breaths are, or smiles) followed me to California, where I didn't answer it (letters do not have to be answered either, any more than thought does, or praise) . . . (p. 243). This suggests the closeness of their friendship. Subsequent letters about various projects and interests cover a wide range of materials by them and others, including their mutual friend Robert Lax. It must have seemed that they could keep writing forever, and so it was a terrible shock for Van Doren to get the telegram about Merton's death. His letter to Lax is poignant:

> Tom dead in Bangkok
> The Abbot just telephoned me
> -- no details.
> I never felt so bad.
> I'll never get over it.
> And I know you won't.
> (p. 259)

A letter to Lax written on 30 December 1968 fills in more details. Again, a scholarly project waits for some researcher; Van Doren explains:

> *America* asked me for a piece about him, and I made it up mostly out of his last letter to me (July), talking with great joy about the trip he was to take. Heartbreaking now, and yet because it was so funny -- almost like his letter to you -- it somehow preserves him without loss. (p. 260)

In that letter Merton had joyfully celebrated the possibility of flying away from his life at Gethsemani. The final paragraph of Merton's 23 July 1968 letter, in a way, goes full circle back to the wit and joy in language which must have been so common in Greenwich Village in 1939 and 1940 when these two poets first corresponded:

> Right now, as I say, I am taken up with getting shots and visas, and cleaning up my premises and finishing up all the absurd jobs I took on when I was a low creature of earth and not a prospective world traveler. I assure you I hope to make the best of it while it lasts! (Think of all the cablegrams saying "RETURN AT ONCET" being shot to Bali, Tibet, Kamchatka, Ceylon, the Maldives, the Endives, the Southern Chives, the Lesser Maundies, the Nether Freeways, the Outer Salvages.) (Columbia University Library)

This book of letters is quite valuable beyond what it says about Van Doren's relationship with Merton. What I have begun to demonstrate here about Merton could, in fact, be done for many other friends, students, and associates of Van Doren's. The book is partially a record of someone who remained excited about writing and about life throughout his own long life. It is a repository of material which will help readers to understand *both* Van Doren and his many correspondents with whom he was able to carry on many different conversations.

It must have been sad for Van Doren, during the last years of his life --the loss of Merton, the suicide of John Berryman, the death of Delmore Schwartz, etc. -- yet he remained clearheaded and hopeful. A letter about Frost (3-20-71) says a lot: "There is only one thing that matters: he was a wonderful poet. All the rest is biography and balderdash." Van Doren's letters are testament to his continual love of and work for the recognition of good poetry.

NOTES ON CONTRIBUTORS

JOHN ALBERT, O.C.S.O., is a monk of Holy Spirit Monastery at Conyers, Georgia. His recent writings include "Two Studies in Chuang Tzu: Thomas Merton and Oscar Wilde," *Merton Seasonal* 12:1 (Winter 1987) and "Thomas Merton and the Dalai Lama: A Special Friendship Remembered," *Merton Seasonal* 12:4 (Autumn 1987).

JOHN EUDES BAMBERGER, O.C.S.O., is abbot of Our Lady of the Genesee in Piffard, New York. A frequent reviewer of Merton materials, his essay "The Monk" was included in *Thomas Merton/ Monk: A Monastic Tribute* (rev. ed. 1983).

JAMES CONNER, O.C.S.O., a monk of Gethsemani Abbey, is currently chaplain to the Benedictine Community of Osage Monastery, Sand Springs, Oklahoma. His essay, "The Original Face in Buddhism and the True Self in Thomas Merton," appeared in *Cistercian Studies* 22:4 (1987).

DAVID D. COOPER is Lecturer in English and American Literature at the University of Califonia, Santa Barbara. His book, *Thomas Merton's Art of Denial: The Evolution of a Radical Humanist,* is scheduled for publication in the Fall of 1988. He was recently appointed to edit the fourth volume of *The Letters of Thomas Merton.*

LAWRENCE S. CUNNINGHAM is Professor of Religion at the Florida State University at Tallahassee. Recent writings on Merton include "The Black Painting in the Hermit Hatch: A Note on Thomas Merton and Ad Reinhardt," *Merton Seasonal* 11:4 (Autumn 1986) and "High Culture and Spirituality" in *The Legacy of Thomas Merton* (1986).

ROBERT E. DAGGY is Director of the Thomas Merton Studies Center at Bellarmine College in Louisville, Kentucky. He is co-editor (with Marquita E. Breit) of *Thomas Merton: A Comprehensive Bibliography* (1986) and editor of the second volume of Merton correspondence, *The Road to Joy: The Letters of Thomas Merton to New and Old Friends,* scheduled for publication in September 1988.

PAUL E. DINTER is Catholic Campus Minister and Director of the Merton Center at Columbia University in New York. He is a frequent lecturer on Merton and sponsor of Merton programs.

RUTH FOX, O.S.B., is a member of Sacred Heart Priory at Richardton, North Dakota. She was previously formation director and prioress, and currently director of the Newman Center at Dickinson State College. She has published in *The American Benedictine Review*.

PATRICK HART, O.C.S.O., is a monk of Gethsemani Abbey at Trappist, Kentucky. He has edited several books by and about Merton including *The Asian Journal of Thomas Merton* (1973); *Thomas Merton/ Monk: A Monastic Tribute* (1974); and *The Legacy of Thomas Merton* (1986). He is editor of the third volume of *The Letters of Thomas Merton*, titled *The School of Charity*.

MATTHEW KELTY, O.C.S.O., a monk of Gethsemani Abbey, was formerly a hermit in Papua New Guinea. Author of *Flute Solo, Sermons in a Monastery*, and other books, his writings on Merton include "Some Reminiscences of Thomas Merton," *Cistercian Studies* 4 (1969) and "The Man" in *Thomas Merton/ Monk: A Monastic Tribute* (rev. ed. 1983).

DEWEY WEISS KRAMER is Professor of German and Humanities at DeKalb College in Clarkston, Georgia. She is the author of *Open to the Spirit: A History of the Monastery of the Holy Spirit* (1986) and co-editor (with Victor A. Kramer) of *An Oral History of the Abbey of Our Lady of the Holy Spirit* (1985).

VICTOR A. KRAMER is Professor of English at Georgia State University in Atlanta, Georgia. He has written extensively on Merton and is the editor of *A Thomas Merton Oral History* (1985). His Twayne U. S. Authors Series book, *Thomas Merton* (1984), will be re-issued by Cistercian Publications in 1988 as *Thomas Merton: Monk and Artist*.

ROBERT LAX is a resident of Patmos, Greece. He was a Columbia University classmate and long-time friend of Merton's. A selection of their letters was published in *A Catch of Anti-Letters* (1978).

PATRICK F. O'CONNELL is Professor of English at Villa Maria College in Erie, Pennsylvania. His writings on Merton include "Sunken Islands: Two and One-Fifth Unpublished Merton Poems" (1987) and "Is the World a Problem?: Merton, Rahner and Clark on the Diaspora Church" (1986).

KARL A. PLANK is Assistant Professor of Religion at Davidson College in Davidson, North Carolina. He is the author of "Meditating on Merton's Eichmann," *Christian Century* 102 (1985) and "Harvesting the Fruits of Monastic Contemplation," *Books and Religion* 14 (1986).

GAIL RAMSHAW currently lives in Philadelphia, Pennsylvania, and is on the Editorial Board of *Worship*. She wrote her doctoral thesis, *The Poetry of Thomas Merton: An Introduction*, at the University of Wisconsin/Madison.

MICHAEL RUKSTELIS, C.O., is a lay member of The Oratory of St. Philip Neri at Rock Hill, South Carolina. He is currently at work on a study of Merton's interest in the feminine dimension of God.

WILLIAM H. SHANNON is Professor Emeritus at Nazareth College in Rochester, New York and General Editor of The Merton Letters. He is the author of *Thomas Merton's Dark Path* (rev. ed., 1987) and editor of *The Hidden Ground of Love: The Letters of Thomas Merton on Religious Experience and Social Concerns* (1985).

DAVID STEINDL-RAST. O.S.B., a monk of Mt. Saviour Monastery in Pine City, New York, currently resides at New Camoldoli Hermitage in Big Sur, California. Essays on Thomas Merton have been published in *Thomas Merton/Monk: A Monastic Tribute* (1974) and *Thomas Merton: Prophet in the Belly of a Paradox* (1978).

BONNIE BOWMAN THURSTON lives in Bethany, West Virginia, and is on the faculty at Wheeling Jesuit College. Her doctoral thesis, written at the University of Virginia, was titled *Flowers of Contemplation: The Later Poetry of Thomas Merton.*" She is the author of several articles on Merton.

MARY LUKE TOBIN, S.L., is Director of the Thomas Merton Center for Creative Exchange in Denver, Colorado. Her book, *Hope is an Open Door* (1981), included "The Door of Prophetic Friendship: Thomas Merton."

INDEX

Wuhan (China), 335
Wybor Wierszy (Merton), 317

Yale University, 332
Yandell, Lunsford, 3
Yankee in Canada, A
(Thoreau), 277, 309, 309n, 311, 312
Yungblut, June, 299n

Zahn, Gordon Charles, 221n
Zen and the Birds of Appetite
(Merton), 17n, 22, 23, 29-31, 97,
108n, 109, 219, 219n, 223, 278
Zen Dust (Miura/ Sasaki), 277, 296
"Zen Insight of Shen Hui, The"
(Merton), 3-15
"Zen Koan, The" (Merton), 296n
Zilboorg, Gregory, 252